S0-AEC-077

THE
HISTORY HIGHWAY
2000

THE HISTORY HIGHWAY 2000

A Guide to Internet Resources

Second Edition

Dennis A. Trinkle
Scott A. Merriman

M.E. Sharpe
Armonk, New York
London, England

Library of Congress Cataloging-in-Publication Data

The history highway 2000 : a guide to Internet resources / Dennis A. Trinkle and Scott
A. Merriman, editors.—2nd ed.
    p. cm.
Rev. ed. of: The history highway.
Includes bibliographical references and index.
ISBN 0-7656-0477-9 (alk. paper) ; ISBN 0-7656-0478-7 (alk. paper ; pbk)
    1. History—Computer network resources. 2. Internet (Computer network) I. Trinkle,
Dennis A., 1968– II. Merriman, Scott A., 1968–

D16.225.C65 H58 2000
025.06′9—dc21   99-052019

Printed in the United States of America

The paper used in this publication meets the minimum requirements of
American National Standard for Information Sciences
Permanence of Paper for Printed Library Materials,
ANSI Z 39.48-1984.

BM (c)   10   9   8   7   6   5   4   3   2   1
BM (p)   10   9   8   7   6   5   4   3   2   1

In Memory of Elizabeth M. Merriman

Contents

Acknowledgments

One of the great strengths of the Internet is its ability to facilitate cooperation and collaboration. *The History Highway 2000* is a grand tribute to this dimension of the Internet. In addition to the section contributors, many individuals too numerous to mention helped assure the completion of this project with their time, suggestions, support, and generosity.

Dennis Trinkle would like to thank his family, friends, and past teachers for their constant support and examples of life well-lived. DePauw University provides especially fertile ground for a scholar and teacher, and I am grateful for the institutional support the university provides. The DePauw history department is also an outstanding incubator of fine ideas and achievements. It is a true blessing to work amidst such a generous and talented group of faculty and students. Sue Balter, John Dittmer, Bob Garrett, Glen Kuecker, Kerry Pannell, John Schlotterbeck, Carl Singer, Carol Smith, and Barbara Steinson deserve particular collegial thanks. Mike Garrison, Joe Stafford, Josh Diller, Brian Dixon, Ana Sobol, Heather Walker, and all of my students in HIST 300 also deserve special thanks. Community and the liberal arts flourish in collaborative soil.

Scott Merriman would like to thank his family, friends and teachers, both past and present, for their support and guidance. I would also like to recognize the faculty and graduate students of the history department of the University of Kentucky for their financial assistance and encouragement. Especially deserving of gratitude for serving as mentors are Robert Ireland, Eric Christianson, David Hamilton, and Robert Olson. The staff of the department has been of great assistance, particularly Lynn Hiler, Dottie Leathers, Tina Hagee, Brian Moses, and the late Darlene Calvert. This book is dedicated to my grandmother, who to her dying day, was proud and supportive of my work. Finally, for all those who have supported me, but who are not specifically mentioned, thanks!

Introduction

More than ninety million Americans are now online according to the OpenMarket Internet Index, and 760 households gain access to the Internet every hour.[1] The number of Web pages is increasing so rapidly that no reliable estimate exists, though best guesses suggest several hundred million pages and climbing. This growth rate and proliferation is staggering, and it is historically unprecedented. Radio, television, and the telephone became part of American daily life at a comparatively glacial pace. This dizzying expansion and alteration makes the Internet a tremendously exciting phenomenon, but also unsettling and unwieldy.

When we wrote the first edition of *The History Highway* in 1996, we lamented that trying to explore and sample the Internet was like trying to sip water from a fire hose. The metaphor is now even more appropriate. To novices and even seasoned users, the Information Superhighway can be information overload at its worst, and it can often be more intimidating and frustrating than exciting. For anyone interested in history, however, the Internet simply cannot be ignored. The resources are richer and more valuable than ever. There are nearly fifty thousand sites dedicated to the American Revolution alone. Students can find the complete texts of hundreds of thousands of books, work with previously inaccessible primary documents, and explore thousands of first-rate sites dedicated to historical topics. Publishers can advertise their wares, and professors can find enormous databases devoted to teaching suggestions, online versions of historical journals, and active scholarly discussions on a wide variety of research topics. The Internet is quite simply the most revolutionary storehouse of human knowledge in history.

For most of us, however, whether we are students, professors, librarians, editors, or just lovers of history, there are not enough hours in our already busy days to go chasing information down an infinite number of alleyways, no matter how useful or interesting that information might be. This is especially true for those of us who have never logged on to a computer network or who have only a basic acquaintance with the Internet. The aim of this book is to provide a general introduction to the skills and tools necessary to navigate the Information Superhighway and to offer detailed information about the thousands of quality resources that are out there and how to find them.

Chapter One is a short primer for those with little or no experience using the Internet. It discusses what exists and what you can do with it. It explains how to gain access to the Internet and outlines what types of software are necessary. There is also an important section on the manners and rules that govern the Internet—"netiquette" as seasoned users call it.

Chapter Two is the heart of the book. It lists thousands of sites that will appeal to anyone interested in history and which our specialist section authors have determined to be reliable and useful for the serious study of history. This section will allow you to avoid the helter-skelter databases, such as Yahoo!, Excite, and DogPile, which take you to information regardless of quality and utility. You will not find sites created by first graders in Indianapolis or by biased, ahistorical groups like the Holocaust Deniers of America. Of course, since the Internet is growing and changing at an astronomical rate, our specialist authors certainly have not uncovered every worthy and valuable site on the Internet. Fortunately, the Internet offers a solution to its own challenge. *The History Highway* will have its own Internet site at http://www.theaahc.org/ historyhighway/hh2000.htm, where our specialists will list address changes as they detect them and worthy new sites as they come along. *The History Highway* will therefore serve as an evolving road map as you travel down the Internet thoroughfares. Bon Voyage!

Note

1. *The Open Market Internet Index*, Win Treese, compiler, volume 24, May 1999. Available online at http://new-website.openmarket.com/intindex/99=05.htm.

THE
HISTORY HIGHWAY
2000

Chapter One

Getting Started

History of the Internet

Since this book is directed at those interested in history, it seems sensible to begin with a brief history of the Internet itself. The story of the Internet's origins is as varied, complex, and fascinating as the information the Net contains. Ironically, the Net began as the polar opposite of the publicly accessible network it has become. It grew out of the Cold War hysteria surrounding the Soviet launch of Sputnik, the first man-made satellite, in 1957. Amidst paranoia that the United States was losing the "science race," President Eisenhower created the Advanced Research Projects Agency (ARPA) within the Department of Defense to establish an American lead in science and technology applicable to the military. After helping the United States develop and launch its own satellite by 1959, the ARPA scientists turned much of their attention to computer networking and communications. Their goal was to find a successful way of linking universities, defense contractors, and military command centers to foster research and interaction, but also to sustain vital communications in case of nuclear attack. The network project was formally launched in 1969 by ARPA under a grant that connected four major computers at universities in the southwestern United States—UCLA, Stanford, the University of California–Santa Barbara, and the University of Utah. The network went online in December 1969. The age of computer networks was born.

In the early 1970s, it became clear to the initial developers of the ARPANET that the system was already stretching past its Cold War origins. Nonmilitary research institutions were developing competing networks of communication, more and more users were going online, and new computer languages were being introduced—all of which made communication difficult or impossible between networks. To resolve this problem, the Defense Advanced Research Projects Agency (which had replaced ARPA) launched the Internetting Project in 1973. The aim was to create a uniform communications language (a protocol) that would allow the hundreds of networks being formed to communicate and function as a single meganetwork. In an amazing display of scientific prowess comparable to the Apollo Program, this crucial step in the development of the Information Superhighway was accomplished in a single year when Robert Kahn and Vinton G. Cerf introduced the Transmission Control Protocol/Internet Protocol (TCP/IP). This protocol (as the rules governing a computer language are termed) made possible the connection of all the various networks and computers then in existence and set the stage for the enormous expansion of the Internet.

Over the next decade, the Department of Defense realized the significance and potential of the Internet, and nonmilitary organizations were gradually allowed to link with the ARPANET. Shortly after that, commercial providers like CompuServe began making the Internet accessible for those not connected to a university or research institution. The potential for profiting from the Internet fueled dramatic improvements in speed and ease of use.

The most significant step toward simplicity of use came with the introduction of the World Wide Web (WWW), which allows interactive graphics and audio to be accessed through the Internet. The World Wide Web was the brainchild of Tim Berners-Lee of the European Laboratory for Particle Physics, who created a computer language called "hypertext" that made possible the interactive exchange of text and graphic images and allowed almost instantaneous connection (linking) to any item on the Internet. Berners-Lee was actually developing this revolutionary language as the Internet was expanding in the 1970s and 1980s, but it was only with the introduction of an easy-to-use Web browser (as the software for interacting with the Web is called) that the Web became widely accessible to the average person. That first browser— Mosaic—was made available to the public by the National Center for Supercomputing Applications at the University of Illinois, Urbana–Champaign in 1991. Three years later, Mosaic's creator, Marc Andreessen, introduced an even more sophisticated browser that allowed the interaction of sound, text, and images—Netscape Navigator. The next year Microsoft launched a browser of its own—Internet Explorer.

Today, there are many software options for exploring the Internet, and access can be purchased through thousands of national and local service providers. One need no longer be a military researcher or work at a university to "surf the Net." There are now more than one hundred million users logging on to the Internet from the United States alone. Tens of thousands of networks now are connected by TCP/IP, and the Internet forms a vast communication system that can legitimately be called an Information Superhighway.

Uses of the Internet

This section of Chapter One will explain the most useful features of the Internet for those interested in history. It will discuss sending and receiving e-mail, reading and posting messages to Usenet newsgroups and discussion lists, logging on to remote computers with Telnet, transferring files using the File Transfer Protocol and browsing the World Wide Web. The next section will discuss in greater detail the software packages that perform these tasks and explain exactly how to get online.

Sending and Receiving E-Mail

E-mail (electronic mail) is the most popular feature of the Internet. It offers almost instantaneous communication with people all over the world. The Nora Ephron film *You've Got Mail* has made e-mail as widely known as the United States Post Office, and e-mail functions vary similarly, allowing users to send and receive messages or computer files over the Internet. Rather than taking days or weeks to reach their destination, however, e-mail messages arrive in minutes or seconds. A professor in Indianapolis can correspond with a student in Delhi, India in the blink of an eye. A publisher, editor, and author can exchange drafts of a history book they are preparing with no delay. And, e-mail does not involve the high costs of international postage, fax charges, or long distance telephone premiums. E-mail is always part of the basic service arrangement provided with Internet access, and it is quite easy to use with the software packages discussed later.

A Note on E-Mail Addresses

E-mail addresses are very similar to postal addresses. Like a postal address, an e-mail address provides specific information about where the message is to be sent along the Internet. For example, a friend's address might be something like:

Gkuecker@depauw.edenvax.edu

If you look at the end of the address, you will notice the .edu suffix. This means the e-mail message is going to an educational institution. In this case, it is DePauw University, as the second item indicates. Edenvax shows that the message is traveling along the Net to someone on a VAX computer designated as Eden at DePauw University. Finally, the address reveals that the recipient is your friend Glen Kuecker (Gkuecker). This is just like providing the name, street address, city, state, and zip code on regular mail.

The names that individual institutions choose for their Internet address vary widely, but to help make e-mail addresses a little easier to understand, all addresses in the United States are broken down into the computer equivalent of zip codes. We've already noted that the .edu in the above message indicates the recipient's account is at an educational institution. There are six such three-letter designations, which provide a clue as to where your e-mail is going or coming from. They are:

Category	Meaning
.com	commercial organizations
.edu	educational institutions
.gov	government organizations (nonmilitary)
.mil	military institutions
.net	network service providers
.org	miscellaneous providers and nonprofits

A common naming system for American primary and secondary schools has also recently been introduced. This system uses the school name, the k12 designation, and the state where the school is located in the address. A typical address might read:

KeithTrinkle@howe.k12.in.us.

This indicates that a student, teacher, or administrator at Howe High School in Indiana sent the e-mail. The k12.state.us will always be present in e-mail coming from a primary or secondary school.

These designations do not apply to e-mail addresses for accounts located outside the United States, but an equally simple system exists for identifying foreign messages. All mail going to or coming from foreign accounts ends with a two-letter country code. If you have a colleague in France, you might receive an e-mail message ending with .fr. You may receive an e-mail message from an editor in Canada ending in .ca. Or, if you met a historian with similar interests on that last trip through Tanzania, you might soon receive mail ending with .tz. These extensions are:

AF   Afghanistan

AL	Albania
DZ	Algeria
AS	American Samoa
AD	Andorra
AO	Angola
AI	Anguilla
AQ	Antarctica
AG	Antigua and Barbuda
AR	Argentina
AM	Armenia
AW	Aruba
AU	Australia
AT	Austria
AZ	Azerbaijan
BS	Bahamas
BH	Bahrain
BD	Bangladesh
BB	Barbados
BY	Belarus
BE	Belgium
BZ	Belize
BJ	Benin
BM	Bermuda
BT	Bhutan
BO	Bolivia
BA	Bosnia-Herzegovina
BW	Botswana
BV	Bouvet Island
BR	Brazil
IO	British Indian Ocean Territory
BN	Brunei Darussalam
BG	Bulgaria
BF	Burkina Faso
BI	Burundi
KH	Cambodia
CM	Cameroon
CA	Canada
CV	Cape Verde
KY	Cayman Islands
CF	Central African Republic
TD	Chad
CL	Chile

CN	China
CX	Christmas Island
CC	Cocos Islands
CO	Colombia
KM	Comoros
CG	Congo
CK	Cook Islands
CR	Costa Rica
CI	Côte d'Ivoire
HR	Croatia
CU	Cuba
CY	Cyprus
CZ	Czech Republic
DK	Denmark
DJ	Djibouti
DM	Dominica
DO	Dominican Republic
TP	East Timor
EC	Ecuador
EG	Egypt
SV	El Salvador
GQ	Equatorial Guinea
ER	Eritrea
EE	Estonia
ET	Ethiopia
FK	Falkland Islands
FO	Faroe Islands
FJ	Fiji
FI	Finland
FR	France
GF	French Guiana
PF	French Polynesia
TF	French Southern Territories
GA	Gabon
GM	Gambia
GE	Georgia
DE	Germany
GH	Ghana
GI	Gibraltar
GR	Greece
GL	Greenland
GD	Grenada

GP	Guadeloupe
GU	Guam
GT	Guatemala
GN	Guinea
GW	Guinea-Bissau
GY	Guyana
HT	Haiti
HM	Heard and McDonald Islands
HN	Honduras
HK	Hong Kong
HU	Hungary
IS	Iceland
IN	India
ID	Indonesia
IR	Iran
IQ	Iraq
IE	Ireland
IL	Israel
IT	Italy
JM	Jamaica
JP	Japan
JO	Jordan
KZ	Kazakhstan
KE	Kenya
KI	Kiribati
KP	Korea
KR	Korea
KW	Kuwait
KG	Kyrgyz Republic
LA	Lao People's Democratic Republic
LV	Latvia
LB	Lebanon
LS	Lesotho
LR	Liberia
LY	Libyan Arab Jamahiriya
LI	Liechtenstein
LT	Lithuania
LU	Luxembourg
MO	Macau
MK	Macedonia
MG	Madagascar
MW	Malawi

MY	Malaysia
MV	Maldives
ML	Mali
MT	Malta
MH	Marshall Islands
MQ	Martinique
MR	Mauritania
MU	Mauritius
YT	Mayotte
MX	Mexico
FM	Micronesia
MD	Moldova
MC	Monaco
MN	Mongolia
MS	Montserrat
MA	Morocco
MZ	Mozambique
MM	Myanmar
NA	Namibia
NR	Nauru
NP	Nepal
NL	Netherlands
AN	Netherlands Antilles
NT	Neutral Zone
NC	New Caledonia
NZ	New Zealand
NI	Nicaragua
NE	Niger
NG	Nigeria
NU	Niue
NF	Norfolk Island
MP	Northern Mariana Islands
NO	Norway
OM	Oman
PK	Pakistan
PW	Palau
PA	Panama
PG	Papua New Guinea
PY	Paraguay
PE	Peru
PH	Philippines
PN	Pitcairn

PL	Poland
PT	Portugal
PR	Puerto Rico
QA	Qatar
RE	Réunion
RO	Romania
RU	Russian Federation
RW	Rwanda
SH	Saint Helena
KN	Saint Kitts and Nevis
LC	Saint Lucia
PM	Saint Pierre and Miquelon
VC	Saint Vincent and the Grenadines
WS	Samoa
SM	San Marino
ST	São Tomé and Principe
SA	Saudi Arabia
SN	Senegal
SC	Seychelles
SL	Sierra Leone
SG	Singapore
SK	Slovakia
SI	Slovenia
SB	Solomon Islands
SO	Somalia
ZA	South Africa
ES	Spain
LK	Sri Lanka
SD	Sudan
SR	Suriname
SJ	Svalbard and Jan Mayen Islands
SZ	Swaziland
SE	Sweden
CH	Switzerland
SY	Syria
TW	Taiwan
TJ	Tajikistan
TZ	Tanzania
TH	Thailand
TG	Togo
TK	Tokelau
TO	Tonga

TT	Trinidad and Tobago
TN	Tunisia
TR	Turkey
TM	Turkmenistan
TC	Turks and Caicos Islands
TV	Tuvalu
UG	Uganda
UA	Ukraine
AE	United Arab Emirates
GB	Great Britian
UK	United Kingdom
US	United States
UM	United States Minor Outlying Islands
UY	Uruguay
UZ	Uzbekistan
VU	Vanuatu
VA	Vatican City State
VE	Venezuela
VN	Vietnam
VG	Virgin Islands
VI	Virgin Islands
WF	Wallis and Futuna Islands
EH	Western Sahara
YE	Yemen
YU	Yugoslavia
ZR	Zaire
ZM	Zambia
ZW	Zimbabwe

A Note on E-Mail Security

Because sending e-mail is so similar to sending a letter by postal service, many people forget that there is a major difference—federal laws discourage anyone from looking at (or intercepting) your mail and sealed packaging provides a fairly reliable way to detect tampering. Unfortunately, e-mail is not protected in the same ways. As your electronic message passes through the Internet, it can be read, intercepted and altered by many individuals.

Some security measures have been developed to protect e-mail just as an envelope secures letters. The latest versions of many programs that process e-mail now include the ability to encrypt messages. Encryption converts your e-mail into a complex code that must be deciphered by an e-mail program or

Web browser that is designed to convert the encoded message back into regular text. The latest versions of Netscape Communicator, Microsoft Internet Explorer, Qualcomm Eudora, and Pegasus Mail include the ability to code and decode encrypted e-mail, but no e-mail program automatically converts a message into a secured code. If you want your messages or files encrypted you will have to follow the directions provided with your e-mail package for doing it. If you purchase products and services over the Internet, you will also want to be certain that your account or credit card numbers are insured by some sort of encryption. Nevertheless, it is prudent to keep in mind that no security measure is completely reliable.

Reading and Posting Messages on Usenet Newsgroups

For anyone interested in history, Usenet newsgroups are another rewarding feature of the Internet. They are the electronic equivalent of the old New England town meetings in which anyone could pose a question or make an observation and others could respond to it. At present, there are nearly ten thousand newsgroups dedicated to thousands of different topics, and many of these relate to history. Each is regulated by a moderator who, like the editor of a newspaper, sets the quality and tone of the posts. There are groups that regularly discuss the Holocaust, the American Revolution, historical publishing, library concerns and cartography, just to mention a few areas.

The software that allows one to easily locate and participate in these newsgroups will be discussed later. Before passing on to the next topic, however, there are several clues to determining the content and nature of groups that will help down the road. Like e-mail addresses, the addresses of newsgroups provide some insight into the nature of the group. Take the newsgroup:

alt.civilwar

This address indicates that the group discusses the alternative topic—the Civil War. Each newsgroup will have a similar address revealing its type and topic. The following categories will aid in determining which of the nearly ten thousand newsgroups are worth investigating:

Category	Meaning
Alt.	Alternative themes [Most groups relating to history carry the Alt. designation]
Comp.	Computer related topics

Misc.	Miscellaneous themes
News.	Posts about Newsgroups
Rec.	Recreational topics
Sci.	Scientific discussions
Soc.	Social concerns
Talk.	Talk radio style format

Reading and Posting Messages on Discussion Lists

Discussion lists are a hybrid mixture of e-mail and newsgroups. With discussion lists, the posts and replies that anyone can access in newsgroups are sent by e-mail only to those who have subscribed to the list. As with most newsgroups, there is an editor who screens the posts before they are sent to subscribers, maintaining quality and decency. There are discussion lists that target students, professors, editors, publishers, librarians, and general readers. Almost any historical topic imaginable has a list devoted to it. How open the discussion lists are to subscribers is determined by the moderators. Some limit membership to those with a special interest, while others permit anyone who wishes to join. Chapter Two discusses the lists focusing on history and explains their qualifications for subscription in more detail.

Chapter Two will also provide more specific instructions on how to subscribe to each group. All discussion lists share a basic subscription format, however. To subscribe (or to unsubscribe), one simply sends an e-mail message to the computer that receives and distributes the messages. This computer is called the listserver (or listserv) because it serves the list. For example, to send a message to a list discussing the history of dogs (H-Dog), one would send the e-mail message:

> Subscribe H-Dog yourfirstname yourlastname
> to the e-mail address: Listserv@ucbeh.san.uc.edu.

The listserv would quickly acknowledge your registration as a member, and e-mail posts from the other list members would begin arriving in your box.

A Word of Warning about Discussion Lists

You should be careful only to join subscription lists that are truly of interest and be certain to read your e-mail several times a week. Most discussion lists are very active, sending out fifteen or more messages per day. If you get carried away at first, you may find yourself buried under an avalanche of several hundred e-mail posts awaiting your eager attention. So, be careful to only subscribe to those lists that most interest you until you gain a feel for how much mail you are likely to receive.

Multi-User Virtual Environments

Unlike Discussion lists, multi-user virtual environments allow real-time conversations between participants anywhere in the world, that is, they can speak to each other at the same time as if on a conference telephone call. The most popular and widely known version of a multi-user environment is the chat room. There are now thousands of "rooms" on the Internet were people come together daily to discuss philosophy, politics, or the latest NBA game. Chat rooms are generally informal arenas. Another variation of MUVE, the Multi-User Domain, Object Oriented, or MOO as they are commonly called, has been widely adopted for educational and serious use. MOOs allow the same real-time conversation of chat rooms, but the participants interact within a textually described world created by other participants.

MOOs offer every user the opportunity to construct and describe the spaces and objects of this textual world. For example, a history class on the American Revolution could create a room simulating the Constitutional Convention, complete with robots of the leading delegates programmed to interact with visitors to the room on key themes and with copies of various constitutional drafts and other documents readily available for reading. Each robot, draft, document, and chair would be an object created by the instructor or student and endowed with the inalienable properties they chose to give it.

Many universities and scholarly societies now sponsor MOOs that are open to the pubic. On some of these MOOs one can take a virtual class, engage in a historical recreations, or simply converse about historical issues. The MOOs related to history are discussed in more detail in Chapter Two. A good directory to educational MOOs and to tutorials for those who would like more guidance can be found at http://www.itp.berkeley.edu/~thorne/MOO.html.

Logging on to a Remote Computer with Telnet

Anyone who has ever used an electronic library catalog is familiar with the computerless screens and keyboards that allow patrons to access the library's catalog. These machines do not have their own microprocessors, but are linked to a central computer that shares information with all of the terminals connected to it. Telnet is a program offered by all Internet service providers that permits your home or office computer to act just like the terminals at the library. It enables you to temporarily connect to a remote computer and access its information as if it were on your own computer. Those interested in history will find Telnet particularly important because almost every major library in the world now allows Telnet access to its catalogs. Anyone can do subject searches or find out which libraries possess a specific work they are looking for.

Transferring Files with File Transfer Protocol (FTP)

File Transfer Protocol (or FTP) is similar to Telnet. Like Telnet, it is a program that connects you to a remote computer. FTP does not allow you to read the material on the remote machine; rather, it actually allows you to copy the files or programs and transfer them to your own computer. You can use FTP to get a copy of the United States Constitution or to download (as retrieving information with FTP is called) a program that teaches you the history of the Vietnam War. Thousands of sites with downloadable files, programs, and historical information are out there waiting to be tapped. Many of the best and most useful FTP sites will be discussed in Chapter Two.

As with Telnet, there are many packages that permit FTP access. For now, we will only mention that there are three main types of FTP access that exist. There is anonymous FTP, identified FTP, and restricted FTP. A computer with anonymous FTP allows anyone to connect and download files without identification. Identified FTP also allows anyone to copy materials, but it requires you to give your e-mail address and name, so that the sponsors of the site can maintain statistical information about the use of their site. Restricted FTP is used by some commercial and private institutions which only allow FTP for a fee or for authorized users. The sites mentioned in Chapter Two specify that of these categories the sites fall into and explain how to gain access when a fee or password is required.

Browsing the World Wide Web

For most computer users, time on the Internet will mean exploring the World Wide Web (WWW) and working with a Web browser (as the programs that allow access to the WWW are called). The Web is the most popular and fastest growing section of the Internet because it combines text, sound and graphics to create multimedia sites. History buffs can find everything from an audio track of the *Battle Hymn of the Republic* to short film clips of JFK's assassination to a complete version of the French *Encyclopédie*. The most powerful Web browsers also perform all of the other Internet functions such as e-mail, Telnet and FTP, so new users need only learn to use one basic software package.

The Web and Web browser packages owe much of their popularity and potential to their multimedia format, but they also profit from their ability to link information. With the World Wide Web, Web page developers can create links to any other page on the Web. A mere point-and-click of your mouse on linked image or section of text brings up related information almost instantly on your computer. Thus, a link on a home page (the first page of information that a person sees when they connect to a Web site is called the home page) can connect you to any other site, just as a cross reference in a textbook sends you to other related information. This makes the WWW an amazingly easy-to-use source of information or recreation (for those who become Web junkies).

The next section discusses the software which makes connecting to the Web possible, but as with e-mail, you will need to understand Web addresses to find information on the WWW. These addresses are called URLs—uniform resource locators—which is simply techno-talk for addresses. Every page on the Web has a unique URL. This makes it very easy to go directly to the information you need. They look something like this:

http://www.theaahc.org/index.htm

Some addresses are longer than this. Some are shorter. All contain three basic parts. Looking from right to left, the first designation you notice is index.htm. This tells you that you are retrieving a file called index in the html format. HTML (Hypertext Markup Language) is the standard language of the Web for saving multimedia information, and index is the default name many individuals and html editors give to the opening page of a Web site. Other possibilities include .gif and .jpeg, which indicate graphic images files; .aif, .avi, and .wav, which indicate audio files; or .mpg and .mov, which signals a movie.

The middle part of the address: /www.theaahc.org is just like an e-mail address, specifying what network and computer stores the information so that your software package can find it on the Internet. The .org extension tells you the information is an organization's or nonprofit's Web site and as with e-mail, there will always be a three-letter code revealing the type of institution that sponsors the site.

The http:// lets you know that the browser is using the Hypertext Transfer Protocol to get the information. This is the standard language that governs the transfer and sharing of information on the Web. If you were using your browser to Telnet or FTP, the http:// would be replaced by ftp:// or telnet:// and then the address, showing which function your computer is performing.

Of course, you can use the Internet and profit from the World Wide Web without spending hours studying their technical background, history, and terms. The next section tells you how to get on the Internet and what software you need.

Getting on the Internet

Once upon a time, getting connected to the Internet was the hardest part of going online. In the early days, if you did not work for the military or a research institution, you were out of luck. The introduction of commercial providers in the 1980s made access easier to obtain, but it might cost you as much as a new car. Today, there are thousands of local and national Internet service providers, and the competition has made Internet access amazingly inexpensive. In most markets, you can now get almost unlimited access for $10 or $15 per month. For those fortunate enough to work for a library, college, university, or publisher, the price is often even better—free. Getting on the Internet has never been easier or less expensive.

Internet access is offered by three basic categories of service providers—corporate/institutional, national commercial, and local commercial providers. For those who work at companies or institutions offering Internet access to their employees, the best way to learn about your options is to speak directly to your system manager or computer support staff.

For those who do not have access to the Internet at work or school, there are several factors to consider in choosing a provider. Perhaps most important is finding a service that offers a local phone number or a toll-free number, so that you need not pay long distance charges for your Internet access. The attractiveness of the Internet vanishes quickly in the presence of a $400 phone bill. Fortunately, there are now so many service providers it is usually easy to find a provider that offers a local phone number in your area. Cable and satellite providers are also scurrying to offer other access options besides telephone connections.

The second consideration is the type of service you desire. Many national and local service providers in your city or state will offer almost unlimited access to the WWW, e-mail, FTP, and other basic services for very affordable rates ($5 to $20 a month). [Local service providers can be found by looking in your local phone book under "Internet Service Providers" or "World Wide Web Service Providers."] There are also several national service providers such as America Online and CompuServe that provide special services in addition to basic Internet access. These services include such things as access to electronic versions of national newspapers, up-to-the-minute stock market reports and special discussion lists and newsgroups only available to subscribers. Because these national service providers offer features you cannot find elsewhere, they are more expensive. The best way to decide if any of the national service providers feature packages you want is to contact each of them directly, keeping a record of the benefits and limitations of each service.

The Hardware

Convenient use of the Internet and its many tools is governed by speed. The faster your computer can send and process information, the more pleasurable and productive your time on the Net will be. Thus, there is a simple rule of thumb that guides the purchase of computer equipment for use on the Internet: Buy the best machine you can realistically afford. This does not mean to mortgage your house just to get better equipment. All new computers sold today are more than adequate for exploring the resources described in this book. For those with older computers, machines with the minimum configurations listed in table 1.1 and 1.2 will allow you to access the resources of the Internet. More memory (RAM), a faster processor, and a speedier modem will all enable you to interact with the Net more quickly, however. If you want to start with the basic system described on the following page and gradually upgrade, make sure the first addition you make is more RAM. Upgrading from 4 megs to 8 or 16 megs of RAM or more will make the most noticeable difference in the performance of your computer. Improving your processor should be second and trading in your old modem should be done last. At present, the speed of phone lines restricts the effectiveness of modems, so you will get the least improvement in your system from the purchase of a faster modem.

The Software

While many educational institutions and the national service providers such as AOL and CompuServe offer their own software packages with directions and tutorials, those who choose local service providers can select the soft-

Table 1.1

Windows-Based Configurations

Processor	486 or Higher
RAM	32 MB with Windows 95, 98, or NT
Modem	28.8 KBS or Faster Recommended
Hard Drive	35 MB Free Space Recommended
Sound Card and Speakers	Recommended for Multimedia
VGA Monitor	Required
Network or Dial-Up Connection	Required

Table 1.2

Apple Configurations

Processor	PowerPC with OS 7.6.1 or Higher
RAM	24 MB or Higher
Modem	28.8 kbs or Faster Recommended
Hard Drive	35 MB Free Space Recommended
Sound Card and Speakers	Required
VGA Monitor	Required
Network or Dial-Up Connection	Required

ware they wish to use to access the Internet. Most local service providers will also give new users software needed to access the Internet along with detailed instructions. In principle, however, you can use any package you wish to connect to the Internet through a local provider. This section will present brief descriptions of some of the best packages and explain where to obtain them.

Netscape Communicator and Microsoft Internet Explorer

The two powerhouse packages (Web browsers as they are called) that most Internauts use are Netscape Communicator and Microsoft Internet Explorer. They combine all the tools for accessing the Web, sending e-mail, Telnetting, and using FTP. Both can display the combinations of graphics and text that make the Internet a lively and exciting resource. They are simple to use, come with tutorials and a help feature, and are good choices for all users from novices to experts.

Netscape Communicator and Microsoft Internet Explorer also can both be downloaded on the Internet. You can download Netscape at the following address (please note, addresses are case sensitive):

http://www.netscape.com/computing/download/

Microsoft Internet Explorer can be downloaded at:
http://www.microsoft.com/windows/ie/default.htm

Both Netscape and Internet Explorer are currently available free for students, faculty and staff of educational institutions and to employees of non-profit organizations. Others are asked to pay a small registration fee after a complimentary evaluation period.

Qualcomm Eudora and Pegasus Mail

Netscape and Internet Explorer perform all of the functions you need to explore the Internet, including e-mail. Not everyone wishes to use an e-mail package linked to a browser, however, and there are a number of fine stand-alone e-mail packages. Qualcomm's Eudora and Pegasus Mail are currently two of the best programs for handling e-mail that are available on the Internet at no cost to students, faculty, and staff. Both packages can send messages to lists of recipients, permit the use of special filters to sort and screen e-mail, allow secure protection of files (given the sender and receiver have the same encryption keys), can send files in addition to or along with text, and feature attractive graphic environments and menus that make them easy to use.

Eudora is available via FTP at:
http://www.eudora.com/

Pegasus Mail is available via FTP at:
http://www.pegasus.usa.com/

Netiquette and Copyright

Because electronic communication is still new, the rules governing online expression are still evolving. There are already, however, some basic courtesies that help keep the free and open communication of the Internet polite and enjoyable. With this in mind, here are some Netiquette hints that can help keep you from accidentally offending someone.

General Netiquette

The most important thing to remember is that Internet communication is just like writing a letter. Electronic messages can be seen by many individuals other than the intended recipient. They can be forwarded to countless people. They can even be printed and posted in public areas. Thus, the golden rule of Internet communication should never be forgotten:

Never write anything you would not want a stranger to read.

It is also important to remember that e-mail is judged by the same standards as other written communication. Sometimes, the ease and speed of electronic communication lulls users into forgetting to check grammar and spelling. This can lead to an error-filled e-mail being forwarded to thousands of individuals, and you do not want people all over the Internet laughing because you innocently asked if it was Vasco de Gama who circumcised the world with a 40-foot clipper.

There are also several special grammatical conventions that govern the Internet. One important rule is not TO WRITE EVERYTHING OUT IN CAPITAL LETTERS or to underline everything, *italicize everything,* or **to put everything in bold.** Seasoned e-mail readers consider this the equivalent of shouting at the top of your lungs, and it is considered the mark of a "newbie," or someone who has not yet learned the rules of courtesy for the Internet.

Because e-mail lacks a convenient way to convey emotion through text, you will also often encounter special symbols in e-mail correspondence. For example, a :) or :(is often put after a sentence to express happiness or sadness. A :0 may be added to express surprise. A :; may be inserted to indicate confusion, and history buffs who think they are Abe Lincoln may include a =|:-)= somewhere in their messages. These symbols add a bit of charm to Internet communication, but it is important to remember that they are only appropriate in informal correspondence. They also should not be overused. Too many emotive symbols are considered to be another mark of a newbie.

Since many e-mail users receive hundreds of messages each day, it is also considered polite to put a clear note indicating what the message is about on the header line. This is especially important when using the reply function of e-mail packages. Most e-mail software will automatically insert a reply header. For example, in a reply to a message originally titled "Fourth of July Celebrations," most software packages would add a header that reads: "RE: Fourth of July Celebrations." Such a reply title leaves much ambiguity about the contents of the message, so netiquette dictates that one should instead use a clear header. In this example, a more specific title such as "Fourth Celebrations— Williamsburg the Best" would be more appropriate.

Rules for Newsgroup and Discussion List Posts

Besides the Netiquette governing general Internet communication, there are also some rules for those who wish to participate in newsgroups and discussion lists.

1. Before you make a post to a group or list, it is wise to follow the group's posts for a while. This will help you to know what has already been asked and what type of questions/statements are considered appropriate. Asking repetitive or uninformed questions can get you off to a bad start.

2. Think before you write. Do not send off emotional or ill-considered responses to posts. (This is called "flaming" in Internet parlance.) Take time to consider criticisms, sarcasms, and insults carefully. Remember the Internet is not an anonymous frontier, and online remarks can be just as hurtful to a person as any others.

3. Do not send private correspondence to groups or lists. If you just want to thank someone, send the message to the person directly. And, be very careful when you reply to a message. You do not want to accidentally tell several thousand readers about your date last night because you replied to the wrong address.

4. Do not post advertisements to groups or lists. This is considered extremely rude and intrusive, and it is the surest way to become the victim of vicious flaming. Internauts are being careful to avoid the spread of junk mail to the Internet.

Copyright

The question of copyright is an important one for students, teachers, librarians, publishers, and all those on the Internet. Everyone wants to know what the laws are governing copying and sharing information on the Internet, and lawyers and lawmakers are working to develop clear rules that govern electronic mediums. For now, the issues of copyright as they pertain to the Internet are still somewhat hazy, but there are some certainties that can guide your steps. Most importantly, all online correspondence, files, and documents are handled like other written documents. They are automatically held to be copyrighted in the individual author's name. When an Internet item is copyrighted by some other party, the copyright holder generally identifies him, or herself at the end of the document.

Students, teachers, and general users will be glad to know that a judge has just ruled that Internet documents can be copied according to the fair use rules that govern printed sources. You can make personal copies of online documents and images, and you can incorporate them in instructional packages (if you are a student, teacher, or librarian) as long as the package is in no way intended to generate a profit and you follow the general standards for fair use. Other more precise codes governing copyright will undoubtedly be developed in the near future. The Stanford University Libraries maintain an excellent information page on copyright and fair use at http://fairuse.stanford.edu/. Those interested in copyright issues should consult the Stanford site for additional information and periodic updates.

Chapter Two

Internet Sites for Historians

The history sites on the Internet present an astounding amount of information. No one could ever hope to examine and read everything that is now online. Of course, no one could ever read every book in the Library of Congress either. This is why the Library of Congress is meticulously organized and cataloged. When you need to find a book or fact, you can go to an index or turn to a librarian for assistance. There is no Internet librarian, but the subject area specialists who have written the following sections offer the same guidance and assistance one gets from a knowledgeable librarian or seasoned teacher. This section of *The History Highway 2000* is designed to help you find specific information when you are looking for it and guide you to interesting and useful sites that are worth examining for pleasure or serious study.

As you read this guide, you will notice that the historical sites on the Internet have been created by a wide variety of people, ranging from history professors and students to publishers and history buffs. There is also a broad range of content on the Internet. Some sites are scholarly; others are more informal. Some are composed entirely of links to other sites. The resources described here have been screened for quality, utility, and reliability. In an age of information superabundance, it is important that everyone become a skilled critic of electronic information, however. To help you make personal determinations about each site, whenever possible the names and sponsoring institutions or organizations are clearly indicated. Nevertheless, we urge you not to assume that every argument or resource that you encounter on one of the following pages is credible or valid. Just as many excellent books contain some errors and misinterpretations and every library contains fallacious books, so some of the sites mentioned here contain a mixture.

GENERAL HISTORY

Dennis Trinkle and Scott Merriman

A Walk Through Time

http://physics.nist.gov/GenInt/Time/time.html

A Walk Through Time is an interesting look at the history of timekeeping. Beginning with an explanation of various ancient calendar systems, the site then discusses early clocks—such as sundials and water clocks—modern time-keeping methods, and time zones. The National Institute of Standards and Technology maintains the site.

Archnet

http://archnet.uconn.edu/

Archnet is sponsored by the University of Connecticut and contains field reports, images, conference information, electronic exhibits, fieldwork opportunities, and more. It covers archaeology throughout the world, and the site is an excellent way to learn about field practices and the scholarship of historical archaeology.

Arctic Circle

http://arcticcircle.uconn.edu/index.html

Arctic Circle presents information on the history and culture of the Arctic regions. The site focuses on the people of the Arctic, but there is also much information on the natural resources and environment of the area. Norman Chance, a cultural and environmental anthropologist at the University of Connecticut, manages the site.

ArtServ: Art and Architecture

http://rubens.anu.edu.au/

ArtServ provides access to 16,000 images relating to the history of art and architecture around the world. The site is maintained by Michael Greenhalgh, Professor of Art History at the Australian National University.

Bill Douglas Centre for the History of Cinema and Popular Culture

http://www.ex.ac.uk/bill.douglas/

This archive houses the Bill Douglas and Peter Jewell Collection at the University of Exeter, which contains over 60,000 items, including 25,000 books and thousands of films.

A College Web Index of Significant Historians and Philosophers

http://www.corvinia.org/history/histphil.html

This is a site with many links to significant historians and philosophers, including George Berkeley and Thomas Paine. It is the effort of Peter Ravn Rasmussen, a history doctoral student at the University of Copenhagen.

Eighteenth-Century Resources

http://andromeda.rutgers.edu/~jlynch/18th/

Eighteenth-Century Resources contains a wide variety of material on the eighteenth century, from electronic texts to calls for papers. There is a large collection of digitized primary sources and many links to other sites. These pages are the labor of love of Jack Lynch, an English professor at Rutgers University, Newark, New Jersey.

En Garde!

http://www.gt.kth.se/~bjornh/eg/

En Garde! is a clever, interactive, online game that combines history and a lot of role playing. It sets you in the seventeenth century and challenges you to climb the social ladder, teaching you European history as you play. The simulation is the work of Bjorn Hedin, a research scientist at the Division of Media Technology at the Royal Institute of Technology in Sweden.

Galaxynet

http://galaxy.einet.net/galaxy/Social-Sciences/History.html

Galaxynet is a large, searchable database of links to sites on all subjects. This address takes you to Galaxynet's links to history sites.

Great Books of Western Civilization

http://www.geocities.com/Athens/Atlantis/4360/index.html

This site is arranged around eight "great books" courses offered by Mercer University. Each section has a course description and full electronic versions of the texts used for the course.

Guide to Maritime History Information on the Internet

http://ils.unc.edu/maritime/home.html

The Guide to Maritime History Web page provides general information on all aspects of maritime history, including ships, music, art, and nautical archaeology. The pages are maintained by Peter McCracken of the University of North Carolina–Chapel Hill's School of Information and Library Science.

H-Net Home Page

http://h-net2.msu.edu/

H-Net is a National Endowment for the Humanities–sponsored project to bring the humanities into the twenty-first century. H-Net's home page contains links to the more than seventy discussion lists they sponsor, to the Web pages of each of those discussion lists, to their extensive book review project, and to hundreds of other resources for historians.

History Departments around the World

http://chnm.gmu.edu/history/depts/

This is an alphabetical listing of links to history department home pages in the United States and foreign countries. It is managed and updated by the Center for History and New Media at George Mason University.

History of Money from Ancient Times to the Present Day

http://www.ex.ac.uk/~RDavies/arian/llyfr.html

This is an interesting collection of essays by Glyn and Roy Davies of the University of Exeter on a range of topics dealing with money and currency. The topics include: "Warfare and Financial History," "The Significance of Celtic Coinage," "Third World Money and Debt in the Twentieth Century," and "Origins of Money and Banking."

History/Social Studies Web Site for K-12 Teachers

http://www.execpc.com/~dboals/boals.html

This is a large annotated metasite aimed at K-12 teachers and students. Its sources should be critically scrutinized, however; some of them are nonscholarly advocacy groups. The site is maintained by Dennis Boals.

The Horus History Links

http://www.ucr.edu/h-gig/

Created and maintained by history faculty members at the University of California–Riverside, Horus History Links is one of the best general gateways to historical Web sites. The Horus project contains links to more than one thousand sites, and it features excellent interactive graphics and a multimedia format.

HyperHistory Online Project

http://www.hyperhistory.com/

The HyperHistory Project attempts to present world history as a flowing, illustrated timeline. In ten-year increments, major figures and events are presented, with clickable biographies and descriptions. The project is still under construction.

Joan's Witch Directory

http://www.rci.rutgers.edu/~jup/witches/

Joan's Witch Directory contains information on witchcraft trials from around the world, some historical diaries, letters and testimonials, and links to other sites of interest.

Professional Cartoonists' Index

http://www.cagle.com/teacher

This site offers the largest collection of newspaper editorial cartoons on the Web. Current cartoons from seventy-one newspaper editorial cartoonists are presented with the permission and participation of the creators, who include the top names in the field, such as Pulitzer Prize winners Michael Ramirez, Jeff MacNelly, Jim Borgman, Mike Luckovich, Steve Breen, Dick Locher, Jim Morin, and Mike Peters. Along with the cartoons is a rich network of resources for students and teachers, including lesson plans for using the editorial cartoons as a teaching tool in the social sciences, art, journalism, and English at all levels. The goal is to help teachers and students use cartoons for interactive learning.

Tennessee Technological University History Resources

http://www.tntech.edu/www/acad/hist/history.html

Created by the Department of History at Tennessee Technological University, this is a good general starting point for gopher resources on the Internet, including essays on why one should study history and careers for historians.

University of Kansas History Resources

http://www.ukans.edu/history/VL

This site, sponsored by the University of Kansas, is one of the oldest and largest collections of links to sites on all topics of history. It is an excellent starting point for research.

World Rulers

http://www.geocities.com/Athens/1058/rulers.html

World Rulers lists the past and present leaders of every state in the world. Birth and death dates are provided, as well as pictures for some. Monthly updates are posted.

ANCIENT HISTORY

Keith Nightenhelser

A NOTE ON "ANCIENT" SEARCH TERMS

WWW resources do not consistently use the term "ancient" for the oldest manifestation of a culture. (Library classification systems do not either!) "Ancient" is used most often for the Near East, Egypt, Greece, and Rome, but outside those areas you may need to employ other terms, such as "pre-Columbian" for the Western Hemisphere, "Old European" or "Celtic" for ancient Europe, "Harappa" for India, or "classical Chinese" for China. Reference tools (including the WWW, most of our library classification systems, and this book!) tend to classify materials about antiquity by region, except for the ancient Mediterranean civilizations. So if you do not find what you are looking for in this section of *The History Highway 2000*, try looking in a relevant regional section.

SEARCH ENGINES FOR ANCIENT HISTORY

Altavista and Miningco

A word of advice about commercial search engines: materials for ancient history will turn up not just under the headings "History" or "History, Ancient," but also under headings such as Myth, Religion, or a geographical designation. For instance, in what appears to be the best commercial search engine at present for ancient history, Altavista, at *www.altavista.com,* following the category "Reference and Education," leads to a link for "Arts and Humanities," and that subcategory presents a choice between sub-subcategories "Classics," "History," and "Mythology." All of these lead to useful ancient history Web sites. Furthermore, the "History" link gives a choice between "Ancient" and "History by Region." "Ancient" leads to links mostly about ancient Greece, Rome, Egypt, Britain, and the Near East. Virtually all other ancient history resources known to Altavista appear under "History by Region."

Suppose you wanted to find Internet resources about ancient Korea. With Altavista, you would not find it in any ancient category under "History"; instead, it will show up within "History" under "History by Region" and then under "Asia." Or you would have been able to find it if at the start of your search you had selected "Social Sciences" rather than "Arts and Humanities," and had looked there under "Cultures and Regions."

In Miningco, *www.miningco.com* (not as clearly organized for someone seeking information about ancient history, and probably less comprehensive than Altavista, but quite user-friendly and plainly the best of the rest), the "Guidesite" for Ancient/Classical History (including Greco-Roman, Egyptian, and Near Eastern materials) appears under "Education's" subcategory "History" alongside a Guidesite for "Archaeology," which also offers resources in Ancient History. If you want Miningco's links on Ancient India, you will have to select the "Society/Culture" category, and look in one of its "Cultures" subcategories under India. (That is where you will find ancient history links for many other world cultures.) Or, more simply, just search Miningco for "Ancient India."

ANCIENT HISTORY METASITES

Ancient World Web

http://www.julen.net/aw

This superb metasite, created by Julia Hayden, can be searched by region or subject, and has worldwide coverage; it is an excellent starting point.

Archnet

http://archnet.uconn.edu

Archnet organizes WWW archaeological resources both by region and by subject, is very comprehensive, and is frequently updated. It is produced by Thomas Plunkett (City University of New York) and Jonathan Lizee (University of Connecticut).

Argos Limited Area Search Engine

http://argos.evansville.edu

Argos is the WWW's first peer-reviewed limited area search engine. It covers mostly the Near East, Greece, Rome, and medieval Europe, and assures the quality of its information by limiting its search to links already accepted by approved Associate Sites. It was created at the University of Evansville by Anthony F. Beavers and Hiten Sonpal.

GENERAL ANCIENT HISTORY SITES

The Amazing Ancient World of Western Civilization

http://www.omnibusol.com/ancient.html

This chronologically organized basic online textbook on the Near Eastern and Greco-Roman origins of Western Civilization is used in the for-credit Internet course that its author, Konnilyn Feig, teaches at Foothill College (wwwfh.fhda.edu/foothill/). It is a lively introduction to these cultures, includes a substantial annotated library of links, and ends with a collection of related Web rings. (Web rings are sites that are enrolled in a common group register. At the bottom of a Web page, there is an icon that connects to the index for member sites and to the prior and subsequent sites in the "circle" or "ring.")

Encyclopedia Mythica

http://www.pantheon.org/mythica

Micha F. Lindemans coordinates the work of many volunteers to create this guide to 4,700 plus gods and supernatural and legendary creatures and places from cultures all over the world. The site is advertising-free.

Exploring Ancient World Cultures

http://eawc.evansville.edu/index.htm

EAWC is an online course supplement edited by Anthony F. Beavers and hosted by the University of Evansville. It presents, in an introductory fashion, a picture of the civilizations of ancient Egypt, Mesopotamia, Greece, Rome, the Islamic world, India, China, and Europe, and includes well-annotated links to other sites.

The Museum of the Oriental Institute of the University of Chicago

http://www-oi.uchicago.edu

The Oriental Institute Web site includes a virtual museum, reference tools about the ancient Near East, and resources for teachers.

Myths and Legends

http://pubpages.unh.edu/~cbsiren/myth.html

Christopher B. Siren's collection of links to information about myths and legends from all over the world appears to be the most comprehensive available, but includes fantasy and gothic horror materials as well. In his materials are links to high-quality FAQs from the Usenet discussion lists on Near Eastern myths from the Hittites, Canaanites, Sumerians, and Assyrians.

The Smithsonian Institution's National Numismatic Collection

http://www.si.edu/organiza/museums/nmah/csr/cadnnc.htm

Online exhibitions that use ancient coins as evidence about the cultures that produced them.

University of Michigan Papyrus Collection

http://www.lib.umich.edu/pap/

Besides information about what we can learn of the Greco-Roman world from surviving papyri, the University of Michigan Library has excellent online exhibitions at this site on subjects such as daily life in the Egyptian city of Oxyrhynchus, the transmission of the Bible, and ancient magic. Plus there are links to online exhibitions at the University's Kelsey Museum of Archeology, and to other WWW resources about papyri.

University of Pennsylvania Online Museum Exhibits

http://www.museum.upenn.edu

"Cultures: Ancient and Modern" from the University of Pennsylvania Museum includes a variety of materials about ancient Greece, Oceania, and South America.

ANCIENT HISTORY RESOURCES BY REGION

Ancient Africa and Asia

Note: There appear to be few scholarly Web sites that collect links for these subjects, apart from those dealing with Egypt and the ancient Near East. Using the commercial search engines and metasites with search terms such as "Ancient India" or "Ancient Nubia" or "Ancient China" is probably the best approach at present, unless you are looking for information about Egypt or the ancient Near East.

ABZU (a Metasite)

http://www.oi.uchicago.edu/OI/DEPT/RA/ABZU/ABZU.HTML

ABZU is a guide to the ancient Near Eastern resources that are available on the Internet. The materials include electronic journals, museum information, online exhibits, and links to other resources. It is regularly maintained and of high scholarly quality.

Ancient India Links in Miningco.com

http://indianculture.miningco.com/msub13.htm

M.A. Arun edits these links as part of his Miningco.com guide to India.

Ancient Korea

http://violet.berkeley.edu/~korea/ancient.html

Hosted by Korean Studies at the University of California, Berkeley, and created as a history seminar project by students there, this site includes chronology, cultural information, and relevant legendary material from the origins of Korea through the unification of the peninsula in 661 C.E.

Egyptology.com

http://www.egyptology.com

Greg Reeder's collection of images and links about ancient Egypt, including a link to the online magazine *KMT: A Modern Journal of Ancient Egypt.*

Guardian's Egypt Home Page

http://guardians.net/egypt

A collection of historical sketches, images, and links.

History of China

http://www-chaos.umd.edu/history/welcome.html

Leon Poon's adaptation with supplement of the history section from the U.S. Army's Area Handbook on China (done with permission of the copyright owner, the U.S. Department of Commerce). This is a comprehensive history of China, but appears to be the best single WWW source for ancient China as well, and it includes a collection of links. The original history section of the Area Handbook was written by Rinn-Sup Shinn and Robert L. Worden.

Material Culture of Ancient Canaanites, Israelites, and Related Peoples

http://staff.feldberg.brandeis.edu/~jacka/ANEP/ANEP.html

John R. Abercrombie's site provides materials both for students in his Anthropology course at Brandeis and for researchers. It contains a searchable library of images of artifacts from ancient Israel, as well as primary texts.

Overview of Ancient Chinese History

http://www.uis.edu/~www/crowley/c-hist.html

Dr. Robert Crowley's summary history of Ancient China is tantamount to a very full encyclopedia article on the Web. It is part of a set of pages on Asia hosted by the University of Illinois–Springfield. It contains no links to other resources itself, but has a link to his Asia page, which does have a collection of WWW resources.

University of Memphis Institute of Egyptian Art and Archaeology

http://www.memst.edu/egypt/main.html

An online exhibit of artifacts and photographs from Egypt, plus links to other WWW sites.

ANCIENT EUROPE

Anglo-Saxon World

http://www.ccc.nottingham.ac.uk/~aczkdc/asresource.html

A collection of WWW materials relating to the Anglo-Saxons, maintained by Trent & Peak Archaeological Trust at the University of Nottingham.

Archaeological Resource Guide for Europe (a Metasite)

http://odur.let.rug.nl/arge/

ARGE organizes WWW resources about European archaeology by subject, period, and region, and actively seeks out the newest links and evaluates them prior to inclusion. The links lead to documents in a variety of languages, and ARGE is currently working on multilingual access and searching methods. It was organized by Sara Champion and Martijn van Leusen, and is essentially a volunteer effort funded by the European Community.

Archaeology of France

http://www.culture.fr/

This page fires up in French, but there is a button for the English version, and after clicking it you will find online exhibitions of French archeological finds, site guides, and much useful information.

Celtic and Saxon Home Page

http://www.primenet.com/~lconley/index.html

A sizeable collection of links about the Celts and other peoples of ancient Western Europe, compiled by Lawrence V. Conley.

Classics Eireann

http://hermes.ucd.ie/~civilise/Classics_Eireann.html

A collection of articles and links about the influence in Ireland of Greco-Roman civilization, hosted by University College Dublin.

Museum of Antiquities on the WWW

http://www.ncl.ac.uk/~nantiq/

The University of Newcastle-upon-Tyne's online museum, featuring ancient objects from all over Europe.

The Ancient Greco-Roman World

Ancient City of Athens

http://www.indiana.edu/~kglowack/athens/

The Ancient City of Athens is a photographic archive of archaeological and architectural remains of ancient Athens. It includes essays about the sites and monuments depicted. All of its images are from the personal slide collection of Kevin T. Glowacki and Nancy L. Klein, and may be downloaded for non-commercial purposes provided proper credit and copyright notice are included.

Ancient Medicine/Medicina Antiqua

http://www.ea.pvt.k12.pa.us/medant/

Ancient Medicine/Medicina Antiqua includes translations of medical treatises from the ancient Greco-Roman world, and bibliographies and short essays on medicine there from Mycenean times until the fall of Rome. There is an associated listserv, MEDANT-L, described at the site, which is sponsored by The Episcopal Academy (Merion, Pennsylvania) and maintained by Dr. Lee T. Pearcy and an advisory committee.

Ancient Roman Cooking

http://www.cs.cmu.edu/~mjw/recipes/ethnic/historical/ant-rom-coll.html

The Ancient Roman Cooking Web page presents a variety of recipes and an encyclopedia of native Roman ingredients.

Bearers of Meaning: The Ottilia Buerger Collection of Ancient and Byzantine Coins at Lawrence University

http://www.lawrence.edu/dept/art/buerger/

A gorgeous online exhibition of ancient Greco-Roman coins, with accompanying essays about their production and their significance for the study of history.

Bryn Mawr Classical Review

http://ccat.sas.upenn.edu/bmcr

BMCR is the second oldest online journal in the Humanities. Its founders, Richard Hamilton and James J. O'Donnell, together with a very strong staff of advisory editors, have produced for years now a very high-quality review of books about the ancient Greco-Roman world. For informed opinion about recent books in this area, or for a list of prominent recent books in this area, it is the preferred site on the WWW.

Classics and Mediterranean Archaeology (a Metasite)

http://rome.classics.lsa.umich.edu

A very comprehensive index of scholarly sites devoted to the ancient Greco-Roman world—including its Mediterranean neighbors—hosted by the University of Michigan and maintained by Sebastian Heath.

CLASSICS-L

http://omega.cohums.ohio-state.edu/hyper-lists/

The Classical Studies listserv started by Linda Wright at the University of Washington is archived at the above site (and the archive is searchable!). Many topics about the ancient Greco-Roman world have been discussed by experts on this site since its inception, so the archive may be a resource for researchers with patience and ingenuity. This site also contains archives of the inactive ANCIEN-L listserv and of the still active LT-ANTIQ listserv, which is devoted to discussion of Late Greco-Roman Antiquity.

College Course Materials from the APA

http://www.colleges.org/ctts/courses_frames.html

A collection of online syllabi and materials from college courses about the ancient Greco-Roman world, compiled and updated by the Classics, Teaching and Technology Subcommittee of the American Philological Association.

De Imperatoribus Romanis

http://www.salve.edu/~romanemp/startup.htm

An online encyclopedia of rulers of the Roman Empire, from Augustus through the fall of Byzantium. This well-organized, easy-to-use and growing site contains an atlas, Robert Cape's catalog of Roman coins, family trees, and many useful essays and links. It has an editorial board of American and international scholars chaired by Jacqueline Long.

DIOTIMA (a Metasite for Online Bibliography)

http://www.uky.edu/ArtsSciences/Classics/gender.html

DIOTIMA is an interdisciplinary resource for the study of gender patterns around the ancient Mediterranean. It includes course materials, primary and secondary texts, and an abridged hypertext of Mary Lefkowitz and Maureen Fant's book *Women's Life in Greece and Rome*. There is a good collection of materials about ancient Jews and Christians. It has excellent bibliographical resources about sex and gender in the ancient Mediterranean, plus a well-designed bibliographical search engine linked to other online ancient Mediterranean bibliographies. Information about an associated listserv, ANAHITA, is available at the site. DIOTIMA was created by Ross Scaife and Suzanne Bonefas, and is hosted by the University of Kentucky.

Electronic Resources for Classicists: The Second Generation (a Metasite)

http://www.tlg.uci.edu/~tlg/index/resources.html

Maria C. Pentelia's metasite for resources about the ancient Greco-Roman world includes an excellent collection of K-12 links. It is hosted by the University of California at Irvine.

Imperium Romanorum

http://wwwtc.nhmccd.cc.tx.us/people/crf01/rome/

Useful tables and links created by Clifton R. Fox of Tomball College present information about Roman officials and emperors.

Interactive Ancient Mediterranean

http://iam.classics.unc.edu

IAM is an online atlas of the ancient Mediterranean world. It provides a variety of high-quality royalty-free maps derived from the Classical Atlas Project of the American Philological Association, and includes detailed articles about places in the ancient Mediterranean (at present only Carthage, Delphi, and Vindolanda are operational), as well as links to other Web-based resources and a comprehensive reference tool for abbreviations of Greco-Roman authors and works. It is based at the University of North Carolina and directed by Professor Richard J.A. Talbert.

Perseus Project

http://www.perseus.tufts.edu

The Perseus Project is an evolving digital library of resources for the study of the ancient Greek world. It includes texts, maps, diagrams, and images for the study of ancient Greece, and materials for ancient Rome are under construction. (See http://www.perseus.tufts.edu/Texts/latin_TOC.html for available Latin texts and translations.) A highlight is Thomas Martin's "Overview of Archaic and Classical Greek History" among the "Secondary Sources." It links his narrative and analysis directly to primary sources within Perseus. The Perseus Project is located within the Department of Classics of Tufts University.

POMOERIUM (a Metasite)

http://www.pomoerium.com

POMOERIUM was developed by Dr. Ryszard Pankiewicz, and includes an online scholarly journal as well as a library of links. It is the Argus Clearing-house–approved site for ancient history.

Prehistoric Archaeology of the Aegean

http://devlab.dartmouth.edu/history/bronze_age/

A series of lessons on the cultural evolution of humanity in the Aegean basin from the Paleolithic era to the great palatial cultures of Minoan Crete and Mycenaean Greece, this site is drawn from lecture notes by Dr. Jeremy B. Rutter of the Classics Department at Dartmouth College. A glossary and a collection of links are planned, but at present it is basically a well-informed online book. It is jointly sponsored by the College and by the Foundation of the Hellenic World.

The Seven Wonders of the Ancient World

http://ce.eng.usf.edu/pharos/wonders/

Alaa K. Ashmawy's site presents a multimedia look at the Seven Wonders (all from Greek culture except for the Great Pyramid of Giza), and a history and bibliography of the idea of the Seven Wonders through the Middle Ages. It contains discussions of art, history, trivia, and links to related sites.

VROMA (a Metasite and a Content Site)

http://acs.rhodes.edu

VROMA ("Virtual Rome") is a collection of online resources for teaching Latin and ancient Roman culture. It is both an online "place" that models to some degree the ancient city of Rome and allows participants to interact through a MOO, and a collection and filter of Internet resources. One outstanding feature of the site is a growing library of images that are available "for noncommercial purposes." (See http://acs.rhodes.edu/images/image_search.html.)

Warfare in the Ancient World

http://www.fiu.edu/~eltonh/army.html

Hugh Elton's site collects FAQs, bibliographies, teaching materials, and links about warfare in the Greco-Roman world from the Mycenaean era through the Byzantine Empire. The site is based at Florida International University, where he is a faculty member.

ANCIENT WESTERN HEMISPHERE

Note: As with Ancient Africa and Asia, there are few scholarly Web sites collecting links for the cultures of the ancient Americas. Again, the best approach may be to use commercial search engines and metasites.

Mesoamerican Archaeology WWW Page

http://copan.bioz.unibas.ch/meso.html

Here you can find collected scholarly files, links, resources, software, and reports relevant or interesting to Mesoamerican and Pre-Columbian Archaeology.

Mesoweb

http://www.mesoweb.com

A very attractive if elementary presentation of some features of Mesoamerican culture.

Precolumbian Mexican Cultures (Aztecs, Toltecs, Olmecs)

http://udgftp.cencar.udg.mx/ingles/Precolombina/precointro.html

The University of Guadalajara's Web site offers an attractive picture of these ancient Mesoamerican cultures. There is also a version in Spanish at http://udgftp.cencar.udg.mx.

K-12 Resources

Ablemedia's Classics Technology Center

http://ablemedia.com/ctcweb

Wendy E. Owens's consulting firm provides free Web resources for teaching about the ancient Greco-Roman world. She recognizes with her "Silver Chalice" award excellent syllabi and teaching resources submitted from many sources, and provides links to them from her site.

Ancient World Resources for Elementary Teachers

http://www.rmc.edu/~gdaugher/elem.html

A collection of links compiled by Greg Daugherty of Randolph Macon College.

History/Social Studies Web Site for K-12 Teachers

http://www.execpc.com/~dboals/boals.html

Dennis Boals's excellent collection of links is a good place to find ancient history materials for non-Western cultures. Its sources should be critically scrutinized, however; some of them are nonscholarly advocacy groups. The site itself thoughtfully includes a Research/Critical Thinking section to assist the user in careful use of WWW resources.

Latinteach

http://geocities.com/Athens/Styx/1790/index.html

Created for K-12 Latin teachers by Sharon Kazmierski, this site also has many useful resources for K-12 students interested in the Greco-Roman world who are not studying Latin.

Mr. Donn's Ancient History

http://members.aol.com/donnandlee/index.html

Middle school lesson plans and links compiled by Don Donn, with units on everyday life in a number of ancient societies.

Mr. Dowling's Virtual Classroom

http://www.mrdowling.com

A middle school classroom on the Internet, with downloadable lessons on topics such as ancient Africa, ancient Greece and Rome, Mesopotamia, and prehistory.

The Rome Project of the Dalton School

http://www.dalton.org/groups/rome/

An attractive collection of links created at an independent school in New York City and maintained by Dr. Neil Goldberg.

MEDIEVAL HISTORY

Christopher A. Snyder

The American Academy of Research Historians of Medieval Spain

http://kuhttp.cc.ukans.edu/kansas/aarhms/mainpage.html

The American Academy of Medieval Historians (AARHMS) is an affiliated society of the American Historian Association and sponsors sessions at both the AHA's annual meeting and at the International Congress of Medieval Studies. Its Web site, maintained by James W. Brodman of the University of Central Arkansas and Lynn Nelson of the University of Kansas, offers translations of medieval charters, manuscript images, and book reviews.

Angelcynn: Anglo-Saxon Living History, A.D. 400–900

http://www.geocities.com/Athens/2471/index.html

Old English for "the English people," Angelcynn is a "living history" group whose page offers interesting introductions to Anglo-Saxon clothing, weapons, and settlements. Includes links, images, and glossary.

Anglo-Saxon Cemeteries

http://www.gla.ac.uk/Acad/Archaeology/staff/jwh/ascems.html

Jeremy Huggett at the University of Glasgow presents online his research concerning Anglo-Saxon cemeteries and burial customs. Included are maps, plans, and a fully searchable dataset.

Anglo-Saxon History: A Select Bibliography

http://www.wmich.edu/medieval/rawl/keynes1/index.html

Despite its name, this is an extensive bibliography of Anglo-Saxon History compiled by Simon Keynes and presented online by the Medieval Institute at Western Michigan University.

Antique and Medieval Atlas

http://salve5.salve.edu/~romanemp/index.htm

This site contains historical maps of Europe for every century from A.D. 1 to A.D. 1200. Maps are in color and clickable. Maintained by Christos Nüssli.

Arthuriana: The Scholarly Journal about King Arthur

http://dc.smu.edu/Arthuriana/

Arthuriana is the quarterly journal of the International Arthurian Society (North American Branch) and covers many aspects of medieval history and literature. Its Internet site, maintained by editor Bonnie Wheeler of Southern Methodist University, contains article abstracts and good Arthurian links.

Arthurnet Links

http://web.clas.ufl.edu/users/jshoaf/Arthurnet.htm

The home page of Arthurnet, an Internet discussion group sponsored by *Arthuriana* and located on the University of Florida server. Mostly a metasite with links to excellent Arthurian and medieval resources.

Bede's World

http://www.bedesworld.co.uk/

The Museum of Early Medieval Northumbria at Jarrow sponsors a Web page for exploring the world of the Venerable Bede (A.D. 673–735) through his writings and related archaeological discoveries.

Beowulf Bibliography

http://spirit.lib.uconn.edu/Medieval/beowulf.html

This online bibliography by Robert Hasenfratz attempts to cover all scholarship relating to *Beowulf* published from 1979 through 1994, derived mostly from Hasenfratz's *Beowulf Scholarship: An Annotated Bibliography, 1979–1990*, Garland Medieval Bibliographies, 14 (New York: Garland, 1993).

Britannia: The Arthurian Reenactment Society

http://www.arthurian.freeuk.com/

This is the Web site of one of the more reputable medieval reenactment groups. The site contains some good discussion of early medieval military history, along with images of reconstructed weapons and armor.

Britannia Internet Magazine

http://www.britannia.com/history/

This Internet tourist magazine features such departments as the Age of Arthur, the Anglo-Saxons, and Medieval Britain. Mostly introductory articles, lavishly illustrated.

Byzantium: Byzantine Studies on the Internet

http://www.bway.net/~halsall/byzantium.html

One of the most extensive online resources for Byzantine Studies. Contains texts, images, syllabi, conference information, essays, and bibliography. Maintained by Paul Halsall at Fordham University.

The Camelot Project

http://www.lib.rochester.edu/camelot/cphome.stm

The Camelot Project is a significant database of Arthurian texts, images, bibliographies, and basic information. The project is sponsored by the University of Rochester and overseen by Alan Lupack.

The Canterbury Tales Project

http://www.sheffield.ac.uk/uni/projects/ctp/index.html

Though partly an advertisement for the *Canterbury Tales* on CD-ROM, this site at Sheffield University does provide (for free) essays on Chaucer and electronic scholarship as well as links to Chaucer sites. The Web site is maintained by Michael Pidd.

CAPITULUM: Research Group for Medieval Church History

http://www.jate.u-szeged.hu/~capitul/capiteng.htm

This Hungarian academic site features some unique links to sites on The Crusades, medieval medicine, and more.

CELT: Corpus of Electronic Texts

http://www.ucc.ie/celt/index.html

The CELT Project at University College Cork is an online resource for contemporary and historical Irish documents in literature, history, and politics.

Celtic and Medieval History Page

http://www.geocities.com/Athens/Parthenon/3615/

A metasite maintained by Robert Harbison. Some good links to online journals.

Celtic Art & Cultures

http://www.unc.edu/courses/art111/celtic/index.html

This site was developed as part of an Art History course at the University of North Carolina–Chapel Hill. Contains timelines, essays, links, and good images of Hallstatt, La Tène, and medieval Celtic art.

Celtic Studies Bibliography

http://www.humnet.ucla.edu/humnet/celtic/csanabib.html

The Celtic Studies Association of North America (CSANA) sponsors this substantial online bibliography. Fully searchable. Edited by Karen E. Burgess.

The Celtic Twilight

http://www.celtic-twilight.com/

At first glance unscholarly, this quirky nonacademic site offers nevertheless online editions of texts ranging from Gregory of Tours's *History of the Franks* to *Bullfinch's Mythology*. Especially strong collection of Arthurian miscellany. Maintained by Jim Donaldson.

Celts and Saxons Home Page

http://www.primenet.com/~lconley/bookmarks.html

Metasite with extensive links to both academic and popular sites. Maintained by Lawrence Conley.

Diplomatarium Norvegicum

http://www.dokpro.uio.no/engelsk/about_dn.html

A searchable database of transcriptions of some 20,000 diplomas relating to Norway from A.D. 1050 to A.D. 1590. Maintained by Bjørn Eithun, University of Oslo.

DScriptorium

http://www.byu.edu/~hurlbut/dscriptorium/

This project, at Brigham Young University, is devoted to collecting, storing, and distributing digital images of medieval manuscripts. Maintained by Jesse Hurlbut.

Dumbarton Oaks

http://www.doaks.org/Byzantine.html

The Dumbarton Oaks Research Library and Collection, in Washington, D.C., has one of the best collections of Byzantine images, rare books, and research materials. The collection is searchable online.

Early Medieval Resources for Britain, Ireland, and Brittany

http://members.aol.com/michellezi/resources-index.html

This nonacademic site contains good chronologies, bibliographies, links, and translations of early Welsh poetry. Maintained by Michelle Ziegler.

Early Music Institute

http://www.music.indiana.edu/som/emi/

The Web site of the Early Music Institute, at the Indiana University School of Music, offers information about recordings and performances of medieval music as well as scholarly articles and bibliographies.

Electronic Beowulf

http://www.uky.edu/%7Ekiernan/BL/kportico.html

The Electronic Beowulf Project is a huge database of digital images of the *Beowulf* manuscript and related manuscripts and printed texts. Includes bibliographies and links to online Old English dictionaries.

Essays in Medieval Studies

http://www.luc.edu/publications/medieval/

Essays in Medieval Studies: The Proceedings of the Illinois Medieval Association is available online. The general editor of the online version is Allen J. Frantzen.

Every Celtic Thing on the Web

http://og=man.net

One of the most extensive metasites for things Celtic. Contains many nonscholarly links, but also a few gems, including sites on medieval Brittany, Cornwall, and Galicia. Maintained by "Angus Og."

A Gazetteer of Sub-Roman Britain (A.D. 400–600): The British Sites

http://intarch.ac.uk/journal/issue3/snyder_index.html

An article in the refereed online journal *Internet Archaeology*. This electronic version of the author's *Sub-Roman Britain (A.D. 400–600): A Gazetteer of Sites* (Oxford, 1996) includes a clickable map, many color photographs, and a searchable database.

Gregorian Chant Home Page

http://silvertone.princeton.edu/chant_html/

This site is full of links and resources supporting advanced research on Gregorian chant. Maintained at Princeton University by Peter Jeffery.

The Heroic Age

http://members.aol.com/heroicage1/homepage.html

The Heroic Age is a refereed online journal dedicated to the study of Northwestern Europe from the Late Roman Empire to the advent of the Norman Empire. Issues include feature articles, essays, book and film reviews, archaeology news, historical biographies, and "Medievalia on the Web."

Hill Monastic Manuscript Library

http://www2.csbsju.edu/hmml/index.html

The Hill Monastic Manuscript Library at Saint John's University in Minnesota has several medieval manuscripts in its collection. At their Web site you can view images of these manuscripts, hear audio files of medieval music, and connect to related medieval sites.

The Historicity and Historicisation of Arthur

http://www.users.globalnet.co.uk/~tomgreen/arthur.htm

An online article by Thomas Green that examines the historical and archaeological evidence for the existence of King Arthur. Contains a good bibliography with links to other Internet resources.

History Today

http://www.historytoday.com/article/index.cfm?chronology_id=2

History Today, an acclaimed British popular history magazine, has a Web site that features several articles and book reviews in medieval history.

The International Medieval Institute

http://www.leeds.ac.uk/imi/

The Web site of the International Medieval Institute contains information about their annual conference at Leeds, the published proceedings of the conference, and their *International Medieval Bibliography (IMB)*. Trustworthy links as well.

The Internet Medieval Sourcebook

http://www.fordham.edu/halsall/sbook.html

One of the first and most extensive online collections of medieval texts, both excerpts and full texts. Though many are older English translations, the site also includes texts in French, Spanish, and Latin, as well as some secondary literature. Searchable, with texts listed under convenient categories as well as by author and title. Maintained at Fordham University by Paul Halsall.

Irish & Celtic Resources on the Internet

http://english.glendale.cc.ca.us/irish.html

A metasite with lots of links to Irish art and literature, Celtic history, and Gaelic language sites. Maintained by Dennis Doyle at Glendale Community College.

Jorvik Viking Centre

http://www.jorvik-viking-centre.co.uk/

The Web site of the Jorvik Viking Centre, the acclaimed living history museum in York, England, features museum information, links, and Viking sights and sounds. Sponsored by the York Archaeological Trust.

The Journal of Medieval History

http://www.elsevier.co.jp/inca/publications/store/5/0/5/5/9/1/

The Web site of the *Journal of Medieval History (JMH)* features searchable tables of contents, perspective author information, and online ordering of a sample paper copy. Hosted by Elsevier Science.

The Labyrinth: Resources for Medieval Studies

http://www.georgetown.edu/labyrinth/labyrinth-home.html

One of the first and most highly acclaimed medieval Internet sites. In addition to its impressive collection of texts and images, the Labyrinth provides connections to databases, services, texts, and images on other servers around the world. The Labyrinth is sponsored by Georgetown University and is fully searchable.

Llys Arthur

http://www.webexcel.ndirect.co.uk/gwarnant/arthur/arthur.htm

Welsh for "Arthur's Hall," this nonacademic site offers hard-to-find medieval Welsh poetry and genealogies in addition to speculation on the historical Arthur. Maintained by Jeff Davies.

Maps of Medieval Islam

http://ccat.sas.upenn.edu/~rs143/map.html

An online collection of color maps tracing the development of Islam in the Middle Ages. Part of Barbara R. von Schlegell's Islamic Religion course at the University of Pennsylvania.

Marginality and Community in Medieval Europe

http://www.kenyon.edu/projects/margin/margin.htm

Designed as a class project at Kenyon College, this site has good articles, bibliographies, and links to primary source documents.

Mediæval Sword Resource Site

http://www.aiusa.com/medsword/

This noncommercial site provides information of interest to students and collectors of medieval European swords and other edged weapons. Good bibliography. Maintained by Lee A. Jones.

Medieval Academic Discussion Groups

http://www.towson.edu/~duncan/acalists.html

Maintained by Edwin Duncan. Contains descriptions of the lists and subscription addresses.

Medieval Academy of America

http://www.georgetown.edu/MedievalAcademy/

The Medieval Academy's Web page has information about publications (including its journal, *Speculum*), conferences, awards, and jobs for medievalists.

Medieval & Renaissance Europe—Primary Historical Documents

http://library.byu.edu/~rdh/eurodocs/medren.html

Part of the Primary Historical Documents project at Brigham Young University, this metasite has links to medieval manuscript facsimilies, original language texts, and English translations.

Medieval & Renaissance History

http://www.nyu.edu/gsas/dept/history/internet/geograph/europe/medieval/

Good metasite from the history department at New York University.

Medieval Art and Architecture

http://www1.pitt.edu/~medart/index.html

Alison Stones of the University of Pittsburgh has a Web site that features images of medieval art and architecture as well as a useful glossary of terms.

Medieval Canon Law

http://www.maxwell.syr.edu/maxpages/faculty/penningk/

Ken Pennington's home page includes very useful essays, bibliographies, and texts concerning medieval canon law. Professor Pennington has also made available online his medieval course syllabi and information about the Medieval and Renaissance Studies program at Syracuse University.

Medieval Drama Links

http://www.leeds.ac.uk/theatre/emd/links.htm

A good (and selective) metasite that offers links not just to drama but also music, costume, and dance. Created by Sydney Higgins and sponsored by the Workshop Theatre of the University of Leeds.

Medieval English Towns

http://www.trytel.com/~tristan/towns/towns.html

Stephen Alsford's very useful site provides capsule histories of select English towns, primary sources, and links to other sites on medieval towns.

Medieval History Lectures

http://www.ukans.edu/kansas/medieval/lecture_index.html

Lynn Nelson at the University of Kansas has made available online several of his undergraduate medieval history lectures.

Medieval Literary Resources

http://andromeda.rutgers.edu/~jlynch/Lit/medieval.html

An excellent metasite with links to primary sources (in several languages), modern criticism, academic sites, journals, and organizations for medievalists. Maintained by Jack Lynch at Rutgers University.

The Medieval Review

http://www.hti.umich.edu/b/bmr/tmr.html

This book review journal (formerly the *Bryn Mawr Medieval Review*, now published by Western Michigan University) is searchable and has put all of its reviews since 1993 online.

Medieval Scandinavia and Anglo-Saxon Britain

http://www.fas.harvard.edu/~layher1/medscan.html

A metasite featuring links to Norse and Old English texts, runic inscriptions, fonts, and museum collections with Viking artifacts. Maintained on the Harvard University server by William Layher.

The Medieval Science Page

http://members.aol.com/McNelis/medsci_index.html

A metasite with links related to all aspects of medieval and Renaissance science. Edited by James McNelis.

Medieval Studies at Oxford University

http://firth.natcorp.ox.ac.uk/cgi-bin/humbul/section.pl?SECTION=medieval

This metasite features good links to primary sources, manuscript facsimiles, images, bibliographies, journals, and academic sites.

Medieval Studies at UC–Davis

http://philo.ucdavis.edu/MST/index.html

A good metasite, housed at the University of California at Davis, with lots of links to primary sources.

The Middle English Collection

http://etext.virginia.edu/me.browse.html

The Middle English Collection at the Electronic Text Center at the University of Virginia includes everything from mystery plays to the works of Chaucer. Fully searchable.

The Miller Project

http://www.icemt.iastate.edu/~timmyg/miller/index.html

A unique site featuring computer-aided reconstructions of historic buildings. Includes still images and VRML models of the cathedrals of Speyer and Notre Dame (Paris). The Miller Project is a cooperative effort between the Iowa Center for Emerging Manufacturing Technology (ICEMT) and the Iowa State University Department of Architecture.

The Miningco Guide to Medieval Resources

http://historymedren.miningco.com/

This popular metasite/search engine has devoted a lot of effort to collecting medieval links. The sites represented are a mixed bag, but include online essays, scholarly journals, map collections, and images.

NetSERF

http://netserf.cua.edu/

A metasite with over 1,000 medieval-related links, located at the Catholic University of America. Also contains an excellent glossary of medieval terms and a guestbook for visiting medievalists.

Old English Pages

http://www.georgetown.edu/cball/oe/old_english.html

The most diverse and perhaps useful of the Old English Web sites, maintained by Cathy Ball at Georgetown University. Here are links to dependable history and language sites, plus information about software, courses, manuscript images, and even sound recordings (in Real Audio) of early English poetry.

The Online Medieval and Classical Library (OMACL)

http://sunsite.berkeley.edu/OMACL/

English translations of more than thirty medieval and classical texts (not excerpts). Searchable, with links to other primary source collections. Housed at the University of California–Berkeley and maintained by Douglas B. Killings.

ORBCOnline Reference Book for Medieval Studies

http://orb.rhodes.edu

This is an ambitious project to create an online textbook for medieval studies. Contains links, primary sources and images, instructional materials, and original "encyclopedia" essays on over a dozen medieval topics.

Peritia

http://www.ucc.ie/peritia/index.html

Peritia is the journal of the Medieval Academy of Ireland. Its Web site features contents and abstracts from past issues as well as related links. Maintained at University College, Cork.

The Pictish Arts Society

http://www.kapnobatai.demon.co.uk/pictarts/

The official home page of the Pictish Arts Society, a charitable organization dedicated to the study and discussion of Pictish and Early Scottish history. The site includes contents of their journal, online book reviews, bibliography, and related links.

The Pictish Nation

http://members.tripod.com/~Halfmoon/index.html

The first Internet site devoted to the Picts, the obscure inhabitants of early medieval Scotland. A nonacademic site, with an impressive collection of links (though of varying quality) and a good bibliography. Maintained by Catriona Fraser.

Plague and Public Health in Renaissance Europe

http://jefferson.village.virginia.edu/osheim/intro.html

A hypertext archive of narratives, medical consilia, governmental records, religious and spiritual writings, and images documenting epidemic disease in Western Europe between 1348 and 1530. Published by the Institute for Advanced Technology in the Humanities at the University of Virginia.

PORTICO: The British Library

http://www.bl.uk/

The British Library's Web site features images, translations, and bibliographies of three important medieval manuscripts in their collection: *Beowulf*, the *Lindisfarne Gospels*, and the *Magna Carta*.

PSC Medieval Society

http://oz.plymouth.edu/~medsoc/links.html

The Plymouth State College Medieval Society has a links page with a significant number of both academic and nonacademic medieval sites.

Richard III Society

http://www.richardiii.net/

The Web site of the Richard III Society (London) is dedicated to the study of fifteenth-century England and to the scholarly reassessment of the much-maligned English king. It features essays, links, and information about the Society's journal and conference. The North American branch also has an excellent Web site (http://www.r3.org/).

The Robin Hood Project

http://www.lib.rochester.edu/camelot/rh/rhhome.stm

The Robin Hood Project is designed to make available in electronic format a database of texts, images, bibliographies, and basic information about Robin Hood. The project is sponsored by the University of Rochester and is overseen by Alan Lupack.

ROMIOSINI: Hellenism in the Middle Ages

http://www.greece.org/Romiosini/

This site, sponsored by the Hellenic Electronic Center, includes essays, maps, genealogies, bibliographies, and photos of Byzantine churches and icons. Maintained by Professor Nikolaos Provatas and Yiannis Papadimas.

Secrets of the Norman Invasion

http://www.cablenet.net/pages/book/index.htm

This rather unique Web site features essays, primary sources, and aerial photographs relating to the landing of the Normans in England in 1066. Included are photographs of the Bayeaux Tapestry. Created by Nick Austin of The Landscape Channel (UK).

The Sutton Hoo Society

http://www.suttonhoo.org/

The Web page of the Sutton Hoo society contains bibliography, maps, photos, and an interactive tour of the famous Anglo-Saxon royal burial.

The Texas Medieval Association

http://www.towson.edu/~duncan/tmahome.html

The home page of the Texas Medieval Association (or TEMA) serves as a good medieval metasite as well as offering information about their organization and conferences. Maintained by Edwin Duncan at Towson University.

Thesaurus Musicarum Latinarum

http://www.music.indiana.edu/tml/start.html

The Thesaurus Musicarum Latinarum (TML) is an evolving online database of the entire corpus of Latin music theory written during the Middle Ages and the Renaissance. Sponsored by the Center for the History of Music Theory and Literature at Indiana University, Thomas J. Mathiesen, Director.

The Très Riches Heures du Duc de Berry

http://humanities.uchicago.edu/images/heures/heures.html

Online images of and background text to this early fifteenth-century "book of hours," considered by many to be the greatest example of late medieval manuscript illumination.

The Viking Home Page

http://www.control.chalmers.se/vikings/indexframe.html

A Swedish metasite with several good links to academic sites and texts. Maintained by Lars Jansson.

The World of Dante

http://www.iath.virginia.edu/dante/

A hypermedia project for the study of the *Inferno*, using VRML to search and navigate the text. Created by Deborah Parker and the Institute for Advanced Technology in the Humanities at the University of Virginia.

The World of the Vikings

http://www.pastforward.co.uk/vikings/

A Viking metasite with international links to museums, texts, ship images, and essays.

The WSU Anglo-Saxon Homepage

http://www.wsu.edu:8080/~hanly/oe/503.html

This home page for Michael Hanley's Old English course at Washington State University serves essentially as a good Anglo-Saxon metasite with some images thrown in. Links to other Old English course Web pages.

RENAISSANCE AND REFORMATION HISTORY
Julia Landweber

METASITES

Discoverers Web

http://www.win.tue.nl/cs/fm/engels/discovery/

Maintained by Dutch historian Andre Engels, the Discoverers Web is an enormous set of links to Web sites about discovery and exploration. The site is especially strong on quality links for the Age of Discovery and European expansion.

Electrifying the Renaissance: Hypertext, Literature, and the World Wide Web

http://humanitas.ucsb.edu/depts/english/coursework/rar/index.html

Electrifying the Renaissance is a visually beautiful site that proposes to illustrate intellectual connections between the Renaissance and the World Wide Web, while at the same time offering an alternative guide for students of the Renaissance and Early Modern periods. The site promises more than it delivers, but it offers a terrific array of links to other Renaissance material on the Web.

European Renaissance and Reformation

http://www.execpc.com/~dboals/rena.html

This is a lengthy list of sites put together primarily for the use of K-12 teachers.

The Fourteenth Century and the Black Death

http://www.eyebeater.com/14.html

This site contains several brief essays and a chronology about the plague in the fourteenth century, combined with a good set of external links to primary documents and current historical and scientific information about the Black Death and its sociocultural backdrop.

Medieval and Renaissance Europe—Primary Historical Documents

http://www.lib.byu.edu/~rdh/eurodocs/medren.html

A subset of the Eurodocs Web site, Medieval and Renaissance Europe offers links to a variety of mostly primary historical documents.

Medieval, Renaissance, Reformation: Western Civilization Act II

http://www.omnibusol.com/medieval.html

This site is a great compendium of links to topics ranging from Machiavelli to the Black Death, to the Spanish Inquisition, and on through castles, cathedrals, medicine, food, drink, and more.

The Reformation

http://www.mun.ca/rels/hrollmann/reform/reform.html

This site links to a variety of texts, in original languages and in English translation, by Luther, Melanchthon, Calvin, Zwingli, Bullinger, the Mennonites, and Catholic reformer St. Ignatius of Loyola. The site also includes a portrait gallery of Reformation figures.

Texts and Documents: Europe

http://history.hanover.edu/europe.html

Maintained by Hanover College, the Texts and Documents: Europe site links to a number of important primary documents for the study of early modern

Europe. Good sources are present for the study of both the Protestant and Catholic Reformations, philosophy, theology, literature, the Renaissance, the Age of Exploration, the Scientific Revolution, and witch hunts.

Witchcraft Craze History

http://www.geocities.com/Athens/2962/witch.html

Privately maintained by a person with an academic background, this site contains a wide variety of links to many areas of early modern witchcraft research. Also included are a precis of current scholarly views on the subject, a regularly updated list of academic publications, timelines of witchhunts in Britain and on the Continent, and other resources.

General Renaissance and Reformation Sites

The Arte of Defense

http://jan.ucc.nau.edu/~wew/fencing.html

The Arte of Defense, run by a bona fide fencing instructor, is dedicated to fifteenth- and sixteenth-century fencing. It includes information on period fencing masters, online instruction manuals, terminology, theatrical combat, and contemporary groups who take part in period fencing demonstrations.

Centre for Reformation and Renaissance Studies

http://citd.scar.utoronto.ca/crrs/index.html

The Centre for Reformation and Renaissance Studies, located in Toronto, Canada, is a library and research center with a strong collection of rare books on the topics of northern humanism, Reformation history, English drama, French literature, and confraternity studies. A particularly rich resource is the Erasmus collection. The Centre also hosts lectures and seminars, and publishes Renaissance and Reformation texts in translation.

Columbus and the Age of Discovery

http://marauder.millersv.edu/~columbus/

A searchable database of over 1,100 text articles pertaining to Columbus and themes of discovery and encounter. The site was built by the History Department of Millersville University of Pennsylvania in conjunction with the U.S. Christopher Columbus Quincentenary Jubilee Commission of 1992, and has unrestricted access.

The Columbus Navigation Home Page

http://www1.minn.net/~keithp/

This top-notch Web site, built by Keith A. Pickering, examines the history, navigation, and landfall of Christopher Columbus, and more generally discusses fifteenth-century navigation and voyages of discovery. It is a wonderful site about early mapmaking and navigational tools, and would make an excellent teaching tool.

Creating French Culture

http://lcweb.loc.gov/exhibits/bnf/bnf0001.html

Creating French Culture is an exhibit of illuminated manuscripts from the collections of the Bibliothèque Nationale de France first presented by the Library of Congress in 1995. The site traces the history of France from Charlemagne to Charles de Gaulle, and it has valuable highlights from the fifteenth through seventeenth centuries, including a focus on the Wars of Religion, which make it a good site for the study of Renaissance and Reformation history.

The Decameron Web

http://www.brown.edu/Departments/Italian_Studies/dweb/dweb.shtml

In addition to the full text of Boccaccio's *Decameron* in its established critical English edition, the Decameron Web provides the reader with very good background information on the literary, historical, and cultural context of the work. The site is intended for college and high school teachers and students.

Del's Dance Book

http://www.pbm.com/~lindahl/del/

Del's Dance Book is a guide to the Renaissance dance styles of Italy, Burgundy, France, and England. The site includes audio and sheet music files for many of these dances.

Digital Dante

http://www.ilt.columbia.edu/projects/dante/index.html

Digital Dante, a project of Columbia University, provides multimedia versions of Dante's works that can serve as research and teaching tools. The site contains, in comparative format, the complete text of *The Divine Comedy* in its original language and in two standard English translations, as well as teaching aids, image collections, and Dante in recent news and exhibits.

Discovery and Reformation

http://www.wsu.edu/~dee/REFORM/

Discovery and Reformation is a cyberspace "research textbook" created by Washington State University. It is intended to be used as a resource for students who seek background material to enhance historical projects about the period of European discovery, the Reformation, and the Northern Renaissance. Resources provided include a historical text, an atlas, a glossary of terms, a collection of primary readings, and an image gallery. The site is still very much a work in progress; nonetheless, it is an exciting portent for the rich future of online textbooks for serious student use.

The Elizabethan Costuming Page

http://www.dnaco.net/~aleed/corsets/general.html

This site began as "The Elizabethan Corset Page," a how-to guide for making an authentic sixteenth-century English corset. Over time the author has expanded her site enormously to include detailed instructions, illustrations, and historical information for designing a complete Elizabethan outfit. It is an excellent site both for historical costume buffs and for those interested in making period clothing.

The Florence Art Guide

http://www.mega.it/eng/egui/hogui.htm

The Florence Art Guide is a succinct and informative hypertext guide to the history, art, and architecture of this most quintessentially Renaissance city. The map-based navigation is an especially helpful feature for learning your way around Florence.

Florentine Renaissance Resources: Online Catasto of 1427

http://www.stg.brown.edu/projects/catasto/overview.html

This is an online version of the tax data for the city of Florence from 1427 to 1429, originally collected by David Herlihy and Christiane Klapisch-Zuber. The site has its own search engine, which helps users to find information for specific people, places, or topics.

The Folger Shakespeare Library

http://www.folger.edu/

This site provides information about the holdings and activities of the Folger Library in Washington, D.C., home to the world's largest collection of Shakespeare's printed works and a large collection of other rare Renaissance books and manuscripts. It also links to the Folger Institute (http://www.folger.edu/institute/nintro.cfm), the center for advanced study and research in the humanities sponsored by the Folger Shakespeare Library and a consortium of other universities.

The Galileo Project

http://es.rice.edu/ES/humsoc/Galileo/

The Galileo Project is a hypertext site on the life and work of Italian astronomer Galileo Galilei and the science of his time. It includes textual and pictorial information about his family, his contemporaries, and his career, a detailed timeline of his life, searchable maps, and links to other resources on the Web about Galileo and also about current astronomy.

The Geometry of War

http://www.mhs.ox.ac.uk/geometry/title.htm

Presented by the Museum of the History of Science, Oxford, United Kingdom, The Geometry of War is a virtual exhibition about the relationship between warfare and geometry from 1500 to 1750. The exhibition highlights how advances in early modern warfare and technology led to many new developments in practical mathematics, and vice versa.

The Internet Renaissance Band

http://www.csupomona.edu/~jcclark/emusic/

This site offers midi files of music from the Middle Ages and Renaissance, sequenced by Curtis Clark. The music is available for free use for noncommercial purposes.

Iter: Gateway to the Renaissance

http://iter.library.utoronto.ca/iter/index.htm

Developed in part by the Renaissance Society of America, Iter is a nonprofit research project that has the goal of creating a collection of online bibliographic databases to increase access to all published materials relating to the Renaissance. To access the databases, a paid subscription (available on an individual and group basis) is required. Free guest access allows entry to a sample subset of the database.

Life and Times of Martin Luther

http://www.reformation.org/luther.html

This is a good image-oriented synopsis of Martin Luther's career as a reformist, although written with a heavily anti-Catholic bias. The site also succinctly explains the origins of the Reformation.

Medieval and Early Modern Data Bank

http://scc01.rutgers.edu/memdb/

The Medieval and Early Modern Data Bank is a project established at Rutgers University and codirected by Professors Rudolph M. Bell of Rutgers University and Martha C. Howell of Columbia University. Its aim is to provide scholars with an expanding library of information in electronic format on currency exchanges and prices in the medieval and early modern periods of European history.

Medieval and Renaissance Brewing Home Page

http://www.pbm.com/~lindahl/brewing.html

The Brewing Home Page is a collection of reference works and guides to medieval and Renaissance brewing. The home page also offers recipes for brewing your own period ale, and links to groups interested in the practice of brewing period ales.

Medieval and Renaissance Embroidery Home Page

http://www.staff.uiuc.edu/~jscole/medembro.html

This site has information about medieval and early modern techniques of embroidery, as well as links to sites on famous tapestries.

Medieval and Renaissance Food Home Page

http://www.pbm.com/~lindahl/food.html

The Medieval and Renaissance Food site provides many articles and recipes to help you recreate period dishes dating before 1600, including the texts of several Renaissance cookery books.

National Geographic Interactive Salem Witchcraft Trials

http://www.nationalgeographic.com/features/97/salem/index.html

The Salem Witchcraft Trials is a moderately interactive approach to understanding the seventeenth-century witchcraft trials in New England. The hook is to let you, the reader, "experience the proceedings first-hand as you assume the identity of a town resident accused of sorcery." The site was designed by *National Geographic* with assistance from historian Richard Trask.

The Newberry Library Center for Renaissance Studies

http://www.newberry.org/nl/renaissance/L3rrenaissance.html

The Newberry Library houses a world-class collection of manuscripts and printed matter from the late medieval and Renaissance periods. The Center for Renaissance Studies, located at the Library, offers programs at graduate and postdoctoral levels, including research training in paleography and other archival skills, workshops, and conferences.

Plague and Public Health in Renaissance Europe

http://jefferson.village.virginia.edu/osheim/intro.html

This site is a hypertext archive of medical consilia, governmental records, and religious writings documenting the arrival, impact, and handling of the Bubonic Plague in the three Italian towns of Florence, Pistoia, and Lucca in 1348.

Le Poulet Gauche

http://www.lepg.org/index.html

Le Poulet Gauche, in its real world incarnation, is a living history recreation of a sixteenth-century tavern in Calais, France, that makes biannual appearances at Society for Creative Anachronism events in the United States. The Web site is an impressively detailed guide to the history, culture, religion, and daily life of sixteenth-century France as seen from the bottom up. This site is designed to be a resource for historical recreation, and in the process it offers nonspecialist readers an unparalleled insight to life in Calais four hundred years ago.

Project Wittenberg

http://www.iclnet.org/pub/resources/text/wittenberg/wittenberg-home.html

Project Wittenberg is a collection of online documents by Martin Luther and related materials by other Lutheran scholars from the sixteenth through nineteenth centuries. The documents are posted both in their original languages and in English translation.

The Renaissance Society of America

http://www.r-s-a.org/

The Renaissance Society of America is the leading organization in the Americas for scholars dedicated to the study of the late medieval, Renaissance, and early modern periods. The home page describes the RSA's activities, membership, publications, annual conference schedule, and an online directory of all members of the RSA.

Rome Reborn: The Vatican Library & Renaissance Culture

http://www.ncsa.uiuc.edu/SDG/Experimental/vatican.exhibit/
Vatican.exhibit.html

This exhibit was originally presented in 1993 by the Library of Congress in Washington, DC. Through a display of rare maps, manuscripts, and books possessed by the Vatican, "Rome Reborn" tells the story of the Vatican Library as "the intellectual driving force behind the emergence of Rome as a political and scholarly superpower during the Renaissance."

Sixteenth-Century Renaissance Fashion, 1500–1530

http://www.marquise.de/

A collection of sixteenth-century paintings by noted artists (Cranach, Dürer, Holbein, Pontormo, and others) that minutely illustrate the clothing of the period.

Tudor England

http://tudor.simplenet.com/

Tudor England is one enthusiast's guide to the Tudor family of England. Also present are pages about the society and architecture of Tudor England, as well as maps, a chronology, and current events related to the Tudors, such as their appearances in recent literature and in theater and film productions.

Tyburn Tree: Public Execution in Early Modern England

http://www.unc.edu/~charliem/index.htm

The Tyburn Tree site contains documents, images, bibliographies, and transcripts of last words. It was originally created by Zachary Lesser of Columbia University in 1995. Charlie Mitchell of the University of Colorado at Boulder has greatly expanded the original site and now maintains it.

The Virtual Sistine Chapel

http://www.rm.astro.it/amendola/sistina.html

A short introduction to the Chapel's construction is followed by a series of high-resolution images of Michelangelo's masterpieces.

Web Gallery of Art

http://gallery.euroweb.hu/

The Web Gallery of Art is an exceptional site for Renaissance and Reformation art history, presenting over 3,500 digital reproductions of European paintings and sculptures created between the years 1200 and 1700. Informative biographies are presented for the more significant artists, and commentaries accompany each high-resolution image. Guided tours and a good search engine are also available.

WebMuseum: La Renaissance

http://metalab.unc.edu/wm/paint/glo/renaissance/

The Renaissance WebMuseum is an excellent introduction to the artistic wealth of the period in Italy, the Netherlands, Germany, and France. High-quality images of famous and lesser-known artworks are paired with good explanations.

Women Philosophers of the Renaissance

http://www.geocities.com/Athens/Forum/9974/ren.html

This site consists of information on a few influential women thinkers of the Renaissance, including Catherine of Siena, Saint Teresa of Avila, Christine de Pisan, Julian of Norwich, and Birgitta of Sweden.

AFRICAN HISTORY
Kathryn L. Green

Africa South of the Sahara
http://www-sul.stanford.edu/depts/ssrg/africa/

This site, developed and maintained by Karen Fung of Stanford University, arose from the 1994 meeting of the African Studies Association Electronic Technology Group. This site is the best starting point for finding links for the study of African history. There are hundreds of links under the "Topics-History" section, and links are also accessed through a separate Countries/Regions section. The site has a "Breaking News" section, which gives numerous links for current events. Fung keeps the site current and has forms to reply to her if broken links, incorrect URLs, or other inaccuracies are found on the site.

African Studies WWW
http://www.sas.upenn.edu/Afrcan_Studies/AS.html

This site is a major gateway for scholarly information on African Studies. Linkage sections include Africa Web Links and Feeds from Africa, Country-Specific links, Black/African Resources, K-12 resources for teachers, and Multimedia and Book links dealing with African Studies. It is maintained by Ali B. Ali-Dinar at the University of Pennsylvania.

An A-Z of African Studies on the Internet
http://docker.library.uwa.edu.au/~plimb/az.html

A gateway site developed by Dr. Peter Limb (University of Western Australia and online editor for H-Africa of the H-Net listserv group). Arranged alphabetically to link users to several hundred Web sites and listservs. A rich resource from which to begin a search.

Columbia University–African Studies Internet Resources
http://www.columbia.edu/cu/libraries/indiv/area/Africa/

A gateway site for news, topical, and geographic Internet resources on Africa.

H-Net African Gateway

http://www.h-net.msu.edu/gateways/africa/

H-Net Humanities and Social Sciences Online is an interdisciplinary organization of scholars interested in the use of the Internet in teaching and research. One of its strongest components is the African section. From this URL gateway, users are taken to links with nine African Studies discussion listservs, to which thousands of scholars are subscribed. Of particular interest to historians of Africa are H-Afresearch, dedicated to the discussion of issues surrounding the use of primary sources in African humanities and social sciences research (edited by Susan Tschabrun and Kathryn Green at California State University–San Bernardino) and H-Africa, dedicated to discussions of Africa's history and culture and African Studies in general (edited by nine scholars from universities around the globe). Each of the listservs has a Web page with archived posted messages and discussion threads.

University of Illinois Center for African Studies

http://wsi.cso.uiuc.edu/CAS/

This is a gateway with numerous links useful for historians and educators dealing with Africa. The site is managed by Professor Al Kagan.

World Wide Web Resources—Africa

http://www.uky.edu/Subject/africa.html

A gateway of various links to African Studies resources presented by the University of Kentucky.

The Abyssinia Cyberspace Gateway

http://www.cs.indiana.edu/hyplan//dmulholl./acg.html

Contains multiple links, including photographs, general information, and mailing lists for Djibouti, Eritrea, Ethiopia, Somalia, and Somaliland. The author seems to be several years behind in updating his postings. Authored by Daniel Yacob.

Adminet—Africa

http://www.adminet.com/Africa/

This is a French commercial site with entries for Africa by topic and country.

Africa.com: History

http://www.africa.com/history.html

This site has a varied assortment of essays and photographic displays of the continent and its history. It is dominated by South African topics and photos. Copyright holder is ATIO Corp.

AfricaNews Online

http://www.africanews.org/

This site has daily headline news from around the continent, various other news links, rich archives and background papers, and is searchable by region, country, and topics. The site also offers a gateway link for Africa Resources Online.

Africa Policy Information Center (APIC)

http://www.africapolicy.org/

APIC produces documents on major issues in Africa in which the United States has an interest. The site contains APIC documents, full-text archives on this site from 1995 and of selected APIC publications, surveys, and survey reports. It also has several policy/development links for African issues. It is an important site for more recent African history.

Africa Research Central: A Clearinghouse of African Primary Sources

http://africa-research.csusb.edu/index.htm

This site, developed by Kathryn Green and Susan Tschabrun, serves as a gateway to archives, libraries, and museums that have important collections of African primary sources, focusing on collections in Africa, Europe, and North America. The site is aimed at both researchers and repository professionals and seeks to bring these two professional groups together to facilitate research and to better preserve the primary sources—written, audio, photographic, and material culture—that are at risk in many areas of the continent. Some full-text documents and archival guides are available on the site. Future plans for the site—which is constantly updated through questionnaires and user input—include a "For Educators" section to publicize creative efforts to use African primary source material in teaching and learning.

African Art: Aesthetics and Meaning: An Electronic Exhibition Catalog

http://viva.lib.virginia.edu/dic/exhib/93.ray.aa/African.html

This online exhibition catalog of the Bayly Art Museum at the University of Virginia is part of the university's extensive audio and visual collections of their digital media center. The exhibition catalog contains a short discussion of African aesthetics.

African History and Studies

http://www.tntech.edu/WWW/ACAD/HIST/African.html

This site, constructed by the History Department of Tennessee Technological University, is a page of links to over forty-five Web sites on African history and studies, and sites of some American Universities with African Studies programs and a few discussion lists and journals for African history.

African Indigenous Science and Knowledge Systems

http://members.aol.com/afsci/africana.htm

This site presents abstracts of articles and book-length works on various aspects of African science and technology. It also presents Africana links to various regional and topical Web resources on African history, science, and technology. Presented by Gloria Emeagwali of the History Department at Central Connecticut State University.

African Internet Resources Relevant to Museums

http://www.icom.org/africom/africa1.htm

This page, authored by Andrew Roberts, is produced by the International Committee for Documentation of the International Council of Museums and consists of links to Internet home pages of museums in Africa or with African collections, as well as related organizations on the Internet, African programs of international organizations on the Internet, African subject information relevant to museums on the Internet and general interest African Internet resources relevant to museums. The page was produced in 1996, and some of the links are no longer extant.

The African Media Review Project

http://www.und.ac.za/und/ccms/afriprog/afriproj.htm

This media (film, TV, and video) review project of the University of Natal Cultural and Media Studies Program is linked to the African Media Program at Michigan State University. Both projects are designed to "assist...teachers, instructors, and students in identifying appropriate teaching and research materials for classroom use on film and video." Numerous links on the site lead the user to full text articles on cultural and media issues in Africa. The site has articles discussing films about apartheid, as well as critical reviews and articles of other media productions.

African National Congress

http://www.anc.org.za/

The home page of the major anti-apartheid resistance group and post-apartheid political party, this is a rich site with links to the home pages of the first two post-apartheid presidents, as well as to a very rich "government info" link that contains verbatim texts of legislation, commission reports (including the full text of the Truth and Reconciliation Commission report), conference documents, discussion documents, policy documents, notices, press statements, proclamations, regulations, reports, speeches, summits, and white papers. There are also links from the government information page to other South African Internet resources.

The African Studies Association

http://www.sas.upenn.edu/African_Studies/Home_Page/ASA_Menu.html

This home page for the American African Studies Association gives all the pertinent information about the organization, as well as links to its journals, papers, and book publications in African Studies. This site is maintained by Ali B. Ali-Dinar of the University of Pennsylvania.

African Studies at Central Connecticut State University

http://www.ccsu.edu/Afstudy/

In addition to information on the university's program, the site contains full-text articles from their publication *Africa Update* and a gateway for a few online resources in African Studies.

L'Afrique à Paris VII

http://www.sedet.jussieu.fr/sedet/Afrilab/Afrhome.htm

This site of the University of Paris-VII has links that bring up francophone sites that are not listed in many other gateway sites.

Afrique francophone

http://www.lehman.cuny.edu/depts/langlit/french/afrique.html

This is a site of assorted links to sites on francophone Africa. It contains some links for francophone Africa that are not always found on anglophone gateway sites. Authored by Bob Peckman, Professor of French at the City University of New York.

The Atlantic Slave Trade: Demographic Simulation

http://www.whc.neu.edu/simulation/afrintro.html

This simulation was developed by Patrick Manning and Computer Science Department members of Northeastern University. Manning writes: "This simulation, in summarizing available information on slave trade— and combining it with what is known of normal human patterns of birth, death, and migration—has made it possible to offer a coherent picture of African and diaspora population in the era of slave trade. In exploring the simulation, you are invited to vary the demographic conditions and see their implications."

BBC World Service Online: Africa

http://news.bbc.co.uk/hi/english/world/africa/default.htm

This is an important site for recent African history, archived from November of 1997 with a searchable database.

Center for Middle Eastern Studies, University of Texas–Austin

http://link.lanic.utexas.edu/menic/

This site has extensive topical and geographical links, as well as country-specific links for the traditionally included African countries of the "Middle

East" rubric: Algeria, Egypt, Libya, Mauritania, Morocco, Sudan, and Tunisia, including links to K-12 educational resources for teachers.

Central Oregon Community College Humanities 211

http://www.cocc.edu/cagatucci/classes/hum211/index.htm

This site is the home page for Cora Agatucci's interdisciplinary African humanities class at Central Oregon Community College. There are extensive and annotated links on topics regarding African literature, history, and film, and the site seems to be updated fairly frequently. It is a very good resource for teachers and students.

Eric Chary's Home Page

http://www.wesleyan.edu/~echarry/

Professor Chary, an ethnomusicologist of Mande and West African music, has created a site with good links for the history of West African music and instruments as well as world music sites. Sound, graphics, and videos illustrating some of his articles are also posted.

Clio en afrique: L'histoire africaine en langue française

http://www.africanews.org/

This site was created by Jean-Louis Triaud of the Université de Provence. It is dedicated to African history in the French language. The site contains issues of their review bulletin of African history on-line. Each bulletin contains editorials, thematic articles, bibliographical studies, reviews, and conference notices. Some full-text articles and published papers are also presented.

CODESRIA—Council for the Development of Social Science Research in Africa

http://www.sas.upenn.edu/African_Studies/codesria.html

This council, headquartered in Senegal, works on various project initiatives surrounding development issues and the social sciences. The page contains information on current projects, funding and grants, documentation, and publications. The site is edited by Ali A. Ali-Dinar of the University of Pennsylvania.

COSATU—Congress of South African Trade Unions

http://www.cosatu.org.za/

This home page of COSATU is a good starting point for labor history in Africa, and in South Africa in particular. The site has many links to other labor Internet resources, policy papers, documents, resolutions, submissions, and speeches of the organization.

Egypt and the Ancient Near East, Web Resources for Young People and Teachers

http://www-oi.uchicago.edu/dept/ra/abzu youth_resources.html

This site is a project and publication of The Research Archives of the Oriental Institute, Chicago. It contains extensive links dealing with ancient Egypt for students and for teachers. It is authored, edited, and maintained by Alexandra A. O'Brien.

Egyptian Government CultureNet Home Page

http://www.idsc.gov.eg/culture/index.htm

This site is divided into five sections: Ancient, Coptic, Islamic, Sites, and Museums. The sections include photography and text introductions. Some of the introductions suffer from poor copyediting. The Museums section has a comprehensive listing of Egyptian museums, with links to those with Web pages, as well as 140 international museums with Egyptian collections.

Eloquent Elegance

http://minotaur.marques.co.za/clients/zulu

This site gives a history of African traditional beadwork, traditional beadwork in the Zulu nation, and a history of the Zulu nation. In addition, illustrations of the various beadworks discussed are given. Presented by Dr. H.S. Schoeman.

"Ethiopia: Land of Plenty," *One World Magazine*

http://www.envirolink.org/oneworld/focus/etiopia/index.html

This site is a 1996 production of an online environmental publication focused on Ethiopia. It contains beautiful photography, and the text is divided into sections produced by established scholars into "The Past," "The Land," and "The People."

Fourth World Documentation Project: Africa

http://www.cwis.org/africa.html

This site is a project of the Center for World Indigenous Studies and contains the full text of approximately twelve studies on various regions in Africa where indigenous peoples are at risk.

Human Rights Watch Reports in Print

http://www.hrw.org/hrw/pubweb/

This site gives full-text documents of various Human Rights Watch reports on Africa, on their analysis of U.S. policy in Africa, and of various specific African countries that have been deemed by this international organization to have human rights issues that need to be addressed.

INCORE (Initiative on Conflict Resolution and Ethnicity) Guide to Internet Sources on Conflict and Ethnicity in Algeria

http://www.incore.ulst.ac.uk/cds/countries/algeria.html

This is a must-see site for anyone interested in the history of Algeria. It has a multitude of links for North African and Islamic sources, as well as Algeria-specific sites. It also contains links to full-text articles on the specific topic of ethnic strife in Algeria.

Internet African History Sourcebook

http://www.fordham.edu/halsall/africa/africasbook.html

This site is a subsite derived from three other Internet History Sourcebooks (Ancient, Medieval, and Modern) produced by Paul Halsall of the Fordham University History Department. "In addition to direct links to documents, links are made to a number of other Web resources." The African sourcebook contains materials on: General African History (including documents/articles on debates in the Africanist communities) human origins, ancient Egypt and other ancient African societies; Greek and Roman Africa, Africa and Islam, Ethiopia and Christianity, Slavery, European Imperialism, Modern Africa, Gender and Sexuality in Modern Africa, and Further Resources on African History. An important site for teachers of all age groups.

The Kennedy Center African Odyssey Interactive

http://artsedge.kennedy-center.org/odyssey.html

"The purpose of African Odyssey Interactive (AOI) is to promote an ongoing exchange of ideas, information, and resources between artists, teachers, and students of African arts and culture." The program focuses on culture, dance, music, textiles, storytelling, and theater, and the site has links to online resources for the study of African history and culture.

The Living Africa

http://hyperion.advanced.org/16645/contents.html

This site is of interest for K-12 teachers in particular. It was completed in August of 1998 as part of the Thinkquest 98 contest involving student world collaboration on creating educational resources for the Internet community. This particular site was produced by three students from the United States, the Netherlands, and India, and involves multiple text and photographic links about Africa, its peoples, its wildlife, and its lands. It also includes feedback forms for communicating with the authors.

Mamluk Bibliography Home Page

http://www.lib.uchicago.edu/LibInfo/SourcesBySubject/MiddleEast/MamBib.html

This site is part of an ongoing project of the Middle East Documentation Center of the University of Chicago. It is a project dedicated to compiling all research and discussion, scholarly and popular, germane to the Mamluk sultanate of Egypt and Syria. The bibliography is divided into nineteen categories and is searchable.

MANSA/Mande Studies Association

www.oswego.edu/other_campus/stud.org/mansa

This multidisciplinary organization's Web site contains information on the organization, the Mande peoples of West Africa, photographs submitted by various researchers of this region, and links to Internet resources and information on MANSA conferences and history. The site is still under construction, by David Conrad, SUNY–Oswego.

Repositories of Primary Sources: Africa and the Near East

http://www.uidaho.edu/special-collections/africa.html

Prepared by T. Abraham of the University of Idaho, this site gives links to African archives that have Web sites as well as additional links to various archival and museum collection sites on the Web.

South African Truth and Reconciliation Commission

http://www.truth.org.za/final/index.html/

This rich site has a searchable database, audio recordings of interviews with Desmond Tutu, a photo gallery, an amnesty database, reports of the various committees of the commission, and numerous links to related sites. The site is designed, authored, and maintained by Steve Crawford, an "independent computer consultant" and is not an official government site.

South African War Virtual Library

http://www.uq.net.au/~zzrwotto/

This rich site, authored by Robert Wotton, has photographs, a variety of links on military history and the Boer War, and a searchable database by subject for numerous issues on the history of this period in South African history.

Swiss Society of African Studies (SAG-SSEA)

http://www-sagw.unine.ch/members2/sag-ssea/Home.htm

This is a trilingual site (French, German, English) offering numerous links. In addition, the Webmaster of the site, Roger Pfister, has published a work entitled Internet for Africanists and others interested in Africa, through the Swiss Society of African Studies, that has over five hundred Internet addresses on Africa. It is currently out of print, but the author continues to update the information through the site listings.

United Nations High Commissioner for Refugees—Africa

http://www.unhcr.ch/world/afri/afri.htm

This site gives country profiles for most African countries, and each profile has a series of links dealing with issues of interest in refugee studies and historical background on the conflicts involved. There is also a section "For

Teachers" that links to discussions, articles, and sites on the history of asylum and various refugee issues. There are a multitude of links and descending levels on this site. A rich resource.

United Nations Reliefweb/IRIN (Integrated Regional Information Network)

http://www.reliefweb.int/IRIN

From the site: "The regions covered by the IRINs—sub-Saharan Africa and the Caucasus and Central Asia—are often underreported, misunderstood, or ignored....By fostering greater awareness and understanding of regional issues and events, the IRINs contribute to better-informed and more effective humanitarian action and media coverage, including emergency preparedness and advocacy....As well as producing their own reports daily and weekly, the Networks collect publications from UN agencies, local and international NGOs, the Red Cross and Red Crescent Movement, the OAU, governments, academia, and more. These are then made available either in response to specific inquiries or by subscriptions to a suite of mailing lists." The mailing lists of this organization are very important for anyone interested in contemporary Africa.

University of Chicago—Oriental Institute Nubia Salvage Project and Exhibitions

http://www-oi.uchicago.edu/OI/PROJ/NUB/Nubia.html

This site has good historical introductions to the salvage project of ancient Nubia and two exhibitions (1987 and 1992) of the institute's museum coming from the salvage expeditions. Many of the pieces from the UNESCO expedition are part of the institute's permanent collection, and there are quite a few photos of these objects, along with good historical introductions available on this site.

WoYaa!

http://www.woyaa.com/

Searchable database with numerous thematic entries. Advertises its mission: "to promote Digital Africa by easing and making cost-effective navigation and communication as well as increasing the visibility of African Web sites and resources."

ASIAN HISTORY
Jeffrey G. Barlow

METASITES

Asian Studies Online Bookshops

http://www.ciolek.com/WWWVLPages/AsiaPages/VLBookshops.html

Another resource-oriented site, this is the guide to online bookstores in Asian Studies. These shops have a strong Internet presence, including online ordering procedures in several cases.

Asian Studies WWW Virtual Library

http://coombs.anu.edu.au/WWWVL-AsianStudies.html

In Asian Studies the grandest of the WWWVL sites is this metasite at the Australian National University (Coombs) maintained by Dr. T. Matthew Ciolek. The Coombs site is staggering in its extent and will lead the visitor to literally thousands of additional sites in every conceivable field of Asian Studies.

Council on East Asian Studies

http://darkwing.uoregon.edu/~felsing/ceal/welcome.html

Though not precisely a metasite, the Council of East Asian Libraries, maintained at the very rich University of Oregon Darkwing server can lead the researcher to a host of specific resources. It also links to a series of pages on how best to access character-based Asian languages on the Internet. Some of these pages have unfortunately not been updated recently, but many of the links are useful ones.

Internet Resources for East Asian Studies: China

http://lark.cc.ukans.edu/~eastasia/linkcall.html

Another metasite, this one at the University of Kansas at Lawrence, has been nominated by Geoff Wade, Research Officer at the Center of Asian Studies, University of Hong Kong. This is an astonishingly large and diverse site. Its many materials on using Asian languages on the Internet are particularly useful, as this is a key problem for Asianists on the WWW.

Library of Congress Experimental Search System

http://lcweb2.loc.gov/catalog/

While more a general search engine than a metasite, the Library of Congress's search system, again nominated by Geoff Wade, is among the best places to look for Asian Studies resources. It searches the enormous holdings of the library and has facilities for very sophisticated narrowly defined searches.

World Area Studies Internet Resources

http://www.wcsu.ctstateu.edu/socialsci/area.html

This metasite, "World Area Studies Resources," sponsored by Western Connecticut State University, is one of those surprising sites that appears to be largely the work of a single zealous individual, in this case "J. Bannister." It covers not only Asian Studies but many other areas as well and has won a number of awards.

World Wide Web Virtual Library: Subject Catalogues

http://www.fisk.edu/vl/Overview2.html

This is the "distributed subject catalogue" of the WWW Virtual Library (WWWVL), a massive cataloguing project where each topic or division is maintained by experts in that field. Almost any search in any field should begin here, but particularly one in Asian History.

East Asia

Asian-Pacific Economic Cooperation Web Site

http://www.apecsec.org.sg/

This is an area wide site, also nominated by Geoff Wade, and is maintained by the organization for Asian-Pacific Economic Cooperation. It is a gigantic site with many free publications to download. This would be particularly useful for those working in recent history, and in economic issues.

Asian Studies—WWW Search Engines Guide

http://www.ciolek.com/SearchEngines.html#asia

The metasites listed above are a useful gateway into Asia on the Web, but subject area sites devoted to geographic areas or to individual countries are also very important ones. This is a good place to begin for country-specific search engines. While the entire article "Annotated Guide to WWW Search Engines," edited by Dr. Ciolek, is a very useful one, by scrolling down to the entry "Simple Search Engines, Asia Databases," one encounters a wide variety of search engines in individual countries of Asia. Most are commercial sites, but as they contain search engines for sites specific to that country or culture, each is an important resource for that country and will presumably uncover materials not found in larger sites or search engines.

China

China Home Page

http://solar.rtd.utk.edu/~china/china.html

This is one of the oldest WWW sites maintained in China, at the Institute for High Energy Physics, Beijing.

Chinese Window

http://china-window.com/northusa/chinw97.htm

The Chinese Studies field is unavoidably politicized because of the Cold War and the continuing rivalry between China and Taiwan. This site is that of a large commercial agency that is attempting to avoid these issues while facilitating the expansion of the WWW for business purposes in China.

European Association of Sinological Librarians

http://www.uni-kiel.de/easl/easl.html.

This very useful site is maintained by the European Association of Sinological Librarians. This site provides entry into a wide variety of collections and resources in Chinese studies.

Internet Guide for China Studies

http://sun.sino.uni-heidelberg.de/netguide/netguide.htm

This site is the WWWVL Internet Guide to Chinese Studies, maintained by Hanno Lecher at Heidelberg University.

Selected Works of Mao Tse-tung

http://www.maoism.org/msw/mao_sw.htm

This site is another example of the high degree of politicization of the Chinese Studies field, as well as an example of how scholars may benefit from it. This is an extensive online archive of the works of Mao Zedong. This homage to a Chinese revolutionary is in English, was digitized in India, and apparently is maintained by the Communist Party of Peru, and is hosted on a server in the United States.

U.S. Embassy in China

http://www.usembassy-china.org.cn/

This is the site of the U.S. embassy in Beijing and has many useful resources for study of or travel to the People's Republic of China.

Taiwan

Academia Sinica

http://www.sinica.edu.tw/

This is the site of the central scholarly institution in Taiwan, the Academia Sinica. Its site is a true treasure for Asia historians, as it permits full-text retrieval of ninety-two million characters of ancient Chinese texts.

Taiwan, Ilha Formosa

http://www.taiwandc.org/index.html

This site provides an index of Taiwanese organizations.

Taiwan WWW Virtual Library

http://peacock.tnjc.edu.tw/taiwan-wwwvl.html

This, the WWWVL site for Taiwan, is maintained at Tung Nan (Dong Nan) Junior College of Technology in Taiwan. While this site is an exhaustive one, it should be mentioned that it has apparently not been updated since September of 1997 and must be badly dated.

Japan

Japan Information Network

http://www.jinjapan.org/index.html

This is a specifically Japanese metasite. It has a very sophisticated (if annoyingly slow) search engine that will turn up both graphical and textual files. As of this writing there were many bad links in the site and one wonders if it is being maintained adequately.

Japan Policy Research Institute

http://www.nmjc.org/jpri/

The Japan Policy Research Institute, begun by Chalmers Johnson, is a very active rapidly growing site with a great deal of information relating to historical and contemporary issues affecting Japan, and U.S.–Japanese relations.

Network Pacific Asia

http://law.rikkyo.ac.jp/npa/indx.htm

The Network Pacific Asia is an interesting site in Japanese Studies maintained at Rikkyo University in Tokyo. It provides entrée to a number of journals, book reviews, etc., all of use to scholars in this field.

Stanford University U.S.-Japan Technology Management Center

http://fuji.stanford.edu/

The U.S.–Japan Technology Management Center at Stanford University has long been one of the important centers for contemporary economic issues in Japanese studies. It also hosts many important sites, such as that of the Japanese Diet. The "J-Guide" accessible from this site is also the WWW Virtual Library for Japanese Studies.

Korea

WWW Virtual Library—Korea

http://www.duke.edu/~myhan/b_SK.html

This is the WWW Virtual Library for Korean Studies, found at Duke University.

Vietnam

Vietnam Online

http://www.vietnamonline.net/

This is Vietnam Online, a useful commercial site in Hanoi.

Vietnam Web

http://home.vnn.vn/index_e.html

Nominated by William S. Turley, a noted Vietnam specialist, this site is maintained by the Vietnamese government. It has, at this writing, some problems in trying to mix Vietnamese and English scripts. But it is a very useful gateway into a great deal of information in and about Vietnam.

WWW Virtual Library—Vietnam

http://coombs.anu.edu.au/WWWVLPages/VietPages/WWWVL-Vietnam.html

The WWW Virtual Library for Vietnam. This seems to be the most highly commercialized of the WWWVL portals.

Teaching the Vietnam War

Bibliography of the Vietnam War

http://hubcap.clemson.edu/~eemoise/bibliography.html

A wonderful bibliography is maintained at this site by the scholar Edwin Moise of Clemson. This site is an exemplar of what one scholar can do to assist others less knowledgeable in teaching a particular area.

The History of the ARVN

http://mcel.pacificu.edu/mcel/barlow/TR2/tianrong2/arvnhist.htm

This site, also one which I maintain, is one of the few with a statement by ARVN (Army of the Republic of Vietnam, Saigon) veterans.

Pacific University Asian Studies—Resources

http://mcel.pacificu.edu/as/home/resources.html

I hope I can be pardoned here for mentioning one of my own sites, if only because it has some original materials in it: These pages contain many interviews with American veterans and have received considerable attention.

The Wars for Vietnam

http://students.vassar.edu/~vietnam/

An excellent university site is this Vietnam War site at Vassar.

South Asia

South Asia Resource Access on the Internet

http://www.columbia.edu/cu/libraries/indiv/area/sarai/

This is the South Asian metasite for the WWW Virtual Library, found at the South Asia Resource Access on the Internet (SARAI) site at Columbia University, and maintained by David Magier. Of all the Virtual Library sites, this has one of the cleanest and most useful opening pages, from which one can move quickly to a wide range of specific materials.

India

WWW Virtual Library—India

http://webhead.com/WWWVL/India/

This is the WWW Virtual Library site for India.

Southeast Asia

Guide to Southeast Asian Resources

http://www.library.wisc.edu/guides/SEAsia/

Also nominated by Geoff Wade, the Southeast Asian site at the University of Wisconsin–Madison, is an impressive one. It is very easy to use in that the opening or splash page quickly opens a wide variety of well-considered and deeply arrayed resources.

South-East Asia Information

http://sunsite.nus.edu.sg/asiasvc.html

A metasite for South-East Asia, this site is a pleasure in that it opens quickly with a minimalist menu that directly leads the reader into a wide variety of electronic resources.

World Wide Web Virtual Library—Southeast Asian Studies

http://iias.leidenuniv.nl/wwwvl/southeast.html

This is the WWW Virtual Library for Southeast Asian Studies, hosted at the University of Leiden. Here one can find good portals for eleven different countries of this region.

Asian Art

National Palace Museum

http://www.npm.gov.tw/indexe.htm

This is the site of the National Palace Museum, Taiwan, which is among the great Chinese art collections of the world.

World Art Treasures

http://sgwww.epfl.ch/berger/

This site includes a wonderful trove of professionally produced photographs of Asian sites and Asian art.

WWW Virtual Library—Chinese and Japanese Art History

http://www.nyu.edu/gsas/dept/fineart/html/chinese/index.html

This is the WWW Virtual Library for Asian art and is hosted by the indefatigable Nixa Cura.

WWW Virtual Library—Museums Around the World

http://www.comlab.ox.ac.uk/archive/other/museums/world.html#museums

This site provides a list of world museums that are on the Internet, indexed by country and region.

Philosophy and Religion

Chinese Philosophical E-text Archives

http://www.wesleyan.edu/~sangle/etext/index.html

This site is the wonderful Confucian e-text project, which provides originals and translations of classical texts.

World Wide Web Virtual Library—Religion

http://www.vlib.org/Religion.html

This site is the index for the WWW Virtual Library for Religions. However, this site is not highly developed in religions outside East Asia.

Buddhism

Buddhism in Europe: An Annotated Bibliography

http://www.sunderland.ac.uk/~os0dwe/bs10.html

One site worth mentioning, although it has not been updated for several years, is that hosted by Martin Baumann in the United Kingdom. It contains a wonderful series of links to English-language bibliographies on Buddhism in Europe.

Buddhist Studies and the Arts

http://www.artsci.wustl.edu/%7Errscott/

This site contains gorgeous Buddhist art, including recent electronic art.

Resources for the Study of East Asian Language and Thought

http://www.human.toyogakuen-u.ac.jp/~acmuller/index.html

This site, maintained by an individual enthusiast, Charles Muller, Professor of East Asian Philosophy and Religion at Toyo Gakuen University, Chiba, opens into a number of Buddhist and Japanese resources. Professor Muller also shows a degree of thoughtfulness too often lacking in Asian-related sites in that he provides links necessary to download useful software for viewing his site and other encoded ones. This site also contains the Electronic Buddhist Texts Initiative, a promising resource for scholars and students in this field.

Taoism/Daoism

Taoism Information Page

http://www.clas.ufl.edu/users/gthursby/taoism/

This is the WWW Virtual Library site for Taoism, the best entry point for this religion/philosophy.

Organizations

Asia Society

http://www.asiasociety.org/

This site is maintained by the Asia Society, which, according to its own Web pages, is America's leading institution dedicated to fostering an understanding of Asia and communication between Americans and the peoples of Asia and the Pacific. A nonprofit, nonpartisan educational institution, the Asia Society presents a wide range of programs, including major art exhibitions, performances, international corporate conferences, and contemporary affairs programs.

The Association for Asian Studies

http://www.aasianst.org/

The Association for Asian Studies, with its many regional associations, is the leading professional organization for Asianists.

AUSTRALIAN AND NEW ZEALAND HISTORY

Christine de Matos

AUSTRALIA

General Australian History Sites

Australian Association for History and Computing

http://www.unimelb.edu.au/infoserv/ahc/index.html

This site provides information about the Australian and New Zealand branch of the Association for History and Computing.

Australian Council of Professional Historians Associations, Inc. (ACPHA)

http://enterprise.powerup.com.au/~acpha/

The ACPHA is the national body representing professional historians in Australia. The site hosts links to the state representative professional historian bodies, as well as links to other Australian history Web sites.

Australian History on the Internet

http://www.nla.gov.au/oz/histsite.html

This is a high-quality index of Australian history Web sites provided by the National Library of Australia. It includes links to reference libraries, historical documents, online journals, resources at Australian universities, current issues and debates, and more.

Australian History Resources

http://sunsite.anu.edu.au/austudies/info/docs.html

This is a vast collection of links to various Internet sites dealing with Australian history, with an emphasis on primary resources. They include major Australian archives, documents, e-journals, historical societies, and resources on Australia in the United States

Banks's (Sir Joseph) Papers

http://www.slnsw.gov.au/Banks/index.html

Sir Joseph Banks (1743–1820) was a naturalist who sailed with Captain James Cook on the *Endeavour* and was actively involved with Pacific exploration and early Australian colonial life. The State Library of New South Wales holds approximately 10,000 of Banks's manuscript pages, which includes correspondence, reports, invoices and accounts, journals, and a small quantity of maps, charts, and watercolors. Indexed facsimiles of all these have been made available via this site, creating an extremely accessible primary resource for researchers.

The Bushranger Site

http://wwwcream.une.edu.au/OtherSites/Bushrangers/HOME.HTM

Sponsored by the University of New England CREAM server, this is a great site to discover the infamous collection of Australian bushrangers, especially designed for school students. It includes information about bushrangers in pictures, poetry, and song, as well as text biographies. Links are also provided to further bushranger Web sites.

The Dismissal of the Whitlam Government 11 November 1975

http://vcepolitics.com/dismiss/intro.htm

The dismissal of the Whitlam government (Australian Labor Party—ALP) in 1975 remains the most controversial political event in Australia. This site gives an overview of, and background to, these events, along with texts of some key documents, and lists key questions for Australian politics arising from the dismissal. A great resource is the sound file archive included on the site, which includes *It's Time* (the 1972 ALP campaign theme), Whitlam's *Kerr's Cur* speech and Malcolm Fraser's (Liberal Party) policy speech from November 1975.

Explorers of Australia

http://werner.ira.uka.de/~maier/australia/explore/

This site provides a brief overview of Australian explorers after European settlement. Pictures and maps are included for each explorer, as well as links to further Web sites. It is a useful site for school students and teachers.

Gold 150

http://www.ballarat.edu.au/krause/external/sovhill/gold150//sovhill.htm

Gold 150 is a project sponsored by Sovereign Hill, the National Maritime Museum, the University of Ballarat and the Australia Foundation to celebrate 150 years of Australian Gold Rush history. The site includes images, documents, essays, and guides to other sources on the gold rushes.

HERA (Heritage Australia Information System)

http://www.environment.gov.au/heritage/infores/HERA/index.html

HERA is a searchable bibliographic database about significant places in Australia's natural and cultural environment, produced by the Australian Heritage Commission. Although HERA is accessible to the public, it is not full access. The full version of HERA is one of thirty-six databases available on the Ozline Information Network, but this is only available via subscription. Information concerning subscription is available on the site.

History of Places in Australia

http://www.zades.com.au/ozindex/ozindex.html

Part of *Project 2000,* this site has the ambitious aim of indexing all existing histories of locations in Australia on the Internet before the year 2000. The project has been "adopted" by the Melbourne Dead Persons' Society.

Life on the Goldfields

http://www.slv.vic.gov.au/slv/exhibitions/goldfields/

This is a beautifully presented virtual exhibit by the State Library of Victoria. The story of life on the goldfields is told through images and extracts of documents (letters, diaries, newspapers, and books) created by those who participated in the gold rush era. Find out about the entertainment, mining techniques, and Australia's own rebellion on the goldfields, the *Eureka Stockade.*

Pictures of Health

http://www.cimm.jcu.edu.au/hist/main.html

This developing site, housed by The Centre for Interactive Multimedia at James Cook University, is attractively constructed and provides information on the history of health in Australia. It is organized in a module format designed for use by students and educators. Some of the interesting modules include the health of those who joined the Australian Imperial Force in the First World War (War's Cruel Scythe) and the health of Australians living in isolated areas (Fever).

Women and Politics in South Australia

http://www.slsa.sa.gov.au/int_pubs/women/index.html

South Australia was the first state in Australia (indeed one of the first places in the world) to grant women's suffrage in 1894. This site, hosted by the State Library of South Australia and sponsored by The Women's Suffrage Centenary Steering Committee and the Office for the Status of Women, South Australia, looks at the role of women in politics in South Australia in historical context. Topics covered include women's suffrage, Federation, and key individuals.

Aboriginal and Torres Strait Islander History

Aboriginal Studies WWW Virtual Library

http://www.ciolek.com/WWWVL-Aboriginal.html

Part of the WWW Virtual Library, this site boasts a wide collection of Aboriginal Studies Internet sites.

Frontier Online

http://www.abc.net.au/frontier/

This site has been designed to accompany the Australian Broadcasting Corporation's (ABC) television series *Frontier*, but it is a valuable site in its own right. Transcripts of live Internet discussions that have taken place on contemporary issues raised by the series, on topics such as treaties and reconciliation, are also included. There are educational resources and ideas for teachers and students, and a guestbook area to contribute your own comments on indigenous issues.

The Hidden Histories

http://www.mov.vic.gov.au/hidden_histories/index.html

The Hidden Histories Project, sponsored by the Museum Victoria, the Department of Education (Victoria), and the Global Classroom, aims to document the oral histories of Koorie communities and to increase the wider community's understanding of Koorie culture. The site is "interactive," as questions can be asked about Koorie life and history, or oral history interviews can be contributed to the site's collection. This project is very appropriate and useful for school communities.

Papers of Edward Koiki Mabo (1936-1992)

http://www.nla.gov.au/1/ms/find_aids/8822.html

Edward Koiki Mabo was an indigenous community leader and human rights activist who came to national prominence in Australia after his death in June 1992 as the successful principal plaintiff in the landmark High Court ruling on native land title. This decision challenged the 205-year-old legal doctrine of *terra nullius*. Mabo's papers are held by the National Library of Australia and this site is a guide to those papers. There are also some images and biographical information about Mabo included on the site.

Archives and Libraries

Australian War Memorial

http://www.awm.gov.au/

Research on Australia's involvement in overseas conflicts necessitates a visit to the Australian War Memorial's Web site. It includes searchable databases on the Memorial's vast collection (art, books, film, official records, private records, photographs, roll of honor, sound recordings), information about the Australia–Japan Research Project, and an online journal, the *Journal of the Australian War Memorial*.

Directory of Archives in Australia

http://www.asap.unimelb.edu.au/asa/directory/

The Directory is a comprehensive database of information about archives in Australia developed by the Australian Society of Archivists Inc. and the Australian Science Archives Project. The site can be browsed alphabetically or geographically, or searched via keywords.

National Archives of Australia

http://www.naa.gov.au/

This is an essential starting point for historical research pertaining to the Australian Commonwealth government. The site has general information about the archives, two searchable databases on the collections (Angam and Rinse), a notice board of events, examples of exhibits, and more. Included is an interesting online exhibit of digitized resources on Federation, *Federation Gallery*.

The National Archives of Ireland Transportation Records

http://www.nationalarchives.ie/search01.html

The National Archives of Ireland has developed this site to provide an online facility to search for the records of convicts sent from Ireland to Australia from 1788 to 1868.

National Library of Australia

http://www.nla.gov.au/

The National Library of Australia provides an exhaustive entry point to information on Australian History, both within its own collections and as a starting point to accessing other collections via the Internet. The site provides comprehensive descriptions of the library's collections and an online search catalogue. Links are provided to other high-quality Internet sites, including the Australian Libraries Gateway, the latter allowing you to search for any library in Australia. The National Library has developed a number of online databases, including the *Register of Australian Archives and Manuscripts* (RAAM).

Register of Australian Archives and Manuscripts (RAAM)

http://www.nla.gov.au/raam/

This database is provided by the National Library of Australia. It allows you to search for nongovernment records held in Australian archival repositories. The RAAM database can be searched in a variety of ways, including keyword searches.

State and Territory Archives

http://www.aa.gov.au/AA_WWW/StateAs.html

This site lists the links to the various state and territory government archives in Australia.

Australian History E-Journals

Electronic Journal of Australian and New Zealand History

http://www.jcu.edu.au/aff/history/

This journal is an initiative of the School of History and Politics at James Cook University and the Department of History at Melbourne University. The site has a wide variety of content, including articles, history on the Net, and resources for teaching.

Journal of the Australian War Memorial

http://www.awm.gov.au/journal/

This online journal publishes current research on Australia's military history.

Genealogy

Australian and New Zealand Genealogy Pages

http://freepages.genealogy.rootsweb.com/~kemp/aust_genealogy.html

This site has links to genealogy societies, professional genealogists, libraries and archives, ships and passenger lists, and other genealogy records.

Genealogy in Australia

http://www.pcug.org.au/~mpahlow/welcome.html

Genealogy in Australia is a useful starting point to contact genealogy societies in Australia. The site includes software reviews, lists of genealogy BBSs, contact details of genealogy societies around Australia, and genealogy guides. It is sponsored by the Canberra Dead Persons' Society.

Australian Military History

Australians at War 1788–1998

http://www.iol.net.au/~conway/index.html

This is an informative Web site concerning Australian involvement in overseas conflicts from Sudan in 1885 to the Gulf War in 1991.

Local Heroes: An Oral History of World War Two

http://www.localheroes.8m.com/

This site contains a collection of one hundred and thirty interviews conducted and recorded by Year 10 History students in the Melbourne area (Victoria).

The AIF (Australian Imperial Force) Project

http://www.adfa.oz.au/HISTORY/andrew/diggers.html

The AIF Project is a database hosted by the Australian Defense Force Academy that provides detailed information on all 332,000 Australian men and women who served in the First World War. Members of the public must pay a fee to access the database.

The Great War in Australia

http://www.pitt.edu/~novosel/aussi.htm

Part of the Great War Web site (http://www.pitt.edu/~novosel/ww1.html), this page is an exhaustive index of Web sites and other information related to Australian involvement in World War I.

Australian Museums

Australian Museum Online

http://www.austmus.gov.au/index.htm

The Australian Museum has developed an extensive online guide to its collection and exhibits, with online search facilities. Selected images from the collections are included.

Australian Museums and Galleries Online

http://amol.org.au/

Developed through the collaboration of the Cultural Ministers Council and the Heritage Collections Council, this site provides guides to the collections and other useful information on over 1,000 Australian Museums and Galleries. Some examples from the larger collections are shown as digital images and the site has a comprehensive search facility.

National Museum of Australia

http://www.nma.gov.au/

This site gives information about the Museum's collection, which is divided into three broad themes: Australian Social History, Gallery of Aboriginal Australia, and People and the Environment.

NEW ZEALAND

General New Zealand Indexes

New Zealand—Ancient and Modern History

http://www.enzed.com/hist.html

This site is part of the larger *eNZed* Web site, which provides links to information on New Zealand. This is a very comprehensive index, with everything from the arrival of the Maori to recent economic reforms.

New Zealand History Resources on the World Wide Web

http://www.vuw.ac.nz/~agsmith/847/resguide/pearson/nzhist_main.html

The aim of this site is to "provide a guide to any New Zealand history pages or fragments of pages, even where they form a very small part of a site whose overall purpose is something other than historical." The site can be browsed in four ways: by place, by subject, by organizational body, or by time.

New Zealand Archives and Libraries

Alexander Turnbull Library

http://www.natlib.govt.nz/docher/atl.htm

The Alexander Turnbull Library is described as "a library within a library," as it is actually part of the National Library of New Zealand. It holds the nation's collection of books, photos, letters, drawings, maps, music, and sound recordings. The library hosts *Timeframe*, an online searchable database of images from its collection.

National Archives of New Zealand

http://www.archives.govt.nz/

The National Archives Web site contains information about the archives' holdings.

National Library of New Zealand

http://www.natlib.govt.nz/

This attractive site hosts information on the collections (including how and when to use the online catalogue), information for educators, and links to other Web resources. The Alexander Turnbull Library's online image database, *Timeframe,* can be accessed from the site's home page.

National Register of Archives and Manuscripts (NRAM)

http://www.nram.org.nz/

The NRAM Web site is a database that helps archivists and researchers find archival collections held in museums, local government bodies, libraries, historical societies, community repositories, and in-house business, religious, and sporting archives throughout New Zealand. The database can be browsed in a variety of ways, including collection name or subject, or searched via keywords. The New Zealand Society of Archivists funds the site.

New Zealand History E-Journals

Electronic Journal of Australian and New Zealand History

http://www.jcu.edu.au/aff/history/

This journal is an initiative of the School of History and Politics at James Cook University and the Department of History at Melbourne University. The site has a wide variety of content, including articles, history on the Net, and resources for teaching.

New Zealand Genealogy

Australian and New Zealand Genealogy Pages

http://opax.swin.edu.au/andrew/aust_genealogy.html

This site has links to genealogy societies, professional genealogists, libraries and archives, ships and passenger lists, and other genealogy records.

Genealogy New Zealand

http://www.voyager.co.nz/~ianclap/icc1.htm

A range of information on, or links to, genealogy resources in New Zealand can be found on this site.

GENEoNZ—NZ and Maori Genealogy

http://www.geocities.com/Heartland/Park/7572/nz.htm

Listed on this site is a huge range of sources and services for genealogy in New Zealand.

General New Zealand History Sites

New Zealand Association for History and Computing

http://www.unimelb.edu.au/infoserv/ahc/index.html

This site provides information about the Australian and New Zealand branch of the Association for History and Computing.

The Declaration of Independence

http://www.wcc.govt.nz/poneke/tow/independ.txt

This site hosts the text of the *Declaration of Independence of New Zealand*, signed by James Busby (the British Resident) and thirty-five northern Maori chiefs on October 28, 1835. The text is in both Maori and English.

Historical Timeline

http://www.nzhcottawa.org/aboutnz/histtimeline.htm

The New Zealand High Commission Ottawa has provided this historical timeline on the Web from C.E. 1300 to 1997.

Land Ownership and Settlement Timeline

http://www.maf.govt.nz/MAFnet/schools/kits/ourland/timeline/httoc.htm

The Ministry of Agriculture and Forestry, New Zealand has supplied this very comprehensive timeline of land ownership in New Zealand from pre-1840 to 1995.

New Zealand Historic Places Trust

http://www.historic.org.nz/

Information concerning historic places in New Zealand can be found on this site.

Treaty of Waitangi 1840

http://www.wcc.govt.nz/poneke/treaty.htm

Three versions of the Treaty of Waitangi are found on this New Zealand government site (Maori, English, and a modern English translation), as well as a summary of the treaty's history and images of the treaty (the latter two hosted by the National Archives of New Zealand).

New Zealand Historical Museums

The Museum of New Zealand

http://www.tepapa.govt.nz/default.html

The Museum of New Zealand (Te Papa Tongarewa) Web site provides information about the museum's resources, activities, and more. The *New Zealand Museums Online* database is accessible from this site.

New Zealand Museums Online

http://www.nzmuseums.co.nz/default.html

This site is a database of information on museums in New Zealand that can be searched by collection, region, or name. New Zealand Military History

New Zealand Military History

New Zealand and the Great War

http://www.ake.quik.co.nz/phoar

The main concern of this site is to give an overview of the social and cultural effects of the Great War on New Zealand.

CANADIAN HISTORY

Scott Merriman and Dennis Trinkle

METASITES

Association for Canadian Studies in the United States

http://canada-acsus.plattsburgh.edu/index.htm

The Association for Canadian Studies in the United States (ACSUS), a multidisciplinary association of scholars, professionals, and institutions, is dedicated to improving understanding of Canada in the United States. Founded in 1971, ACSUS encourages creative and scholarly activity in Canadian studies, facilitates the exchange of ideas among Canadianists in the United States, Canada, and other countries, enhances the teaching of Canada in the United States, and promotes Canada as an area of academic inquiry. Their site offers a rich array of resources and links.

British Columbian History

http://www.freenet.victoria.bc.ca/bchistory.html

This site is dedicated to tracking Internet and World Wide Web resources for the study of British Columbian history. The compilation is intended to be as comprehensive and broad as possible, rather than selective.

Canadian Archival Resources on the Internet

http://www.usask.ca/archives/menu.html

The purpose of this site is to provide a comprehensive list of links to Canadian archives and associated resources on the Internet. Created and maintained by Cheryl Avery, University of Saskatchewan Archives and Steve Billinton, Archives of Ontario, the pages include links to individual repositories, multirepository databases, archival listservs, archival associations, educational opportunities, and other related sites. Links are generally limited to archival repositories, but museums and library special collections departments have been included when they contain reference to nonpublished materials.

Canadian History Learning and Teaching Resources

http://web.uvic.ca/hrd/history.learn-teach/learning.html

This is an excellent scholarly guide to the best resources for studying Canadian history. The site was designed by Hilary Street, under the direction of Stewart Arneil of the University of Victoria Language Centre. The content was initially vetted by John Lutz and Lorne Hammond of the University of Victoria history department.

Canadian History on the Web

http://www.interchange.ubc.ca/sneylan/cdnhist.htm#graphics

Compiled by Susan Neylan, a professor in the University of British Columbia department of history, this site is a rich gateway to resources on Canadian history.

GENERAL SITES

Canadian History Archives

http://neal.ctstateu.edu/history/world_history/archives/archive46.html

This site contains a variety of materials for teachers and students of Canadian history. There are links to images, essays, movies, sound clips, journals, and other multimedia resources.

Canada's National History Society

http://www.historysociety.ca/

Canada's National History Society was incorporated in December, 1993 as a nonprofit organization devoted to popularizing Canadian history. It aims to make Canadians more aware and appreciative of their heritage.

Canada SchoolNet

http://www.schoolnet.ca/

One of the most useful sites for students and teachers. SchoolNet offers the classroom advantage of interactive learning and the teacher advantage of easy access to a wide range of educational sources. You can communicate with educators in any part of Canada and collaborate on educational learning projects with schools and students all over the country.

Canadian Communities, Local History

http://ellesmere.ccm.emr.ca/ourhome/

Canadian Communities, Local History is a general gateway to Canadian local history sites.

Canadian Heritage

http://www.magi.com/~westdunn/

Using sound clips, videos, photographs and essays, this site captures Canadian history in a variety of ways.

Canadian Information By Subject

http://www.nlc-bnc.ca/caninfo/ecaninfo.htm

Canadian Information By Subject is an information service developed by the National Library of Canada to provide links to information about Canada from Internet resources around the world. The subject arrangement is in the form of a "Subject Tree," based on the structure of the Dewey Decimal Classification system. This service is updated regularly and is constantly developing and expanding. Be sure to check back often to see the latest additions.

Canadian Women in History

http://www.niagara.com/~merrwill/

This Web site provides histories of Canadian women from various walks of life. Some thirty biographies are now available. The site also includes trivia, a woman of the week, and links to related sites.

H-Canada

http://h-net.msu.edu/~canada

Sponsored by H-Net, this is the Web site of the H-Canada discussion list. The site contains information about the discussion list and allows one to subscribe. It also includes calls for papers, conference announcements, bibliographies, book reviews, articles, and links to related sites.

The Historical Atlas of Canada Online Learning Project

http://www.geog.utoronto.ca/hacddp/hacpage.html

The Historical Atlas of Canada Online Learning Project is under development in the Geography Department at the University of Toronto. The present site lists the proposed contents and illustrates the interface that has been created for the project. Approximately twenty-five percent of the maps listed here have been designed and are available through an interactive mapping package on our internal development site. This should be made public in the spring of 2000.

The National Library of Canada

http://www.nlc-bnc.ca/catalog/ecat.htm

The National Library Catalogue is now available to individuals and libraries without charge through the Internet.

GENERAL EUROPEAN HISTORY
Patrick Callan

Andorra

http://www.sigma.net/fafhrd/andorra/history.htm

Andorra provides a history of the world's smallest nation, a 450-square-kilometer territory located between France and Spain. The site also links users to information about the area, people, and economy of Andorra.

Encyclopedia of the 1848 Revolutions

http://cscwww.cats.ohiou.edu/~Chastain

This is an exemplary site, showing how the international community of historians can collaborate in producing an innovative and challenging site, expanding historical awareness and understanding in a manner rarely encountered on the Internet. Hosted by James G. Chastain at Ohio University, it calls on over 170 extensive articles on the experience of the revolutions throughout Europe, from Ireland in the west to Russia in the east. The authors are specialists in their fields, and the net result is a top-quality resource.

Eurodocs

http://library.byu.edu/~rdh/eurodocs/

This is Brigham Young University's excellent collection of on-line primary historical documents from Western Europe, including selected transcriptions, facsimiles, and translations. The entries cover political, economic, social, and cultural history.

Modern History Sourcebook

http://www.fordham.edu/halsall/

One of the first and most extensive online collections of primary historical documents, both excerpts and full texts. Though many are older English translations, the site also includes texts in French, Spanish, and Latin, as well as some secondary literature. It is searchable, with texts listed under convenient categories as well as by author and title. Maintained at Fordham University by Paul Halsall.

Olympics Through Time

http://fhw.dartmouth.edu/projects/olympics/

An interesting account of the Olympics of Hellenic antiquity, at the *Foundation of the Hellenic World* site, with a review of athleticism in prehistoric times, as well as a succinct outline of the revival of the Games in the late nineteenth century under the inspiration of Baron de Coubertain. The site has useful links to relevant sites dealing with the history of the Olympics, as well as complementary features on ancient history, including the Homeric Age and Mycenaean Greece.

Royal Genealogical Data

http://www.dcs.hull.ac.uk/public/genealogy/royal/catalog.html

Royal Genealogical Data is a searchable database on European royalty from ancient times to the present.

WESSWeb

http://www.lib.virginia.edu/wess/

The WESSWEB site aims to provide specialists in Western European studies with professional information and data about ongoing and recent Western European research efforts.

WWW-VL History Links

http://history.cc.ukans.edu/history/

The WWW Virtual Library history section is a metaguide created by Lynn Nelson of the University of Kansas. It links to more than 4,000 history-related Web sites.

Yale Avalon Project

http://www.yale.edu/lawweb/avalon/avalon.htm

Sponsored by the Yale Law School, the Yale Avalon Project focuses primarily on American texts, but it also contains many documents of interest to Europeanists, including The Communist Manifesto, Franco-American diplomacy, Spanish-American diplomacy, Nazi-Soviet relations, and the Nuremberg Trials. Arranged by period from pre-eighteenth century through the twentieth century.

BRITISH HISTORY
Todd Larson

METASITES

The AITLC Guide to British History

http://tlc.ai.org/histbrit.htm

This is a British history metasite run by the Access Indiana Teaching & Learning Center. It contains primary and secondary resources and a large list of links.

American and British Resources on the Web (Rutgers University)

http://www.libraries.rutgers.edu/rulib/socsci/hist/amhist.html

This enormous metasite, run by Rutgers University, contains links to the most useful British history Web sites. A great starting place for any search.

Arts and Humanities Data Service

http://ahds.ac.uk/

This site works "on behalf of the academic community to collect, catalogue, manage, preserve and promote the re-use of scholarly digital resources." AHDS is a British national service funded by the Joint Information Systems Committee of the UK's Higher Education Funding Councils that is hosted by King's College—London, and is working to promote and collect online resources related to all aspects of British history. Has many good primary resources.

British Library Home Page

http://www.bl.uk/

Snug in its new home in St. Pancras, the British Library Web site has many useful resources for teachers of British history, and is of course a required resource for most British historians and graduate students. The Digital Libraries are excellent, especially the Digital Beowulf Project.

Britannia

http://www.britannia.com/

An enormous commercial site broadly covering British history, culture, and current events. There is some useful historical information once you wade through all the advertising banners; it has some very good general information for high school teachers.

Early Modern England Source

http://www.quelle.org/emes/research.html#BES

Nice list of resources for Early Modern England run by Quelle. Especially good is the online list of bibliographies for topics such as Thomas More, the plague, and witchcraft. Also has useful links to online British libraries and public record offices.

H-Albion Web Page

http://www.h-net.msu.edu/~albion/

Another in a series of H-Net Web sites, the H-Albion Web page allows access to backlogs of its moderated discussion group, a list of pertinent British history sites, reviews of current literature, fellowship listings, job notices, etc. Has become an indispensable resource for British historians.

History Net's American and British History Research Links

http://www.historian.org/research/links.htm

A metasite with many links to British history sites. A good starting place for any search.

Online Resource Book for Medieval Studies (ORB): British Links

http://orb.rhodes.edu/

This massive Web site, created and maintained by Medieval scholars from around the globe, contains an enormous number of useful materials for Medieval British historians and teachers, ranging from the Roman occupation of Britain to the Anglo-Saxon period, to the Viking and Norman invasions, to the High Middle Ages. Excellent resource for anyone having to teach the first half of the British survey.

Victoria Research Web

http://landow.stg.brown.edu/victorian/victov.html

Patrick Leary of Indiana University has put together the Victoria Research Web, a collection of resources associated with the VICTORIA discussion list. It is dedicated "to the scholarly study of the nineteenth century in Britain, and to aiding researchers, teachers, and students in their investigations of any and all aspects of this fascinating period." Particularly good are the tips on studying for the first time in Britain.

The Victorian Web

http://landow.stg.brown.edu/victorian/victov.html

Brown University professor George Landow's The Victorian Web is a searchable metasite devoted to the cultural, historical, literary, and scientific study of Victorian Britain. Has a number of biographical entries and some primary source material.

Victorian Web Sites

http://lang.nagoya-u.ac.jp/~matsuoka/Victorian.html

A large metasite run by Mitsuharu Matsuoka of Nagoya University in Japan, this is perhaps the most comprehensive list of links to Victorian sites currently on the Web. An excellent place to begin a search in nineteenth-century British history.

Voice of the Shuttle's English Literature Pages

http://vos.ucsb.edu/shuttle/english.html

This site, part of the acclaimed University of California–Santa Barbara's Voice of the Shuttle metasite, has a large number of links helpful to British historians wishing to integrate British (and other English-language British Empire countries) literature into their courses and research. Particularly good on the Romantic and the Victorian period.

General British History Sites

Anglo-Saxon Britain: Literature, Culture, History

http://www.fas.harvard.edu/~layher1/medscan.html

William Layher of Harvard University has put together a very useful site on the literature, culture, and history of Anglo-Saxon Britain. It is well-organized and has links to other similar resources.

Jane Austen Information Page

http://www.pemberley.com/janeinfo/janeinfo.html

A useful Web site containing many of Austen's literary works, commentaries on Austen, several useful bibliographies, chat rooms, and some images of the author. This site is a nonacademic one hosted by a volunteer organization called the Republic of Pemberley in conjunction with Amazon.com.

The Battle of Britain Historical Society

http://www.bobsoc.demon.co.uk/

A well-organized site run by The Battle of Britain Historical Society—an organization "pledged to uphold the memory of the largest air battle in history. A time when brave young men flocked to Britain from all over the world to join the RAF and fight to prevent invasion and defeat at the hands of Nazi Germany." Well done in every way.

The Black Presence in Britain

http://www.blacknet.co.uk/history/index.htm

A Web site designed to fill the much-needed gap on ethnicity, Britain, and the Internet. This is an incomplete and often interesting commercial site that has an overview of slavery in Britain and the empire, biographies of famous Britains of African and Afro-Caribbean backgrounds, and a list of other links. An important if underdeveloped site.

Bob Speel's Victorian Art and Culture

http://www.speel.demon.co.uk/index.htm

This is an interesting site run by Bob Speel containing, among other things, a Sculpture Walk in Hyde Park, London; the Great Exhibition of 1851; London and Victorian Art; and Victorian Art in Britain. Some useful images and overviews.

A Brief History of Scotland

http://britannia.com//celtic/scotland/history_scotland.html

Britannia's short history of Scotland, like its Welsh counterpart, is a nice overview of the political and social development of this country.

A Brief History of Wales

http://britannia.com/wales/whist.html

A nice Web site run by Brittania that has a concise and useful history of Wales, this site is divided up into convenient chapters for faster download. It has a nice link to the Wales Home Page, which has links to similar sites.

The British Council on British Studies

http://www.britcoun.org/studies/index.htm

An excellent resource for high school teachers of British history and culture, this site includes an online bibliography of British Studies, a list of useful links, and a library of pertinent documents. Run by The British Council on British Studies.

The British Empire

http://www.edunltd.com/empire/empire.htm

This is a comprehensive and useful Web site dealing with the very broad subject of the British Empire. Created by a British teacher, this site—while at times a bit historically sketchy—is still a good overview of British imperialism. Particularly good is the section on the Imperial Armed Forces.

British Pop Culture in the 1960s

http://home.clara.net/digger/sixties/

Struggling to explain the Beatles to your Modern Britain class? Interested in finding out why Austin Powers is such a dead-on parody of 1960s British culture? Then this entertaining site is for you. From James Bond and Emma Peel to David Lean and Mick Jagger, many aspects of pop culture are touched upon, including musical groups, television shows, celebrities, trivia, and enduring images. Run by David "Digger" Barnes.

The Winston Churchill Home Page

http://www.winstonchurchill.org/index.html

An impressive site run by The Churchill Center in Washington, D.C. It contains speeches, texts, debates, sound recordings, a listserv, and many other categories of Churchillian topics. The place to begin your search to find out what witty sayings Churchill actually said and which have been wrongly attributed to him over time.

The Clans and Tartans of Scotland

http://www.scotclans.com/

Sgian Dhu Interactive's Clans and Tartans Web site contains everything you ever wanted to know about the main Scottish clans including details of clan tartans, crests, and clan homelands.

The Dickens Project

http://humwww.ucsc.edu/dickens/index.html

The Dickens Project is a product of the University of California. It is a "scholarly consortium devoted to promoting the study and enjoyment of the life, times, and work of Charles Dickens." Has a useful online archive and a large list of links.

Electronic Historical Publications: The London Gazette

http://www.history.rochester.edu/London_Gazette/

This Rochester University site contains access to five editions of this seventeenth-century journal/newspaper. A nice but small resource.

The Emancipation of Women, 1860–1920

http://www.spartacus.schoolnet.co.uk/resource.htm

John Simkin of Spartacus Educational, a teaching materials company in Great Britain, has put together a searchable site of biographies of famous British feminists, primary sources, and bibliographic resources. The site is expanding to include information covering British history back to 1700.

The English Civil War Society

http://www.jpbooks.com/ecws/

A site run by the English Civil War Society, a historical reenactment group, with lots of resources on the mechanics and specifics of the conflict. A good list of links makes this a good jumping-off point for the subject.

English Heritage Home Page

http://www.english-heritage.org.uk/

This is the official site of the government organization founded in 1984 and dedicated to preserving the historical environment through education and outreach programs. A nice place to get a feel for English customs and culture.

A General Study of the Plague in England 1539–1640

http://www.gmtnet.co.uk/plague/

A local history Web site concentrating on Loughborough, this gives a good overview of the impact of the plague on the local economy and society of Britain during the middle ages. Run by Ian Jessiman.

The Gilbert and Sullivan Archives

http://diamond.idbsu.edu/GaS/GaS.html

An outstanding searchable site containing the musical scores and texts to all of Gilbert and Sullivan's famous operas. There are lots of links to other Gilbert and Sullivan sites, as well as online music, biographies, bibliographies, etc. This site is run by Jim Farron, Curator, and Alex Feldman, Webmaster.

Glorious Revolution of 1688

http://www.lawsch.uga.edu/~glorious/index.html

This Web site was created by Professor Donald E. Wilkes Jr. and Matthew Kramer of the University of Georgia Law School. Has information, documents, and links to this important event in British history. Has an extremely useful encyclopedia of major characters of the Revolution.

Great Britain Historical Database

http://www.geog.qmw.ac.uk/gbhgis/database/db_index.html

This is a comprehensive Web site devoted to providing a large integrated database of geographically located historical statistics for Great Britain, mainly drawn from the period 1851–1939. This impressive site is directed by three University of London scholars: Humphrey Southall, David Gilbert, and Ian Gregory.

Greenwood's Map of London 1827

http://www.bathspa.ac.uk/greenwood/home.html

Mark Annand's Greenwood's Map of London 1827 is an online resource map scaled at eight inches to the mile, covering London and surroundings and stretching out to Earls Court in the West, to the River Lea and Greenwich in the East, to Highgate to the North, and to Camberwell to the South. An excellent site that clearly shows the intersection between geography and history.

Thomas Hardy Resource Library

http://pages.ripco.com:8080/~mws/hardy.html

An interesting Web site devoted to the works and life of Thomas Hardy. Constructed and maintained by Mark Simons, this site contains an impressive number of Hardy's works, as well as a biography, a list of Hardy works in the media, and a nice compendium of other links.

Hellfire Corner: Tom Morgan's Great War Web Pages

http://www.fylde.demon.co.uk/welcome.htm

A very nice site with lots of interesting and original articles about Britain and its role in the catastrophe known as The First World War. Great articles and a huge list of links make this an extremely worthwhile site.

Her Majesty's Stationery Office's Official Documents Home Page

http://www.official-documents.co.uk/

This is a governmental Web site being developed by The Stationery Office to aide Internet users in locating official documents. It provides access to material published by The Stationery Office and other authoritative bodies.

Houses of Parliament Home Pages

http://www.parliament.uk/hophome.htm

Official Web sites of the House of Commons and the House of Lords. It contains useful information on the history of both bodies. Includes a helpful link to the House of Commons Library Research Papers.

The Huxley File

http://aleph0.clarku.edu/huxley/index.html

The history of science is a field that sometimes gets lost in the shuffle. Two Clark University professors—Charles Blinderman and David Joyce—have put together the kind of site that rectifies this situation. Dedicated to the works of the Victorian scientist Thomas Henry Huxley, this extraordinary Web site contains hundreds of articles, pictures, and commentaries on this very important scientist and his work. Anyone interested in how to properly put up an educational, informative, and interesting academic Web site owes it to themselves to visit these pages.

Hwæt! Old English in Context

http://www.georgetown.edu/cball/hwaet/hwaet06.html

An excellent overview of Old English by Georgetown University's Catherine Ball, this site is an informative resource for student and novice alike, especially for those interested in understanding how English became the national language. Has a basic overview of Old English.

Ian's English Calendar

http://www.albion.edu/fac/engl/calendar/

Ian MacInnes of Albion College has put together a very useful Web site that will convert the Ecclesiastical Calendar, Old and New Style Dating, days of the week, and Regnal Years, eliminating the need to use unwieldy handbooks that are always missing from the library.

Internet Library of Early Journals

http://www.bodley.ox.ac.uk/ilej/

This is an exciting Web site devoted to eighteenth- and nineteenth-century British journals. This Digital Library is a joint project by the Universities of Birmingham, Leeds, Manchester, and Oxford, and aims to "digitize substantial runs of eighteenth- and nineteenth-century journals, and make these images available on the Internet, together with their associated bibliographic data."

Internet Resources for the Anglo-Saxon World

http://www.ccc.nottingham.ac.uk/~aczkdc/asresource.html

A nice list of links related to Anglo-Saxon Britain run out of Nottingham. It has links to archaeological excavations, including the famous Sutton Hoo.

The Invitation to a Funeral Tour: A Free-Style Jaunt Around Restoration London

http://www.okima.com/

This Web site is built on the historical novel *Invitation to a Funeral* by Molly Brown. The site is a kind of online game that has the added bonus of being historically instructive as well. A nice example of where in the river of thought commercial and educational sites should meet.

The Jacobite Heritage

http://sites.internetcorp.net/~mcferran/

Noel S. McFerran's site on Jacobitism, containing among other things biographies of Jacobite royals, primary documents, songs, essays, and a list of other resources.

King Arthur and the Early English Kingdoms

http://britannia.com/history/h12.html

This site is a good starting place for researching the ever popular King Arthur and the Arthurian Legends. It is a branch of the main Britannia site.

LLRX: Guide to British Legal Databases

http://www.llrx.com/features/europe.htm#england

Nice Web site for British legal historians. Contains links to such resources as the Times Law Reports, Government Information Services, and full texts and summaries of Acts of Parliament.

Medieval English Architecture

http://vrlab.fa.pitt.edu/medart/menuengl/maineng.html

Run by Alison Stones at Pittsburgh University, this Web site has a nice clickable image map that allows the user to jump around the map and view different architectural marvels from the Medieval period. Lots of nice pictures of cathedrals on this site.

Medieval English Towns

http://www.trytel.com/~tristan/towns/towns.html

A site put together by Stephen Alsford and devoted to the urban history of Medieval England. A nice overview that promises to be a very useful site when more fully developed.

Montpellier Early Modern English Documents (MEMED)

http://alor.univ-montp3.fr/memed/

This project promises to be an interesting one. Run by the Centre d'Études et de Recherches sur la Renaissance Anglaise in Montpellier and with an esteemed editorial board that includes the likes of Colin Lucas and Glenn Burgess, this site contains only a few primary sources at the time of writing but promises to publish politically seminal pamphlets, pious ballads, legal documents, and comical songs in addition to the standard fare. Will be an important site when it is developed.

Monuments and Dust: The Culture of Victorian London

http://www.iath.virginia.edu/mhc/

This ambitious project, directed by Michael Levenson (University of Virginia) and David Trotter (University of London), is the work "of an international group of scholars now assembling a complex visual, textual, and statistical representation of Victorian London." When completed it will be an invaluable tool for researchers, students, teachers, and anyone interested in this topic.

The William Morris Home Page

http://www.ccny.cuny.edu/wmorris/morris.html

This site details the writings and career of the Victorian socialist William Morris, who was also a famous craftsman, designer, and writer, among other things. This site contains a number of his works, commentaries, and information on Morris-related conferences and events worldwide. It is hosted by City College of New York.

Norman Invasion of England, 1066

http://www.ibiscom.com/bayeux.htm

A general Web site detailing the events of William the Conqueror's invasion of Britain in 1066. Nice images taken from the Bayeaux tapestry make this a visually appealing and useful site.

The Oxford Text Archive

http://ota.ahds.ac.uk/

The Oxford Text Archive, one of the oldest electronic text centers in the world (founded in 1976), is based out of Oxford University and has a stated goal to "collect, catalogue, and preserve high-quality electronic texts for research and teaching." It currently contains more than 2500 resources in over twenty-five different languages.

Penny Magazine Online

http://www.history.rochester.edu/pennymag/

This Rochester University site aims to digitize the *Penny Magazine*, a Victorian publication that came out every Saturday and was aimed at the working classes. It was part of the Society for the Diffusion of Useful Knowledge's program for liberal reform. Currently there are twelve issues from 1832–35 available.

Photographic A to Z of Royal Navy Ships, 1880–1950

http://www.geocities.com/Pentagon/Quarters/6629/

An excellent site containing rare photographs of Royal Navy ships from 1880–1950. This site, run by Steve Johnson of Cyberheritage, is easy to access and offers an opportunity to view 728 Royal Navy ships.

Royal Commission on Historical Manuscripts

http://www.hmc.gov.uk/main.htm

Nice governmental Web site that allows limited access to historical documents from British history, including the National Register of Archives, ARCHON (the Archive gateway), and the Manorial Documents Register.

Royal Navy History

http://www.royal-navy.mod.uk/history/index.htm

A comprehensive official history of the Royal Navy, with sections on the surface fleet, submarine flotilla, the Fleet Air Arm, the Royal Marines, and uniforms. Extremely accessible information.

The Royal Palace

http://www.camelotintl.com/royal/index.html

A Web site run by a commercial travel company, this site nonetheless has good information on the ever popular subject of British royalty. Has some information on heraldry and investitures as well.

Scottish Economic History Database, 1550–1780

http://www.ex.ac.uk/~ajgibson/scotdata/scot_database_home.html

Limited but useful database on Scottish economic history, allowing for queries on such things as crop yields, demographic data, and weather statistics. Created by Alex Gibson of Exeter University.

Scotweb's Scottish History Online Magazine

http://www.clan.com/history/mainframe.html

A Scottish history site run by Robert Gunn, this site has lots of information on the famous battles and people of Scotland, including Falkirk, Stirling Bridge, and, of course, William Wallace (of *Braveheart* fame). It also has a good section on the clearing of the Highlands of the Clans and contains a Scottish timeline complete with links.

Sherlockian Holmepage

http://watserv1.uwaterloo.ca/~credmond/sh.html

A list of sites on British history would be incomplete without a mention of one of the many Sherlock Holmes sites. The Sherlockian Holmepage, despite the pun, is an exceptional ode to the characters created by Arthur Conan Doyle and contains the original Holmes stories, as well as an overwhelming list of other Sherlock information and links. This enormous site is maintained by Chris Redmond of the University of Waterloo.

Spartacus Internet Encyclopedia British History 1700–1950

http://www.spartacus.schoolnet.co.uk/industry.html

Online encyclopedia covering a large portion of modern British history. Particularly useful are the biographical entries for prominent Members of Parliament.

Shakespeare Online

http://www-tech-two.mit.edu/Shakespeare/works.html

The first Web site to make Shakespeare's complete works available online. This site is run by Jeremy Hilton at MIT and is searchable.

The Spanish Armada

http://www.knight.org/advent/cathen/01727c.htm

A good general site outlining the events leading up to the defeat of the Spanish Armada by the forces of Queen Elizabeth I in 1588. This is an entry from *The Catholic Encyclopedia* published in 1913.

Edmund Spenser Home Page

http://darkwing.uoregon.edu/~rbear/

Impressive site run by Richard Bear of the University of Oregon that seeks to collect the complete works of this influential British writer. Includes a complete copy of *The Faerie Queene*.

Stonehenge on the Net

http://members.aol.com/madelefant/PathFndr.html

One of many Stonehenge sites, this is one of the more accurate ones. This site is a basic overview that will take you through a huge list of links down whatever theories you choose to explore, and there are many. The site was created and is maintained by Michael Neal at the Wayne State University Library.

Tudor England

http://tudor.simplenet.com/

Laura Eakins's glossy site dealing with the Tudor period of British history. Subdivided nicely into categories such as "Life in Tudor England" and "Tudor Architecture."

Tyburn Tree Home Page

http://www.unc.edu/~charliem/index.htm

Zachary Lesser of Columbia University and Charlie Mitchell of the University of Colorado at Boulder have put together an interesting little site on capital punishment in early modern Britain. Contains texts, images, and links to other sites.

The UK & Ireland Genealogical Information Service (GENUKI)

http://www.genuki.org.uk/

This is an excellent gateway for anyone interested in local history or the genealogy of Britain. Contains everything you need to know to begin making inquiries on a local level.

Victorian Census Project

http://www.staffs.ac.uk/schools/humanities_and_soc_sciences/census/vichome.htm

Demographic history lends itself well to the use of the Web, as evidenced by the Victorian Census Project, a site directed by David Alan Gatley of Staffordshire University. The goal of this site is to digitize demographic primary source documents relating to Great Britain in the mid-nineteenth century, including census abstracts, registration statistics, Poor Law reports, and Pigot's Typology of England and Wales. Although at present it is incomplete, this promises to be an important and useful site.

Victorian Women's Writers Project

http://www.indiana.edu/~letrs/vwwp/

Indiana University's Victorian Women's Writers Project, whose stated goal is to produce highly accurate transcriptions of works by British women writers of the nineteenth century, is an excellent resource on this underrepresented area of British history. It has a large number of primary documents, ranging from works by Josephine Butler to the poetry of Amy Levy. An excellent site.

Views of the Famine

http://vassun.vassar.edu/~sttaylor/FAMINE/

A site run by Steve Taylor of Vassar College, this has a pictorial history of the devastating famine through the major political cartoons of the day, including those from *Punch*, *The Illustrated London News*, *The Cork Examiner*, and *The Pictorial Times*.

Virtual Teacher's Center British History Page

http://www.timeplan.com/vtc/histbhis.htm

Good resource for high school teachers of British history, containing many links to subjects and themes such as Richard III, Tudor England, and Victorianism.

War of 1812–14

http://members.tripod.com/~war1812/

Rob Taylor's large site dealing with many details of this often overlooked by-product of the Napoleonic Wars. Has a large page of links to other similar sites. A good page for military history buffs.

EASTERN EUROPEAN AND RUSSIAN HISTORY
Igor Yeykelis

METASITES

Armenian Embassy Web Site

http://www.armeniaemb.org/index.html

This site has a large collection of Armenian links on the Internet arranged alphabetically, without annotations. There are several history-related sites, dealing mainly with the Armenian Genocide of 1915–16. Maintained by the Embassy of the Republic of Armenia, Washington, D.C.

A Belarus Miscellany (ABM)

http://solar.rtd.utk.edu/~kasaty/miscellany.html

A collection of links to resources from and about Belarus. Organized by subject and featuring a separate history links page, which in turn contains annotated links to onsite and external resources. Maintained by Peter Kasaty and hosted by the University of Tennessee in Knoxville. Mirror site in Belarus.

Central and Eastern Europe Internet Resources

http://src-h.slav.hokudai.ac.jp/eng/server-e-fr3.html

A companion site to the Internet Resources for Russian Studies site (see below), this site covers the states of Central Europe and the Balkans. Extremely well-organized geographically and by subject. All of the country pages have history sections. Most of the links are reliable in their connection. Maintained by the Slavic Research Center, Hokkaido University, Japan.

Central Eurasia Project Resource Page

http://www.soros.org/central_eurasia.html

This site focuses on Armenia, Azerbaijan, Tajikistan, Uzbekistan, Georgia, and Kyrgyzstan. Each of these Central Eurasian countries has a separate resource page, with links grouped according to subjects, with some history links, although the amount and quality of the material varies from country to country. Maintained by the Soros Foundation.

Cilicia.com

http://www.cilicia.com/

A large Armenian information site with extensive resources and outside links. Many of the history-related links are located on the Armenian Genocide page. External links are grouped together following the internal resources, and it is easy to recognize one from another. Maintained by Raffi Kojian and hosted by Cilicia.com. Part of the Armenian Web Ring.

Doug and Colleen Hartman's Links Galore!

http://ourworld.compuserve.com/homepages/DouglasHartman/homepage.htm

A large and fairly well-designed metasite with links to Russia, the countries of the former Soviet Union, and a number of other European countries. Organized by country and subject. Russian history links are accessible through *History* listing. Most of the links are annotated. Privately maintained by Douglas Hartman and hosted by OurWorld CompuServe.

European History Resources

http://public-affairs.levitt.hamilton.edu/gambit/soc_links/history/regions.html

A collection of links to various resources dealing with European history, grouped by country. None of the pages devoted to Eastern European countries have many links, but most are reliable as far as their connections are concerned, and they are a good starting point. Maintained and hosted by the Arthur Levitt Public Affairs Center at the Hamilton College, Clinton, New York.

Faculty of History, Moscow State University

http://www.hist.msu.ru/Menu/index_english.htm

The site is still under construction, but it contains very useful links to materials not available from other metasites. Materials available include sites dedicated to the eight hundred and fiftieth anniversary of Moscow and to the two hundredth anniversary of the birth of Alexander Pushkin. Maintained and hosted by the Faculty of History, Moscow State University.

F and P History

http://www.friends-partners.org/friends/history/opt-tables-unix-english-

This metasite provides links to resources in Russian, Soviet, and American history, as well as to historical documents, like the constitutions of the Russian Federation and the United States, and the 1867 Alaska treaty. Many of the links lead to Russian language resources. Hosted and maintained by Friends & Partners, a Russo-American citizens's organization.

Funet Russian Archive

http://www.funet.fi/pub/culture/russian/index.html

A links and resources site on Russia and the former Soviet Union. History-related links are located at *Funet Russian Archive Index and Links*, which is arranged alphabetically. The whole site itself is at its best in providing onsite historical resources. Maintained by and hosted by Finnish University and Research Network, Espoo, Finland.

History of the Czech Republic at SunSITE Czech Republic

http://sunsite.ms.mff.cuni.cz/czechrep/history/

A part of the *SunSITE Czech Republic* site, this small links page contains a number of internal and external links connected with Czech history. The external links have not been updated for a long time, and consequently many lead to dead ends. Maintained by Jakob Jelínek and Vaclav Sklenar, and hosted by Charles University, Prague, Czech Republic.

History/Social Studies Web Site for K-12 Teachers

http://www.execpc.com/~dboals/boals.html

An important metasite in that it is virtually the only site to provide links to history resources that are specifically chosen for K-12 teachers. The Russian history area is large (sixty-six links), with links to general resources and resources of specific interest to the schoolteachers. Maintained by Dennis Boals and hosted by Xplore Company.

Horus' History Links

http://www.ucr.edu/h-gig/horuslinks.html

This metasite from the History Department, University of California–Riverside gives an overview of sites relating to all geographical and thematic areas of historical study. The site is still under construction, but a large number of Russian history sites is already available. Maintained and hosted by the History Department, University of California–Riverside.

H-RUSSIA WWW Links

http://h-net2.msu.edu/~russia/links/

A selection of links to Russian resources from H-Net. Some history materials are available from the Politics and Miscellaneous subject sections. Highlight: Russian Revolution page from the Military History section of the New York Public Library, with rare photographs of the early Soviet Union. Hosted by Michigan State University.

Illustrated History of Russia and the Former USSR

http://www.cs.toronto.edu/~mes/russia/history.html

This is a collection of links to sites dealing with artifacts, photographs, and other graphic material from the various periods in Russian history, from the era of Genghis Khan to the July 1996 presidential elections in Russia. Privately maintained by Mikhail Soutchanski and hosted by the Department of Computer Science at the University of Toronto.

Important Places

http://www.vwc.edu/wwwpages/dgraf/places.htm

A general metasite, organized by region, with links to Russia and the former Soviet Union, Central Europe, and the Balkans, among other regions. Related metasites with Russian links: e.g., Exhibits and Museums, Military History. Maintained by Professor Dan Graf and hosted by Virginia Wesleyan College.

Institute of Baltic Studies

http://europa.ibs.ee/Arts/index.html

An Estonian site with links to resources on Estonia and other Baltic states. Organized by subject. History subject area is small, with both internal and external links listed together. Highlight: Department of History, University of Tartu site, with its Electronic Library of Estonian History page. Maintained and hosted by the Institute of Baltic Studies, Estonia.

Internet Resources for Russian Studies

http://src-h.slav.hokudai.ac.jp/eng/server-e-fr1.html

Probably the best metasite for materials on Russia, the Commonwealth of Independent States, and the Baltic States. Extremely well-organized geographically (by region and country) and by subject. All of the country pages have a history section, with history links on the Slavic and Baltic pages further sub-divided chronologically. Many of the links on this metasite lead to the re-sources compiled within the former Soviet Union, and cannot be found on other metasites. Most of the links are reliable in their connection. Maintained by the Slavic Research Center, Hokkaido University, Japan.

Links Slavica

http://www.geocities.com/~celtoslavica/links/links_slavica.html

A part of the larger CeltoSlavica site, this metasite deals with the various facets of Slavic life, including history of the Slavic countries and peoples. History links are scattered throughout the site, within areas dedicated to vari-ous countries. Maintained by CeltoSlavica and hosted by Geocities.

Medieval Russia—Medieval History Net Links

http://historymedren.miningco.com/msubrus.htm

A small but well-organized metasite on Medieval Russian history. Links to chronologies of Russian history, overviews of Russian ruling houses and me-dieval Russian cities, and compilations of medieval Russian law. Equipped with its own search engine. Maintained by the Miningco.

Military History

http://www.cfcsc.dnd.ca/links/milhist/index.html

This metasite provides links to internal and external resources in military his-tory. Russian, Soviet, and East European resources are scattered throughout entries on various wars. Hosted and maintained by the Information Resource Center, Canadian Forces College, Toronto, Canada.

Orthodox Christian Resources on the Internet

http://www.hrweb.org/orthodox/

This well-designed metasite is unique in bringing together the links related to the Russian and other Slavic Orthodox Churches. Arranged by subject. His-tory page is small but very useful. Highlights: ERP Church History, a compre-hensive history of the Orthodox Church, including the Russian Orthodox Church. Maintained by Catherine Hampton and hosted by The Human Rights Web.

REIIweb: Internet Resources

http://www.indiana.edu/~reeiweb/internet.html

Extensive and well-designed site linking material on Russia, the former Soviet Union, Eastern and Central Europe, and the Balkans. The links for each country are grouped together and are not annotated, and therefore they have to be explored in order to locate history-related sites. Maintained and hosted by the Russian and East European Institute at Indiana University.

REESWeb

http://www.ucis.pitt.edu/reesweb/rstest.html

One of the oldest links sites dealing with Russia, the former Soviet Union, and Eastern Europe, this site has fallen into a state of disrepair, with many dead links. Highlight: ArcheoBiblioBase, which presents vital data about individual archival repositories in Russia and the Ukraine and a structured bibliography of their finding aids. There also are a large number of national home pages. Maintained by the University of Pittsburgh.

Russia on the Web

http://www.valley.net:80/~transnat/index.html#Russia

A well-designed metasite with links to Russian sources. Organized by subject with a small History page. Many of the sites on this page can, however, be found on other larger metasites. Hosted by the Transnational Institute.

Russian and East European Network Information Center (REENIC)

http://reenic.utexas.edu/reenic.html

A large metasite with links to resources on Russia, the countries of the former Soviet Union, and Eastern Europe. Most country pages have a history subject listing, but these are not abundant in resources. The site is at its best as a starting point to other relevant metasites on the World Wide Web. Maintained by the Center for Russian, East European, and Eurasian Studies at the University of Texas in Austin.

Russian History

http://www.departments.bucknell.edu/russian/history.html

A well-organized and well-maintained Russian metasite. The links are generally arranged in chronological order, although there are large thematic sections. A number of links lead to photographic and genealogical material, as well as Russian and Soviet historical documents. Maintained by Bucknell University, Lewisburg, Pennsylvania.

Russian History on the Internet

http://www.ucr.edu/history/seaman/

An information and links site on Russia and the Soviet Union. Contains a links page with some history-related links. Main strength is the photo archive of the Bolshevik leaders and the bibliography of the materials related to Russian history. Maintained by James Seaman, History Department, University of California–Riverside.

Russian History on the Web

http://www.russianhistory.org/

Recently launched by Marshall Poe of the School for Historical Studies at the Institute for Advanced Study, this valuable gateway provides academic researchers, educators, and students with a collection of critically evaluated Internet resources relevant to the study of Russian history. This selective, well-organized gateway offers an annotated index of high-quality information resources including metasites, guides, indices, bibliographies, dissertations, scholarly articles, journals, maps, surveys, archives, professional organizations, research centers, discussion lists, primary texts, image databases, and much more.

Russian Regions Internet Resources—Tatarstan

http://src-h.slav.hokudai.ac.jp/eng/Russia/tatar-e.html

A part of the Volga Region Internet Resources, a larger metasite from the Slavic Research Center at the Hokkaido University. Highlight: History of Tatarstan site from Kazan State University, a concise but richly illustrated history of Tatarstan and peoples that have lived there throughout the ages. Maintained by the Slavic Research Center, Hokkaido University, Japan.

The Russian Revolution

http://www.barnsdle.demon.co.uk/russ/rusrev.html

A fairly small but very useful metasite with particular emphasis on the February and October Revolutions of 1917 in Russia and the Russian Civil War. It also contains links to political parties, figures, and movements, images and maps, and critiques of the events in the years after the Russian Revolutions of 1917. Privately maintained by David Barnsdale.

Russophilia!

http://www.dove.net.au/~rabogna/russian/russian1.htm

An excellent Russian links page from Adelaide in Australia. Arranged by subject, with a large and varied History & Social Sciences section. Major topics include the Romanov Dynasty, Soviet Russia, and regional histories, with many sites not listed in other metasites. Maintained by Rita Bogna.

The Society for Romanian Studies

http://www.huntington.edu/srs/

This site contains a large Romanian Studies Internet Gateway, with links to outside sites on Romania, organized by subject. While history is not one of those subjects, a significant amount of history-related links can be found in the Scholarly Publications and Cities areas. Maintained by Paul E. Michelson and hosted by Huntington College, Huntington, Indiana.

Ukraine

http://www.physics.mcgill.ca/WWW/oleh/ukr-info.html

One of the oldest national sites on the former Soviet Union, this site dates back to at least 1994. History links are located in the Historical Items subsection of the General Information area. The section is small, but it contains links to a diverse range of materials. Maintained by Oleh Baran and hosted by the physics department of McGill University, Canada.

UNCG's Slavic Studies Trails

http://www.uncg.edu/~lixlpurc/russian.html

A collection of links to resources on and from Poland, Russia, and the Ukraine. The Russian links are the most numerous and reliable, and some of them lead to history sites. This site is best used as a starting point to other larger and more history-oriented metasites. Maintained by the Department of German and Russian at the University of North Carolina, Greensboro.

The University of Kansas History Group

http://kuhttp.cc.ukans.edu/history/WWW_history_main.html

A part of the WWW Virtual Library, this site is an important starting point for research in history. Russian and East European resources are located in the Russia and Eastern Europe section, the Central Europe section and in the sections on Slovakia and Romania. The links are not annotated. Maintained by the University of Kansas History Group under the auspices of the WWW Virtual Library and hosted by the University of Kansas.

Virtual MOLDOVA

http://www.info.polymtl.ca/Moldova/

A small metasite with annotated links to material in and about Moldova (formerly Moldavia), including the history of Moldova. A number of links lead to Jewish history, including the Kishenev pogrom of 1903. Maintained by Tavi Ureche and hosted by École Polytechnique de Montréal, Canada.

World History Compass

http://www.SchillerComputing.com/whe/index.htm

A large and important metasite with links to history materials throughout the world. Russian, former Soviet Union, and East European links are indexed under *Europe,* where in turn they are indexed under separate countries. No annotations for sites are provided. Maintained by Schiller Computing, Stratford, Connecticut, and hosted by LexiConn Internet Services, Colchester, Connecticut.

WWW-VL History Index

http://www.ukans.edu/history/VL

A general metasite with worldwide links to sites devoted to history. Organized by subject and geographical area. Sites are neither annotated nor organized by subheadings. Highlights: a number of links to the nineteenth-century maps of Russia and Central and Eastern Europe. Jointly maintained by the Department of History of the University of Kansas and the Lehrstuhl für Ältere deutsche Literaturwissenschaft der Universität Regensburg. Managed by Eric Marzo of Regensburg and Lynn Nelson of Kansas.

REFERENCE SITES

ArcheoBiblioBase

http://www.iisg.nl/~abb/

An important information source on federal and regional archives of the Russian Federation. The information for each archive includes name, address, phone number and e-mail, hours, outline of holdings, library facilities, and finding aids. Maintained by Patricia Kennedy Grimsted in collaboration with Rosarkhiv, the Federal Archival Service of Russia, and hosted by the International Institute of Social History, Amsterdam, Netherlands.

Armenian Research Center

http://www.umd.umich.edu/dept/armenian/

A U.S.-based resource site that deals with various aspects of Armenian history and culture. The most useful part of the site is a collection of bibliographies on the Nagorno-Karabakh conflict and the Armenian Genocide, which constitute an important starting point in a study of these two topics. Maintained by the Center for Armenian Research and Publication and hosted by the University of Michigan–Dearborn.

Brokgaus Online

http://www.agama.com/bol/

The core material presently at this site is the *Brokgaus-Efron Encyclopedia*, and the pre-Revolutionary dictionaries by Pavlenkov, Mikhelson, and Starchevskii. The encyclopedia is a very important source of information on pre-Revolutionary Russia, a source that may not be readily available elsewhere. The site is in Russian, and a knowledge of the language, as well as a Russian-English keyboard, is needed to access the site. Compiled and maintained by Sergei Moskalev and jointly hosted by Agama WWW Server and Cityline Internet Service Providers (Moscow).

Chronology/Timeline of Russian History

http://ourworld.compuserve.com/homepages/DouglasHartman/
chronology.htm

A chronology of Russian history, from the times of Rurik to modern days, written by Douglas Hartman as a part of his metasite. Included are links to relevant material and other Russian history articles by Hartman on the site. Privately maintained by Douglas Hartman and hosted by OurWorld CompuServe.

Fabergé Timeline

http://merlin.alleg.edu/WebPub/Groups/hulmer/timeline.html

A chronology of the Fabergé family, the jewelers to the Romanov Tsars, from their arrival in Russia in the 1600s to the death of Carl Fabergé in Paris in 1920. Maintained by Benjamin Allison and hosted by Allegheny College, Pennsylvania.

H-RUSSIA WWW Site

http://www.h-net.msu.edu/~russia/

H-RUSSIA, a member of H-NET, encourages scholarly discussion of Russian and Soviet history. Makes available diverse bibliographical, research and teaching aids, and features a review project. Maintained by H-NET Humanities & Social Sciences Online and hosted by the Michigan State University.

History_Index

http://www.slip.net/~rufrisco/History_index.html

A collection of short chronologies of several former Soviet republics and Baltic states. Includes chronologies of Russia, Ukraine, Latvia, Georgia, Armenia, and of the Jewish people. The site is still under construction. Maintained by Grigoriy Milgram as a part of his Russian San Francisco site and hosted by Slip.Net Internet Service Provider.

The House of Romanov

http://www.departments.bucknell.edu/russian/facts/romanov.html

The detailed family tree of the Romanov Tsars and emperors who ruled Russia between 1613 and 1917. The site appears to be under construction, and key figures in the dynasty will have links to more detailed information about themselves and their contribution. Maintained by Robert Beard and hosted by the Russian Studies Department, Bucknell University, Lewisburg, Pennsylvania.

The House of Rurik

http://www.departments.bucknell.edu/russian/facts/rurik.html

The detailed family tree of the Rurik Dynasty, Russia's first ruling dynasty descended from Viking princes. The site appears to be under construction, and key figures in the dynasty will have links to more detailed information about themselves and their contribution. Maintained by Robert Beard and hosted by the Russian Studies Department, Bucknell University, Lewisburg, Pennsylvania.

Information about Lithuania

http://neris.mii.lt/homepage/liet1-1.html

An important reference site on Lithuania. Features a short outline of the country's history, with links to a cultural timeline and a list of rulers. The site also contains detailed information on the major urban centers in the country. Maintained by Danute Vanseviciene and hosted by Lithuania Academic and Research Network at the Institute of Mathematics and Informatics.

ISCIP Database

http://www.bu.edu/iscip/database.html

This Web-based database consists of over 60,000 full-text items dealing with various aspects of the former Soviet Union, post-Soviet Russia, and the newly independent states. Maintained and hosted by the Institute for the Study of Conflict, Ideology, and Policy at Boston University.

The Lost Churches of Kyiv

http://www.kiev.ua/oldkiev/

This site is an important reference source on the churches in the Ukrainian capital destroyed during the Stalinist era. Each link leads to a separate page with the photograph of the church in question, and a description of its history and the circumstances of its destruction. Maintained and hosted by the Global Ukraine ISP under the auspices of the Ukraine Online project.

Moldova: Important Events

http://admin.ici.ro/moldova/MoldavianSoccer/eventsMOLDOVA.htm

A chronology of the history of Moldova, from Roman times (105 A.D.) to the present. Maintained and hosted by the Embassy of Moldova in Washington, D.C.

Political Leaders, 1945–99

http://personales.jet.es/ziaorarr/00index.htm

A continually updated index of leaders of the countries in the world, from 1945 to the present day. Heads of states, prime ministers, and the leaders of ruling parties are featured. Maintained by Roberto Ortíz de Zárate and hosted by Jet Internet, Spain.

Reference Sources: Russian History and Literature

http://www.lib.berkeley.edu/Collections/Slavic/russref.html

This online bibliography of reference material is extremely useful as a starting point in research on Russian and Soviet history and literary heritage. Sources listed include general guides, encyclopedias, serial reference publications, and guides to archival materials and émigré sources. Library of Congress classification numbers are provided. Maintained by Allan Urbanic and hosted by the Library of the University of California—Berkeley.

Romanov Dynasty WWW Encyclopedia (Russian Edition)

http://www.online.ru/sp/cominf/romanovs/index.rhtml

This site is based on the Dinastiia Romanovikh (The Romanov Dynasty) CD-ROM, published by the Cominfo Electronic Publishers of Moscow. Information is accessible through Tsars, famous individuals, or by using a chronology. Includes photographs of the artifacts connected with the dynasty. The site is available in Russian only, but an English version is under construction. Maintained by Cominfo Publishers, Moscow, and hosted by Russia Online.

The Russian Archive Series

http://www.ucr.edu/history/russia/RAS.html

The Russian Archive Series publishes up-to-date guides to the main Russian archives. Maintained by the Center for Russian and East European Studies, The University of Pittsburgh, Pennsylvania, and hosted by the History Department at the University of California–Riverside.

Russian History

http://merlin.alleg.edu/WebPub/Groups/hulmer/history.html

A short chronology of Russian history, from early Russia to the Bolshevik Revolution of 1917. Concentrates on the rulers of Russia during this period.

Hyperlinks to the glossary of related terms. Maintained by Kristen Magee and hosted by Allegheny College, Pennsylvania.

Russian Revolution in Dates

http://www.barnsdle.demon.co.uk/russ/datesr.html

A detailed chronology of the Russian Revolution, from the Bloody Sunday in January of 1905 to the death of Lenin in 1924. Privately maintained by David Barnsdale as a part of his Russian Revolution site.

Sites by T.F. Boettger

http://www.geocities.com/~tfboettger/

T.F. Boettger has a number of extensive sites dealing with Russian and Georgian nobility. All areas of the site are still under construction, but they are an important source of information for those researching the members of the upper echelons of Russian and Georgian nobility and their descendants. Maintained by T.F. Boettger and hosted by GeoCities.

Soviet Leaders

http://artnet.net/~upstart/soviet.html

A chronology of Soviet leaders from Khrushchev to Gorbachev. Features a minute-by-minute chronology of the August 1991 Coup, and the seventy-three slogans advanced by the Central Committee of the CPSU in celebration of the sixtieth anniversary of the October Revolution, among other items. Hosted by aNet Communications, Los Angeles, California.

Ukraine—History

http://www.freenet.kiev.ua/ciesin/Ukraine/ukr-hist.html

This site, which is under construction, currently features an outline of Ukrainian history, and a set of pages featuring information on the regions of Ukraine, their history from the Ukrainian point of view, and historical towns. Maintained by Elena Kuzmenko on behalf of the Consortium for International Earth Science Information Network (CIESIN) and hosted by Kyiv FreeNet as a part of the UN Internet Project in Ukraine.

ONLINE EXHIBITIONS AND VIRTUAL TOURS

The Alexander Palace Web Sites

http://www.alexanderpalace.org/.

The palaces showcased include the Alexander Palace, the Great Catherine Palace of Tsarskoe Selo, and the Yelagin Palace of St. Petersburg. Each of the sites includes a virtual tour of the palace in question, its history, and its connection with the various members of the Romanov dynasty. Other exhibits showcased include the Romanov Jewels. Maintained by the Alexander Palace Association and hosted by PalasArt Web Design and Hosting, Austin, Texas.

Alexander Rodchenko Museum Series Portfolios

http://photoarts.com/schickler/portfolios/rodchenko/

Alexander Rodchenko (1891–1956) was a consummate artist in all media: his painting, design work, and photography were fundamental to the founding of abstract art in Revolutionary Russia. From the historical point of view, the second portfolio is the most important, as it features the portraits of the famous Soviet artists, actors, and intellectuals in the 1920s and 1930s. Maintained by Howard Schlicker Fine Arts, New York, and hosted by PhotoArts.

Beyond the Pale: The History of Jews in Russia

http://www.friends-partners.org/partners/beyond-the-pale/

This site explores the history of Jews in Russia and the Soviet Union. The exhibition explores from Jewish life during the Middle Ages to the resurgence of anti-Semitism in the post-Soviet period. Each section outlines events, policies, and ideas, and is accompanied by images of artifacts, paintings, and photographs. English and Russian versions are available. Maintained by M.F. Miller and Matvey B. Palchuk. Hosted by Friends and Partners.

The Chairman Smiles

http://www.iisg.nl/exhibitions/chairman/

An online exhibition of posters from the former Soviet Union, Cuba, and China. The Soviet section features thirty-three posters dating between 1919 and 1938. A brief introduction is given, followed by images of the posters. Each image contains an explanatory note, giving the author, translation of the slogan, and a brief historical background. Maintained and hosted by the International Institute of Social History, Amsterdam, Netherlands.

Estonia: Land, People, Culture

http://www.erm.ee/pysi/engpages/index.html

An online version of the permanent exhibition from the Estonian National Museum in Tallinn. The site covers all historical facets of Estonian life, including peasant life, holidays and festivities, and regional peculiarities, through Tsarist, interwar, Soviet, and post-Soviet eras. Maintained and hosted by the Estonian National Museum, Tallinn, Estonia.

The Face of Russia

http://www.pbs.org/weta/faceofrussia/

An online companion to the acclaimed PBS series of the same name. This well-developed site includes an interactive timeline of Russian history and culture, a description of the series, and reference material. Maintained and hosted by the Public Broadcasting Service, Alexandria, Virginia.

The Jewels of the Romanovs

http://mfah.org/romanov/index.html

Based on an exhibition by the same name hosted by the Museum of Fine Arts in Houston, this WWW site showcases images of jewels, costumes, paintings, icons, and religious artifacts of the Romanov dynasty from the eighteenth century to its fall in 1917. Maintained and hosted by the Museum of Fine Arts in Houston.

Kyiv-Pechersk Lavra

http://www.lavra.kiev.ua/lavra/

A virtual tour of Kiev-Pechersk Lavra, the oldest monastery complex in the Russian Orthodox Church, dating back to the tenth century. The site showcases the monastery's architectural and religious landmarks, and includes a home page of the functioning monastery. Maintained by Igor Romanenko and hosted by LuckyNet Internet Service Provider, Kiev, Ukraine.

Moscow Kremlin Virtual Tour

http://www.online.ru/sp/cominf/kremlin/english/

This site is a well-designed and well-developed online guide to the Moscow Kremlin. The site is organized corresponding to architectural elements of the

Moscow Kremlin. Each area is described textually, with hyperlinks to important persons, buildings, and organizations connected with the Kremlin. The site is available in Russian and in English. Maintained by Cominfo Publishers, Moscow, and hosted by Russia Online.

Nicholas and Alexandra

http://www.nicholasandalexandra.com/

This online exhibition proceeds chronologically, from the youth and courtship between Nicholas II and Alexandra to their exile and execution in Yekaterinburg in 1918. The site also contains Russian maps of the period, a Nicholas and Alexandra timeline, a list of the Romanov rulers, and related links. Maintained and hosted by Broughton International, an organizer and promoter of exhibitions based in St. Petersburg, Florida.

Pictures of Russian History

http://metalab.unc.edu/sergei/Exs/His/His.html

A selection of illustrations completed by S. Ivanov in 1908–13 for *Pictures of Russian History* published in Moscow. The original work was in a series of albums, and it gives an important insight into how the history of Russia was perceived in the Russian Empire at the beginning of the twentieth century.

Revelations from the Russian Archives

http://lcweb.loc.gov/exhibits/archives/

The documents presented in the exhibition come from the archives of the Communist Party of the Soviet Union and cover a wide range of chronological periods and themes, such as Lenin's attitudes, Stalin's purges, Chernobyl, and the changes in relations between the Soviet Union and the United States. Each page describes historical background of a given theme, then presents scanned images of illustrative documents relating to that theme and period, together with translations. Maintained and hosted by the Library of Congress.

The Romanovs: Their Empire, Their Books

http://www.nypl.org/research/chss/slv/exhibit/roman.html

This exhibit presents a selection of some items from a collection of over 3,000 Romanov volumes acquired by The New York Public Library during the 1920s and 1930s, organized thematically according to six broad areas: Empire, War, Exploration, Work and Leisure, Culture, and Faith. Each area contains a short summary and one or two sample illustrations. Maintained by R. Davis and hosted by the New York Public Library.

Rudolf Abel—Legendary Soviet Spy

http://members.tripod.com/~RUDOLFABEL/

A biography of Rudolf Abel (real name, William August Fisher), the legendary Soviet spy in Britain and the United States, where he was arrested in 1957 and freed in 1962 in exchange for U-2 pilot Gary Powers. Features an online exhibit of photographs and documents associated with Abel. Maintained by Alex Heft and hosted by Tripod Inc.

Russian Art from the Hulmer Collection

http://merlin.alleg.edu/WebPub/Groups/hulmer/index.html

An online exhibition of Russian religious art bequeathed to Allegheny College by Eric C. Hulmer. Maintained by Amelia Carr and hosted by Allegheny College, Pennsylvania.

The Russian Church and Native Alaskan Cultures

http://lcweb.loc.gov/exhibits/russian/s1a.html

This online exhibit deals with the relationship between the Russian Orthodox Church and the native peoples and cultures of Alaska and the Aleutian Islands between 1741 and 1915. It includes scanned images of the lithographs, documents, and photographs that illustrate the various facets of the relationship between the Russian Orthodox missionaries and the native Alaskans and Aleutians. Maintained and hosted by the Library of Congress.

Russian Empire, 1895–1910

http://cmp1.ucr.edu/exhibitions/russia/russia.html

A selection of photographs from Moscow, St. Petersburg, and Kiev dating 1895–1910 that are part of the Keystone-Mast collection of some 900 stereoscopic images of Russia housed at the California Museum of Photography. Maintained and hosted by the California Museum of Photography at the University of California–Riverside.

Russian Icons

http://www.auburn.edu/academic/liberal_arts/foreign/russian/icons/

A large collection of digitized images of Russian icons dating from the twelfth to the late seventeenth century. Maintained by George Mitrevski as a part of his resources page and hosted by Auburn University, Alabama.

Soviet War Photography

http://photoarts.com/schickler/exhibits/sovietwar/index2.html

A collection of thirty-three Soviet World War II photographs by the country's most noted master photographers of the time. Covers a wide range of topics, from the partisans gathering to thwart the Nazi advance into Belorussia to the subsequent war crimes trials at Nuremberg in 1946. Maintained by Howard Schlicker Fine Arts, New York, and hosted by PhotoArts.

Treasures of the Czars

http://www2.sptimes.com/Treasures/

An exhibition of the Tsars' treasures that was mounted in 1995 at the Florida International Museum in St. Petersburg, Florida. The site contains the exhibits as well as historical information about the Rurik and the Romanov dynasties, including an interactive timeline of the Tsars and a detailed tour of the exhibition itself. Maintained and hosted by *St. Petersburg Times*, St. Petersburg, Florida as a part of its WWW site.

Yevgeni Khaldei

http://photoarts.com/schickler/exhibits/khaldei/exhibit/exhibit.html

A selection of the photographs of Yevgeni Khaldei, one of the most preeminent Soviet news photographers of the World War II era. The photographs include such famous images as the raising of the Soviet flag over the Reichstag, the portrait of Churchill, Truman, and Stalin seated at the Potsdam Conference, and the images of the Nuremberg Trials. Maintained by Howard Schlicker Fine Arts, New York, and hosted by PhotoArts.

ONLINE ARCHIVES

The Armenian Genocide

http://www-scf.usc.edu/~khachato/genocide/

This site aims to provide documentary material concerning the massacres of Armenians in the Ottoman Empire in 1915–16. It is divided into four sections. Section II provides references to the coverage by the contemporary American press (1915–19) of the massacres, as well as statistical tables. Section III provides photographic material of the massacres, historically the most significant part of the site. Privately maintained by Reynold Khachatourian and hosted by the University of Southern California.

Armenian National Institute

http://www.armenian-genocide.org/

Armenian National Institute is an organization based in Washington, D.C. Its Web site has an extensive *Research* area, which contains photographs, a selection of documents from American and British archives, statements from various official sources on the subject, and press coverage in the United States of the massacres between 1915 and 1920.

Cold War Document Library

http://cwihp.si.edu/cwihplib.nsf

An online collection of documents connected with the Cold War and the participation of various powers (e.g., the Soviet Union, the United States, and China) in it. Maintained and hosted by the Woodrow Wilson International Center for Scholars as a part of its Cold War International Project site.

The Development of the R.S.F.S.R.

http://www.marxists.org/history/ussr/index.htm

A significant repository of the material relating to the establishment and the early days of the Soviet Union, in the form of the R.S.F.S.R. (Russian Soviet Federative Socialist Republic). Contains Soviet documents on foreign policy, American–Soviet relations, and the Constitution of the R.S.F.S.R., as well as photographs of leading Bolsheviks and leaders of the White movement. Maintained by Brian Basgen and hosted by the Marxists Internet Archive.

From Marx to Mao

http://gate.cruzio.com/~marx2mao/

An online archive of English translations of works by leading socialist thinkers, from Marx and Engels to Mao Tse-tung. The material related to Russian history is featured in the online collection of works—arranged chronologically—by Lenin and Stalin. The works are mostly sources from the English editions published by the Foreign Languages Publishing House in Moscow in 1950s and 1960s. Hosted by Santa Cruz County, California.

Marxist Writers

http://csf.Colorado.edu/psn/marx/Other/

This site provides English translations of selected works of important Marxist theorists, both Russian and non-Russian. The Russian Marxists include Lenin, Stalin, Anatoly Lunacharsky, and Leon Trotsky. Archives of Lenin and Stalin also contain a number of digitized photographs. Maintained by the Syber-Marx International and hosted by the University of Colorado under the auspices of the Communications for a Sustainable Future project.

Materials of Russian History

http://www.alina.ru/win/magister/library/history/history1.htm

This Russian-language online archive features the classics of Russian historical thought written in the eighteenth and nineteenth centuries. The material includes Klyuchevskiy's *Lectures* (under construction), and Karamzin's groundbreaking *The History of the Russian State*. Also included are the three versions of the medieval epic poem *The Song of Igor's Campaign*. Maintained and hosted by Alina-Moscow Bank, Moscow, Russia.

Modern Customs and Ancient Laws in Russia

http://www.socsci.mcmaster.ca/~econ/ugcm/3ll3/kovalevsky/

A series of six lectures on the ancient laws of Russian society and their influence on the nineteenth-century Russian customs, delivered in 1891 by Maksim Kovalevsky, a prominent Russian thinker in the field. Maintained and hosted by the Faculty of Social Sciences, McMaster University, Ontario, Canada.

Modern History Sourcebook: Catherine the Great

http://www.fordham.edu/halsall/mod/18catherine.html

A selection of materials in English translation related to Catherine the Great. Includes the characterization of Catherine by Baron de Breteuil, the French diplomat in Moscow, Catherine's proposals for the Russian law code, and an excerpt of her decree on the serfs. Maintained by Paul Halsall and hosted by Fordham University, New York.

Moscow Trials 1936, Court Proceedings

http://art-bin.com/art/omoscowtoc.html

An online version of the official transcript of the 1936 trial of Zinoviev and others accused of belonging to the so-called Trotskyite-Zinovievite United

Terrorist Center. This was one of the first large show trials in the Stalinist Soviet Union and it led to the execution of Zinoviev, Kamenev, and other members of the Left Opposition. Maintained and hosted by the *Art Bin* online magazine, Sweden.

Patriotic History

http://www.lants.tellur.ru/history/index.htm

This Russian-language site has a wealth of information on Russian history. The highlights of the archive are, however, the online versions of the classic works of Russian history, including *Lectures* by V.O. Klyuchevskiy and *The History of Russia from the Earliest Times* by S.M. Soloviev. Maintained by Oleg Lantsov, and hosted by Tellur Network Technologies, Moscow.

The Peace Treaty of Brest-Litovsk

http://www.lib.byu.edu/~rdh/wwi/1918/brestlitovsk.html

A complete text of the peace treaty of Brest-Litovsk, which took Russia out of World War I, set the stage for invasion by various powers, and was a starting point for the Russian Civil War. Maintained by Jane Plotke as a part of the World War I Document Archive and hosted by the Brigham Young University Library.

Russian History Home Page

http://www.dur.ac.uk/~dml0www/Russhist.html

An important and useful online archive providing Russian historical texts in English. A wide chronological and thematic range of documents is provided, from the founding of the city of Kiev in the medieval Russian chronicles to the documents on the trial of Soviet dissidents in the 1960s. Maintained by John Slatter and hosted by the University of Durham, United Kingdom.

Russian History on the Internet

http://www.ucr.edu/history/seaman/

This site is significant for its collection of photographs of Bukharin, Lenin, Stalin, and Trotsky, the key figures in the Russian Revolution and the Bolshevik movement. An AVI movie clip of Lenin is also included. A significant bibliography of sources related to Russian and Soviet history is available, but still under construction. Maintained by James Seaman, History Department, University of California–Riverside.

Russian Philosophy on the Internet

http://www.cc.emory.edu/INTELNET/rus_philosophy_home.html

An archive of material connected with Russian philosophers and the history of Russian philosophy of the nineteenth and twentieth centuries. Features an overview of the history of Russian philosophy, the major ideas of four Russian thinkers—Vladimir Solovyov, Nikolai Fedorov, Vasily Rozanov, and Nikolai Berdyaev—a portrait gallery, related links, and a number of other works. Maintained by Mikhail N. Epstein, Associate Professor, Department of Russian, Eurasian, and East Asian Languages and Cultures, Emory University.

The Song of Igor's Campaign

http://home1.gte.net/artiom/slovo/slovo.htm

A translation of the *Song of Igor's Campaign (Slovo o polku Igoreve)*. This is one of the Russian epic poems, and as such, an important primary source of early medieval Russian history. Privately maintained by Artiom Kochukov and hosted by GTE Internet.

VENONA Home Page

http://www.nsa.gov:8080/docs/venona/venona.html

VENONA was the code name used for the U.S. Signals Intelligence effort to collect and decrypt the text of Soviet KGB and GRU messages from the 1940s. These messages provided extraordinary insight into Soviet attempts to infiltrate the highest levels of the United States government. The site features the images of the VENONA documents, the chronology of the project, and the document release monographs. Maintained and hosted by the National Security Agency, Fort Meade, Maryland.

YIVO Institute for Jewish Research: Photo Collection

http://www.baruch.cuny.edu/yivo/test1.htm

YIVO is the New York-based Institute for Jewish Research and a repository of Jewish archival materials. These materials include some 100,000 photographs relating to Jewish life in Europe and America from the mid-nineteenth century. The photos on the site are also searchable by caption. Maintained by YIVO Institute for Jewish Research and hosted by Baruch College, CUNY.

YIVO Institute for Jewish Research: Poster Collection

http://www.baruch.cuny.edu/yivo/posters.html

A companion site to the YIVO photo collection (see previous page), this site highlights several large collections of Jewish posters. The posters shown online date between 1919 and 1938, most come from Poland, with some coming from Russia. Together with photos, these constitute an important body of online primary material on Jewish history of Russia and Eastern Europe. Maintained by YIVO Institute for Jewish Research and hosted by Baruch College, CUNY.

ACCOUNTS AND OPINIONS

1700 Years of Christianity in Armenia

http://www.freespeech.org/oneworld/1700/english/e_hist.htm

This site commemorates the coming seventeen-hundredth anniversary of the introduction of Christianity in Armenia. The site contains three history-related documents: Armenian khachkars or cross-stones, their origins and their connection to the pre-Christian Armenian culture; medieval Armenian churches and their significance in Armenian history; and a brief overview of the history of the introduction of Christianity to Armenia. This site is likely to be further extended. Maintained and hosted by ArmScape, a U.S.-based site with mirror sites in Armenia and Australia.

Armenia-Azerbaijan Conflict

http://www.azembassy.com/confl/browse.htm

A selection of official views and supporting diplomatic documents on the Armenia-Azerbaijan conflict from the Azerbaijan embassy in Washington, D.C. Historical background to the conflict is featured on a separate page, where the conflict between the two peoples is traced to the official policies of the Russian Empire from the early 1700s onward, in which the Armenians with their Christian religion were allegedly favored over the Moslem Azeris. Maintained and hosted by the Embassy of the Republic of Azerbaijan in Washington, D.C.

Armenians

http://www.calpoly.edu/~pkiziria/pub-files/history.html

A detailed historical overview of the history of Armenia and Armenians from antiquity to the modern days, written by Dennis R. Papazian, Professor of History, The University of Michigan–Dearborn. Linked to a page on the Armenian Genocide on the same site. Both pages are maintained by Paul Kizirian and hosted by California Polytechnic.

Articles on the History of Armenia

http://wotan.wiwi.hu-berlin.de/~houssik/Armenia/History/Index.html

A collection of a number of newspaper articles, letters to the editor, and press releases, dated from June to October of 1995 and mainly from the United States. These articles deal with the Armenian Genocide of 1915–23 and the perceived revisionist attempts to negate the existence of these events in Armenian and Turkish history. Maintained by Houssik Hovhannisian and hosted by the Institute of Statistics and Econometrics, Humboldt-Universität of Berlin.

Azerbaijan's History

http://www-scf.usc.edu/~baguirov/azeri/azerbaijan4.htm

A brief history of Azerbaijan and the Azeri people within brief encyclopedic format. History material spans from the pre-Islamic period, beginning with the ninth century B.C. and extending to modern days. There are hyperlinks to modern and historical maps of Azerbaijan. Maintained by Adil Baguirov as a part of Virtual Azerbaijan site, and hosted by the University of South California Student Computing Facility.

The Baltic Heritage Page

http://www.globalserve.net/~latvis/baltic/fr_home.htm

This U.S.-based site was created for the purpose of introducing people to the ancient customs and religious beliefs of the Baltic people in general and the Latvian people specifically. Features a historical overview that covers the history of Baltic peoples from prehistoric times to modern days. Maintained and hosted by GlobalServe Communications Inc., Mississauga, Ontario, Canada.

Cossacks

http://home1.gte.net/artiom/cossacks/kazaki.htm

A very informative history of the Cossack movement in Russia, from its beginnings in late medieval Russia to its revival in the post-Soviet Russian Federation. The main text has hyperlinks to other Cossack-related materials on the site. Includes photographs of the Cossacks during the Late Imperial era. Maintained by Artiom Kochukov and hosted by GTE Internet.

Did Lenin Lead to Stalin?

http://www.geocities.com/CapitolHill/2419/lensta.html

An analysis of Lenin and his connection to Stalin from an Anarchist perspective. Argues that Lenin actively pursued policies that eventually became the hallmarks of Stalinism, namely socialism in one country, one party rule, and totalitarianism. Maintained by Andrew Flood and hosted by the Capitol Hill server of GeoCities.

Electronic Library of Estonian History

http://www.history.ee/library2.htm

A collection of materials on the history of Estonia from the Tartu University. Consists of two main sections. *Dissertations* is an entrance point to the online copies of dissertation abstracts on various areas of Estonian history, either in German or in English. The second section is the home page of *Kleio. The Estonian Historical Journal*, and an entrance point to the online versions of its English-language articles. Maintained and hosted by the Department of History, Tartu University, Estonia.

The Establishment of the Kiev Rus

http://xyz.org.ua/russian/win/discussion/hold_rus.rus.html

An online article in Russian (the Ukrainian version is available as well) by Sergei Datsyuk tracing the establishment, the rise, and the eventual demise of the Kievan Rus and the lessons that can be learned from this medieval state by the modern Ukrainian state in its economic, social, and cultural policies. Maintained and hosted by the *XYZ Online Magazine*, Ukraine.

Estonia Country Guide—History

http://www.ciesin.ee/ESTCG/HISTORY/

A concise historical overview of the history of Estonia from prehistoric times to current days. The country's history is portrayed from a distinctly nationalist point of view, with the interwar independence (1920–40) portrayed in the greatest detail and as the country's best period. World War II Estonia is portrayed as the victim of double aggression from the Soviet Union and Nazi Germany. There are hyperlinks to other materials in the Estonia Country Guide site. Maintained by Toomas Mölder and hosted by CIESIN Baltics Regional Node WWW in Estonia.

Factory Committees in the Russian Revolution

http://flag.blackened.net/revolt/talks/russia_fac.html

A discussion by Ray Cunningham of the factory committee's role in establishing the eight-hour day and other improvements to workers' conditions following the February Revolution of 1917. Maintained by Workers Solidarity Movement, an Irish Anarchist Group, and hosted by Flag.Blackened.Net server.

Funet Russian Archive Directory/pub/culture/Russian history

http://www.funet.fi/pub/culture/russian/history/

This site contains an online version of *A Brief History of Russia and the Soviet Union* (1971), which was used to train American military personnel. It also contains a detailed chronology of Russia with relevant links and numerous miscellaneous accounts of different periods in Russian history. Maintained and hosted by Timo Hamalainen.

History & Culture of Russia

http://www.interknowledge.com/russia/rushis01.htm

An overview of the history of Russia, in which the authors aim to go beyond the usual Acompendium of hazy legends and sensationalist rumors. Throughout the text there are hyperlinks to other Russian material. Maintained by the Russian National Tourist Office and hosted by InterKnowledge Corporation.

History of Belarus

http://www-cat.ncsa.uiuc.edu/~zelenko/history.html

A detailed account of the history of Belarus, from ancient times to modern days, including the current politics of Belarus. Short notes and bibliography. Maintained by Dmitry Zelenko and hosted by the National Computational Science Alliance (NSCA), University of Illinois.

History of Belarus

http://www.lang.uiuc.edu/HUM382/belarus/history.html

An overview of Belarus from 980 A.D. to modern days. Illustrated with historical maps and images of historical architectural landmarks. Maintained by Vladimir Novik, the Deputy of the Supreme Soviet of the Republic of Belarus, and hosted by the University of Illinois at Urbana–Champaign.

History of Belarus (Great Litva)

http://jurix.jura.uni-sb.de/~serko/history/history.html

A history of Belarus from the sixth century A.D. to modern days. Includes a chronology of Belarus, followed by a number of documents excerpted from recent works, dealing with such sensitive areas as the Stalinist repression and executions of Belarussians in the 1930s. Links to other Belarus and Lithuania sites. Maintained by Aliaksiej Sierka and hosted by the Institute for Computers and Law, University of Saarland, Germany.

History of Kazakstan

http://members.tripod.com/~kz2000/history/

This page is part of a more general Kazakstan Online site, and it deals with the history of Kazakhstan and especially the origins of the various ethnic groups that have populated the country throughout the ages. More modern historical events connected with Kazakhstan are dealt with in the chronology of Kazakhstan. Maintained by Yerzhan Yerkin-uly and hosted by Tripod Inc.

History of Modern Russia

http://mars.acnet.wnec.edu/~grempel/courses/russia/lectures.html

The site features, among other things, a complete set of forty-eight course lectures by Professor Gerhard Rempel. These lectures deal with a wide variety of topics in Russian history, from the democratic tradition in Medieval Russia to the 1989 revolutions in Eastern Europe. Maintained by Professor Rempel and hosted by Western New England College, Springfield, Massachusetts.

The History of a National Catastrophe

http://www.ilasll.umn.edu/bashiri/Masov%27s%20History/frame.html

Rahim Masov's analysis of the nationalities policies of Soviet Russia in Central Asia during 1917–24, and the detrimental effects that these policies had on the Tajiks and other peoples of Soviet Central Asia. Well-referenced, with a selection of relevant official Soviet documents in an appendix. Maintained by Professor Iraj Bashiri of the Department of Slavic and Central Asian Languages and Literatures at The University of Minnesota.

A History of Russia

http://palimpsest.lss.wisc.edu/~creeca/

Online versions of lectures on the history of Russia from 800 to 1917, delivered in 1987 by Michael Petrovich, Professor of Balkan and Russian History at the University of Wisconsin–Madison. The lectures are in RealAudio format, with maps and images displayed. Maintained and hosted by the Center for Russia, Eastern Europe, and Central Asia, University of Wisconsin–Madison.

The History of the Russian Navy

http://www.neva.ru/EXPO96/book/book-cont.html

An online version of the book by the same name, which gives a detailed overview of the history of the Russian navy from the times of Kievan Rus' to the Bolshevik Revolution. Illustrated, but no references are provided. Maintained and hosted by RUSNet, St. Petersburg, as a part of the Russian Pavilion in the 1996 Internet World Exhibition.

The Kronstadt Uprising 1921

http://www.cs.utah.edu/~galt/kuprise.html

An online account and analysis of the Kronstadt Uprising in Soviet Russia's Baltic Fleet in 1921 written by Ida Mett from the Anarchist perspective. Examines the events that led to the uprising, its causes and effects, and the connection between the uprising and other events in Soviet history at the time. Bibliography included. Maintained by Greg Alt and hosted by the University of Utah Computer Science Department.

Moldova

http://www.moldova.org/html/moldova.htm

An information site on all aspects of Moldova. The history of the country is located in the *General Information* section, where brief accounts of early history and recent history can be found. A chronology of important historical events connected with Moldova and its historical predecessors is also published. Maintained and hosted by the Embassy of Moldova in Washington, D.C.

Moldova—A Bit of History

http://www.info.polymtl.ca/tavi/archive/moldova.hist.html

An online version of "From Moldavia to Moldova: The Soviet–Romanian Territorial Dispute" by Nicholas Dima (1991). This work examines the history of territorial disputes over Moldavia/Moidova between Romania and the Russian Empire and the Soviet Union, between 1812 and 1940, when Moldavia formally became a part of the Soviet Union under Stalin. Well-researched and thoroughly referenced. Maintained by Tavi Ureche and hosted by Le Génie Informatique à l'École Polytechnique de Montréal, Canada.

Origins of the Rus

http://www.geocities.com/Athens/9529/scanrus.htm

Online version of "An Inquiry into a Scandinavian Homeland for the Rus," a paper by Hugh R. Winfrey in which he examines the Scandinavian origins of the founders of Russia. Well-written and extensively footnoted, with a large bibliography. Maintained by Hugh R. Winfrey and hosted by GeoCities.

Reforms of Peter the Great

http://www.chat.ru/~jian/refpetra1.htm and http://www.chat.ru/~jian/refpetra2.htm

Online version of a thesis by D.O. Kutishenko examines in significant detail the reign and reforms of Peter the Great. Includes such materials as the Table of Ranks and the structure of rural and municipal government under Peter. In Russian. Maintained by Andrey Smirnov (Jian Web Studio) and hosted by CHAT.RU Internet Server.

Republic of Azerbaijan

http://www.president.az/azerbaijan/azerbaijan.htm

An official WWW site of Azerbaijan from the Office of the President of the Republic, featuring brief historical outline. In keeping with the official viewpoint of the site, the responsibility for the conflict is placed jointly on the Soviet central authorities and the then Armenian SSR and subsequently the independent Armenian state. Maintained and hosted by the Office of the President of the Republic of Azerbaijan.

The Role of the Zemskii Sobor in Russian History

http://www.odu.edu/~hanley/history1/Hawkins.htm

This article by Patrick H. Hawkins appears in the online version of *The Old Dominion University Historical Review* (1994). In it, the author explores the institution of *Zemskii Sobor* (The Assembly of the Land) in sixteenth-century Russia, and the role of this selectively representative body in governing the country in the late Middle Ages. Maintained by *The Old Dominion University Historical Review* and hosted by Old Dominion University, Norfolk, Virginia.

Russia.Net History

http://www.russia.net/history.html

A well-written outline of Russian history, from the early Slavs and Kiev Rus to a detailed account of the August 1991 coup, and the collapse of the Soviet Union. Maintained and hosted by Russia.Net, a U.S.-based Russian server, with a mirror site in Russia.

The Russian Post-Emancipation Household

http://www.uib.no/hi/herdis/HerdisKolle.html

This master's thesis in history by Herdis Kolle of the University of Bergen examines Russian peasant households of the two villages in the Moscow area following the emancipation of the serfs in 1861. Covers demography, family life, and the occupations pursued by the freed peasants. Maintained by the Department of History, University of Bergen, Norway.

Window to Armenia

http://wotan.wiwi.hu-berlin.de/~houssik/Window/armenia.html

An exploration of all facets past and present of Armenia and its people. History-related material is featured in the history page and the page on the Armenian Genocide. Maintained by Nelson Baloian and hosted by the Institute for Statistics and Econometrics, Humboldt-Universität of Berlin.

EASTERN EUROPE

REFERENCE SITES

Association of Polish-American Professionals Recommendations

http://www.informatics.sunysb.edu/apap/recomm/index.html

Bibliographies on all aspects of Polish history and society. History-related topics include General Polish History, Polish Military History, and Holocaust/ Polish-Jewish Relations. Maintained by John Radzilowski on behalf of the Association of Polish-American Professionals and hosted by the Department of Informatics at the State University of New York–Stony Brook.

Czech Open Information Project

http://www.open.cz/

This site is an important reference point on the various aspects of history, geography, and present-day society of the Czech Republic. Divided by subject. Hyperlinks to information on historical cities and other landmarks. Maintained and hosted by Czech Open Information Project, Brno Czech Republic.

Hapsburg Source Texts Archive

http://h-net2.msu.edu/habsweb/sourcetexts/index.html

These excerpts or entire documents in the Hapsburg Source Texts Archive are intended for college students; included are the memoirs of Prince Metternich, *The Eastern Crisis of 1875-78*, and an article by Mark Twain on "Stirring Times in Austria" (1898).

Historical Text Archive—Hungary

http://www.msstate.edu/archives/history/hungary.html

The Historical Text Archive section on Hungary has a wide-ranging series of full texts. A series of Hungarian images prefaces a library of eight substantial texts on history and Hungarian affairs. C.A. Macartney, a specialist on Hungary, contributes *Hungary: A Short History* (1962), which is a history of Hungary from its earliest known origins down to the end of the Hungarian Republic in 1956; the site also refers to the plight of Hungarians caught in territorial realignment, e.g., in Romania.

Hungary in 1848–49

http://h-net2.msu.edu/~habsweb/sourcetexts/hungsources.html

This strong selection of documents, from 1848 to 1852, focuses on the impact of the revolutions on Hungary, including communications between King Ferdinand and the Hungarian Diet, and the Hungarian Declaration of Independence, April 14, 1849.

Hungary: Battles for Freedom 1848–49

http://mineral.umd.edu/hal/projects/1848-49/

This reference source provides a day-by-day account of the Revolution of 1848 in Hungary, and the role of various figures in it, including Louis Kossuth, the military and political leader of the Hungarian Revolution of 1848–49. Materials include text, illustrations, and an 1890 recording of Louis Kossuth. Includes a photo gallery of Kossuth and the memorials in the United States and Hungary connected with him. Maintained by Hungarian American List and hosted by Mineral WWW Server at the University of Maryland.

Hungarian History Page

http://www2.4dcomm.com/millenia/dates.htm

A collection of materials, in English and Hungarian, relating to the history of Hungary and Hungarian people from 5000 B.C.. to modern days. Text, digitized maps, and links to other Hungarian history sites are included. The site is still under construction. Maintained as a part of the *Hungarian Heritage Homepage* site and hosted by Global Internet Services, 4D Communications Inc.

The Imperial House of Hapsburg

http://www.hapsburg.com/

This site on the Hapsburg monarchy is hosted by Juraj Liöiak, of McGill University, Montreal, Canada. While difficult to navigate, it contains worthwhile information on the origins of the dynasty, its symbols, the Holy Roman Empire, and the achievements of the Hapsburgs. However, it does not develop the history of the dynasty as comprehensively as it might.

New Sources on the 1968 Soviet Invasion of Czechoslovakia

http://www.seas.gwu.edu/nsarchive/CWIHP/BULLETINS/b2a4.htm

A historiographical essay by Mark Kramer on the new sources of the 1968 Soviet invasion of Czechoslovakia that became available since the late 1980s and the collapse of the Eastern bloc and the Soviet Union. Maintained by the Cold War International History Project and hosted by the School of Engineering and Applied Science, George Washington University.

Polish Kings

http://www.to.utwente.nl/masters/spizewsk/pl_kings/pl_kings.htm

A well-designed reference site dealing with the Polish monarchy from 960 A.D. to 1795 and the partition of Poland between Russia and Prussia. Features sections on Polish royal dynasties, a timeline of Polish monarchy, and an alphabetical listing of all Polish kings, among other things. The site is intended as a teaching resource for setting up lessons about rulers in Poland. Maintained by Justyna Lanzing-Spizewska, and hosted by the University of Twente in Enschede, The Netherlands.

Romania

http://risc.ici.ro/docs/romania.html

A comprehensive reference site dealing with various periods of Romanian history, from the late Middle Ages to modern days. One of the aims of this site is to debunk the commonly held myths about Romanian history. Much of the site is divided into geographical areas roughly corresponding to what the compilers of the site see as traditional Romanian regions, most of which have historical material. The site is still under construction. Maintained and hosted by the Research Institute for Informatics, Bucharest.

The Romanian History—A Virtual Travel

http://nt1.ici.ro/history/

A reference site of Romanian history from the Romanian Academy and National Museum of History. Features a brief history of Romania, the country's chronology, an online gallery of historical artifacts, landmarks and monuments, and an online historical atlas of Romania. Maintained by Cornelia Lepadatu on behalf of the Romanian Academy and the National Museum of History, and hosted by the Research Institute for Informatics, Bucharest.

ONLINE EXHIBITIONS AND VIRTUAL TOURS

St. Wenceslas Crown Jewels at SunSITE Czech Republic

http://sunsite.ms.mff.cuni.cz/czechrep/crown/

A part of a large SunSITE Czech Republic site, this online exhibit features the St. Wenceslas Crown Jewels, created for the coronation of Charles IV, the ruler of Bohemia and the Holy Roman Emperor regarded as the national symbol of the Czech state. Maintained by Jakub Jelínek and Vaclav Sklenar, and hosted by the School of Informatics, Faculty of Mathematics and Physics, Charles University, Prague, Czech Republic.

Velvet Revolution '89 at SunSITE Czech Republic

http://sunsite.ms.mff.cuni.cz/czechrep/history/revolution/

This exhibit portrays the political and religious leaders, the dissidents, and the common people during the Velvet Revolution of 1989 in Czechoslovakia, an event that brought down communism in that country. The images are by themselves powerful and self-expressive. However, a short note for each noting the circumstances under which the image was taken and/or person portrayed would make these images even more important as a historical source. Maintained by Jakub Jelínek and Vaclav Sklenar, and hosted by the School of Informatics, Faculty of Mathematics and Physics, Charles University, Prague, Czech Republic.

ONLINE ARCHIVES

Hungarian Electronic Library (MEK)

http://www.mek.iif.hu/

The Hungarian Electronic Library (MEK) was established in 1993 and currently this archive consists of some 2,500 documents. The history collection is a significant one, with areas covered including the general history of Hungary, local and regional history, history of neighboring countries, and related subjects. Texts are mainly in Hungarian, but a significant number of English texts are available as well. Maintained by Moldován István and Drótos László, and hosted by the National Information Infrastructure Development Program of the government of Hungary. Best viewed with the Central European character set.

Hungarian History

http://www.net.hu/corvinus/

A collection of digitized texts on Hungarian history from the Corvinus Library in Hungary. American and Hungarian (translated) historical texts are presented, as are important memoirs of the witnesses to various periods in Hungarian history. The texts can be read online or downloaded as Microsoft Word files. There are links to other Hungarian sites. Maintained and hosted by Hungary.Network.

Hungary

http://www.msstate.edu/archives/history/hungary.html

A collection of digitized texts on Hungarian history. The collection includes *The Hungarian Revolt October 23—November 4, 1956,* by Richard Lettis and William I. Morris (1961), a collection of sources on the Hungarian Revolution of 1956, and the memoirs of Admiral Miklos Horthy, the collaborationist Hungarian leader during World War II. There are links to several other Hungarian sites. Maintained by Don Mabry and hosted by Mississippi State University under the auspices of the Historical Text Archive.

The Wolf Lewkowicz Collection

http://web.mit.edu/maz/wolf/

Between 1922 and 1939, Wolf Lewkowicz, of Poland, engaged in a lengthy and intimate correspondence in Yiddish with his nephew Sol J. Zissman. This correspondence consists of 179 letters that document various aspects of life of the Jewish community in Poland, culminating with the Holocaust, which took the lives of Wolf Lewkowicz and most of his family. Translated from Yiddish. Family photographs and recordings of excerpts of some of the letters are included here. Maintained by Marc Zissman and hosted by WWW Server, Massachusetts Institute of Technology.

ACCOUNTS AND OPINIONS

A.I.P.C.—Polish History

http://www.ampolinstitute.org/polish_history.html

This Polish history site features a brief history of Poland, including portraits of all Polish kings, and the chronology of Polish history from 966 A.D. to the present. Maintained and hosted by The American Institute of Polish Culture, Miami, Florida.

Backward Through the Looking Glass: The Yugoslav Labyrinth in Perspective

http://boserup.qal.berkeley.edu/~gene/looking.glass.html

This is an extensive and detailed academic essay by E.A. Hammell (University of California–Berkeley) about the deep-seated roots of the ethnic conflicts in the Yugoslav area, from the Roman Empire to the modern conflict.

Brief History of Hungary

http://www.users.zetnet.co.uk/spalffy/h_hist.htm

By the author's own admission, this is a "broad outline" of the history of Hungary. It is arranged in reverse chronological order, going back to the tenth century. Includes links to downloadable texts and books and to online archives on Hungarian history. Maintained by Stephen Pálffy and hosted by Zetnet Internet Service, United Kingdom.

Bulgaria.com—History of Bulgaria

http://www.bulgaria.com/history/index.html

This section of the Bulgaria.com site is divided into two parts. The first provides a chronological account of the country's history, from prehistoric antiquity to 1944, and the second provides biographies of Bulgarian rulers, from pre-Christian Khan Kubrat to post-Communist President Zhelyu Zhelev. Both sections are well-translated and well-illustrated. Maintained and hosted by Bulgaria.com, Santa Clara, California.

Bulgarian History and Politics

http://www.b-info.com/places/Bulgaria/ref/05HIST.html

The Bulgarian History and Politics site contains a bibliography for Bulgarian history from medieval times to the present. Each source listed in the bibliography is described fully, and there are accompanying pictures.

Columbus and the Age of Discovery

http://marauder.millersv.edu/~columbus/mainmenu.html

This project is a massive database system offering access to over 1,100 articles from magazines, journals, newspapers, speeches, official calendars, and other sources relating to various encounter themes. The site is a joint effort of the History Department and Academic Computing Services at the University of Pennsylvania, Millersville, and was awarded the status of an "Official Project" by the U.S. Christopher Columbus Quincentenary Jubilee commission, Spain 1992, and the Pennsylvania Historical and Museum Commission.

Crisis in Kosovo

http://homepages.luc.edu/~jgresse/kosovo.html

This Web site teaches students to think critically and historically through an interactive simulation. The simulation was created by Judy Gressel of Loyola University–Chicago, and it models the complexity of the recent crisis in Kosovo. The site is a model for how students can study current events with a critical and historical perspective through the Internet.

The Czech Republic—History

http://www.travel.cz/travel/history.asp

A detailed chronology of Czechoslovakia and its predecessor and successor states, as well as the peoples living on the territory of the country, from pre-history to current days. Well-written and illustrated. Maintained by Gabriela Beranova and hosted by Tom's Travel, Prague.

Documents on Bosnia

http://www.mtholyoke.edu/acad/intrel/bosnia.htm

A substantive list of documents, texts, and contemporary material on Bosnia, hosted by Vincent Ferraro, Professor of International Politics at Mount Holyoke University.

History of Slovakia

http://www.adc.sk/english/slovakia.htm

An outline of the history of Slovakia, from 500 B.C. to current days. The Czecho-slovak period of the Slovak history (1918–89) is looked at from the Slovak nationalist point of view. Maintained by Professor Jozef Komornik, Department of Applied Mathematics, Comenius University, Bratislava, and hosted by ADC Ltd., Trnava, Slovakia.

The Hungarian Revolution of 1956 & How it Affected the World

http://www.cserkeszek.org/scouts/webpages/zoltan/1956.html

Zoltán Csipke examines the causes of the Hungarian Revolution of 1956 in relation to the independence struggle of the Hungarian people, the events of the revolution, and its effects throughout the Hungarian society and world in general. Privately maintained by Csipke and hosted by Cserkeszek Online, the official site of the Hungarian scout troops 8 and 49 in the Los Angeles area.

Intermarium

http://www.columbia.edu/cu/sipa/REGIONAL/ECE/intermar.html

This online journal provides an electronic medium for noteworthy scholarship and provocative thinking about the history and politics of Central and Eastern Europe following World War II. Jointly maintained by Andrzej Paczkowski, Institute for Political Studies, Polish Academy of Sciences, and John S. Micgiel, Institute on East Central Europe, Columbia University. Hosted by the School of International and Public Affairs, Columbia University.

Jan Hus

http://gray.music.rhodes.edu/musichtmls/Papers120/Hus.html

A concise biography of Jan Hus, the famous Bohemian church reformer during the early Reformation, who was burnt at the stake as a heretic on July 6, 1415, and is considered a national hero by the Czech nation. Contains a small bibliography, which can be a good starting point for studies of Hus and his movement. Written and maintained by Chris Gerrish and hosted by the Music Department of the Rhodes College, Memphis, Tennessee.

Jews in Poland

http://www.cyberroad.com/poland/jews.html

This site outlines the history of Poland's Jewish community from 965 to the outbreak of World War II in 1939. It discusses Jews in Poland during World War II and present-day conditions for Jews in Poland. Maintained by LNT Poland and hosted by Cyberville Webworks.

The Magyars of Conquest-Period Hungary

http://www.net.hu/Magyar/hungq/no141/p3.html

In this article for the *Hungarian Quarterly,* Gyula László, a retired professor of Eötvös University, examines Byzantine and Arabic sources on the arrival of Magyars in present-day Hungary, in support for his argument that the Magyars arrived in two separate waves, centuries apart. Maintained and hosted by Hungary.Network Ltd.

Romania—History

http://home.sol.no/~romemb/history.htm

A detailed outline of Romanian history, from Roman times to modern days. Illustrated with images of historical landmarks, artifacts, and portraits and photographs of Romanian rulers and statesmen. Maintained by the Romanian Embassy, Oslo, Norway, and hosted by Scandinavia Online.

Twenty-Five Lectures on Modern Balkan History

http://www.lib.msu.edu/sowards/balkan/

This series of online lectures deals with the turbulent history of the modern Balkans from 1500 to current days. While most of the lectures deal with the Balkans proper, a number of those lectures examine the Eastern European states of Hungary and Romania. Compiled and maintained by Steven W. Sowards and hosted by Michigan State University Libraries.

The Warsaw Uprising

http://www.cs.princeton.edu/~mkporwit/uprising/

An account of the Warsaw Uprising of 1944 by the Polish Resistance (AK). An overview of the situation before the uprising, followed by accounts of the events of August and September of 1944, and the aftermath. Maps and photographs of the uprising and the key people involved are also provided. The page is still under construction. Maintained by Marcin Porwit and hosted by the Department of Computer Science, Princeton University.

FRENCH HISTORY

Charles H. MacKay

METASITES

Dr. Zoë Schneider's French History Web Links

http://www.georgetown.edu/faculty/schneidz/web.html

Created and maintained by Dr. Zoë Schneider of Georgetown University, this site features an extensive but selective categorized list of links relating to all fields of French history.

ARCHIVES AND LIBRARIES

Le Ministère de la culture et de la communication

http://www.bnf.fr/index.htm

Home page for the French Minister of Culture and Communication. Virtual exhibits, links, and searchable lists for art, architecture, archeology, dance, literature, music, and photography, among other subjects. France's National Archives falls under the jurisdiction of the Minister of Culture. (See separate entry below.)

Centre d'accueil et de recherche des Archives nationales (CARAN)

http://www.culture.fr/culture/sedocum/caran.htm

Home page for France's National Archives. Practical information on hours of operation, contacts, general description of holdings, information on obtaining catalogs, temporary holdings, and exhibits. Includes links to the Centre des archives d'outre-mer, Centre des archives du monde du travail, and the Centre des archives contemporaines.

Archives du service historique de l'Armée
Archives du service historique de la Marine

http://www.culture.fr/culture/nllefce/fr/rep_ress/an_00481.htm

http://www.culture.fr/culture/nllefce/fr/rep_ress/an_00300.htm

French army and naval archives with contact information. Both under construction.

Archives et documentation du Ministère des affaires étrangères

http://www.culture.fr/culture/nllefce/fr/rep_ress/an_75351.htm

General listing of holdings, along with contact information.

Bibliothèque nationale de France

http://www.bnf.fr/index.htm

Home page for France's National Library. Contains lists of collections, updates, practical information, hours of operation, contacts, a virtual tour of the new facility, special exhibits, and several limited searchable online catalogs. A limited English version is available, including the online catalogs.

La Nouvelle France

http://www.culture.fr/culture/nllefce/fr/indlieux.htm

Hot links to many of France's archival institutions, including the Archives Nationales, other archives of the state (army, navy, foreign affairs, etc.), many departmental and communal archives, several archives from Chambers of Commerce, various associations, the Bibliothèque Nationale, other libraries (including Arsenal, National Assembly, Senate, Marine, and the Institute of France), Centers of Study, and museums. All contain basic contact information and some idea of their holdings.

Pre-Medieval History

GIS and Remote Sensing for Archeology: Burgundy, France

http://deathstar.rutgers.edu/projects/france/france.html

This site shows how mapping technology and satellite imagery can be used in historical research. It offers an evolving presentation of aerial photography and survey data that reveals long-term interactions between cultures and the physical environment.

Paleolithic Cave Paintings in France

http://www.culture.fr/culture/arcnat/chauvet/en/gvpda-d.htm

This site discusses the paintings and engravings dating from the Paleolithic Age that have been found in the caves of southern France. The material is in both French and English and includes excellent images of the cave paintings along with historical descriptions.

Medieval History

The Age of King Charles V (1338–80)

http://www.bnf.fr/enluminures/aaccueil.htm

One of many exhibits sponsored by the Bibliothèque Nationale. This site features 1,000 images of illuminated text. The quality of the reproductions is high and the site is available in English or French. The site is also organized around five themes—History, Religion, Science and Technology, Sports and Entertainment, and Miscellaneous—with more refined subcategories under each theme listing. Viewers can choose any of these themes to access a thumbnail gallery of images falling under the subcategory.

Early Modern and Old Regime History

Château de Versailles

http://www.chateauversailles.com/

Official site for Versailles. A rich, well-written and well-illustrated site with an interactive map, thousands of images—including Marie Antoinette's Hamlet—several 360° panoramic views, descriptions, practical information and contacts, and resources for French students. English version available.

The Home Page for Eighteenth-Century France

http://www.geocities.com/Paris/Metro/2549/index2.html

Contains quite a few well-known paintings of the royal court and family, as well as text. Eighteenth-century France is slickly presented, complete with music. However, some visitors, without the necessary equipment to play the music, will find the presentation and the Geocities format irritating.

Eighteenth-Century Resources

http://andromeda.rutgers.edu/~jlynch/18th/

Site dedicated to scholarly resources online. Eighteenth-Century Resources is not limited to France or even Europe, nor is it limited to the study of History. Other disciplines include Art, Architecture, Literature (and Electronic Texts), Music, Philosophy, Religion & Theology, and Science & Mathematics.

French 208 Introduction à la littérature du XVIIIe siècle

http://tuna.uchicago.edu/homes/jack/course.materials.html

Prepared for the American and French Research on the Treasury of the French Language, University of Chicago (ARTFL) Project at the University of Chicago, this site is a thorough and well-organized course packet for students. It includes links to electronic sources, hundreds of images of maps, architecture, and art, chronologies, text on authors, philosophes, and artists.

Modern Editions of Early Modern French Sources Translated into English compiled by Jeffrey Merrick and David A. Bell

http://jhunix.hcf.jhu.edu/~dabell/sources.html

Impressive bibliography of primary and secondary sources to early modern French sources. Works are organized topically including sections on art, colonialism, correspondence, crime, economic thought, education, several enlightenment groupings, literature, memoirs, politics, revolution, science, travel, witchcraft, women, and others.

The National Huguenot Society

http://huguenot.netnation.com/

Site dedicated to the study of French Huguenots. Operates like similar Scottish clan Web pages. Contains information on Huguenot history, an adequate bibliography—particularly for primary sources—and links to other Huguenot-related sites and resources.

French Revolution and First Empire

The Era of the French Revolution

http://mason.gmu.edu/~gbrown6/french-rev.htm

Part of a course syllabus by Gregory S. Brown placed online, this site has a brief selection of online documents and maps as well as an excellent link list to an extensive array of French Revolutionary Web sites.

French Revolutionary Pamphlets

http://humanities.uchicago.edu/homes/mark/fr_rev.html

Another ARTFL project from the University of Chicago, this site contains three full-text pamphlets.

Images of the French Revolution

http://chnm.gmu.edu/revolution/index.html

Lynn A. Hunt and Jack Censer edit this site sponsored by the American Social History Project and the Center for History and New Media of the Department of History at George Mason University and supported by grants from the National Endowment for the Humanities and the Florence Gould Foundation. At the time of publication, access was password-protected, but based on the interest this site has generated among academics, it will likely have general access soon.

Links on the French Revolution

http://www.hs.port.ac.uk/Users/david.andress/frlinks.htm

Sponsored by Dave Andress, this site is more than just a list of links. Links are annotated and separated into scholarly and "buff" sections. The site also contains sample writing of the author.

Napoleon

http://www.napoleon.org/

Site includes a library section, which includes basic textual information, images, primary material, and bibliographies, a museum with a comprehensive section on Napoleonic caricatures, and links to other resources.

The Napoleon Series

http://www.historyserver.org/napoleon.series/

Comprehensive site with information (in many cases images) about treaties, music, art, videos, civilian and military maps, and a vast set of links to other Napoleonic and military history sites. The best starting point for information about the First Empire.

Napoleonic Literature

http://napoleonic-literature.simplenet.com/

Contains full-text translations of nine prominent works, including the contemporary memoirs and the military maxims of Napoleon. Has links to various art images of the period.

Proctor Jones Publishing

http://www.napoleonfirst.com/

Online catalog of works published by the Proctor Jones Publishing Company. Of particular interest is the book *An Intimate Account of the Years of Supremacy,* which includes three hundred color and two hundred black-and-white art images.

Nineteenth Century

Encyclopedia of 1848 Revolutions

http://cscwww.cats.ohiou.edu/~Chastain/index.htm

An online encyclopedia of the 1848 Revolutions with close to seventy contributing scholars and 180+ entries. Although the 1848 Revolutions site is not specific to France (Poland is very well represented, for instance), there are many entries on France's role in the revolutions. Site includes entries on biographies, events, institutions, and concepts. Most entries include a current bibliography.

Georgetown University Centennial Conference, February 1998: The Dreyfus Case: Human Rights vs. Prejudice, Intolerance and Demonization

http://www.georgetown.edu/guieu/colqtop.htm

Web page of a one-day interdisciplinary conference on the historical aspects of the Dreyfus case. Speakers included French and American historians, political scientists, linguists, and religious studies intellectuals. In addition to the conference poster and contact information, the site includes full-text versions of many of the papers presented and the statement by President Jacques Chirac on the centennial of Emile Zola's *J'accuse!* The host, Jean-Max Guieu, has links to his home page, which includes links to other Dreyfus sites.

The Siege and Commune of Paris, 1870–1871

http://www.library.nwu.edu/spec/siege/index.html

This page contains more than 1,200 digitized photographs and images drawn from the Northwestern University Library's Siege and Commune Collection.

Twentieth Century

Be Realistic—Demand the Impossible!: Posters from the Revolution, Paris, May 1968

http://burn.ucsd.edu/paristab.htm

Collection of twenty-nine posters and accompanying text from the Paris Revolution of 1968. Quality of the posters is good, and French captions have been translated into English.

Images de la France d'autrefois

http://france.mediasys.fr:8060/

Collection of 80,000 black-and-white postcards of France. The site is organized by traditional regions, and one can search for specific departments or by size of settlement (small, medium, or large). Most photographs date from the turn of the twentieth century.

Paris Libéré!

http://www.paris.org/Expos/Liberation/

Created for the 50th anniversary of the Liberation of Paris. Contains a time line, photo archive, map of the attack, text on the attack, its leaders, the surrender, prisoners, an index, and a bibliography.

The World War I Document Archive

http://www.lib.byu.edu/~rdh/wwi/

Assembled by members of H-Net's WWI Military History List, this site is organized into several categories: Conventions, Treaties and Official Papers, Documents by Year, Memorials, Personal Reminiscences, WWI Biographical Dictionary, WWI Image Archive, Special Topics and Commentary Articles, and WWI Sites: Links to Other Resources. The picture archive is well-organized and contains 1,072 images. The content, production, and quality are excellent.

General, Documents, and Reference

Hanover Historical Texts Project

http://history.hanover.edu/project.html

Initiated by the History Department of Hanover College in Indiana, this site contains full-text versions of documents from Ancient Greece and Rome to the present. Although the site contains documents from American and various non-Western regions, there is quite a bit on France, including many significant works from Louis XIV's reign, several Revolutionary cahiers, the Civil Constitution of the Clergy, and documents from the 1848 revolution. Quite a few texts are in the process of being prepared.

History of France—Primary Documents

http://library.byu.edu/~rdh/eurodocs/france.html

A rich, eclectic collection of hundreds of primary documents in French, German, Spanish, and English covering Medieval France through modern times. Many documents have been expertly photoreproduced from the Bibliotèque Nationale and other archives, and the quality of the selections and their reproduction is high. A considerable number of documents have been translated. Some selections include *Les Très riches heures du Duc de Berry,* the Declaration of the Rights of Man and of the Citizen, Émile Zola's *J'accuse!,* and impressive sections on WWI, WWII, and the Liberation of France.

Internet Modern History Sourcebook

http://www.fordham.edu/halsall/mod/modsbook.html

An indispensable library of documents from the Early Modern Period to the present. Hundreds of primary source documents are reproduced here, and the site contains valuable links to similar sites, visual resources, and printed reference sources. Other sites in the same series (but not referenced here) include Ancient, Medieval, African, East Asian, Indian, Islamic, Jewish, Women's, Global, Science, and Lesbian, Gay, Bisexual, and Transgendered people.

La France à travers les âges

http://www.as.wvu.edu/mlastinger

An interesting encyclopedic potpourri of images and text covering all aspects of French culture from prehistory to the present. Numerous links and other resources.

Le Louvre: Official Web Page

http://www.louvre.fr

Official Web page of the Louvre. Contains hours of operation, contacts, information about temporary exhibitions, holdings, and upcoming events. The site is available in English as well as in several other languages.

Musée d'Orsay

http://www.musee-orsay.fr:8081/ORSAY/HTML.NSF/By+Filename/mosimple+index?OpenDocument

Official Web page of the Musée d'Orsay, housing many nineteenth-century masterpieces. Contains hours of operation, contacts, information about temporary exhibitions, holdings, and upcoming events, and an online gift shop.

Project for American and French Research on the Treasury of the French Language, University of Chicago (ARTFL)

http://humanities.uchicago.edu/ARTFL/ARTFL.html

ARTFL contains electronic versions of nearly two thousand texts, which range from classic works of French literature to nonfiction prose to technical writing. The subjects covered include literary criticism, biology, history, economics, and philosophy. The database is available only to members of universities who are associated with the ARTFL project, but those with access can perform an impressive variety of intratextual and comparative textual searches.

Paris Maps

http://www.columbia.edu/cu/arthistory/courses/parismaps/

Paris Maps houses one hundred full-color historical maps of eighteenth- and nineteenth-century Paris.

Treasures from the Bibliothèque Nationale de France: Creating French Culture

http://lcweb.loc.gov/exhibits/bnf/bnf0001.html

Sponsored in part by the Library of Congress, this is an exhibit that traces the relationship between power and culture in France from Charlemagne to Charles de Gaulle by using images from manuscripts and books from the French National Library. This site is available in English or French.

GERMAN HISTORY

Claire Gabriel

METASITES

DINO—Wissenschaft—Geschichte

http://www.dino-online.de/seiten/go14h.htm

Of the various German-language search engines, DINO (Deutsches InterNet-Organisationssystem) offers the most convenient and extensive listing of history-oriented sites. The DINO history section is divided into subcategories by time period and special interest.

German History

http://www.uni-heidelberg.de/subject/hd/fak7/hist/c1/de/

This section of the WWW Virtual Library is a directory of resources arranged by epoch and historical subfield. Although the sections are uneven, it is a useful starting point for exploration.

H-GERMAN Home Page

http://www.h-net.msu.edu/~german/

HABSBURG Home Page

http://www.h-net.msu.edu/~habsweb/

Both of these sites, which are sponsored by the H-NET group of electronic discussion lists, provide a variety of resources, including archives of discussion threads, book reviews, news about professional conferences and meetings, teaching materials, and selected links to other sites of historical interest. H-GERMAN focuses on the scholarly study of German history of all time periods; HABSBURG is devoted "to the history and culture of the former Habsburg lands and peoples from about 1500 until this century" (HABSBURG welcome). Material provided by these sites may be in English or German.

Nachrichtendienst für HistorikerInnen

http://www.crispinius.com/nfh2/index.htm

A site crammed with information for anyone interested in history, but somewhat difficult to navigate. Provides information on and links to—among other subjects—German television programs, news articles, research institutes, conferences, and meetings. Also included are a chatroom and a newsboard.

General History Sites

Archive in der Bundesrepublik Deutschland

http://www.bawue.de/~hanacek/info/darchive.htm

Archive in Österreich

http://www.bawue.de/~hanacek/info/aarchive.htm

These sites, compiled by Andreas Hanacek, are directories of German and Austrian archives by type: governmental, religious, military, etc. Contact information and hours are provided, along with citations to guides or articles about archival collections. With some exceptions, this site does not provide links to home pages of archives on the Web. In German and English.

Archive in Deutschland

http://www.uni-marburg.de/archivschule/deuarch.html

This site is a directory of links to individual archival repositories on the Web, arranged by category: governmental, religious, literary, political, etc. Sponsored by the Archivschule Marburg.

Deutsches Historisches Museum/German Historical Museum, Berlin

http://www.dhm.de/

An overview of the museum founded amid some controversy in 1987 and devoted to the history of the German nation. The site provides general information about the aims and organization of the museum as well as its collections and exhibitions. In addition, descriptions and images of selected items from the permanent collections and selections from previous exhibitions are available. In German and English.

Deutschland: Könige, Kaiser, Staatschefs

http://userpage.chemie.fu-berlin.de/diverse/bib/de-kks.html

This reference site provides birth and death dates and period of rule for German leaders from Charlemagne to Gerhard Schroeder. Compiled by Burkhard Kirste of the Freie Universität, Berlin.

Gedenkstätten in Baden-Wörttemberg

http://www.lpb.bwue.de/gedenk/gedenk1.htm

Gedenkstötten in Berlin und Brandenburg

http://www.brandenburg.de/~mwfk/kultur/deutsch/gedenkst/index.html

KZ-Gedenkstätte Dachau

http://www.infospace.de/gedenkstaette/index.html

Zum Beispiel Dachau

http://members.aol.com/zbdachau/index.htm

These pages serve as an introduction to the many Web sites dedicated to victims of the Nazi regime. The Länder of Baden-Württemberg and Berlin/Brandenburg have provided pages with links to various sites within their boundaries. The infamous concentration camp Dachau, outside Munich, is represented by an official site with historical information and photographs, as well as by a site created by the Study Group for the Investigation of Contemporary Dachau History. Pages on Dachau are in German and English.

German, Austrian, Swiss Cultural History

http://www.stthomas.edu/www/language_http/German/culthist.html

This site has several useful components: a biographical dictionary of several hundred prominent persons from German-speaking Europe (in German); a chronology of important events in German and world history; and a calendar of significant events in the German-speaking countries, arranged by month and date (in English). Created by Paul A. Schons of the University of St. Thomas.

Haus der Geschichte der Bundesrepublik Deutschland

http://www.hdg.de/

The Haus der Geschichte der BRD presents the history of the two post-war German states—the Federal Republic of Germany and the German Democratic Republic—with particular emphasis on the development of political institutions. In German and English.

History of Austria, Austro-Hungarian Empire: Primary Documents

http://library.byu.edu/~rdh/eurodocs/austria.html

History of Germany: Primary Documents

http://library.byu.edu/~rdh/eurodocs/germany.html

The EuroDocs site at Brigham Young University is the most comprehensive resource for primary documents in German and Austrian history. Documents may be in a variety of formats and in German or English. The time period covers spans from the end of the classical period to the present. Highlights include the Works of Marx and Engels and the World War I Document Archive. Compiled by Richard Hacken.

Philipp Melanchthon

http://www.melanchthon.de/

An online exhibit commemorating the five-hundredth anniversary of the birth of the reformer and humanist. The site details Melanchthon's life and involvement in the Protestant Reformation. In German and English. This site and the site on Martin Luther were created by the Kommunale Datenverarbeitungsgesellschaft Wittenberg.

Österreichische Historische Bibliographie

http://www.uni-klu.ac.at/groups/his/his_oehb/info

This searchable database corresponds to annual printed volumes, beginning in 1945, that report professional publications in Austrian history. Books, periodical articles, conference proceedings, dissertations, and essay collections are included. Produced at the Institut für Geschichte an der Universität Klagenfurt. For scholars only!

Virtual Library Geschichte "Drittes Reich"

http://www.hco.hagen.de/history/index.html

This page devoted to the Third Reich, compiled by Ralf Blank of the Ruhr-Universität, Bochum, is one of the standouts of the German History section of the WWW Virtual Library (above). It offers information about various aspects of the Nazi regime, including "Politik," "Wirtschaft," and "Widerstand."

WebMuseen: Museen und Austellungen im deutschsprachigen Raum

http://webmuseen.de/

This site provides information and links for museums of all types in Germany, Austria, and Switzerland. The "Themen" option allows a search for historical museums.

Willkommen bei der Bundesregierung Deutschland

http://www.bundesregierung.de/

Auswärtiges Amt

http://www.auswaertiges-amt.de/

Der Bundespräsident

http://www.bundespraesident.de/

Deutscher Bundestag

http://www.bundestag.de/index.htm

These official sites of the German federal government are good starting points for recent history and political events. Of particular historical interest is the site of the Auswärtiges Amt (Foreign Ministry), with information about its organization, history, and publications.

Martin Luther Historical Site

http://www.luther.de/

This site is a good source of information about the life and times of Germany's most famous religious reformer. It includes a detailed biography, discussion of the historical background, and legends associated with Martin Luther's life. In German and English.

GREEK HISTORY (Modern)
deTraci Regula

Armed Forces of Greece

Hellenic Air Force—History

http://www.hellas.org/hafhist.html

Detailed account of the air force since its inception in 1911. Gives founders' names, some background, pictures, and basic specifications of early aircraft.

Hellenic Armed Forces

http://www.hellas.org/militar.html

Brief breakdown of the different branches of the armed forces, including manpower, major equipment, and photos.

Hellenic Army

http://www.hellas.org/harmy.html

Rundown on equipment and manpower of the Greek army.

Hellenic Army Aviation

http://www.evansb.gr/haa/haae.htm

Unofficial page collecting information previously published in military journals. Some good photos and links to additional information. Not much content per page.

Hellenic Army General Staff

http://www.army.gr/english/index.htm

Thorough, official site covering everything from the history of the army and the chain of command to the equipment, military schools, uniforms, and medals, broken down by period.

Hellenic Navy

http://www.hellas.org/hnavy.html

Quick basic specifications on the Hellenic navy, with details on number and type of crafts.

Books, Journals, and Magazines

Greek University Library Catalogs Online

http://galaxy.einet.net/hytelnet/GR000.html

From MGSA, quick access to many Greek libraries, with instant search capability.

Hellenic Bookspace

http://book.culture.gr/

Site devoted to modern literature and books of all types.

Hellenism and Modern Greece

http://weber.u.washington.edu/~egkioule/books/greece_today/

Listing of books in Greek and English, with links to bibliographical information.

Journal of Modern Greek Studies

http://jhupress.jhu.edu/press/journals/titles/mgs.html

Online editions are available for subscribers. General information only here.

Modern Greek History Resources

http://www.webexpert.net/vasilios/history/history.htm

Excellent selection of Greek and English-language materials on all aspects of modern Greek history.

National Book Centre of Greece

http://book.culture.gr/2/nbc.html

Government-sponsored archive and program provider for Greek books. Includes bibliographies of folklore, lists of political books written under the dictatorship, events, and links to literary journals. Searchable bibliographical index.

Newsletters, Journals, and Magazines

http://www.nyu.edu/pages/onassis/other/magz.html

Listing of English-Language and Greek-language periodicals pertaining to Hellenic studies.

Synthesis: Review of Modern Greek Studies

http://www.lse.ac.uk/depts/european/synthesis/

Home page for this Greek journal. There's also a U.S.-based mirror site at *Synthesis*.

Recent Events

Athens News Agency

http://www.ana.gr/

Streaming headlines, daily news, photo of the day. A great quick look at news in Greece from the major English-language newspaper.

Ministry of Foreign Affairs—What's New

http://www.mfa.gr/whatnew/

Constantly updated list of material relating to current events. Many entries only in Greek; scroll down for more English-language listings.

Defense Industry

Greek Defense Industry Directory

http://www.deloscomm.gr/defenc98.htm

Information on annual volume published about the Greek Defense industry, listing more than 5,000 organizations.

Government and Government Agencies

Election Results Since 1952

http://www.glavx.org/greece/election.htm

Election results broken down by party and number of seats won. Followed by a list of presidents of Greece, noting those who seized power through a coup rather than an election. From the Vryonis Society.

Hellenic Ministries

http://www.fossnet.com/mneng.htm

Listing of all the government ministries.

Hellenic Parliament

http://www.parliament.gr/en/today/uk/

Includes listing of members, constitutional history, and photos.

Ministry of Culture

http://www.culture.gr/

Includes: The Identity of the Ministry; Museums, Monuments, and Archaeological Sites of Hellas; Modern and Contemporary Cultural Creation; Cultural Organizations; Cultural Events; Selected Cultural Events; Special Issues; Announcements—Press Releases; and a Guide to the Internet.

Ministry of Foreign Affairs

http://www.mfa.gr USA mirror site: http://www.hri.org/MFA/

The Hellenic Republic's official office of foreign affairs, with abundant links to documents pertaining to foreign policy and current events.

Greek Language Tools

Download Greek Fonts

http://www.ana.gr/gr/greek.html

Selection of fonts available for different operating systems, including Windows, Macintosh, and others.

Fonts and Tools for Greek

http://www.nyu.edu/pages/onassis/top-level/tools.html

Links to fonts and other tools for reading Greek on the Internet.

Greek Alphabet

http://sunsite.unc.edu/koine/greek/lessons/alphabet.html

From Little Greek 101, this is a great quick introduction to reading and writing the Greek alphabet. Pronunciations are Erasmian rather than Modern, but it is a good place to start.

Greek–English and English–Greek Dictionary

http://www.kypros.org/cgi-bin/lexicon

Enter any common word and find its translation.

Greek Spell Checker

http://www.kypros.org/Orthographic/

In Greek. Copy Greek-font text into the spell check window for a quick confirmation of spelling.

Hellenic Study Programs

Hellenic Studies Center at Dawson College

http://www.hol.gr/mirrors/hec/HSDC/brochure.html

Online information brochure about this program in Quebec, Canada.

Onassis Program in Hellenic Studies

http://www.nyu.edu/pages/onassis/

Starting point for information about this NYU-based program.

Princeton—Program in Hellenic Studies 98–99

http://www.princeton.edu/pr/catalog/gsa/214-hellenic.html

Information on this graduate program, including committee members, faculty, general focus, and required courses.

University of Manitoba Centre for Hellenic Studies

http://www.umanitoba.ca/faculties/arts/classics/chc/index.html

Information on this program, originally funded by the Hellenic Ministry of Culture.

Modern Greek History—The Cyprus Question

Images of the Invasion of Cyprus

http://www.hellas.org/cyimages.html

Selection of photos taken during this event.

Lobby for Cyprus Home Page

http://www.lobbyforcyprus.org/

Well-organized, award-winning page promoting the solution of the Cyprus problem from the Greek perspective.

Modern Greek History—Chronology

Chronology of Events

http://www.glavx.org/greece/chronology.html

From the Vryonis Society, decade-by-decade breakdown of key political events in Greece from 1950 to 1997.

Modern Greek History—Demographics

http://www.glavx.org/greece/demos.htm

Brief details of the population statistics of Greece, up to 1994.

Modern Greek History—Documents

Greece-FYROM Dispute

http://www.hri.org/docs/fyrom/

From Hellenic Resource Network, various online documents pertaining to the conflicts between Greece and the former Yugoslav Republic.

History of Modern Greece—Primary Documents

http://library.byu.edu/~rdh/eurodocs/greece.html

Extensive online collection of key documents, including the Greek Constitution, World War II, the Aegean Dispute, and much more. Maintained by Richard Hacken, European Studies Bibliographer, Harold B. Lee Library, Brigham Young University.

Internet Law Library—Greece

http://law.house.gov/63.htm

Listing of online documents prepared for the U.S. House of Representatives. Includes the constitution, treaties, Athens Convention, NATO documents, Lausanne Treaty, and more.

Ministry of Foreign Affairs—European Union

http://www.mfa.gr/foreign/euro_union/

Links to documents and statements pertaining to Greece's participation in the European Union. Includes: Memorandum—For a European Union with Political and Social Content; Greece's Contribution to the 1996 Intergovernmental Conference; Resolution on the political situation following the UN-sponsored talks on Cyprus and the European Commission, Representation in Greece.

Ministry of Foreign Affairs—Foreign Policy—Greece and Turkey

http://www.mfa.gr/foreign/bilateral/

Includes the following official statements, among many others: Greek-Turkish relations; Turkish claims in the Aegean; The Imia Crisis; State of the Union; Map of Imia rocks; Agreements between Italy and Turkey of 1932 (in French); The Cyprus Issue: A revealing fact of the situation in Northern Cyprus—increasing numbers of Turkish-Cypriots seek asylum in the United Kingdom; Greek Minority of Turkey.

Treaties and Conventions

http://www.mfa.gr/foreign/treaties/

From the Hellenic Ministry of Foreign Affairs, numerous online documents pertaining to Greece.

Modern Greek History—World War II

German Campaign in the Balkans—Greece

http://www.army.mil/cmh-pg/books/wwii/balkan/20_260_3.htm

Account of "Operation Marita," which also discusses some of Italy's attacks on Greece. Includes maps. From documents posted by the U.S. Army via the Center of Military History. Lack of link-backs conceal author and other details.

Maritime History

http://mykonos.forthnet.gr/general/aegean/history.htm

An abundantly detailed history of ships and seafaring in the Aegean, focusing on Delos and Rhodes.

Museums and Societies

Historical and Ethnological Society of Greece

http://www.fhw.gr/projects/vouli/en/museum/society.html

Information about this organization devoted to the study of middle and modern Greek history and literature.

Institute of International Economic Relations

http://idec.gr/iier/aims.htm

Industry group presenting conferences, seminars, and publishing materials related to Greek economic involvement.

National Historical Museum—Greece

http://www.fhw.gr/projects/vouli/en/museum/museum.htm

Virtual tour of this museum devoted to the history of Modern Greece.

The Speros Basil Vryonis Society for the Study of Hellenism

http://www.glavx.org/

Organization devoted to the promotion of Hellenistic studies.

Search Engines

Ariadnet

http://www.ariadne-t.gr/

Research-oriented search engine operated by NCSR Demokritos, the "oldest and largest Physics and Sciences Research establishment in Greece."

Phantis

http://www.phantis.com

Well-organized and regularly maintained search site, with good coverage of sites within Greece. Many Greek entries, but enough English-language ones to make a visit worthwhile even if Greek is a challenge.

RoBBy—The Greek (Hellenic) Search Engine

http://www.robby.gr/

Well-categorized search engine focusing entirely on sites pertaining to Greece. The main page also offers daily links to international exchange rates and news in Greece. Strong coverage of politically oriented sites.

Thea—Complete Greek Indexer

http://www.thea.gr/

Thorough general search machine for Greek or Greek-related sites worldwide.

IRISH HISTORY

Patrick Callan

A to Z of Ancient Ireland

http://www.atlanticisland.ie/atlanticisland/arts/flatozex.html

This extensive glossary of terms associated with Celtic Ireland runs the gamut from "airbre druad" (or "druid's hedge") to "yew sticks" used by magicians. It is based on a text, *Ancient Ireland—The Users' Guide*, by Conan Kennedy, and provides a substantial context for the study of pre-Christian Ireland. There is a wry sense of humor throughout, as well as references to other contemporary European civilizations, and religions.

About Local Ireland: 1798 Rebellions

http://www.local.ie/history/1798index.html

This is a clear, illuminating site, a good introduction to the 1798 rebellions; it gives a clear sense of context (back to 1601), the military background, the armies and the soldiers, and the aftermath, as well as five clear maps.

Aspects of Ulster

http://ourworld.compuserve.com/homepages/martin_sloan/

This site by Martin Sloan features a timeline related to events in Ulster from prehistoric times to modern times. While taking a longitudinal perspective to the conflict, it is often slipshod in judgment, e.g., that it was only the establishment of the Gaelic League in 1893 that ushered in Gaelic nationalism. A useful companion to other timelines, as the site also features biographies of lesser known people born in the nine-county province.

Ballinamuck and '98

http://www.local.ie

Father Owen Devaney writes extensively on the battle of Ballinamuck, the last conventional land battle fought on Irish soil, when the English forces defeated the French.

The Battle of Antrim

http://www.antrim.gov.uk/battle/index.html

The 1798 rebellion as manifested in County Antrim is covered in a clear manner. A. Smyth, the author, shows its background, the principal participants, the battle of Antrim, and its aftermath. Included are outlines of the battle, which are supplemented by artwork, contemporary pictures, and maps. Smyth intended to "explore history with respect for the truth we may learn."

The Battle of the Boyne

http://www.grandorange.org.uk/

Hosted by the Orange Order, the site contains the Boyne battle plan, pictures of the protagonists and the battlefield, as well as paintings by VanWyck. A description of the battle is supplemented by the account of the eminent historian Froude.

Battle of the Boyne Day Pages

http://www.bcpl.lib.md.us/~cbladey/orange.html

The battle of the Boyne is commemorated by the Orange Order at its annual 12 July parades. Conrad Bladey's site includes a substantial account of the battle, information about the armies and soldiers, and songs of the Orangemen. Contemporary illustrations give a strong visual sense. The site puts forward an impassioned defense of the Orange tradition, e.g., William III's victory brought about the "defeat of James II, an Absolutist monarch rejected by England, by a tolerant ruler subject to the rule of Parliament."

Battle of the Yellow Ford

http://www.thehistorynet.com/MilitaryHistory/previous/1998/0898_cover.htm

Jon Guttman's article on the Battle of the Yellow Ford is a substantial scholarly account of one of the few decisive victories by the native Irish over a militant English army during the Tudor period. According to the author it was England's worst defeat on Irish soil.

Bawnboy Workhouse

http://www.cavannet.ie/history/archeo/sites/work-hse.htm

Photographs of the remains of a typical workhouse, giving a flavor of the scale of these publicly funded buildings.

George Berkeley

http://www.maths.tcd.ie/pub/HistMath/People/Berkeley/

David Wilkins, of Trinity College, Dublin, authors this site on Ireland's most eminent philosopher. There is a biographical guide, lectures, and essays on his philosophy, as well as selections from his works, including "A Treatise concerning the Principles of Human Knowledge" and "A Defence of Free Thinking in Mathematics."

CAIN Web Service

http://cain.ulst.ac.uk/

CAIN (Conflict Archive on the Internet) is the most comprehensive and scholarly site dealing with Northern Ireland. Aimed at college students, it provides comprehensive bibliographies, chronologies, and an examination of the media and the arts. Dividing events into sixteen units eases navigation. It covers themes such as discrimination and housing, as well as "women and the conflict." The element on "Bloody Sunday" gives an indication of the quality of the site.

CELT: Corpus of Electronic Texts

http://www.ucc.ie/celt/

Corpus of Electronic Texts (CELT), is a rigorously scholarly project that intends to place online many valuable texts relating to Irish history, from Celtic to modern times. Currently, gems such as the 1921 Anglo-Irish Treaty debates, James Connolly's *Labour in Irish History*, the works of Oscar Wilde and Patrick Pearse, and James Stephens's *Insurrection in Dublin* are included.

Chronicon: An Electronic History Journal

http://www.ucc.ie/ucc/chronicon/contents.html

This electronic journal provides scholarly articles on Irish history, along with high-quality postgraduate reports, as well as a historian's forum.

Michael Collins

http://www2.cruzio.com/~sbarrett/mcollins.htm

Suzanne Barrett's biography is brief and well-written, and she appends a bibliography relating to Collins.

The "Confessio" of St. Patrick

http://www.mcs.net/~jorn/html/jj/patrick.html

Kidnapped at sixteen years of age and sold into slavery in Ireland, St. Patrick went on to convert the Irish to Christianity. His *Confessio*, originally written in Latin, offers a clear and enthralling view of life in the British Isles.

Michael Davitt: Mayo's Most Famous Son

http://www.mayo-ireland.ie

Davitt died in Dublin in 1906. By the time of his death at the age of sixty, land for the people had largely become a reality, prison reform had begun, and he himself had become an international champion of liberty.

Discovering the Bronze Age

http://www.iol.ie/~discovry/lbapack.htm

This site gives an illuminating outline of the main characteristics of the Bronze Age in Ireland, with color line drawings. It includes material on ritual and religion, trade, mining, clothing, jewelry, homes and settlements, as well as farming, food, and cooking. Hosted by the Discovery Programme (Ireland).

The Famine—"The Times" and Donegal

http://www2.magmacom.com/~jward/famcont.html

Thomas Campbell Foster's reports from County Donegal provide excellent material on the local famine experiences in Donegal. Published originally in *The Times* (London), they were published in 1846, in a book running to 771 pages. Here, they are selected by John Ward, from County Donegal, who has a deep knowledge of local history, and he integrates the famine reports with relevant local and national materials and sources.

Forgotten Man of Irish History

http://www.mayo-ireland.ie

The year 1879 proved to be a busy and fruitful year for James Daly. He was first elected chairman of the historic Westport meeting addressed by Charles Stuart Parnell. On August 16th, he became vice-president of the Land League of Mayo in Castlebar. He was also elected to the committee of the Irish National Land League founded in Dublin on October 21, 1879.

The Great Irish Famine

http://www.wisc.edu/history/famine/

Thomas Archdeacon, University of Wisconsin–Madison, provides a navigation site to other main famine sites. The unique elements include links to contemporary data on farms and social indicators (from Joel Mokyr), as well as three maps relating to the famine era, of poor law unions, of public works, and of the extent of cholera infection.

The Great War, 1914 to 1918

http://dnausers.d-n-a.net/dnetDkjs/

Karl Murray writes principally about the story of the 36th (Ulster) Division in the Great War, especially its experience on the first day of the Battle of the Somme.

History of Ireland's National Police Force

http://www.geocities.com/CapitolHill/7900/

The Garda Síochána Historical Society has excellent material of the history of Irish policing from 1770 to 1922, and many modern controversies.

Ireland: History in Maps

http://www.fortunecity.com/bally/kilkenny/2/iremaps.htm

Dennis Walsh has included many maps of Ireland, charting the main transitions of Irish history (e.g., the age of Brian Boru). Each map is complemented by an explanatory text. The site also includes supplementary material on old Irish kingdoms, the Normans, and castles, as well as the "Cambro-Norman Invasion of Ireland." There are external links to many ancient and genealogical sites, as well as to other map sites.

The Irish Constitution

http://www.maths.tcd.ie/pub/Constitution/index.html
http://www.uni-wuerzburg.de/law/ei00000_.html

A copy of the 1937 constitution, introduced by De Valera, and which provides the touchstone for many contemporary debates in Ireland today.

Irish Diaspora

http://www.brad.ac.uk/acad/diaspora/

The site includes detailed scholarly reviews of recent works in emigration, and highlights important reissues, such as Hugh Heinrick's *A Survey of the Irish in England* (1872). There is also an interesting essay on

Patrick Magill from Donegal, and a substantial number of links to other sites dealing with the Irish Diaspora. The Irish Diaspora list provides an e-mail discussion forum, dedicated to the scholarly study of the Irish Diaspora. It is hosted by the Irish Diaspora Research Unit from the University of Bradford, England.

Irish Famine

http://www.local.ie/history/famine/

This is the best introductory site to the Great Famine, as it incorporates excellent text and uses some primary documents. It examines the prevailing social order (e.g., community life, housing), gives a chronological history from 1845 to 1851, contains a unique glossary of terms and a bibliography, and includes links to other famine sites.

Irish Famine, 1845–50

http://avery.med.virginia.edu/~eas5e/Irish/Times.html

The Virginia University site presents excellent selections from reports of *The Times* (London) and includes the paper's own index on the famine articles. Topics range from requests for outdoor relief in 1846, to reports of alleged cannibalism in June 1849. Thomas Campbell Foster's reports from County Donegal can also be viewed. There is also a useful bibliography.

Irish History on the Web

http://wwwvms.utexas.edu/~jdana/irehist.html

Jacqueline Dana, M.A. in History (Irish and American) from the University of Missouri–Columbia, hosts a very useful general site that is regularly updated, with links to genealogy and history, timelines and famine sites, reading lists, and documents, with a segment on Northern Ireland's history. It has a disproportionate number of sources reflecting the well-established pedigree of republican history.

John F. Kennedy's Address before the Irish Parliament

http://www.cs.umb.edu/~rwhealan/jfk/

John F. Kennedy was the first American President to visit Ireland during his term of office. During this spirited address to the Dáil (Irish parliament) in 1963, President Kennedy spoke on the Irish contribution to the United States and the shared democratic principles of the two countries.

Local History

http://www.local.ie/history

This is the best brief introduction to Irish history, going from prehistory to the modern problems concerning the continuing conflict in Northern Ireland. The site, part of Telecom Eireann's information age initiative, asserts that it tries "to be as fair and balanced as possible."

Navan at Armagh

http://www.navan.com/

Navan Fort, the ancient Emain Macha of Irish history and legend, was the earliest capital of Ulster. It was the royal seat of the kings of Ulster, and the setting for the tales of Macha, C' Chulainn and the heroes of the Red Branch. Today, Navan is a premier archaeological monument and one of Europe's most important Celtic centers. The site, hosted by the Navan Interpretative Centre, contains clear outlines of the history of Navan Fort, and guidelines to dynamic interactive displays bring the mystery and mythology of Emain Macha to life.

Newgrange Monument

http://www.paddynet.com/island/newgrange/ancient.html

Covering an area of one acre, Newgrange is one of the most impressive prehistoric monuments in Europe, older than the pyramids and Stonehenge. The burial mound dominates the grouping of forty tombs known as Brugh na Bóinne, and it was regarded as the otherworld dwelling of the divine Aonghus Mac Óg—Aonghus the Youthful. The site outlines the archaeology of Newgrange and contains speculations about the possible purpose of this five-thousand-year-old monument.

Newshound

http://www.nuzhound.com

This site allows surfers the facility to access a special index on Irish history articles published in Irish newspapers. The index contains articles published during the previous two years and gives an indication of many controversies and anniversaries in Irish historiography.

The Northern Ireland Election Sites

http://www.explorers.whyte.com/

Nicholas Whyte, a Ph.D. from Queen's University of Belfast, posted this well-moderated text on the history of Westminster parliamentary elections and constituencies, and provides links to local political parties.

Patrick Pearse

http://wwwvms.utexas.edu/~jdana/pearsehist.html

John L. Murphy (California) provides a lively biography, not simply concentrating on the 1916 experience, but also on his formative personal, educational, and political influences.

Personalities of Ireland in the Period 1798–1803

http://unet.univie.ac.at/~a8700035/biograph.html

Stiofan MacAmhalghaidh includes eleven biographies of individuals associated with the 1798 rebellions, although Daniel O'Connell and Robert Emmet go beyond that era.

Potato Blight

http://www.cavannet.ie/nature/spuds.htm

This site describes the nature of the disease that hit the Irish potato crop; uniquely, there are color photographs of healthy leaves that then become infected by the blight.

The Red Flag: The Song, the Man, the Monument

http://www.dcu.ie/~comms/hsheehan/connell.htm

Jim Connell wrote "The Red Flag" in 1889. Dr. Helena Sheehan's site provides substantial information on labor songs in general.

Reinterpreting the 1798 Rebellion in County Wexford

http://www.iol.ie/~pressecw/whelan.htm

Kevin Whelan, one of Ireland's leading historians, reinterprets the rebellion in County Wexford, casting a cold eye on the detail.

Remembering Bloody Sunday

http://www.larkspirit.com/bloodysunday/

This site is hosted by republicans; it features many eyewitness accounts of the internment march and its aftermath, material from Irish Northern Aid, submissions to the UN, photographs of the day, as well as memorials and murals. There is much material republished in the late 1990s, when this event once more gained a high profile due to the corpus of material gathered by the Irish government.

1798 Rebellions in Wexford

http://www.iol.ie/~pressecw/98index.htm

Students of Presentation Secondary School, Wexford give the background to the rebellion in Wexford, as well as a substantive daily account from May 27 to June 24, 1798.

A View of the Present State of Ireland

http://darkwing.uoregon.edu/~rbear/veue1.html

Author of the well-known poetry classic, *The Faerie Queen*, Edmund Spenser penned *A View of the Present State of Ireland* (1596), reflecting the gulf between the English overlords and the native Irish. It establishes the context for the Englishing of Ireland over the following centuries. The edition was prepared by Richard Bar of the University of Oregon, who admits that he "cheered on the Irish the whole time."

Views of the Famine

http://vassun.vassar.edu/~sttaylor/FAMINE/

This site contains many contemporary illustrations from publications including the famous *Illustrated London News* and *Punch*. The graphics show laborers, their cabins, beggars, landlords, evictions, funerals, and emigration. The site also has an excellent article from *The Irish Times* on the artist responsible for the artwork in the *Illustrated London News*. Taylor has also included text that originally accompanied the illustrations. (Access from ~sttaylor/ if any problem with access.)

Visit the Counties

http://www.local.ie/visit_the_counties/

This site brings surfers to each of the thirty counties in Ireland, each of which has a history element. The quality is uneven, but can reward a visit.

The Wild Geese Today—Erin's Far Flung Exiles

http://www.thewildgeese.com/

An excellent metasite for Irish resources, although it includes more than historical information, with many items that are neither sourced nor substantiated. However, the eclecticism of its authors makes it a curio with many nuggets, placing side by side the 1798 rebellions, the 1916 rising, Ian Paisley, and sites on some Irish units in the British army, e.g. 16th (Irish) Division. It hosts an anniversary site, *This week in the history of the Irish*, as well as a *Wild Geese* forum, which contains many interesting comments on Irish history.

Williamite War

http://www.local.ie/history/williamite.

The Williamite War was the "only full scale conventional war ever fought in Ireland" (according to the anonymous authors of this site, sponsored by Telecom Eireann). There is substantial background, material on weapons and tactics, maps, a chronology, and a bibliography, as well as biographies of Williamites and Jacobites.

Workhouse Famine Records

http://www.magma.ca/~jward/workhouse1.html

The material on workhouse famine records were drawn up by a local history group under the guidance of Anthony Begley, County Donegal. It deals extensively with the experience of famine as exemplified through the records of the regionally funded workhouses, as well as attempts to alleviate the suffering in some of the poorest areas of Ireland. (Go to homepage of ~jward if a problem accessing this.)

ITALIAN HISTORY
Ernest Ialongo

Archivi–Sistema Archivistico Nazionale

http://archivi.beniculturali.it

This is a list of the central state and city archives in Italy that lists addresses, phone and fax numbers, and contact persons. The site includes various other archive Web sites.

Archivio Storico della Camera dei Deputati (Historical Archive of the Chamber of Deputies)

http://www.camera.it/camera/mappa/mappafr.htm

This site contains the archives of the Chamber of Deputies. The list is not for those seeking a detailed outline of everything this archive contains. The site attempts to highlight some of its special collections, such as the records of the Neapolitan parliament of 1848–49, and the records of the Camera regia from 1848–1943. The home page, www.camera.it, provides all the information needed for someone planning a research trip to the archive.

Archivio Storico Italiano

http://www.storia.unifi.it/_PIM/ASI-DSPT/ASI/Apertura.htm

This journal, the oldest in Italy, has posted its contents for 1998, along with abstracts of its articles. For the years 1993–97 you can find a table of contents, but no abstracts. 1993 is the earliest year for a listing of contents, but the site provides titles that index the contents of the entire journal.

Cronologia

http://www.goldnet.it/francomputer/storia/welcome.html

This is a very basic chronology from the beginning of time to the present day. Its use for Italianists is that it provides quick information about the major political, social, and cultural events on a year-by-year basis with an emphasis on Italy.

Divine Comedy

http://www.italianstudies.org/dante

The Center for Italian Studies at SUNY–Stony Brook provides this full translation of Dante's *Divine Comedy* by James Finn Cotter (with explanatory notes) on their Web site. The site includes a link to their journal   *Forum Italicum.* (See below.)

Europaea, Journal of the Europeanists

http://www.vaxca1.unica.it/europaea/index.html

This is a journal of European ethnology and anthropology. It has been in existence since 1995 and has recently made all of their issues available online for downloading. Every issue contains either an article or book review of interest to Italianists.

Fondazione Istituto Gramsci

http://www.gramsci.it

The institute's Web site lists its publications, a detailed list of its library, a link to their journal *Studi Storici* (see page 200), and, most importantly, a very detailed list of its archives. They are divided according to organizations, personal archives, and general collections. Within each section there are even more detailed descriptions of the collection. Any student of Italian Communism or the Left should browse this site.

Forum Italicum, A Journal of Italian Studies

http://ws.cc.sunysb.edu/cistudies/forum.htm

The journal is primarily for those interested in Italian literature. However, as literature is increasingly being used as a primary source by historians, some of the articles in the journal are of historical interest. The journal provides a list of its contents from Fall 1995 onward, and from Spring 1996 book reviews, poetry, and fiction are available online.

Garibaldi's Campaign in Southern Italy

http://www.italgen.com/garibal.htm

"This list with 1,089 people given by the Ministry of War was published in the *Giornale Militare* (Military Journal) in 1864 as a result of an enquiry by a State Committee. This Committee had been created to determine, through proofs and witnesses, the names of the volunteers who actually landed at

Marsala on May 11, 1860." The list contains surnames, first names, father's name, place of birth, and province for each entry.

H-Italy

http://www.h-net.msu.edu/~italy/

The H-Italy Web site forms part of the H-Net system out of Michigan State University. The H-Italy site provides announcements of interest to Italianists, links to the H-Net archive of book reviews, and links to resources in Italian art, architecture, and literature (the texts of major Italian authors). Links to Italian libraries are also provided.

History of Italy—Primary Documents, Harold B. Lee Library, Brigham Young University

http://www.lib.byu.edu/~rdh/eurodocs/italy.html

This is a wide-ranging collection of primary documents for Italy, everything from Machiavelli's *The Prince* to the Italian Constitution of 1947 and its Civil Code. Most of the site links to other more comprehensive sites. This site's biggest problem is that it has nothing on the Italian Enlightenment, the French Revolution in Italy, the Risorgimento, or unified Italy up to 1914.

International Institute of Social History

http://www.iisg.nl

This is a large site of interest to historians of any national and international field. For Italianists, this site provides a list of its archives, which are strong in the field of anarchism, communism, labor, etc., and many links to Web sites of direct interest to Italianists in the *WWW Virtual Library of Labour and Business History* (which is much more wide-ranging than it sounds). This is a highly recommended site.

Italian Index, Brigham Young University

http://humanities.byu.edu/classes/ital420/index.html

The Departments of French and Italian maintain this Web site, which is a list of links to other sites spanning Italian history from the Etruscans to today. There are brief comments on the links they provide. Some of the links you will find provide, for example, texts of Leopardi's poetry, reproductions and brief histories of the city-states that formed united Italy, and various links to pertinent archives for each time period. This is a highly recommended site.

J. Calvitt Clarke III Home Page

http://users.ju.edu/~jclarke

Dr. Clarke's home page has links to several of his lengthy articles on Italian diplomacy in the 1930s, which concentrate on Italian relations with the Soviet Union and Japan, and Italy's conquest of Ethiopia. Several of Dr. Clarke's book reviews, which cover the same period, are also posted on his Web site.

Journal of Modern Italian Studies

http://www.brown.edu/Research/Journal_Modern_Italian_Studies

This new journal, under the editorship of David Kertzer (Brown University) and John Davis (University of Connecticut) is one of the few journals in English dedicated to Italian history after the Renaissance, and by far the best. The site has a list of every article and book review published, plus a biography of published authors. Most importantly, each article is abstracted.

Liber Liber

http://www.liberliber.it/biblioteca

Liber Liber is a not-for-profit cultural association that has been putting Italian—but also general European—texts online since 1993. Most of the texts are accompanied by short biographies of the authors, and can be viewed online. Many of the longer texts can be downloaded. There is no charge for this service. Some of the authors Liber Liber represents include Karl Marx, Cervantes, Giosuè Carducci, Vincenzo Cuoco, Cesare Beccaria (*Crime and Punishment*), Giovanni Boccaccio (*Decameron*), and Niccoló Machiavelli (*The Prince,* plus many others). Moreover, Liber Liber has been posting numerous dissertations of interest to Italian historians.

Ministero degli Affari Esteri a Roma (Ministry of Foreign Affairs, Italy) Historical Diplomatic Archive

http://www.esteri.it/eng/backgroundfact/histoarchiv/index.htm

This is a detailed list of the Historical Diplomatic Archives pertaining to the Ministry of Foreign Affairs. Some of the archives available include: the records of the Sardinian legations to the major European capitals, Washington and Rio de Janeiro prior to Unification, the archives of the Italian diplomatic missions to Berlin, Paris, London, St. Petersburg-Moscow, Vienna, and Washington after Unification, a host of archives belonging to the central administration, and a large selection of archives dealing with Italy's colonial empire. The site also lists a host of personal archives available at the Historical Diplomatic Archive. An invaluable list of publications that give specific reports on particular archival holdings is also included. The location, rules of use, and document reproduction policies of the Historical Diplomatic Archive are also listed. Lastly, an English translation of this site is available.

Music and Anthropology, Journal of Musical Anthropology of the Mediterranean

http://gotan.cirfid.unibo.it/M&A

"Music and Anthropology (M&A) is an online multimedia interactive journal, founded by the Study Group on "Anthropology of Music in Mediterranean Cultures" of the International Council for Traditional Music. M&A is hosted by the Dipartimento di Musica e Spettacolo (Università di Bologna), and supported by the Fondazione Olga e Ugo Levi, Venezia." This is an electronic journal that first appeared in 1996. One issue appears per year and articles on Italy have already appeared. There are also links to other anthropological sites.

National Archives and Records Administration (United States of America)

http://www.nara.gov

This site provides links to search engines of various federal archival collections in the United States. Subjects on Italy were located using NAIL (NARA Archival Information Locator). These documents are also available for ordering. The GILS (Government Information Locator Service) is also worth a look.

Passato e Presente, Rivista di Storia Contemporanea

http://www.storia.unifi.it/_paspres

This journal only has its last six issues indexed online (back to 1997). You can find basic reproductions here of the table of contents, but, more importantly, there are English summaries of each article. It is primarily a journal of twentieth-century politics and history.

Polo Informatico Medievistico, University of Florence, History Department

http://www.storia.unifi.it/_PIM

This Web site has two really important features for Italian medievalists: 1) it has links to three comprehensive articles and site lists for medieval Internet resources located at http://www.storia.unifi.it/_PIM/AIM/risorse, and 2) it has an ongoing list of medieval conferences located at http://www.storia.unifi.it/ ._PIM/CM.

Resources on Antonio Gramsci

http://www.soc.qc.edu/gramsci

This site has been put together by the Sociology Department of Queens College, and is the best source for Gramscian studies. The following is a direct quote from the site. "Available resources include an online searchable version of the complete *Bibliografia gramsciana*, a complete list of Gramsci's writings, related appendices and introductory materials, and the first eight issues of the Newsletter of the International Gramsci Society. The research bibliography, which includes some 11,430 items, contains volume 1, the *Bibliografia gramsciana, 1922–88* by John M. Cammett, Rome: Editori Riuniti, 1991, and volume 2, the *Bibliografia gramsciana, Supplement Updated to 1993*, by John M. Cammett and Maria Luisa Righi, Rome: Fondazione Istituto Gramsci, 1995. The newest October 1997 version of the online bibliography includes the Second Supplement, an additional 1,175 references compiled by John Cammett. The published volumes were sponsored and supported by the Fondazione Istituto Gramsci in Rome, Italy." The site includes a search engine of all of its references, as well as a list of Gramsci's own writings in Italian and in translation. The full run of the *International Gramsci Society Newsletter* are available online along with other useful links.

Royal House of Savoy

http://www.knightlyorders.org/savoia.html

This is a site dedicated to the House of Savoy that includes various biographies of its members, a history of the House, and a list of all the heads of the House. English translations of the texts are available.

Servizio Bibliotecario Nazionale (National Library Service)

http://www.sbn.it
http://www.cineca.it/sbn

These useful sites allow you to access many libraries in Italy with every request. Their primary use to scholars outside Italy is that they allow you to see much more of the sources available on a topic than what can be deduced from accessing the Web sites of the bigger libraries in North America, such as the New York Public Library and the Library of Congress.

Studi Storici

http://www.gramsci.it/ststor.htm
http://www.liberliber.it/biblioteca/riviste/studistorici

Studi Storici is a publication of the Fondazione Istituto Gramsci, and one of
the leading journals for historians of the Left in Italy. The sites index the
journal's contents from 1985–94. Most importantly, the 1995 articles are available online for viewing, though they cannot be downloaded or printed. The
journal has yet to add any subsequent issues for online viewing.

Unione Romana Biblioteche Scientifiche

telnet://librs6k.vatlib.it

This Internet library group allows you to search various libraries in Italy, such
as: The American Academy in Rome (AAR), Accademia di Danimarca (AD),
Archivio Segreto Vaticano (ASV), Biblioteca Apostolica Vaticana (BAV), British School at Rome (BSR), Deutsches Archaeologisches Institut (DAI), Escuela
espanola (EE), École Française de Rome (EFR), Istituto Austriaco di Cultura
in Roma (IAR), Istituto Patristico "Augustinianum" (IPA), Institutum Romanum
Findlandiae (IRF), Istituto di Norvegia (IRN), Istituto Svedese di Studi Clas-
sici (ISV), Libera Università "Maria SS. Assunta" (MSA), and Pontificia
Università Lateranense (PUL). Acronyms in parentheses represent the codes
used by this library group to denote where titles are located.

Windows on Italy—History

http://www.mi.cnr.it/WOI/deagosti/history

This is a collection of twenty-four essays covering the history of Italy from
prehistoric times to the Republic. These are very general essays, and are a quick
read for someone not familiar with a particular time period. Each essay contains
links to more specific essays on each of the major cities mentioned in the original text.

NORDIC (SCANDINAVIA) HISTORY
Bente Opheim and Frode Ulvund

METASITES

CultureNet Sweden

http://www.kulturnat.iva.se/english/

The CultureNet Sweden is under the editorial office of the Swedish Ministry of Culture, and presents links to hundreds of Web sites containing and presenting Swedish culture in English. The site has links to archives, libraries, museums, and other cultural institutions.

Medieval Scandinavia and Anglo-Saxon Britain

http://www.fas.harvard.edu/~layher1/medscan.html

This is a metasite with links to informational sites and electronic text sites on Scandinavian and Norse history and culture.

Medieval Studies

http://www.hist.uib.no/middelalder/

This is a site compiled by the Department of History at the University of Bergen, which provides a gateway to medieval source material, articles, and discussion lists on the Web. It is aimed at students in universities, and researchers and teachers in the field of medieval history—Scandinavian as well as European.

GENERAL HISTORY SITES

Antique Maps of Iceland

http://egla.bok.hi.is/kort/english.html

The National and University Library of Iceland have made all the antique maps in their collection (maps dating from before 1900) available on the Internet.

Bombs and Babies

http://www.hist.uib.no/bomb/

The project Bombs and Babies—Oral History on the Web was launched in August 1997 as a pilot collaboration project between the departments of history at the University in Bergen and University College London. The site presents students' work on oral history dealing with childhood memories from WWII. The work is documented with audio clips of interviews.

A Brief History of Iceland

http://www.iceland.org/list8.html

The Embassy of Iceland in Washington, D.C. has an overview of Icelandic culture, including a brief history of Iceland.

Danish Data Archives

http://www.dda.dk/

The Danish Data Archives (DDA) is a national databank for researchers and students in Denmark and abroad. The DDA is an independent unit within the Danish State Archives. It holds online demographic and social data.

Database of Wall Paintings in Danish Churches

http://kalk.historie.ku.dk/english/default.htm

The Department of History at the University of Copenhagen has created an online database that contains 5,320 images of wall paintings from Danish churches. The images are of very good quality, and the site also offers statistical data, along with articles and literature on art and related topics.

The Demographic Data Base

http://www2.ddb.umu.se/DDB/eng/index.htm

As a Swedish national research resource, the Demographic Data Base activities are centered on two main areas: data production and research. Data production includes input, filing, and systematizing information. The Demographic Data Base is responsible for ensuring that historical data from parish registers and parish statistics are easily available for researchers from both Sweden and abroad. Hosted by the University of Umeå.

Denmark

http://www.um.dk/danmark/denmark/

Denmark, a publication by The Royal Danish Ministry of Foreign Affairs in cooperation with the editors of the Danish National Encyclopaedia, gives an in-depth description of Denmark, including a general history of Denmark. The chapters are written by leading Danish experts.

The Digital Archive of Norway

http://www.hist.uib.no/arkivverket/index-en.htm

The Digital Archive is the result of cooperation between the Department of History, University of Bergen, and the Regional State Archives of Bergen, part of the National State Archives. The archive holds a large collection of online and searchable nominative records from censuses, parish registers, emigration lists, and military records of Norway.

The Documentation Project

http://www.dokpro.uio.no/engelsk/index.html

This site contains information on a wide range of aspects of Norwegian language, history, and culture, located at the University of Oslo. It has searchable databases on a number of historical sources, including the Diplomatarium Norvegicum, which is a large collection of Norwegian official documents prior to 1570. The work of collecting and registration of the documents started 150 years ago, and the collection contains 90,000 documents today. The documents are available at this Web site in a searchable full-text database in the original language (Norse or Latin), with a Norwegian abstract.

Emigration from Norway, The Solem and Swiggum Ship Index

http://digidesk.jbi.hioslo.no/~emigrant/

The information on this site is for research and educational purposes. The site contains the names of ships known to have left Norway for America between 1825 and 1925.

Facts about Genealogy in Denmark

http://www.genealogi.dk/factwors.htm

This article from 1970 provides basic information for anyone who wishes to do genealogical research in Denmark. The article is also updated, with links to a number of sites useful for genealogical research in Denmark.

H-Skand

http://www.hum.ou.dk/projekter/h-skand/

H-Skand is a Web site for the H-Net discussion list of the same. H-Skand focuses particularly on research and teaching interests, new scholarship in the field, discussions of Scandinavian historiography, and the sharing of knowledge and experience about the teaching of Scandinavian history, including posting and discussion of course syllabi and reading lists.

How to Trace Your Ancestors in Norway

http://www.ide-as.com/fndb/howto.html

The Royal Norwegian Ministry of Foreign Affairs has published "How to trace your ancestors in Norway" in nine editions from 1958 to 1996. This edition is written by the head of the State Archive of Bergen and has an extensive introduction on how to trace one's ancestors in Norway. It gives a good overview of Norwegian nominative source material.

The Ninety-Two Medieval Churches of Gotland

http://www.algonet.se/~sorengra/churches/mapindexeng.html

This site describes ninety-two medieval churches in Gotland, Sweden, with texts and images. You may click on maps to locate the right church or search through an index.

Norrøne tekster, sagaer og kvad (Norse texts, sagas, and poems)

http://home.sol.no/~jonjf/n-text.htm

A collection of old Norse poems (kvad) and sagas in the original language or Icelandic. The site is a part of a larger site run by an association called "Foreningen Forn Sed," for the promotion of the Norse religion "Aasatru."

The Norwegian Historical Data Centre (NHDC)

http://www.isv.uit.no/seksjon/rhd/indexeng.htm

The Norwegian Historical Data Centre (NHDC) is a national institution under the Faculty of Social Science at the University of Tromsø (UiTø). Contains searchable online census material from 1865 and onward.

Norwegian Historical Statistics—1994

http://www.ssb.no/www-open/english/statistics_by_subject/
00generalhiststat/

Historical Statistics 1994 is a useful reference to anyone seeking knowledge about the development of Norwegian society from the nineteenth century onward. There is a summary for every item and English text in figures and tables. The statistics are produced and published by the governmental bureau of statistics.

Norwegian Social Science Data Services

http://www.nsd.uib.no/english/

The Norwegian Social Science Data Services (NSD) is a national center servicing the research community. Its main objective is to secure access for the Norwegian research community to data and to provide various services. The institutions hold an extensive data collection on Regional Data, Individual Level Data, and Data on the Political System.

The Online Medieval and Classical Library (OMACL)

http://sunsite.berkeley.edu/OMACL/

This collection of electronic texts also contains Scandinavian texts in English translation, such as the old Norse Heimskringla, by Snorre Sturlasson and the Danish Gesta Danorum by Saxo Grammaticus.

Project Runeberg

http://www.lysator.liu.se/runeberg/

This is a project coordinated by Linköping University, Sweden. Project Runeberg is an initiative to publish free electronic editions of Nordic literature, and contains over 200 texts, ranging from old Norse sagas to novels of Strindberg.

The Saami-People of the Sun and Wind

http://www.sametinget.se/index.html

This site gives a lot of information about the Saami people in northern Scandinavia, their history, culture, religion, and modern government.

A Selection of Events and Documents on the History of Finland

http://www.pp.clinet.fi/~pkr01/historia/history.html

Maintained by Pauli Kruhse, the site contains a large number of primary sources on Finnish history, spanning from 1249 to 1944.

Swedish Institute

http://www.si.se/eng/esverige/esverige.html

An official Swedish site containing information about Sweden in general and an overview of both Swedish history and the Saami people of Sweden.

Virtual Finland

http://virtual.finland.fi/

An official Finnish Web site produced by the Ministry for Foreign Affairs of Finland containing information on a wide range of topics, including history.

The World of the Vikings

http://www.pastforward.co.uk/vikings/index.html

This is a guide to Viking resources on the Internet. The site offers a gateway to topics such as mead, ships, sagas, and runes.

LATIN AND SOUTH AMERICAN HISTORY

H. Micheal Tarver

METASITES

H-LatAm

http://h-net2.msu.edu/~latam

The site is the home page of the Latin American section of the H-Net, Humanities and Social Sciences Online project, hosted by Michigan State University. Included in the site are links to H-LatAm's discussion lists, Announcements, Reviews, Resources, and Internet Links. A good place to start an inquiry into all aspects of Latin America studies.

Internet Resources for Latin America

http://lib.nmsu.edu/subject/bord/laguia

This site provides information and links to Internet resources. This outstanding site contains links that are geared more toward the social sciences, human rights, and indigenous peoples, and has a geographic slant toward Mexico. Compiled by Molly E. Molloy at New Mexico State University.

Latin America and the Caribbean

http://www.info.usaid.gov/regions/lac/

Site at the United States Agency for International Development for Latin American and Caribbean affairs. Includes links for specific countries.

Latin American Country Links

http://www.unites.uqam.ca/gric/pays.htm

Selected links for various Latin American countries. The site is maintained by the University of Quebec at Montreal (in French), although the links include English-language sites as well as French and Spanish.

Latin American Studies Links

http://www.unl.edu/LatAmHis/LatAmLinks.html

Numerous links to sites of concern to Latin America, including specific country resources. The site was created and maintained by DeeAnna Manning, Department of History at the University of Nebraska–Lincoln.

Latin American Links

http://www.ozemail.com.au/~ecuapita/latam.html

This site contains links to several locations with resources relating to Latin American culture and news. There is a variety of themes, countries, and formats.

Rey L. Pratt Center for the Study of Latin America

http://fhss.byu.edu/history/pratt

This site provides invaluable links to sites of interest and importance to the study of Latin America, including, but not limited to, links to over 150 Latin American newspapers and periodicals, links to other Centers for Latin American Studies worldwide, and links to course syllabi. The Rey L. Pratt Center is affiliated with the Brigham Young University History Department.

WWW Virtual Library: Latin American Studies

http://lanic.utexas.edu/las.html

Divided into both Country and Subject Directories, this site provides links for virtually all aspects of Latin American studies. This University of Texas at Austin site was rated one of the top 500 sites on the Web by a 1997 *HomePC* survey.

Latin American Library, Tulane University

http://www.tulane.edu/~latinlib/lalhome.html
http://www.tulane.edu/~latinlib/revistas.html
http://www.tulane.edu/~latinlib/igc.html

These sites contain limited access and links to selected original materials from one of the premier Latin American collections in the United States. There are excellent links to electronic journals relating to Latin America, and access to many Peacenet conferences.

General Latin American Sites

Handbook of Latin American Studies Online

http://lcweb2.loc.gov/hlas/

This is an online, searchable version of the *Handbook of Latin American Studies*, a comprehensive annotated bibliography of selected works in the social sciences and humanities. Updated monthly by the Hispanic Division of the U.S. Library of Congress. It provides abstracts and complete bibliographic information for published materials from and about Latin America on a wide range of topics in the humanities and social sciences and covers more than 60 years of scholarly literature in Latin American studies.

Historical Text Archive—Latin America

http://www.msstate.edu/Archives/History/Latin_America/latam.html

This site provides access to various historical documents in the collection of Mississippi State University. The four major categories are: People Before Columbus, Discovery and Conquest, Colonial Period, and National Histories. There are also direct links provided for specific Latin American nations.

Inter-American Human Rights Database

http://www.wcl.american.edu/pub/humright/digest/index.html

The Inter-American Human Rights Database contains documents in English and Spanish adopted by the Inter-American Commission on Human Rights since its first session, celebrated in 1960. The site includes reports on individual cases, making them available to the general public. The Database wiil include special country reports and thematic reports adopted by the Commission since its inception. The site is maintained by the Center for Human Rights and Humanitarian Law of the Washington College of Law (The American University) and is funded by the Netherlands Ministry of Development Cooperation.

Latin America Database

http://ladb.unm.edu

Provides selected newsletters, economic data on Latin America, and information about the LADB fee-based news service. Also provides access to sites for secondary educators and resources for teaching about the Americas. According to the information presented on the site, the Latin America Database is the first Internet-based news service in English about Latin America, publishing in-depth coverage of Latin American affairs since 1986. The service's professional journalists produce three weekly electronic news bulletins about Mexico, Central America, the Caribbean, and South America. These are available on the Web site or by e-mail with a subscription.

Latin American Lists on the Internet

http://www.msstate.edu/Archives/History/netuse.lists.la

This site is a list of discussion lists that have some connection to events in Latin America. The site includes directions on how to subscribe to (i.e., participate in) the discussions. The list was compiled by Molly Molloy, New Mexico State University Library.

North American Free Trade Agreement (NAFTA) Secretariat

http://www.nafta-sec-alena.org/english/

Official site of the NAFTA Secretariat, comprised of the Canadian, United States, and Mexican Sections, which is responsible for the administration of the dispute settlement provisions of the Agreement and the provision of assistance to the Commission and support for various nondispute-related committees and working groups.

Online Publications from and about Latin America

http://www.lib.utsa.edu/Instruction/helpsheets/pubs.html

Links to online newspapers, wire services, and many other kinds of publications. Compiled by Rita Wilson at the University of Texas at San Antonio.

Perry-Castañeda Library Map Collection—Maps of the Americas

http://www.lib.utexas.edu/Libs/PCL/Map_collection/americas.html

This site provides digitized maps of the Americas, both contemporary and historical. The maps are not copyrighted, and can be downloaded and copied for individual or classroom use. Historical maps for Central America date as far back as the sixteenth century. The collection is maintained by the University of Texas at Austin.

Resources for Locating and Evaluating Latin American Videos

http://www.library.cornell.edu/colldev/video.html

This site provides both general and country-specific information on locating and evaluating Latin American videos. Useful for the social sciences as well as the arts. The page is part of the Seminar on the Acquisition of Latin American Library Materials (SALALM) Web site.

RETAnet, Resources for Teaching About the Americas

http://ladb.unm.edu/www/retanet

A Web site for secondary educators, produced by the Latin America Data Base at the University of New Mexico and funded by the U.S. Department of Education.

United States Department of State Bureau of Western Hemispheric Affairs

http://www.state.gov/www/regions/ara/index.html

Site of the Bureau of Western Hemisphere Affairs, which advises the Secretary of State and guides the operation of the U.S. diplomatic establishment in Latin America, the Caribbean, and Canada. It includes links to press statements, country information, briefings, and current issues in the news.

Venezuela Web

http://venezuela.mit.edu

Sponsored by MIT, this site provides links to many sites in Venezuela and about Venezuela.

Zona Latina

http://www.zonalatina.com/Zlpapers.htm

Links to various newspapers that are available in Latin America.

Selected Library Catalogs with Major Latin American Holdings

Biblioteca Nacional—Argentina

http://www.bibnal.edu.ar

Biblioteca Nacional—Brazil

http://www.bn.br/home1.html

Biblioteca Nacional—Chile

http://www.dibam.renib.cl/ISC137

Biblioteca Nacional—Honduras

http://ns.sdnhon.org.hn/miembros/cultura/binah/index.htm

Biblioteca Nacional—Panama

http://www.binal.ac.pa/

Biblioteca Nacional—Peru

http://www.binape.gob.pe/

Biblioteca Nacional—Portugal

http://www.biblioteca-nacional.pt/bn/bemvindo.html

Biblioteca Nacional—Spain

http://www.bne.es

Biblioteca Nacional—Venezuela

http://www.bnv.bib.ve

Biblioteca Nacional de Antropología e Historia—Mexico

http://www.arts-history.mx/biblioteca/menu.html

Duke University Library
http://www.lib.duke.edu/online_catalog.html

Stanford University Libraries Latin American and Iberian Collections
http://www-sul.stanford.edu/depts/hasrg/latinam/latamint.html

Tulane University Latin American Library
http://www.tulane.edu/~latinlib/lalhome.html

University of California at Berkeley Library
http://www.lib.berkeley.edu/Collections/LatinAm/index.html

University of Florida Library
http://www.uflib.ufl.edu/

University of Illinois Latin American Library
http://www.library.uiuc.edu/lat/

University of Miami
http://www.library.miami.edu

University of North Carolina at Chapel Hill
http://www.lib.unc.edu

University of Texas at Austin
http://www.lib.utexas.edu/Libs/Benson/benson.html

Vanderbilt University
http://www.library.vanderbilt.edu/central/latam.html

GENERAL AMERICAN HISTORY
Ken Kempcke

METASITES

Academic Info: United States History

http://www.academicinfo.net/histus.html

A subject directory of Internet resources tailored to a college or advanced high school audience.

American and British History Resources on the Internet

http://www.libraries.rutgers.edu/rulib/socsci/hist/amhist.html

Produced at Rutgers University, this site provides a structured index of scholarly resources available online. Its contents include Reference Resources, History Gateways and Text Sites, Titles by Historic Period, and Archival and Manuscript Guides.

The Digital Librarian

http://www.servtech.com/~mvail/history.html

Maintained by Margaret Vail Anderson, a librarian in Cortland, New York, this page provides links to hundreds of fascinating Web resources on American history.

Index of Resources for United States History

http://www.ukans.edu/history/usa/usaindex.html

This Web page from the University of Kansas offers links to over twelve hundred sites of interest to students of United States history.

Links for the History Profession

http://www.indiana.edu/~oah/links.html

This site, maintained by the Organization of American Historians, furnishes many links to professional societies, associations, centers, and resources.

The TimePage—American History Sites

http://www.seanet.com/Users/pamur/ahistory.html#us

A general directory with links to hundreds of U.S. history sites.

United States History

http://www.tntech.edu/www/acad/hist/usa.html

A list of links to history sites arranged chronologically and by subject from the History Department at Tennessee Technological University.

Voice of the Shuttle: American History Page

http://humanitas.ucsb.edu/shuttle/history.html#us

Constructed by Alan Liu at the University of California–Santa Barbara, this site provides links to American History resources, academic departments, conferences, journals, discussion lists, and newsgroups.

GENERAL SITES

An Abridged History of the United States

http://www.us-history.com

An online textbook produced by William M. Briton. The text includes photographs and hypertext links to various court cases and other historical documents.

AMDOCS: Documents for the Study of American History

http://history.cc.ukans.edu/carrie/docs/amdocs_index.html

Part of the Electronic Library at the University of Kansas, this site provides access to hundreds of important documents vital to the study of American History. The materials date from the fifteenth century to the present.

American History Online

http://longman.awl.com/history/default.htm

From Longman Publishing Company, this bank of resources includes interactive practice tests, downloadable maps, primary sources, Web activities, and reference links.

American Memory

http://lcweb2.loc.gov/ammem

American Memory is the online resource compiled by the Library of Congress's National Digital Library Program. With the participation of other libraries and archives, the program provides a gateway to rich primary source materials relating to the history and cultural developments of the United States. The site provides multimedia collections of digitized documents, photographs, maps, recorded sound, and moving pictures.

The American Presidency

http://www.grolier.com/presidents/preshome.html

A history of presidents, the presidency, politics, and related subjects. Provides the full text of articles from the *Academic American Encyclopedia* and includes an online exhibit hall, historical election results, presidential links, and a trivia quiz.

American Studies Electronic Crossroads

http://www.georgetown.edu/crossroads

Maintained at Georgetown University, ASEC contains pedagogical, scholarly, and institutional information for the international American Studies community. Includes a collection of resources and tools for use by teachers, administrators, and students, as well as indexes to online courses and projects.

A Chronology of U.S. Historical Documents

http://www.law.ou.edu/ushist.html

Provides hundreds of important documents related to American History from pre-Colonial times to the present. From the University of Oklahoma Law Center.

Douglass: Archives of American Public Address

http://douglass.speech.nwu.edu

Douglass is an electronic archive of American oratory and related documents. It is intended to serve general scholarship and courses in American rhetorical history at Northwestern University.

Historic Audio Archives

http://www.webcorp.com/sounds/index.htm

Audio files containing the voices of famous Americans.

Historical Text Archive

http://www.msstate.edu/Archives/History/USA/usa.html

Mississippi State University provides links to Native American history, U.S. historical documents, the colonial period, the Revolution, the early republic, the nineteenth and twentieth centuries, U.S. wars, and more.

History Buff's Home Page

http://www.historybuff.com/index.html

Produced by the Newspaper Collectors Society of America, this site is devoted to press coverage of events in American history. It includes an extensive, searchable, library with the following categories: Civil War, Baseball, Journalism Hoaxes, Old West including Billy the Kid, Crime Figures such as Bonnie and Clyde, and over a dozen other categories. The Presidential Library includes the inaugural addresses of all U.S. presidents. There is also a primer and price guide for historic newspapers.

History Matters: The U.S. [History] Survey Course on the Web

http://historymatters.gmu.edu

Designed for high school and college teachers of U.S. History survey courses, this site serves as a gateway to Web resources and offers unique teaching materials, first-person primary documents, and threaded discussions on teaching U.S. history. From the American Social History Project/Center for History and the New Media.

The History Net

http://www.thehistorynet.com

Provides access to discussion forums and hundreds of full-text articles on American History from selected journals. Also includes a picture gallery and a list of events and exhibits taking place around the United States. Produced by the National Historical Society.

History's Best on PBS

http://www.pbs.org/history/american.html

Links to American history programs that have appeared on Public Television.

A Hypertext on American History: From the Colonial Period until Modern Times

http://odur.let.rug.nl/~usa

The main body of this hypertext comes from a number of United States Information Agency publications: An Outline of American History, An Outline of the American Economy, An Outline of American Government, and An Outline of American Literature. The text is enriched with hypertext links to relevant documents, original essays, other Internet sites, and to other Outlines.

Making of America

http://www.umdl.umich.edu/moa

Making of America (MOA) is a digital library of primary sources in American social history from the antebellum period through Reconstruction. The collection is particularly strong in the subject areas of education, psychology, American history, sociology, religion, and science and technology. The collection contains approximately 1,600 books and 50,000 journal articles with nineteenth-century imprints.

The National Archives and Records Administration

http://www.nara.gov

The NARA site furnishes electronic access to historical records of government agencies, as well as an online exhibit hall, digital classroom, and genealogy page. The site also includes multimedia exhibits, research tools, and NARA publications.

The National Portrait Gallery

http://www.npg.si.edu

A searchable site that contains photographs, portraits, and biographical information on thousands of prominent Americans.

Presidents of the United States

http://www.ipl.org/ref/POTUS

In this resource you will find background information, election results, cabinet members, notable events, and some points of interest on each of the presidents. Links to biographies, historical documents, audio and video files, and other presidential sites are also included to enrich this site. From the Internet Public Library at the University of Michigan.

The Smithsonian Institution

http://www.si.edu

The Smithsonian Institution's Web page provides access to a fascinating array of historical resources in many subject areas. Its offerings include Smithsonian collections, exhibits, photographs, and publications, as well as links to sites hosted by the Institution's museums and organizations. The Smithsonian's Online Research Information System allows browsers to search the Institution's various online catalogs.

Talking History

http://www.albany.edu/history/talkinghistory

This site provides audio files of the weekly radio program *Talking History,* a coproduction of the History Department of the State University of New York at Albany, the Department of History of Creighton University (Omaha, Nebraska), and WRPI-FM, Troy, New York.

United States Historical Census Browser

http://fisher.lib.Virginia.EDU/census

The data presented here describe the people and the economy of the United States for each state and county from 1790 to 1970.

United States History

http://www.usahistory.com

Information on presidents, statistics, wars, states, history trivia, the Constitution, and more.

U.S. Diplomatic History Resources Index

http://www.tamu-commerce.edu/coas/history/sarantakes/stuff.html

Created by Nicholas Evan Sarantakes, a professor at Texas A&M University–Commerce, this Web page is an index of resources available to historians of U.S. foreign policy. Geared toward scholars in history, political science, economics, area studies, international relations, and journalism, it provides an extensive list of historical archives and papers indexed alphabetically and by subject.

AFRICAN-AMERICAN HISTORY

Marilyn Dell Brady

METASITES

Academic Info: African-American History: An Annotated Resource of Internet Resources on Black History

http://academicinfo.net/africanam.html

This extensive listing provides quality sites on African-American History for researchers, university students, and teachers. It lists and briefly describes meta-indexes, digital libraries and archives, online publications, museum presentations, library and archival catalogs, resources for teaching and some topics such as Martin Luther King, jazz, and slavery. It is a fine source for locating primary materials. The directory is created and kept updated by Academic Info, a private organization compiling subject indexes for respected Web sites on a wide range of topics. Although the Web master is the law librarian at the University of Washington, the site is not sponsored by that institution.

American Identities: African American

http://xroads.virginia.edu/~YP/ethnic.html

Produced by the University of Virginia American Studies Program, this site links to a wide range of sites, some of them historical. Although these and other sites are all from the University of Virginia, they are not directly connected.

African-American Literature

http://curry.edschool.virginia.edu/go/multicultural/sites/aframdocs.html

Links to online sites of classic African-American documents, some more historical than literary. Contains a wide range of documents, familiar and unknown, many of them useful in teaching history. Part of the Multicultural Paths Project at the University of Virginia.

African-American West

http://www.wsu.edu:8080/~amerstu/mw/af_ap.html#afam

A metasite with links to dealing with blacks in the history of the American West. Local sites included.

A–Z of African Studies on the Internet

http://docker.library.uwa.edu.au/~plimb/az.html

A–Z of African Studies on the Internet is another general clearinghouse of links to African and African-American sites. Peter Limb of the University of Western Australia maintains it.

Christine's Genealogy Web Site

http://ccharity.com/

Important for black history as well as genealogy, this privately run site contains a variety of governmental documents and lists. Although the contents are scattered and searching is somewhat difficult, materials include immigration records to Liberia, Freemen's Bureau's lists of "outrages," lynching, census records, and similar records useful in both research and teaching. Links to black history by members of local communities.

Historical Text Archive: African-American History

http://www.msstate.edu/Archives/History/USA/Afro-Amer/afro.html

A metasite created by a professor at Mississippi State University includes a wide variety of links, including some to black history in particular states and regions, exhibits about blacks, primary sources, genealogy sites, and teaching materials. Although Mississippi State University makes the site available, the University takes no responsibility for it.

Social Studies School Services: Black History

http://www.socialstudies.com

This commercial organization offers lesson plans, student exercises, RealVideo clips of materials they sell, catalogs of their other materials, reviews of other sites and links. Extensive, but materials are not guaranteed for accuracy.

GENERAL SITES

Aboard the Underground Railroad

http://www.cr.nps.gov/nr/underground/ugrrhome.htm

Aboard the Underground Railroad explores the historical sites recognized as part of the Underground Railroad. The site includes a bibliography of printed sources and links to state sites involving the Underground Railroad are also presented.

African-American Census Schedules Online

http://www.prairiebluff.com/aacensus

A private project, not yet complete, assembling and putting on line the special slave and free black manuscript census data compiled by the U.S. government before the Civil War. A variety of states, including some in New England and the West, have been completed.

African-American Community

http://www.cmstory.org/african/default.htm

A large collection of online photographs and other information about African Americans for Charlotte and Mecklenberg County, North Carolina, sponsored by the local public library.

African-American Heritage Preservation Foundation, Inc.

http://www.preservenet.cornell.edu/aahpf/homepage.htm

Provides information, photographs, and archeological reports on preservation projects with which the organization is involved.

African-American History in the National Park System,

http://www.nps.gov/pub_aff/courier/feature1.htm

Provides an extensive listing of sites that individuals and classes may want to visit.

African-American Mosaic: A Library of Congress Resource Guide for the Study of Black History and Culture

http://lcweb.loc.gov/exhibits/african/intro.html

The major site and starting place for African-American materials online from the Library of Congress and a rich sampling of their larger collections. Included are a comprehensive text and images from the nearly 500 years of the black experience in the Western Hemisphere. Lesser-known topics, which are covered, include Liberia, abolitionists, western migration, and documents from the Works Progress Administration, the Federal Writers Program, and the Daniel Murray Pamphlet collection. Items within the African-

American Mosaic can be searched online. The American Odyessy is not part of the American Mosaic.

African-American Resources: Electronic Text Center

http://etext.lib.virginia.edu/speccol.html

An extensive collection of original documents ranging from nineteenth-century African-American issues to dozens of letters from such notables.

African-American Resources at the University of Virginia

http://etext.lib.virginia.edu/rbs/rbs16-95.html

This site contains an initial online group of texts of documents and images relating to slavery assembled by a special seminar of the Rare Books Division of the University of Virginia.

Africans in America

http://www.pbs.org/wgbh/aia/home.html

An ambitious site with many of the strengths and weaknesses of the original Public Television production. Extensive documents, text, maps, and images are included along with careful lesson plans for teachers. Although the impressive panel of scholars who assisted with the project is listed, little attention is given throughout to the identity and qualifications of writers and speakers, creating problems for students trying to put materials in historical context.

AfriGeneas

http://www.msstate.edu/Archives/History/afrigen/index.html

This site is the home page for a private mailing list run by the Mississsippi State Historical Archives. The focus is discussion, promotion, and exchange of family history research, especially for people of African descent. The Web site provides a newsletter, information about surnames, and a unique "Slave Data Project," which is an online collection of wills and other documents of slave owners.

Afro-American Sources in Virginia: A Guide to Manuscripts

http://rock.village.virginia.edu/plunkett/

This is an electronic edition of a print guide jointly produced by Michael Plunkett, The University Press of Virginia, and the University of Virginia's Electronic Text Center.

American Slave Narratives: An Online Anthology

http://xroads.virginia.edu/~hyper/wpa/wpahome.html

Texts, photos, and recordings of some selected Work Progress Administration interviews are presented online. Developed for classroom use at the University of Virginia.

Archives of African-American Music and Culture

http://www.indiana.edu/~aaamc/index.html

This is a large database dedicated to all aspects of African-American music and culture, including many links to related sites. The site is a project of the Department of Afro-American Studies at Indiana University.

The Atlantic Monthly: Black History, American History

http://www.theatlantic.com/unbound/flashbks/black/blahisin.htm

The Atlantic Monthly provides digitized articles by black writers who published in their magazine. Included are debates between Washington and DuBois.

Behind the Veil: Documenting African-American Life in the Jim Crow South

http://aaswebsv.aas.duke.edu/docstudies/cds/btv/

Just beginning to be available online are the results of a major project collecting oral histories and photographs recording the experiences of African Americans in the Jim Crow South. Eventually the site will have some of these materials online, along with course information, classroom suggestions, a timeline, and related reading material and links. The Center for Documentary Studies at Duke University is responsible for the project, with involvement from other universities and communities.

Black Pioneers of the Pacific Northwest

http://www.teleport.com/~eotic/histhome.html

Produced from an exhibit in Oregon, this site provides a timeline of blacks in the state, biographies and photographs of early African Americans there, discussion of the state's exclusion legislation and slavery, and a bibliography of sources.

Charlotte Hawkins Brown Memorial, North Carolina Historic Sites

http://www.ah.dcr.state.nc.us/sections/hs/chb/chb.htm

This excellent site, created by the North Carolina Division of Archives and History, gives information about Brown, a leading black educator, and the school that she founded. Online texts of documents by and about her give insight into her own thought. Very extensive bibliographies give references to manuscript collections, theses, and primary material. Articles and reports, books, and pamphlets are listed for those doing additional research.

Civil Rights Oral Histories from Mississippi

http://www–dept.usm.edu/~mcrohb/

This important site makes available to a wider audience the oral histories collected in the fall of 1997 by the staff members at the University of Southern Mississippi's Center for Oral History and Cultural Heritage and at the Tougaloo College Archives. It contains online text of interviews, searchable in various ways, and a bibliography. The Mississippi State Legislature, Mississippi Department of Archives and History, and the Mississippi Humanities Council funded the project.

Database of United States Colored Troops in the Civil War

http://www.itd.nps.gov/cwss/usct.html

The United States National Park Service and the Civil War Soldiers and Sailors created this database and made it available online. In addition to 235,000 names, information is presented in about 180 histories of USCT (U.S. colored troops) units/regiments and links to sites about the most significant Civil War battles in which African Americans fought.

A Deeper Shade of Black

http://www.ai.mit.edu/~isbell/HFh/black/bhcal–toc.html

A Deeper Shade of Black is one of the premier resources on African-American history, film, and literature. Created and maintained by Charles Isbell of MIT, it is an excellent resource for biographies, with well-developed accounts of figures such as Thurgood Marshall and Paul Robeson. Be sure to also explore Isbell's related site This Week in Black History (http://www.ai.mit.edu/~isbell/HFh/black/thisweek.html).

Desegregation of the Armed Forces: Project Whistlestop Harry S. Truman Digital Archives

http://www.whistlestop.org/study_collections/desegregation/large/desegregation.htm

The Truman Presidential Library has digitized Truman's Executive Order 9981 calling for desegregation and other documents from the study leading up to that decision.

Digital Classroom of The National Archives and Records Administration (NARA)

http://www.nara.gov/education/teaching/teaching.html

Primary documents about African Americans from the National Archives and teaching activities for using them in the classroom. Included are the Amistad Case, Black Soldiers in the Civil War, and Jackie Robinson. Other African-American materials can be found by searching the National Archives Digital Library.

Documents Relating to Black Women's History

http://womhist.binghamton.edu/projectmap.htm

This site from the University of New York–Binghamton contains about twenty document sets, dealing with African-American Women's History. Compiled for college and high school classrooms, this site contains materials by and about black women seldom found elsewhere. The project is funded by the National Endowment for the Humanities.

W.E.B. DuBois Virtual University

http://members.tripod.com/~DuBois/

This private site is a clearinghouse for information on DuBois. It offers links to online texts by and about DuBois, a bibliography of articles and dissertations in print by and "about him," and a list of DuBois scholars.

Duke University Library and John Hope Franklin Research Center for African and African-American Documentation

http://scriptorium.lib.duke.edu/franklin/collections.html#guides

In association with the Duke Library's Digital Scriptorium, the Franklin Center publishes digitized versions of finding aids, subject guides, and materials from selected collections. Exhibits include: African-American Women; Retrieving African-American Women's History; and Third Person, First Person: Slave Voices From The Special Collections Library, Duke University.

Exploring Amistad at Mystic Seaport: Race and the Boundaries of Freedom in Antebellum Maritime America

http://amistad.mysticseaport.org/main/welcome.html

This site, produced by the Mystic Seaport Museum, is one of the best teaching sites focusing on a particular event and its participants. Included are brief a narrative, a timeline, and links to other sites. The online historical documents related to the capture of the ship and its occupants provide little-known information, and the teacher's guide presents a variety of activities, including a re-enactment of the capture.

Faces of Science: African Americans in the Sciences

http://www.lib.lsu.edu/lib/chem/display/faces.html

Faces of Science looks at the past, present, and future of African Americans in the sciences. It presents biographies of famous African Americans grouped into scientific discipline, examines the percentages of doctorates granted to African Americans in each area of the sciences, offers a wealth of statistical and demographic data, and contains links to other related sites. The project is supported by the Louisiana State University Libraries.

Frederick Douglass Papers

http://www.as.wvu.edu/coll03/hist/www/douglass/index.html

Information about the project at the University of West Virginia to edit and publish Douglass' papers not included in the Yale volume of Douglass' works. The site includes links to other sites and a bibliography of recommended sources

Freedman and Southern Society Project

http://www.inform.umd.edu/ARHU/Depts/History/Freedman/home.html

Scholars at the University of Maryland are in process of editing a multi-volume collection of papers from the National Archives by and about men and women who became free from slavery during and after the Civil War. The project is funded by the National Endowment for the Humanities.

Harlem 1900-40: An African-American Community

http://www.si.umich.edu/CHICO/Harlem

This impressive site was created at the School of Information at the University of Michigan as part of their Cultural Heritage Initiatives for Community Outreach. Items came from the Schomberg Center and include digitized texts and photographs. Suggestions for teachers using the materials and links to other related sites are also presented.

Inventory of African-American Historical and Cultural Resources in Maryland

http://sailor.lib.md.us/docs/af_am/stmar.html#e.4

A very extensive listing by county of structures, historical sites, and collections materials in Maryland relating to African-American History. The Maryland Commission on African-American History and Culture supports the project.

John H. White: Portrait of Black Chicago

http://www.nara.gov/exhall/americanimage/chicago/white1.html

An digitized exhibit at the National Archives and Records Administration featuring White photographs taken in the Chicago of the 1970s.

Lest We Forget: The Untold History of America

http://www.coax.net

A private site with a variety of information for those doing African-American history. Includes information and links on little-known historical sites, coming events relating to black history, obtaining military records, genealogies, and more.

Library Catalogs of African-American Collections

http://www.library.cornell.edu/africana/Library/Catalogs.html

A listing of some online catalogs of African-American materials produced by the Cornell University Library. A good source for locating materials, even though not all such collections are included.

Martin Luther King Jr.

http://www.seattletimes.com/mlk/index.html

One of the best sites about King for classroom teachers and students. Produced by the Seattle Times, it includes editorials, interviews, news columns, and photographs from their newspaper. King is presented in historical context, with a series of classic pictures from the civil rights movement. The study guide provides probing questions relating to King's holiday and larger questions of racial equality.

Martin Luther King, Jr. Papers Project of Stanford University

http://www.stanford.edu/group/King/

The scholars at Stanford University who are editing and publishing King's writings have begun to make a sampling of his papers available online. Some of his most well-known documents are present. In addition, the site contains a bibliography file containing about 2,700 references to published works dealing with King and the Civil Rights movement.

Montgomery Bus Boycott Home Page

http://socsci.colorado.edu/~jonesem/montgomery.html

This site offers a teaching plan focused around actual documents created by participants in the boycott. Other materials include *U.S. News and World Report* articles on the Boycott, photographs, and summaries collected by an individual at the University of Colorado.

Museum of African Slavery

http://jhunix.hcf.jhu.edu/~plarson/smuseum/welcome.htm

The Museum of African Slavery in the Atlantic is designed to provide accurate, engaging and provocative information to the public about the history of slavery. The site is aimed at primary and secondary students and their teachers. The primary author is Pier M. Larson, a professor of African history at The Johns Hopkins University.

National Civil Rights Museum

http://www.midsouth.rr.com/civilrights/

This site discusses the National Civil Rights Museum, which is in Memphis, Tennessee. It contains a "virtual tour" of the museum's exhibits and their aims. Color and black-and-white photos are included. In addition to the tour, there are links to related sites, membership information, and admission.

Negro League Baseball Archive

http://www.nc5.infi.net/~moxie/nlb/nlb.html

This well-constructed private site provides information on Negro League Baseball. Articles from the Black Ball News, a journal focused exclusively on African-American baseball, are online. In addition, the site includes basic information about teams and major players, including photographs and links.

The Negro Leagues

http://www.negroleaguebaseball.com/

This commercial Web page includes a great deal of information on the history of the Negro Leagues, including team histories and player profiles.

North American Slave Narratives, Beginnings to 1920

http://metalab.unc.edu/docsouth/neh/neh.html

Books, pamphlets, and broadsides written by fugitive and former slaves before 1920 are being collected and put online by scholars at the University of North Carolina. This National Endowment for the Humanities project, when complete, will include all such works.

Our Shared History: Celebrating African-American History and Culture

http://www.cr.nps.gov/aahistory/

This National Park Service site links to various programs relating to African- American history, which they have developed. These include National Register Travel Itineraries for the Underground Railroad and sites in Detroit, Baltimore, and the Gullah coast. Useful for teachers who can take classes to the sites.

Portraits in Black: The Samuel N. Waller Memorial Web Site to the Buffalo Soldier and Sailor

http://www.con2.com/~blacstar/portraits/

Combines informative text with historic photographs and documents. Important because it covers black military history in a number of time periods and activities not widely recognized, such as the Philippine American War, 1899–

1902, and African-American Army Musicians, 1770–1945. It also contains a Roster of Officers & Enlisted Men, 1898–1901. An impressive site compiled by an individual, knowledgeable about African-American military history.

Schomberg Collection of New York Public Library

http://digital.nypl.org/browse.html

The New York Public Library Schomberg Collection is "the world's leading publicly–accessible research institution for the study of the history and culture of peoples of African descent." Notes on its collections appear on its home page and most of its materials appear in the online catalog of the New York Public Library. A number of online exhibits are also being organized.

This is Our War

http://www.afroam.org/history/OurWar/intro.html

A series of articles written by black war correspondents during World War II for the Baltimore Afro-American. This is part of a larger site on black history produced by the newspaper.

Underground Railroad Home Page

http://www.nps.gov/htdocs1/boaf/urrsum~1.htm

Another tour-de-force home page supported by the National Park Service. This site contains narrative accounts, primary documents, image and map collections, and teaching resources.

Voices of the Civil Rights Era

http://www.webcorp.com/civilrights/index.htm

The Voices of the Civil Rights Era is an audio archive sponsored by Webcorp and containing different views of the future from Malcolm X, Martin Luther King, Jr., John F. Kennedy, and others.

Writing Black USA

http://www.keele.ac.uk/depts/as/Literature/amlit.black.html

Writing Black USA contains full-text essays, books and poems documenting the African-American experience in the United States from colonial times to the present.

THE AMERICAN WEST AND NATIVE AMERICAN HISTORY

J. Kelly Robison

Western American history is theoretically the study of a region of the United States. In practice, it encompasses a wide scope of place and time. Geographically, the American West is usually defined as that region of the United States west of the Mississippi River, yet Western historians also study westward expansion, which brings in that area between the Appalachian Mountains and the Mississippi River. Chronologically, Western History is not solely the study of the late nineteenth-century, covered-wagon days, the cattle drives, and the Indian wars, but embraces the entirety of human history of the West, from beginnings to the present day. Additionally, historians who study Native American history are usually classified as Western historians, which brings a larger geographic and chronological area and era into the fold. The study of the America West is a diverse field and the following World Wide Web sites reflect that diversity.

The American West—General

America's West—Development and History

http://www.americanwest.com/

Though at first glance this site seems hokey and interested in the much-mythologized "Old West," it does contain useful articles, some images, and links to other sites.

Gallery of the Open Frontier

http://www.unl.edu/UP/gof/home.html

A great site for those interested in the American West. It contains articles and links to images of the west: cowboys, Native Americans, railroads, etc. At the time of writing, this site is undergoing a complete revision.

New Perspectives on the West

http://www3.pbs.org/weta/thewest/

The Web site for the PBS special on the American West produced by Ken Burns. An extensive site with links to a wide range of primary documents, articles on various western topics, and biographies of western figures.

Sources for the Study of the Southwest

http://www.smu.edu/%7Ecul/southwest_all.html

A well-thought-out and well-organized list of links to sites of interest to those studying the Southwest. Link topics range from the cattle industry to the archeology of the Southwest. Created by Bob Skinner of Southern Methodist University.

WestWeb: Western History Resources

http://www.library.csi.cuny.edu/westweb/

A growing collection of topically organized links to Western history resources. Created and maintained by Catherine Lavendar of the City University of New York. The site is broken down into thirty-one different chapters, each of which contains numerous links to sites that specialize in that topic. Some of the topic chapters also contain image thumbnails linked to National Archives photographs. The site is indexed and should be the first place anyone interested in Western history sites on the Web should go.

The American West—Topical

Borders—Fronteras

http://www.si.edu/folklife/vfest/frontera/start.htm

The Smithsonian Institution's online exhibit on the southern U.S. border. Contains essays on music (samples in .au form), art, language, and culture, as well as a discussion on what constitutes a border. Also available in Spanish.

California Heritage Collection

http://sunsite.Berkeley.EDU/calheritage/

From the Bancroft Library, this site is a collection of over 28,000 images of California's history and culture. Includes resources for K-12 instructors.

California Mission Studies Association

http://www.ca-missions.org/

Dedicated to the study and preservation of California's missions, this organization's Web site contains articles on the missions, a nice glossary of mission-related terms, and some wonderful photographs.

Chinese Historical and Cultural Education Project Curriculum

http://www.kqed.org/cell/golden/glmenu.html

Designed for the K-6 grades, this site contains a wealth of information on Chinese settlement in the United States. There are articles on daily life and culture, as well as information on where the Chinese fit into the settlement of the West.

Cowboys...by Dawn Banks

http://www.hcc.cc.fl.us/services/staff/dawn/cowboy.htm

Like "Cowgirl's Dream," (below) this site is a mixed bag of sites related, in some fashion, to the cowboy.

Cowgirl's Dream

http://www.cowgirls.com/

An eclectic site containing links, articles, essays, poetry, discussions, and random thoughts. Some kernels among the chaff, though.

Crossing the Frontier: Photographs of the Developing West, 1849 to Present

http://www.CalHum.ORG/sfmoma-crossing/

An online version of a traveling exhibition developed by the San Francisco Museum of Modern Art. The site itself contains fifty of the three hundred images in the exhibit. Also contains several articles on the West and teachers' resources.

Exploring the West from Monticello

http://www.lib.virginia.edu/exhibits/lewis_clark/

A well-executed, online exhibit of the Lewis and Clark Expedition co-organized by Heather Moore and Guy Benson. Includes original articles and numerous digitized antique maps.

General George A. Custer Home Page

http://www.garryowen.com/

A site dedicated to the study of Custer and the Plains Indian Wars. Contains a plethora of information, including short articles, primary data, and photographs.

The Interactive Santa Fe Trail (SFT) Home Page

http://ukanaix.cc.ukans.edu/heritage/research/sft/index.html

Created by Nancy Sween for Kansas Heritage, this site's most interesting feature is its extensive list of other sites related to the Santa Fe Trail.

The Japanese-American Internment

http://www.geocities.com/Athens/8420/main.html

Includes a timeline of the Japanese-American internment, basic information on the camps, and remembrances of internees. Numerous links and links to primary documents are also available on this site by John Yu.

Klondike Ho! 1897–1997

http://www.wolfenet.com/~yoame/klon/

Visually impressive site with basic information on the Klondike Gold Rush. The site was created by Alan Taylor to commemorate the centennial of the gold rush.

The Lewis and Clark Expedition

http://www.pbs.org/lewisandclark/

The Ken Burns PBS production companion site. Presents excerpts from the Corps of Discovery journals, a timeline of the journey, maps of the expedition, and numerous other related materials. Also contains interviews with authorities on the expedition and classroom resources for teachers.

Mormon History Resource Page

http://www.indirect.com/www/crockett/history.html

Dave Crockett's site breaks the history of the Mormon Church into several historical periods, including the trek west and the early days in Utah. The site lists many links but also contains some original articles by Crockett.

Mountain Men and the Fur Trade: Sources of the History of the Fur Trade in the Rocky Mountain West

http://www.xmission.com/%7Edrudy/amm.html

A resource for the study of the fur trade era. This site lists online books on the fur trade, includes business records of the fur trade, and has a nice collection of digitized images of period artifacts and art from the period. A nicely done site.

Multicultural American West

http://www.wsu.edu:8080/~amerstu/mw/

Essentially an online, annotated bibliography of sites relevant to the study of the American West. As the site's name implies, most of the resources and links are related to ethnicity in the West. Designed by Washington State University's American Studies program.

Old Montana Virtual West

http://www.virtualwest.com/

A slightly garishly designed site that plays on the image of the "Old West," which, in itself, makes this site of interest to those studying the mythological West. Created by Erin Tamberella and Cathy Starita, this site does contain some interesting links to Western sites.

The Overland Trail

http://www.over-land.com/

A site dedicated to Ben Holladay's *Overland Trail*, created by Elizabeth Larson. Presents a large amount of information, including a clickable map to articles. The articles range from those strictly on the route and stopovers to Indian problems along the route. Links to other sites are categorized by topic and include brief descriptions.

Perry-Castañeda Library Map Collection

http://www.lib.utexas.edu/Libs/PCL/Map_collection/Map_collection.html

This site, based at the University of Texas, contains digitized historical maps of the world, including the Americas and, especially, Texas.

The Silent Westerns: Early Movie Myths of the American West

http://xroads.virginia.edu/~HYPER/HNS/Westfilm/west.html

Mary Halnon's site devoted to the portrayal of the West in silent film. It presents excellent essays on the early film industry and mythologized elements in the Western movies.

The Vigilantes of Montana: Secret Trials and Midnight Hangings

http://montana-vigilantes.org/

This site, maintained by Louis Schmittroth, presents a wealth of information on the Montana Vigilantes. The site contains online books and articles by well-known Montana historians. The politics of the site are apparent, but the information within is well worth perusing.

Who Killed William Robinson?

http://web.uvic.ca/history-robinson/

A wonderful resource for teachers, this site by Ruth Sandwell and John Lutz takes the reader through a historical mystery to determine the identity of a murderer. Contains primary documents and asks pertinent questions dealing with race, politics, and settlement.

Women Artists of the American West, Past and Present

http://www.sla.purdue.edu/waaw/

Created by Susan Ressler of Purdue University. An online exhibit of female artists with essays on those artists or particular groups of artists.

Yukon and Alaska History

http://arcticculture.miningco.com/library/blYAindex.htm

A subsite within the Mining Company, a commercial Web indexer. Includes articles on Yukon and Alaska history and culture, such as articles on early pioneers and mining in the region, with an emphasis on the Klondike Gold Rush.

Native-American History—General

American Indian Studies

http://www.csulb.edu/projects/ais/

Created by Troy Johnson at California State University–Long Beach. Short but useful list of links to Native-American sites. Also includes a large number of images of Native Americans from precontact to the present.

Cherokee National Historical Society

http://www.powersource.com/powersource/heritage/default.html

In 1963, a group of distinguished Cherokees founded the Cherokee National Historical Society, a private nonprofit corporation designed to preserve the history and culture of the Cherokee people—past, present, and future. Beyond this original mission, the Society is committed to educating not only the Cherokee people, but also the general public, through visual and performing arts, the written word, and the development of uniquely Cherokee resources.

Images of Native America: From Columbus to Carlisle

http://www.lehigh.edu/~ejg1/natmain.html

Professor Edward J. Gallagher's students at Lehigh University created a series of online essays on how Europeans and Euro-Americans imagined native peoples. The essays are nicely written and contain links to related sites.

MAPS: GIS Windows on Native Lands, Current Places, and History

http://indy4.fdl.cc.mn.us/~isk/maps/mapmenu.html

Paula Giese's site, which uses client-side image maps as the gateway to articles on Native-American history and culture from precontact to the present.

Native-American Documents Project

http://www.csusm.edu/projects/nadp/nadp.htm

Located at California State University at San Marcos, this site presents primary material related to Allotment, Indian Commissioner Reports, and the Rogue River War and Siletz Reservation.

Native-American Sites

http://info.pitt.edu/~lmitten/indians.html

A very nice list of sites pertaining to Native America. The topically categorized list contains links to Indian nation Web sites, organizations, and upcoming events. Maintained by Lisa Mitten at the University of Pittsburgh.

NativeWeb

http://www.nativeweb.org/

An extensive collection of links and articles both for and about indigenous peoples in the Americas. These links and articles are not just of a historical nature, but political, legal, and social. Includes search engines, message boards, and lists of Native events. An excellent site for beginning research.

Perspectives of the Smithsonian: Native-American Resources

http://www.si.edu/resource/faq/nmai/start.htm

An excellent starting place for information on Native American history and culture. Includes online Smithsonian exhibits, resources for teachers, parents, and students, and a quite extensive list of readings for various topics. No links, but this site in itself is worth looking into.

Native-American History—Topical

The Avalon Project: Relations between the United States and Native Americans

http://www.yale.edu/lawweb/avalon/natamer.htm

A superb collection of primary documents relating to Native peoples compiled and digitized by the Yale Law School Avalon Project. The main focus of this site is treaties between the United States government and Native groups. The site also presents statutes, presidential addresses, and a few court cases involving Natives.

The Aztec Calendar

http://www.xs4all.nl/~voorburg/aztec/

Done by Rene Voorburg, this nicely done site examines the Aztec calendar. The opening screen depicts the current date in Aztec glyphs. Also contains a calculator that converts any date to its Aztec equivalent. The introduction is a brief but thorough essay on the calendar and its meaning.

Cahokia Mounds State Historic Site

http://medicine.wustl.edu/~mckinney/cahokia/cahokia.html

Run by the Illinois Historic Preservation Agency, Cahokia is the location of a pre-European city across the river from St. Louis, Missouri. The site lists upcoming events at the park, and some information on the archeology and history of Cahokia. This site seems to be a work in progress.

Chaco Canyon National Monument

http://www.chaco.com/park/index.html

This is the national monument's site. There are several articles on Anasazi archeology and a great many recent photographs of the sites within Chaco. The site also lists a short bibliography of related readings, some of which are online, and links to related sites.

Native-American Authors

http://www.ipl.org/ref/native/

Part of the Internet Public Library, this section of the larger site can be browsed by author, title, or tribal affiliation. There is no search engine or subject browsing, however. Individual title "cards" contain only basic bibliographic information.

Sipapu: The Anasazi Emergence into the Cyber World

http://sipapu.ucsb.edu/

The site not only begs the reader to explore Anasazi architecture and archeology, but also asks for contributions. The Research section contains a database of Chaco outliers and a bibliography of related print works. It also links to several scholarly papers on the Anasazi. One interesting item is a wonderful little toy that allows 360-degree viewing of the Great Kiva of Chetro Ketl at Chaco Canyon National Monument. Created by John Kanter at the University of California at Santa Barbara.

SouthWestern Archeology

http://www.swanet.org/

An incredible list of links related to the archeology of the Southwest put together by the nonprofit organization of the same name. This site also includes a nice bibliography, book reviews, an e-mail list, and an invitation to submit data.

COLONIAL AMERICAN HISTORY

Scott Merriman and Dennis Trinkle

1492: An Ongoing Voyage

http://metalab.unc.edu/expo/1492.exhibit/Intro.html

1492: An On-going Voyage is an electronic exhibit of the Library of Congress. The site weaves images and text to explore what life was like in pre- and post-Columbian Europe, Africa, and the Americas. The site examines the effect that the discovery of America had on each continent, and the dark elements of colonization are stressed. There are excellent maps, documents, artwork, and supporting text.

1755: The French and Indian War Home Page

http://web.syr.edu/~laroux/

Created by Larry Laroux, a professional writer, this site serves as a prologue to Laroux's forthcoming book *White Coats*, which will examine the soldiers who fought in the French and Indian War of 1755. The site is presently under construction, but Laroux eventually aims to include histories of important battles, a list of French soldiers who fought in the war, and other statistical records. The site already contains a brief narrative account of the war, along with some interesting information and trivia.

American Colonist's Library: A Treasury of Primary Documents

http://www.universitylake.org/primarysources.html

Compiled by Richard Gardiner, a history instructor at University Lake School (Hartland, Wisconsin), the American Colonist's Library is a comprehensive gateway to the early American primary source documents that are currently available online. Included in the list are links to historical sources that influenced American colonists, online collections of the work of major early American political leaders, the text of the Acts of Parliament concerning the American Colonies, numerous American Revolution military documents, and much more. The hundreds of documents are grouped chronologically from 500 B.C. to 1800 A.D. As the site boasts, "if it isn't here, it probably is not available online anywhere."

Colonial Williamsburg

http://www.history.org/twentieth-century/hilite1.htm

The official home site for Colonial Williamsburg, one of the most extensive historical reconstructions in the United States. The well-illustrated site offers tourist information, educational resources, a Colonial dateline; a historical glossary of names, places, and events in Colonial Williamsburg; photos of buildings and people, articles from the *Colonial Williamsburg Journal,* and an extensive section on Colonial lifestyles.

Columbus and the Age of Discovery

http://columbus.millersv.edu/~columbus

A searchable database of over 1,100 text articles pertaining to Columbus and themes of discovery and encounter. The site was built by the History Department of Millersville University of Pennsylvania in conjunction with the U.S. Christopher Columbus Quincentenary Jubilee Commission of 1992, and has unrestricted access.

Early America

http://earlyamerica.com/earlyamerica/index.html

The main focus of Early America is primary source material from eighteenth-century America. The site is the public access branch of the commercial American Digital Library (http://www.earlyamerica.com/digital-library/), which sells reproductions of hundreds of early American documents from the Keigwin and Mathews Collection of eighteenth- and nineteenth-century historical documents, as well as images, maps, etc.

H-OIEACHNET

http://www.h-net.msu.edu/~ieahcweb/

This is the Web site of the H-OIEACHNET discussion list. Affiliated with H-Net, this group focuses on colonial and early American history. Their Web pages contain information about the discussion list and allow one to subscribe. They also include calls for papers, conference announcements, bibliographies, book reviews, articles, and links to related sites.

Jamestown Rediscovery Project

http://www.apva.org/

The Jamestown Rediscovery Project is a ten-year comprehensive excavation of Jamestown that began in 1994. This site gives photographs and progress reports on the project to date, as well as plans for the future.

Mount Vernon

http://www.mountvernon.org/education/index.html

The Mount Vernon educational resource home page.

Plimoth-on-Web: Plimoth Plantation's Web Site!

http://www.plimoth.org/Museum/Pilgrim_Village/1627.htm

The official Web site for the living history museum of seventeenth-century Plymouth. Like the living history museum, the Web site brings 1627 Plimoth back to life.

The Plymouth Colony Archive Project at the University of Virginia

http://www.people.virginia.edu/~jfd3a/

The Plymouth Colony Archive presents a collection of searchable texts, including seminar analysis of various topics, biographical profiles of selected colonists, probate inventories, wills, Glossary and Notes on Plymouth Colony, and *Vernacular House Forms in Seventeenth-Century Plymouth Colony: An Analysis of Evidence from the Plymouth Colony Room-by-Room Probate Inventories 1633–85*, by Patricia E. Scott Deetz and James Deetz, 1998. The site itself is maintained by the Deetz's, pioneers in material culture studies.

Salem Witch Museum

http://www.salemwitchmuseum.com/

This site primarily presents travel information, but it does also offer an interactive FAQ section on witch trials and local history. Other resources are being added rapidly.

Society of Early Americanists Home Page

http://www.hnet.uci.edu/mclark/seapage.htm

The SEA aims to further the exchange of ideas and information among scholars of various disciplines who study the literature and culture of America up to approximately 1800. The society publishes a newsletter, operates an electronic bulletin board, and maintains the Web site. The site contains an excellent list of links on Colonial and Early American history.

Walking Tour of Plymouth Plantation

http://archnet.uconn.edu/topical/historic/plimoth/plimoth.html

This site includes photographs and a narrative description of the living museum at Plymouth Plantation. It addresses many different aspects of early seventeenth-century life in New England, such as housing, cooking, clothing, and tools.

REVOLUTIONARY AMERICAN HISTORY
Robert M. S. McDonald

METASITES

The American Revolution: National Discussions of Our Revolutionary Origins

http://revolution.h-net.msu.edu/intro.html

This metasite, hosted by the NEH-sponsored H-NET, makes available authoritative essays, archives of interesting discussions, and a bibliography of printed sources on the Revolution. For an extensive array of external links, refer to the section entitled "Resources."

Eighteenth-Century Resources

http://andromeda.rutgers.edu/~jlynch/18th

Compiled by Rutgers University English Professor Jack Lynch, this metasite of links to Web pages "that focus on the (very long) eighteenth century" and home pages of scholars researching eighteenth-century topics enables students of the American Revolutionary era to view it from a global (and especially trans-Atlantic Enlightenment) perspective. General categories include art and architecture, history, music, philosophy, religion and theology, science and mathematics, and professional journals.

HistoryOnline: American Revolution

http://mac94.ralphbunche.rbs.edu/history/timeline.html

This metasite provides more than two dozen links. Maintained by the Jackson (Oregon) Education Service District, the emphasis here is on colorful sites geared toward students and the general public.

General Sites

American Revolutionary War Timeline: People, Events, Documents

http://www.ilt.columbia.edu/k12/history/timeline.html

Here, Columbia University's Institute for Learning Technologies provides internal links to biographical sketches, historical narratives, and important documents (such as the Albany Plan of Union, Stamp Act Congress Resolutions, and John Adams's *Thoughts on Government*). Intended for K-12 teachers and students, this site supplies a wealth of information useful to everyone.

The Avalon Project at the Yale Law School— Eighteenth-Century Documents

http://www.yale.edu/lawweb/avalon/18th.htm

This reliable, user-friendly site provides unabridged transcriptions of dozens of important Revolutionary Era documents, including colonial charters, state constitutions, Indian treaties, and the Virginia Declaration of Rights. There is also a keyword-searchable version of *The Federalist Papers*. This site is an extraordinary resource for scholars of early American statecraft.

Battles of the American Revolutionary War

http://mac94.ralphbunche.rbs.edu/history/aha/battles.html

Maintained by Columbia University's Institute for Learning Technologies, this site links users to information on battles and fortifications that figured prominently in the War for Independence. Brief descriptions place these flash points within the context of larger campaigns, describe strategy and important maneuvers, and estimate casualties. Historic illustrations round out the presentations. This site should aid instructors who seek abbreviated but competent descriptions of the military conflict.

Boston National Historical Park—The Freedom Trail

http://www.nps.gov/bost/ftrail.htm

For decades tourists have flocked to Boston's Freedom Trail, the three-mile stretch of historic sites from the Massachusetts State House to Bunker Hill. Now surfers of the Web can also enjoy an enlightening foray into America's revolutionary past. Valuable information about the significance of the Old South Meeting House, Faneuil Hall, the Old North Church, and the U.S.S.

Constitution gives depth to any student's understanding of the heady, early days of the War for Independence and hints at how urban areas constitute especially fertile fields for political unrest.

Center for Military History—War of American Independence

http://www.army.mil/cmh-pg/online/WAI.htm

This site features several useful resources. Among them is Robert K. Wright, Jr.'s *The Continental Army*, a workmanlike text that recounts the contributions of nonmilitia, nonregular state troops. This site also includes bibliographies and traces the lineages of the units of the Continental Army.

Colonial Williamsburg

http://www.history.org

The official home page of Colonial Williamsburg provides teachers and students with a vivid introduction to the recreated eighteenth-century Virginia capital and the world of imperial Anglo-America. The site offers information on Colonial and Revolutionary Williamsburg's most notable people, places, and events. Teachers will find information on electronic field trips, the Colonial Williamsburg Teacher Institute, and lesson plans for topics such as "Colonial Reaction to the Stamp Act" and "Travel in the 18th Century."

Declaring Independence: Drafting the Documents

http://lcweb.loc.gov/exhibits/declara/declara1.html

An online exhibit on the creation of the Declaration of Independence, this Library of Congress–sponsored site features photographs and transcriptions of Thomas Jefferson's drafts of the 1776 document. In addition, it showcases eighteenth-century printed versions of the text and historic illustrations of its creation and ratification. Brief introductions provide context for these materials. Composition teachers will join history instructors in making use of this site, for it provides a compelling case study of the process of writing and revision.

Documents from the Continental Congress and the Constitutional Convention, 1774-1789

http://lcweb2.loc.gov/ammem/bdsds/bdsdhome.html

Sponsored by the Library of Congress, this invaluable page contains 274 keyword-searchable documents relating to the Continental Congress and the ratification of the Constitution. The texts include treaties, resolutions, committee reports, and extracts from the Congress's journals. This site greatly expedites serious research on Revolutionary Era politics.

The Early America Review

http://earlyamerica.com/review

This online historical journal, published since 1996, includes both book reviews and articles (such as "Jefferson and His Daughters," "The Enigma of Benedict Arnold," and "A Conversation with Alan Taylor"). The essays—most of which are footnoted—should interest wide audiences. Accessible and elegantly presented, this is a worthwhile site.

The Heath Anthology of American Literature

http://www.georgetown.edu/bassr/heath/index.html

"The Syllabus Builder," listed under "Instructor Resources," provides writings by Mercy Otis Warren, Benjamin Franklin, J. Hector St. John de Crevecoeur, Thomas Paine, John Adams, Thomas Jefferson, Philip Freneau, Timothy Dwight, Phillis Wheatley, Joel Barlow, and other Independence Era literati. This virtual library of essential texts, which should ably bolster the resources available to educators at smaller institutions, puts early American classics within reach of everyone.

Historic Mount Vernon—The Home of Our First President, George Washington

http://www.mountvernon.org

Maintained by the curators of George Washington's Potomac River estate, this site provides information about the man who commanded the Continental Army and served as the first U.S. president; in addition, it situates his house within the context of a slave-based plantation labor system. Students of the Revolution will appreciate the authoritative biographical information on Washington, along with the virtual tour of the grounds of Mount Vernon, the pages on "George Washington and Slavery," and the narrated image gallery of paintings relating to Washington. A rudimentary "George Washington Quiz" will challenge children in the primary grades.

Thomas Jefferson: A Film By Ken Burns

http://www.pbs.org/jefferson

The Public Broadcasting System inaugurated this Web site to complement its landmark 1997 documentary series on "Thomas Jefferson," a three-hour televised account (now available on videotape) produced by Ken Burns. Like the film, this site chronicles the multifaceted life of the author of the Declaration of Independence. Student study sheets on political, religious, social, intellectual, and personal freedom and an archive of Jefferson's writings will especially interest educators, as will "Does Jefferson Matter?," an online forum of noted scholars who assess the role of Jefferson (and other "great men") in shaping history.

Thomas Jefferson Online Resources at the University of Virginia

http://etext.virginia.edu/jefferson

The University of Virginia's Electronic Text Center sponsors this extraordinarily useful site concerning its venerable founder. More than 1,700 documents written by Jefferson are accessible, all of them keyword-searchable. In addition, electronic versions of Frank Shuffelton's invaluable annotated bibliographies of books and articles about Jefferson (*Thomas Jefferson: A Comprehensive, Annotated Bibliography of Writings about Him, 1826–1980* [New York: Garland Publishing, 1983] and *Thomas Jefferson, 1981–1990: An Annotated Bibliography* [New York: Garland Publishing, 1992]) are also available—sources that truly supersede their printed versions because they, too, are also keyword searchable. This is the essential site for individuals seeking to start research on a Jefferson topic.

Liberty! The American Revolution

http://www.pbs.org/ktca/liberty

This Web site accompanies the 1997 televised PBS documentary (now available on videotape) "Liberty!," a six-hour account of the causes, course, and consequences of the American Revolution. One especially useful feature is the "Chronicle of the Revolution," an illustrated narrative of the independence movement's signal events. This chronological account, which provides a good overview of the era, is supplemented by a number of internal links that give readers more in-depth information about selected topics (such as "The Boston Tea Party" and "Thomas Hutchinson"). A timeline, bibliography, index, and listing of external links round out the very useful presentation.

Loyalist, British Songs and Poetry of the American Revolution

http://www.erols.com/candidus/music.htm

The texts of one dozen Loyalist songs and poems, many of them quite obscure, appear on this attractive page. A number of links to other sites focusing on Loyalism can be found here as well.

Monticello: The Home of Thomas Jefferson

http://www.monticello.org

Sponsored by the Thomas Jefferson Memorial Foundation, this exceptional, award-winning site focuses on America's third president and life at his mountaintop home, Monticello. Notable features include "A Day in the Life," a richly illustrated narrative—complete with fascinating internal links—of Jefferson's waking moments during a typical day at his plantation. "Matters of Fact" includes a clickable index of reports on various subjects prepared by Monticello's research staff, as well as "Ask Thomas Jefferson," which invites youngsters to correspond with the famous Virginian (students's questions and the replies of "Jefferson" are posted on topically indexed archive). The site also features fresh information on Sally Hemings, the slave with whom— recent DNA testing suggests—Jefferson fathered at least one child. A chronicle of interviews with descendants of Monticello slaves, "Getting Word," provides a glimpse into the lives of members of Jefferson's extended plantation "family." Teachers will discover online lesson plans that provide technical and pedagogical suggestions for optimizing classroom use of the site.

National Archives and Records Administration: Charters of Freedom

http://www.nara.gov/exhall/charters/charters.html

This online exhibit features materials relating to the Declaration of Independence, the Constitution, and the Bill of Rights. Sponsored by the National Archives, which serves as custodian for these seminal documents, this site enables visitors to view exceptionally clear images of these texts' early manuscript and printed versions; it also includes authoritative essays that consider them in various contexts. See, for example, "The Declaration of Independence: A History," which discusses the drafting and ratification of the Declaration, as well as how different generations treated the physical document as it evolved from state paper to national icon.

Omohundro Institute of Early American History and Culture

http://www.wm.edu/oieahc

Cosponsored by the College of William and Mary and the Colonial Williamsburg Foundation, the Omohundro Institute of Early American History and Culture publishes the highly regarded *William and Mary Quarterly (WMQ)*, a journal of American history prior to 1815. Here, on its official Web site, individuals may browse recent tables of contents from the *WMQ*, see news of upcoming conferences and colloquia, and read *Uncommon Sense*, the institute's newsletter.

Thomas Paine National Historical Association

http://www.mediapro.net/cdadesign/paine

The home page of the Thomas Paine National Historical Association is a good starting point for basic research on the important trans-Atlantic radical whose 1776 *Common Sense* pushed American colonists toward revolution. The site includes information about his life and his New Rochelle, New York home (where the association is based), as well as links to full-text versions of his writings and other Paine-related Web pages.

Philadelphia's Historic Mile

http://www.libertynet.org/iha/tour/index.html

Maintained by the Independence Hall Association, this site allows people in far-flung locales to tour Philadelphia's most historic Revolutionary Era landmarks. Stops include the old Pennsylvania State House (Independence Hall), where the Continental Congress and Constitutional Convention met, as well as City Tavern, the first and second Bank of the United States, the Liberty Bell, Christ Church, and Franklin Court. Richly illustrated and competently narrated, the tour provides a tantalizing glimpse of not only a young nation's political life but also an old city's streetscape.

From Revolution to Reconstruction: A Hypertext on American History

http://odur.let.rug.nl/~usa/usa.htm

This extraordinarily useful site provides a wealth of reliable information on the American Revolutionary period. Hosted by the University of Groningen in the Netherlands, this page features numerous full-text documents, including thirty authored between the 1763 Peace of Paris and the 1783 Treaty of Paris. Internal links to brief biographies of important contributors to the Independence movement appear here as well. While the documents, supplied by the U.S. Information Agency, are reliably transcribed, a few of the biographical sketches, authored by non-native English-speakers, contain spelling and grammatical errors. Quibbles aside, students and teachers of early American history will frequently resort to this massive resource.

Betsy Ross Home Page

http://www.libertynet.org/iha/betsy/index.html

This interesting Web site, sponsored by Philadelphia's Betsy Ross House and the Independence Hall Association, includes a picture gallery of historic American flags, a brief biography of upholsterer/flagmaker Betsy Ross, and information about flag trivia and etiquette. It also includes a section, arranged in a point-counterpoint format, arguing that the story of Ross sewing the first U.S. flag (described by some as a myth) is, in reality, accurate. As a result, this site might be used as a springboard for a discussion on standards of historical evidence and the development of historical memory.

U.S. Army Military History Institute

http://carlisle-www.army.mil/usamhi

Sponsored by the U.S. Army War College at Carlisle, Pennsylvania, the Military History Institute allows historians of the Revolution to use electronic bibliographical databases to search, with keywords, a variety of important primary and secondary sources.

Virtual Marching Tour of the American Revolution

http://www.libertynet.org/iha/march/index.html

Maintained by Philadelphia's Independence Hall Association, this site, still under construction, currently focuses on The Philadelphia Campaign of 1777. From the landing of British troops at Head of Elk, Maryland, to Brandywine, Germantown, Fort Mifflin, and Valley Forge, this "virtual marching tour" includes a reliable narrative of events. Photographs, illustrations, and music supplement the text. Several dozen links also appear on this site. Broadly focused, the list of authoritative, mostly professionally maintained Web pages includes everything from the National Trust for Historic Preservation and the Maryland State Archives to the Friends of the Saratoga Battlefield.

George Washington Papers Home Page

http://www.virginia.edu/gwpapers

The official home page of *The Papers of George Washington*, a documentary editing project based for thirty years at the University of Virginia, makes selected documents relating to Washington's long public career available as keyword-searchable electronic texts. Internal links also provide information about the Washington papers project and staff.

The World of Benjamin Franklin

http://sln.fi.edu/franklin

Sponsored by the Franklin Institute, this site provides a fascinating introduction to Benjamin Franklin for elementary school students. A brief biography—along with discussions of Franklin as scientist, inventor, statesman, printer, musician, and economist—offers an interesting portrayal of this multifaceted individual. Enrichment activities on the Constitution, Franklin's epitaphs, and other subjects supplement traditional lesson plans.

EARLY AMERICAN HISTORY, 1783–1860
Edward Ragan

From Revolution to Reconstruction

http://odur.let.rug.nl/~usa/usa.htm

This metasite, maintained by the Arts Faculty of the University of Groningen in the Netherlands, is a massive resource for all aspects of American history. The site is divided into five general sections: Outlines, Essays, Documents, Biographies, and Presidents. This site is organized around several United States Information Agency publications: *An Outline of American History, An Outline of the American Economy, An Outline of American Government, and An Outline of American Literature*. While the text of these Outlines has not been changed, they have been enriched with hypertext links to relevant documents, original essays, and other Internet sites.

The Making of America

http://www.umdl.umich.edu/moa/

The Making of America is a digital library of primary sources in American social history from the antebellum period through Reconstruction. Contained in this collection are approximately 1,600 books and 50,000 journal articles on subjects as far-ranging as education, psychology, American history, sociology, religion, and science and technology. The project, which is sponsored by the University of Michigan, "represents a major collaborative endeavor in preservation and electronic access to historical texts." These texts are searchable by keyword with links to digitized copies of the nineteenth-century imprints. This is an outstanding site for those who need access to nineteenth-century documents.

Nineteenth-Century Documents Project

http://www.furman.edu/~benson/docs/

Lloyd Benson has prepared an extensive collection of primary documents. The period is categorized topically, and all topics seem to emphasize increased sectional differences and the coming of the Civil War. The documents are grouped under the following headings: Early National Politics, Slavery/Sectionalism, the Kansas-Nebraska Bill, the caning of Charles Sumner, the Dred Scott Decision, John Brown/Harper's Ferry, 1850s Statistical Almanac, Election of 1860, Secession and the West, War, and post–Civil War.

Abolition

http://www.loc.gov/exhibits/african/abol.htmlhttp//www.loc.gov/exhibits/african/abol.html

The Library of Congress provides information on the history of the antislavery movement in America that led to the formation, in 1833, of the American Anti-Slavery Society. Includes references to Library of Congress holdings such as abolitionist publications, minutes of antislavery meetings, handbills, advertisements, songs, and appeals to women. Demonstrates the tradition of the abolition movement in America before 1833.The Library of Congress provides information on the history of the antislavery movement in America that led to the formation, in 1833, of the American Anti-Slavery Society. Includes references to Library of Congress holdings such as abolitionist publications, minutes of antislavery meetings, handbills, advertisements, songs, and appeals to women. Demonstrates the tradition of the abolition movement in America before 1833.

An Abridged History of the United States

http://www.us-history.com/

William M. Brinton offers this Internet textbook of U.S. history with a specific focus on the U.S. Constitution. He argues that in order to understand the politics of modern America, one must be familiar with the history. His efforts result in a dialogue between the past and the present. Links to related Web sites are provided, and they help to reinforce Brinton's points. On the whole, this text is very readable and provides a useful electronic reference.

Across the Plains in 1844

http://www.pbs.org/weta/thewest/wpages/wpgs620/sager1.htm

Catherine Sager Pringle wrote this essay circa 1860. It is reprinted here from S.A. Clarke's *Pioneer Days in Oregon History*, Vol. II, (1905).

Across the Plains in the Donner Party

http://www.teleport.com/~mhaller/Primary/VReed/VReed1.html

Mike Haller has edited this book of reminiscences by Virginia Reed Murphy about her travel with the Donner party.

African Canadian Heritage Tour

http://www.ciaccess.com/~jdnewby/heritage/african.htm

The African Canadian Heritage Tour celebrates the history of those who made the arduous journey to freedom in Canada via the Underground Railroad. This site is the central Internet presence for a collection of five historical sites that provide information about the Underground Railroad and the African-Canadian settlement of southwestern Ontario: The Buxton Historical Site and Museum, the North American Black Historical Museum, the Sandwich Baptist Church, the Uncle Tom's Cabin–Josiah Henson Interpretive Site, and the Woodstock Institute Sertoma Help Center.

Ain't I a Woman?

http://www.digitalsojourn.org/speech.html

Digital Sojourn maintains this site about the history of Sojourner Truth's "Ain't I a Woman?" speech at the 1851 Women's Rights Convention in Akron, Ohio. Included is the classic account by Frances Gage and a description from the *Anti-Slavery Bugle*.

The American Whig Party (1834–56)

http://odur.let.rug.nl/~usa/E/uswhig/whigsxx.htm

Essay by Hal Morris that describes the rise of the American Whig Party as an opposition to President Andrew Jackson's king-like tendencies. Included is a history of the Whig Party and links to biographies of Whig presidents and political leaders in America.

Anakapia: "Our Protector" of the Treaty of Greenville

http://www.indianahistory.org/anakapia.htm

The Indiana Historical Society describes the history of the Anakapia. Also known as the Anthony Wayne flag, Anakapia was given to a Miami Indian chief by Wayne at the signing of the Treaty of Greenville in 1795.

American Treasures of the Library of Congress

http://lcweb.loc.gov/exhibits/treasures/

This is a substantial virtual exhibit from the Library of Congress collections. It contains a variety of items, including letters by Thomas Jefferson and John Quincy Adams's notes from the *Amistad* case. Substantial detail and historical context is provided for each component of the collection. Thomas Jefferson, whose personal library became the core of the Library of Congress, arranged his books into three types of knowledge, corresponding to three faculties of the mind: memory (history), reason (philosophy), and imagination (fine arts).

Amistad: Race and the Boundaries of Freedom in Antebellum Maritime America

http://amistad.mysticseaport.org/main/welcome.html

This site is part of the Mystic Seaport Museum. It contains information on the *Amistad* slave ship, the revolt of its cargo, and the Supreme Court trial of its slave mutineers. The focus of this site is living history. A timeline of events is provided, as are classroom lessons for teachers.

The *Amistad* Case

http://www.nara.gov/education/teaching/amistad/home.html

The National Archives and Records Administration provides all relevant documents related to the *Amistad* slave mutiny. This site also includes teaching ideas based on the National Standards for History and the National Standards for Civics and Government.

The Annapolis Convention

http://www.yale.edu/lawweb/avalon/annapoli.htm

The Annapolis Convention assembled to discuss economic issues faced by the states under the Articles of Confederation. It resolved to explore alternatives to the Articles. This site contains the report of the commissioners from the states on Sept. 14, 1786, and links to the Articles of Confederation, the Madison Debates, the *Federalist Papers*, and the U.S. Constitution.

The Anti-Federalist Papers

http://odur.let.rug.nl/~usa/D/1776-1800/federalist/antixx.htm

First published in 1787–88, they argue against constitutional ratification. Whereas the Federalists advocated a strong central government, the Anti-Federalists feared that the constitution would subvert the rights and liberties recently won from Great Britain in the American Revolution. This site provides e-text copies of forty-seven documents that serve as the arguments against ratification. These items are bold statements of American political theory, and this online version makes them more accessible than ever before.

The Articles of Confederation

http://www.yale.edu/lawweb/avalon/artconf.htm

The Articles of Confederation established a central government for the thirteen colonies after the American Revolution. It was a weak system where the separate states held the balance of power. This site contains a full-text copy of the Articles and links to the Annapolis Convention, the Madison Debates, the *Federalist Papers*, and the U.S. Constitution.

The Bill of Rights

http://www.nara.gov/exhall/charters/billrights/billmain.html

The National Archives and Records Administration provides coverage of the Bill of Rights. Included here is a high-resolution image of the document.

Boundaries of the United States and the Several States

http://www.ac.wwu.edu/~stephan/48states.html

Ed Stephan of Western Washington University has created a charming animated map that depicts the territorial growth of the United States. This site allows students to visualize how national, territorial, and state boundaries changed over time.

John Brown

http://www.pbs.org/weta/thewest/wpages/wpgs400/w4brown.htm

This PBS-sponsored site contains a biography of the radical abolitionist John Brown.

Cherokee Nation v. Georgia

http://www.pbs.org/weta/thewest/wpages/wpgs620/cherokee.htm

This is a full-text copy of the decision handed down by the Supreme Court (1831).

The Confessions of Nat Turner

http://odur.let.rug.nl/~usa/D/1826-1850/slavery/confesxx.htm

This is the complete text of *The Confessions of Nat Turner* (1831).

The Constitution of the United States

http://www.nara.gov/exhall/charters/constitution/conmain.html

The National Archives and Records Administration maintains this site. The Founding Fathers page features the biographies of the fifty-five delegates to the Constitutional Convention. You can read a transcription of the complete text of the Constitution. This page also provides hyperlinks to biographies of each of the thirty-nine delegates who signed the Constitution. The article "A More Perfect Union" is an in-depth look at the Constitutional Convention and the ratification process. A quiz section gives visitors the chance to test their knowledge.

Constitution of the United States (1787)

http://civnet.org/resoures/teach/basic/constitu.htm

This site is maintained by Civnet. It includes the U.S. Constitution, an introductory essay, and a bibliography for further reading.

James Fenimore Cooper (1789–1851)

http://odur.let.rug.nl/~usa/LIT/cooper.htm

Kathryn VanSpanckeren has authored this literary biography that evaluates this author's role in the development of the American novel. Traces the familial and cultural influences that led Cooper to create Natty Bumppo, his chief protagonist.

Democracy in America: De Tocqueville

http://xroads.virginia.edu/~HYPER/DETOC/home.html

The American Studies program at the University of Virginia maintains this site, which explores American democracy in the 1830s. De Tocqueville traveled across the United States in the 1830s. UVA has taken his itinerary, letters, and journal entries and combined them with cultural artifacts from the period to provide a glimpse of American democracy and culture in the early nineteenth century. Among other things, gender, race, and religion are examined.

The Donner Party

http://www.teleport.com/~mhaller/index.shtml

Mike Haller provides a history of the ill-fated Donner party, which was stranded on its journey during the winter of 1846–47.

The Early America Review

http://www.earlyamerica.com/review/

This electronic "journal of fact and opinion on the people, issues, and events of eighteenth-century America" is edited by Don Vitale. The journal contains wide-ranging articles about the social, political, and military developments of this period. An excellent example of the ways in which modern scholarship seeks to combine traditional formats with technology.

The Federalist Papers

http://www.yale.edu/lawweb/avalon/federal/fed.htm

The collection is searchable by keyword and linked to relevant documents, such as the Articles of Confederation, the Annapolis Convention, the Madison Debates, and the U.S. Constitution.

FindLaw: U.S. Constitution

http://www.findlaw.com/casecode/constitution/

This site contains all articles and amendments to the U.S. Constitution. Each item is completely annotated with explanations and references. Through hyperlinks, users can access the full-text version of relevant Supreme Court decisions. Each decision is placed in its historical context, along with pertinent theories of law and government. This is an invaluable resource for legal professionals.

First-Person Narratives of the American South

http://metalab.unc.edu/docsouth/fpn/fpn.html

This site contains an outstanding collection of electronic texts that documents the American South. It includes diaries, autobiographies, memoirs, travel accounts, and ex-slave narratives. The focus is on first-person narratives of marginalized populations: women, African Americans, enlisted men, laborers, and Native Americans.

The Founding Fathers

http://www.nara.gov/exhall/charters/constitution/confath.html

The National Archives and Records Administration has compiled biographies of the delegates to the Constitutional Convention of 1778. This is an excellent place to start when studying the U.S. Constitution and the Founding Fathers.

Benjamin Franklin: A Documentary History

http://www.english.udel.edu/lemay/franklin/

J.A. Leo Lemay, a professor at the University of Delaware, gives visitors a peek into the research that he is doing for a Franklin biography. He offers a detailed chronology of Franklin's life that is divided into three stages: early life, professional interests, and political career. Each event in Franklin's life is verified with citations that are connected to a bibliography of primary documents.

Benjamin Franklin: Glimpses of the Man

http://www.fi.edu/franklin/rotten.html

The Franklin Institute maintains this site, which celebrates the life and work of Benjamin Franklin. It emphasizes his work as a statesman, a printer, a scientist, a philosopher, a musician, an economist, and an inventor.

A Girl's Life in Virginia before the War

http://metalab.unc.edu/docsouth/burwell/menu.html

This memoir by Letitia M. Burwell describes Southern plantation life before the Civil War. It was originally published in 1895.

Godey's Lady's Book

http://www.history.rochester.edu/godeys/

Selections from the 19th-century popular women's magazine *Godey's Lady's Book*. Issues from the 1850s include "For the Home," "Nor Just for Ladies," and "Fashion Corner" sections. Visitors to this site will find an informative glimpse into the daily life of the mid-19th-century middle class.

A Grandmother's Recollections of Dixie

http://metalab.unc.edu/docsouth/bryan/menu.html

This is a collection of letters from Mary Norcott Bryan to her grandchildren. It was published in 1912. Her letters shed light on Southern plantation life before the Civil War.

Horace Greeley (1811–72)

http://www.honors.unr.edu/~fenimore/greeley.html

David H. Fenimore of the University of Nevada at Reno offers a detailed biography of Greeley, complete with photographs, quotations, links to related information, and a Greeley bibliography.

Sarah Grimke, Angelina Grimke

http://www.gale.com/schools/resrcs/womenhist/grimkes.html

Gale Publishing has created these biographies of Sarah Grimke and Angelina Grimke, which focus on their work for abolition and women's suffrage.

Historic Mount Vernon—The Home of Our First President, George Washington

http://www.mountvernon.org

Visitors to the official Mount Vernon Web site will find information designed to meet a variety of needs. In addition to a virtual tour of the house and grounds, this site contains a biography of Washington written at the fifth-grade level, with teaching aids such as quizzes and an electronic image collection.

Historical Maps of the United States

http://www.lib.utexas.edu/Libs/PCL/Map_collection/histus.html

The University of Texas at Austin has digitized the Perry–Castañeda Library Map Collection. This is an excellent source for digitized copies of rare maps.

History of the Donner Party

http://www.teleport.com/~mhaller/Secondary/McGlashan/
McGlashanTOC.html

Mike Haller has edited this book by C.F. McGlashan about the Donner party.

The Hypocrisy of American Slavery

http://www.historyplace.com/speeches/douglass.htm

This speech was given by Frederick Douglass on July 4, 1852, in Rochester, N.Y. See later in this section, Douglass's speech made the following day entitled, "What to the slave is the Fourth of July."

The Jay Treaty

http://odur.let.rug.nl/~usa/D/1776-1800/foreignpolicy/jay.htm

This treaty between Great Britain and the United States was the most controversial issue of George Washington's presidency. It was proclaimed in February 1796. Its real significance was that it represented Britain's recognition of American nationality.

Thomas Jefferson: A Film by Ken Burns

http://www.pbs.org/jefferson/

This PBS site is the online version of the Ken Burns film about Thomas Jefferson. It features selections of Jefferson's writings used in the film, the transcripts of interviews conducted for the film, tips for educators on teaching about Jefferson, and classroom activities for students.

Jefferson and Adams: A Lifetime of Letters

http://www.monticello.org/Day/cabinet/profile.html

This is the official site of the Thomas Jefferson Memorial Foundation, Inc. This section is devoted to the relationship between Thomas Jefferson and John Adams. It describes their movement from friendship to opposition to reconciliation.

The Thomas Jefferson Memorial Foundation

http://www.monticello.org

The Thomas Jefferson Memorial Foundation has prepared a virtual tour life at Monticello to demonstrate how Jefferson spent an average day. Included here is a discussion about Jefferson's interests, inventions, family, slaves, and grounds. Lengthy essays seek to explain Jefferson's world to the twentieth-century student. Links connect the reader to additional information about Monticello, its owner, inhabitants, and visitors. "The Jefferson–Hemings DNA Testing: An Online Resource" is valuable for understanding the current controversy about Jefferson's legacy.

Thomas Jefferson on Politics and Government: Quotations from the Writings of Thomas Jefferson

http://etext.virginia.edu/jefferson/quotations/

This site, sponsored by the University of Virginia, contains an extensive collection of Jefferson quotations. The stated goal of this site is to constitute a "fair statement of the complete political philosophy of Thomas Jefferson." Also included is a brief biography of Jefferson and links to related sites.

John Brown: An Address by Frederick Douglass

http://lcweb2.loc.gov/cgi-bin/query/r?ammem/
murray:@field(FLD001+07012896+):@@@REF

This speech by Frederick Douglass can be found at the Library of Congress Web site. It is a tribute to John Brown, a radical abolitionist who, in 1859, raided the federal arsenal at Harper's Ferry in a mad attempt to foment a slave revolt. The Virginia authorities hanged Brown. His last words were: "I, John Brown, am now quite certain that the crimes of this guilty land will never be purged away but with blood." Douglass memorialized Brown as a true hero of the abolitionist cause.

A Journey to the Seaboard States (1856)

http://odur.let.rug.nl/~usa/D/1851-1875/olmsted/jourxx.htm

This essay by Frederick Law Olmsted focuses on slavery and the plantation system. It was written in 1856 while Olmsted was on a journalistic assignment for the *New York Daily Times*. Olmsted is critical of slavery as both cruel and inefficient.

The Judiciary Act of 1789

http://civnet.org/resoures/teach/basic/8.htm

This act established the federal judiciary. Civnet sponsors this site and includes an introduction and suggestions for further reading.

Kentucky Resolution (1799)

http://odur.let.rug.nl/~usa/D/1776-1800/constitution/kent1799.htm

This was Thomas Jefferson's Republican response to the Federalists' Alien and Sedition Acts. The resolution advanced the state-compact theory and argued that states retained the right to notify Congress when it had exceeded its authority.

Lewis and Clark

http://www.pbs.org/lewisandclark/

This is the PBS-sponsored online companion to Ken Burns's documentary series on the Lewis and Clark expedition. The site includes biographies for all members of the Corps of Discovery, along with equipment lists, timelines, maps, and excerpts from the journals kept. Also included are short histories of the Native American tribes that were encountered on the journey. Burns discusses the making of the series, and PBS provides teaching resources. Overall, this is an excellent site.

The Louisiana Purchase Treaty

http://www.pbs.org/weta/thewest/wpages/wpgs610/louispur.htm

This treaty was signed in Paris in 1803.

The Madison Debates

http://www.yale.edu/lawweb/avalon/debates/debcont.htm

The Debates in the Federal Convention of 1787 was created from notes taken by James Madison during the Constitutional Convention held in Philadelphia between May 14 and September 17, 1787. The debates are searchable by keyword or can be accessed according to specific dates. Also contained here are links to the Articles of Confederation, the Annapolis Convention, the *Federalist Papers,* and the U.S. Constitution.

Manifest Destiny

http://odur.let.rug.nl/~usa/E/manifest/manifxx.htm

This essay by Michael Lubragge traces the history of this concept in America.

John Marshall

http://odur.let.rug.nl/~usa/D/1801-1825/marshallcases/marxx.htm

Here are the major decisions written by Chief Justice John Marshall, including *Marbury v. Madison* and *Cherokee Nation v. Georgia*. Also included is a biography of Marshall.

Methods of Resistance to Slavery

http://dolphin.upenn.edu/~vision/vis/Mar-95/8677.html

This is an essay by Colette Lamothe that examines slaves' responses to slavery, oppression, and exploitation. Lamothe uses a comparative method to explore African slavery in the Caribbean, Latin America, and the United States from the fifteenth to the nineteenth century.

The Mexican–American War (1846–48)

http://www.pbs.org/kera/usmexicanwar/

This PBS-sponsored site is the online companion to the TV documentary. It provides a detailed analysis of the war from both sides, with the perspective that "there are many valid points of view about a historical event." The war is placed in its larger context as a war for North America. Also included here is a bibliography, a teacher's guide, a timeline of events, historical analysis by experts, and information on the making of the documentary. This site is available in English and Spanish.

The Mexican–American War, 1846–48

http://www.dmwv.org/mexwar/mexwar.htm

Sponsored by the Descendants of Mexican War Veterans, this site offers a history of the war, with sections on the "Countdown to War," "Scott's Invasion," and "The Treaty of Guadalupe Hidalgo." Also provided are maps, documents, images, and links to related resources.

The Mexican–American War Memorial Home Page

http://sunsite.dcaa.unam.mx/revistas/1847/

The Universidad Nacional Autónoma de México sponsors this site. It includes documents, paintings, and a narrative history of the Mexican–American War (1846–48). The war is presented from the perspective of participants and observers. The pages are available in English and in Spanish.

The Monroe Doctrine

http://odur.let.rug.nl/~usa/D/1801-1825/jmdoc.htm

The Monroe Doctrine was an early statement on American foreign policy. It was taken from President Monroe's annual message to Congress on December 2, 1823.

Mountain Men and the Fur Trade: Sources of the History of the Fur Trade in the Rocky Mountain West

http://www.xmission.com/~drudy/amm.html

This site is devoted to the mountain men of the Rocky Mountains through 1850. It includes digitized personal and public records and a bibliography for further reading.

New Perspectives on the West

http://www.pbs.org/weta/thewest/

This is the PBS-sponsored online companion to Ken Burns's and Stephen Ives's eight-episode documentary on the American West. Burns and Ives introduce the production, and they provide a timeline with relevant biographies of key figures. Also included are sample primary source documents that were used to create the series and links to related sites.

"The Night Before Christmas" Made Clement Moore Famous. Go Figure.

http://www.discovery.com/area/obscurity/obscurity961216/obscurity1.html

The Discovery Channel Online provides the history of Clement Moore's famous poem. This site includes biographical information on Moore, some modern parodies of the popular poem, and a short discussion of whether Moore was the poem's actual author. Here, visitors will get a glimpse into the origins of our modern Christmas traditions.

North American Slave Narratives

http://metalab.unc.edu/docsouth/neh/neh.html

This large collection of American slave narratives is part of the Documenting the American South project sponsored by the University of North Carolina at Chapel Hill. This is an excellent resource for better understanding the slaves' world in the antebellum South.

The Northwest Ordinance (1787)

http://civnet.org/resoures/teach/basic/northwes.htm

This act defined the process of adding new states to the Union.

Orphan Trains of Kansas

http://kuhttp.cc.ukans.edu/carrie/kancoll/articles/orphans/

Connie Dipasquale and Susan Stafford present their research about children brought to Kansas from New York on "Orphan Trains." This site includes first-hand accounts, a timeline, newspaper descriptions, and partial name lists of children on the "Orphan Trains."

Peabody Museum: The Ethnography of Lewis and Clark

http://www.peabody.harvard.edu/Lewis&Clark/

The Peabody Museum of Archaeology and Ethnology at Harvard University has developed this site to examine the cultural implications of the Lewis and Clark expedition. Included here are artifacts (with detailed descriptions) from native Americans, route maps, and a resources page with links.

Politics and Sectionalism in the 1850s

http://odur.let.rug.nl/~usa/E/1850s/polixx.htm

Stephen Demkin has written this essay examining the major political issues of the 1850s, such as the Compromise of 1850, the Kansas–Nebraska Act, and the Dred Scott decision. Also included are links to related sites.

The Prairie Traveler: A Handbook for Overland Expeditions

http://kuhttp.cc.ukans.edu/carrie/kancoll/books/marcy/index.html

This survival guide/handbook was published in 1859.

The Presidents of the United States

http://www.whitehouse.gov/WH/glimpse/presidents/html/presidents.html

The official White House Web site provides excellent biographies of each president, along with links to relevant documents and biographies of the first ladies.

The Presidents of the United States

http://www.ipl.org/ref/POTUS/index.html

The Internet Public Library has produced an excellent collection of presidential Web sites. Sections contain presidential election results, cabinet members, notable events, and links to Internet biographies. The information here is laid out in a very accessible format.

The Proclamation of Neutrality (1793)

http://odur.let.rug.nl/~usa/D/1776-1800/foreignpolicy/neutr.htm

President George Washington proclaims American neutrality during the wars of the French Revolution.

A Roadmap to the U.S. Constitution

http://library.advanced.org/11572/

Jonathan Chin and Alan Stern of ThinkQuest have developed this site on the U.S. Constitution. The authors have tried to recreate the milieu out of which the Constitution emerged. In addition to providing an annotated copy of the Constitution, essays explore the origins of this document. The authors also examine Constitutional "crises" and the relevant Supreme Court decisions. This site provides a discussion board for those with specific questions.

Scanned Originals of Early American Documents

http://www.law.emory.edu/FEDERAL/conpict.html

Scanned originals of the Constitution, the Bill of Rights, and the Declaration of Independence.

Secession Crisis, Chronology of the

http://members.aol.com/jfepperson/secesh.html

James F. Epperson charts the chronology of events that culminated with the firing upon Fort Sumter.

The Sedition Act of July 14, 1798

http://kuhttp.cc.ukans.edu/carrie/docs/texts/sedact.htm

Congress passed this act on July 14, 1798.

Selected Letters from Kansas

http://www.pbs.org/weta/thewest/wpages/wpgs640/lovejoy1.htm

These letters, by Julie Louisa Lovejoy, were written between 1855 to 1863 to the *Independent Democrat*, in Concord, New Hampshire. The letters are part of the PBS Web site on the American West.

"She is More to be Pitied than Censured": Women, Sexuality, and Murder in Nineteenth-Century America

http://www.brown.edu/Facilities/University_Library/publications/RLCexhibit/shes/she_is_morems.html

This exhibition is from the collections of the John Hay Library at Brown University. It focuses on sex scandals and sensational murders in the nineteenth century. Included is a brief overview of the subject, a list of references, and descriptions of seven murders.

A Slaveholder's Daughter

http://metalab.unc.edu/docsouth/kearney/menu.html

This memoir by Belle Kearney describes her life in Mississippi.

Slavery a Positive Good

http://douglass.speech.nwu.edu/calh_a59.htm

John C. Calhoun gave this speech on the floor of the U.S. Senate in 1837.

The Gerrit Smith Virtual Museum

http://www.NYHistory.com/gerritsmith/index.htm

The New York History Net has detailed information about the abolitionist leader. This site includes a biographical essay, bibliography, and portrait gallery of Smith and his family. It was developed in cooperation with the Syracuse University Library Department of Special Collections and Hamilton College, both of whom hold substantial portions of Gerrit Smith's papers.

The Star Spangled Banner

http://odur.let.rug.nl/~usa/E/banner/bannerxx.htm

Amato F. Mongelluzzo offers an essay that relates the events and dispels several myths surrounding the creation of this poem that became the National Anthem.

Henry David Thoreau

http://miso.wwa.com/~jej/1thorea.html

Jone Johnson has prepared this essential Thoreau site. Emphasized here are Thoreau's biography, images, electronic texts, and scholarly analysis of Thoreau's work.

To the Western Ocean: Planning the Lewis and Clark Expedition

http://www.lib.virginia.edu/exhibits/lewis_clark/ch4.html

The site is part of a map exhibition at the Tracy W. McGregor Room, Alderman Library, University of Virginia. "To the Western Ocean" is the fourth chapter of a larger exploration of nation building and mapmaking. This site is valuable because it places the Lewis and Clark expedition into a larger historical context.

Treaty of Greenville (1795)

http://odur.let.rug.nl/~usa/D/1776-1800/indians/green.htm

This is the complete text of the American Indian treaty that formally opened the Northwest Territory for settlement.

Sojourner Truth

http://www.gale.com/schools/resrcs/womenhst/truths.htm

Gale Publishing has prepared this biography of Sojourner Truth, with an accompanying bibliography.

Two Bloody Days at Buena Vista

http://www.thehistorynet.com/MilitaryHistory/articles/1997/02972_cover.htm

This article, by Robert Benjamin Smith, details Major General Zachary Taylor's actions at the Battle of Buena Vista in 1847. It includes a full account of the events of the battle, along with a map.

Uncle Sam: An American Autobiography

http://xroads.virginia.edu/~CAP/SAM/home.htm

The American Studies program at the University of Virginia has created this site to discuss the origin of this American icon. The forgotten origin of Uncle Sam during the War of 1812 is placed alongside his evolution as a symbol and national icon, including his official adoption and standardization by the State Department in the 1950s.

Uncle Tom's Cabin

http://xroads.virginia.edu/~HYPER/STOWE/stowe.html

The American Studies program at the University of Virginia provides an e-text of Harriet Beecher Stowe's 1852 novel.

The Valley of the Shadow

http://jefferson.village.Virginia.EDU/vshadow2/

Edward L. Ayers, a history professor at the University of Virginia, has developed this massive archive of primary sources that concern the experiences of Franklin County, Pennsylvania, and Augusta County, Virginia, in the years just preceding the Civil War. These two counties were separated by the Mason-Dixon line. The document archive includes newspapers, letters, diaries, photographs, maps, church records, population census, agricultural census, and military records. Students can research and write their own histories from the documents provided. The project is primarily intended for secondary schools, community colleges, libraries, and universities. This research will be available in CD-ROM form from W.W. Norton Publishers.

Virginia Resolution (1798)

http://odur.let.rug.nl/~usa/D/1776-1800/constitution/virg1798.htm

This was James Madison's Republican response to the Federalist's Alien and Sedition Acts. In it he advances the state-compact theory, which argued that the federal government could operate only within its constitutionally defined limits.

Virginia Statute for Religious Freedom (1786)

http://civnet.org/resoures/teach/basic/8.htm

This act was drafted by Thomas Jefferson and passed by the Virginia legislature in 1786. It served as the precedent for the religious freedom article in the Bill of Rights.

War of 1812

http://www.army.mil/cmh-pg/books/amh/amh-06.htm

This is a discussion of the war, from *American Military History* (chapter 6). This e-text is sponsored by the Army Historical Series, Office of the Chief of

Military History, United States Army. The war is presented as an outgrowth of the Napoleonic Wars. The major battles are narrated in detail, as are comparisons of American and British military capabilities and strategies.

What to the Slave is the Fourth of July

http://douglass.speech.nwu.edu/doug_a10.htm

This speech was given by Frederick Douglass on July 5, 1852. See earlier in this section, Douglass's speech made the day before in Rochester, New York, entitled, "The Hypocrisy of American Slavery."

Woman of Iron

http://www.thehistorynet.com/AmericanHistory/articles/0495_text.htm

"In 1825 Rebecca Lukens took over her late husband's iron mill. The company still thrives—A Testament to the Management Abilities of this Pioneering Woman CEO." This article by Joseph Gustaitis, sponsored by the History Net.

THE CIVIL WAR

Jim E. Jolly

METASITES

The American Civil War

http://homepages.dsu.edu/jankej/civilwar/civilwar.htm

Created by Jim Janke of Dakota State University, this site is an excellent place to begin one's search for American Civil War materials. The page is extremely well-organized into a wide variety of categories and subcategories that are frequently updated.

The American Civil War, 1861–65 World Wide Web Information Archive

http://www.access.digex.net/~bdboyle/cw.html

This site contains links to a wide variety of Civil War–related materials, such as books, documents, orders of battle, reenactment groups, and other historic preservation groups. It even contains e-text versions of Lincoln's First and Second Inaugural Addresses.

The American Civil War Home Page

http://sunsite.utk.edu/civil-war/

The American Civil War Home Page is another excellent place to begin one's search. It contains links to photographic collections, regimental histories, reenactors, and a host of other materials.

The United States Civil War Center

http://www.cwc.lsu.edu/

The United States Civil War Center, located at Louisiana State University, is dedicated to promoting the study of the Civil War. It has assembled an impressive collection of over 2,400 links to Civil War sites. In addition the page contains online documents, tips for tracing one's Civil War ancestors, and links to reenactors and vendors.

General Sites

African-American Civil War Memorial

http://www.afroamcivilwarmemorial.org/

This site contains a host of information about the African-American Civil War Memorial. It contains information about the design and location of the memorial, a photo gallery of the project, and links to African-American Civil War sites.

American Civil War

http://scholar2.lib.vt.edu/spec/civwar/cwhp.htm

Created by the Special Collections Department of the Virginia Libraries at Virginia Tech, this page offers access to a wide variety of letters and diaries of both Union and Confederate soldiers.

Battle Summaries

http://www2.cr.nps.gov/abpp/battles/tvii.htm#sums

Organized either by state or campaign, this site provides Civil War battle summaries. It also contains preservation information and links to the National Park Service.

Battlefield Medicine in the American Civil War

http://members.aol.com/cwsurgeon0/indexJ.html

Battlefield Medicine in the American Civil War contains a wide variety of information related to medicine in the Civil War. Copies of battlefield reports, eyewitness accounts, and even a copy of General Orders No. 147, which organized the Ambulance Corps in 1862, are included.

Captain Richard W. Burt Civil War Letters from the 76th Ohio Volunteer Infantry

http://www.infinet.com/~lstevens/burt/

This site, managed by Larry Stevens, includes the letters, poems, and songs of Richard W. Burt of the 76th Ohio Volunteer Infantry, as well as a copy of the 76th's recruiting ad.

Civil War Diaries at Augustana College Library

http:://sparc5.augustana.edu/library/civil.html

This page contains two diaries from Illinois soldiers during the Civil War.

Civil War Diary and Letters of David Humphrey Blair

http://netnow.micron.net/~rbparker/diary/index.html

This site, managed by Robert B. Parker, consists of the diary and letters of David Humphrey Blair, a soldier with Company D of the 45th Ohio Volunteers.

Civil War Diary of Bingham Findley Junkin

http://www.iwaynet.net/~lsci/junkin/

This site contains the diary entries of Private Bingham Findley Junkin of the 100th Pennsylvania Volunteer Infantry from March 1864 to June 1865.

The Civil War History of John Ritland

http://www.radiks.net/jritland/

This page consists of the narrative of the life of John Ritland, who served with the 32nd Iowa Infantry from 1862 until 1865.

Civil War Letters

http://home.pacbell.net/dunton/SSDletters.html

This site includes a well-indexed collection of twelve letters written by Private Samuel S. Dunton of the 114th New York Infantry written between 1862 and 1865.

Civil War Live

http://library.advanced.org/2873/data/ref/

This page presents a timeline, essay outlining causes, and biographical sketches of both Union and Confederate generals.

Civil War Manuscripts at the Southern Historical Collection

http://ils.unc.edu/civilwar/civilwar.html

This site contains a small collection of eleven Union and Confederate letters written between 1861 and 1865. With two exceptions all the letters come from the eastern theater of the war.

Civil War Resources Virginia Military Institute Archives

http://www.vmi.edu/~archtml/cwsource.html

Virginia Military Institute's Civil War Resource page includes twenty-three different online manuscript collections. The two most famous of these are the Stonewall Jackson Papers and the Matthew Fontaine Maury Papers. Matthew Fontaine Maury was an oceanographer, Confederate States Navy Commander, and served on the VMI faculty. In addition to his Civil War service, topics include his career at the National Observatory in Washington, D.C., colonization efforts in Mexico, and his professorship at the VMI.

Civil War Sites in the Shenandoah Valley of Virginia

http://www2.cr.nps.gov/abpp/shenandoah/svs0-1.html

This site provides a comprehensive study of the battlefields in the Shenandoah Valley. In addition to summaries the site contains information on the historical context, preservation, and heritage tourism.

Civil War Soldiers and Sailors System

http://www.itd.nps.gov/cwss/

This project is an attempt to build a database of basic information about all those who served in the war.

Civil War Women

http://odyssey.lib.duke.edu/collections/civil-war-women.html

This page offers online information about an archival collection at the Special

Collections Library at Duke University. The collection consists of the Rosie O'Neal Greenlow Papers, Alice Williamson Diary, and the Sarah E. Thompson Papers. It also contains links to other sites containing primary sources related to women and the Civil War.

Dwight Henry Cory Letters and Diary

http://homepages.rootsweb.com/~lovelace/cory.htm

This site contains a collection of letters written by Dwight Henry Cory of the 6th Ohio Volunteer Cavalry.

Elmira Prison Camp Online Library

http://www.innova.net/~vsix/elmiradoc1.htm

This site presents information about the Elmira Prison Camp, a Union POW camp located in New York.

The John Freeman Diary

http://www.public.usit.net/mruddy/freeman.htm

This site contains the diary of John Henderson Freeman, who served with Company I of the 34th Mississippi Volunteers.

Edward G. Gerdes Civil War Home Page

http://www.insolwwb.net/~egerdes/

This is a good resource for those interested in Arkansas during the Civil War. It includes lists of Confederate cemeteries, burial lists, regimental rosters, and Cherokee Confederate units.

H-Civwar

http://h-net2.msu.edu/~civwar

This site is part of H-Net and contains a discussion list of the Civil War, as well as links to other sites. Eventually the page will also offer links to conferences, grants, and bibliographies.

The Iowa Civil War Site

http://www.iowa-counties.com/civilwar/

The Iowa Civil War Site discusses Iowa in the Civil War. It includes letters, diaries, unit histories, and photos.

Letters from an Iowa Soldier in the Civil War

http://bob.ucsc.edu/civil-war-letters/home.html

This page, by Bill Proudfoot, contains some letters of Private Newton Robert Scott of the 36th Infantry, Iowa Volunteers.

Letters of the Civil War

http://www.geocities.com/Pentagon/7914/

This site presents a variety of letters from many different sources. Individuals are encouraged to submit letters that they might have for posting to the site. It also contains photos and diaries.

Overall Family Civil War Letters

http://www.geocities.com/Heartland/Acres/1574/

Presented at this site are the letters of Isaac Overall, a private with Company I of the 36th Ohio Volunteer Infantry. The letters were written between 1862 and his death in 1863.

Pearce Civil War Documents Collection

http://www.nav.cc.tx.us/lrc/Homepg2.htm

Navarro College houses this Web site, which consists of a variety of letters, documents, and diaries.

Poetry and Music of the War Between the States

http://www.erols.com/kfraser/

This site contains wartime and postwar poetry and music from both Union and Confederate sources.

The Role of Women in the Civil War

http://www.glue.umd.edu/~cliswp/History/Cwar/

Sponsored by the University of Maryland at College Park, this site includes an online essay about the role of women in the Civil War. The essay contains links to brief biographical sketches of individuals and organizations.

Secession Era Editorials Project

http://history.furman.edu/~benson/docs/

The Secession Era Editorials Project is sponsored by Furman University. Currently the project provides editorials related to four pre–Civil War events: the Nebraska Bill, Dred Scott, Harpers Ferry, and the caning of Charles Sumner. Eventually the project plans to include a complete run of editorials from the major political parties.

Selected Civil War Photographs

http://rs6.loc.gov/cwphome.htmlhttp://lcweb2.loc.gov/ammem/cwphome.html

Part of the American Memory project of the Library of Congress, this site presents over 1,100 photographs, most of which were taken by Matthew Brady. It includes a searchable database, subject index, and links explaining more about Civil War photography.

The Shenandoah 1863 Civil War Museum

http://www.fortunecity.com/victorian/museum/63/index.html

This page contains profiles of Civil War leaders, pictures of battle flags, campaign and battlefield maps, and a list of sources one can use for further research.

Society for Online Civil War Research

http://www.cwresearch.org/

This site includes an online e-text collection of out-of-print books, letters, pictures, book reviews, essays, and an interactive tour of Fort Morgan, which was built to protect Mobile Bay in Alabama.

Ulysses S. Grant Association

http://www.lib.siu.edu/projects/usgrant/

This site, supported by Southern Illinois University, presents information on Grant's military service, an online version of his personal memoirs, and photographs.

U.S. Colored Troops

http://www.itd.nps.gov/cwss/usct.html

Contains a database of over 230,000 names of individuals who served in the United States Colored Troops (USCT). Developed in part by the National Parks Service, this page also contains links to other NPS sites, as well as the African American Civil War Memorial Web page.

The U.S. Navy in the Civil War: Western Theater

http://www.webnation.com/~spectrum/usn-cw/

Created by Gary Matthews, this site includes chronologies, maps, eyewitness accounts, and images of vessels.

Valley of the Shadow Project

http://jefferson.village.virginia.edu/vshadow2/

A Virginia Center For Digital History project, the original Valley of the Shadow Project has now been released on CD-ROM. Currently the project is in its second phase, adding to its original collection of primary documents, images, sounds, and discussions. Part One of the Valley of the Shadow Project is titled "The Eve of War." Part Two deals with the same communities but concerns itself with "The War Years."

Vermont in the Civil War

http://www.geocities.com/Pentagon/1861/vt-cw.htm

This site attempts to document Vermont's participation in the conflict. It contains an index of over 32,000 names of those who served in the war, letters, brief biographies of individuals who served, and a cemetary database of over 3,000 names.

THE GILDED AND PROGRESSIVE AGE

Kenneth R. Dvorak

METASITES

American Memory

http://lcweb2.loc.gov/ammem

Established by the Library of Congress, this Web site is an excellent research Web source providing search features, printed, film, and photographic indexes on all topics related to American history.

America in the 1890s: A Chronology

http://www.bgsu.edu/~wgrant/1890s/america.html

Created by the American Culture Studies Program at Bowling Green State

University, this site provides a thorough examination of the 1890s using a timeline of the decade as its guide. Directed by Dr. William E. Grant, the site uses student contributions to expand and update this Web site on a continuing basis.

Populism

http://www.boondocksnet.com/centennial/index.html

Produced by linkWorld, this collection of Populist topics with related research links is a through examination of Populism. The site contains topical, biographical, and political links that detail the rise of Populism and its appeal to Americans living in the nineteenth century but also shows its cultural influence throughout the twentieth century.

Sentenaryo/Centennial: The Philippine Revolution and Philippine-American War

http://www.boondocksnet.com/centennial/index.html

Produced by Syracuse University historian Jim Zwick, this is an extensive and highly recommended Web site devoted to understanding the cultural and political impact of the Philippine Revolution and the 1898 Philippine–American War. The site includes photographs and essays on a variety of topics relating to the clash of American and Philippine cultures.

The West

http://www.pbs.org/weta/thewest/wpages/wpgs000/w010_001.htm

Based on the film documentary, *The West*, directed by Ken Burns (of PBS Civil War fame), this is a highly recommended Web site for those searching for information on the American West. Part of this site is an extensive timeline with research links detailing historical events occurring from 1890–1900.

The World's Columbian Exposition: Idea, Experience, Aftermath

http://xroads.virginia.edu/~MA96/WCE/title.html

The 1893 World's Columbian Exposition, held in Chicago, Illinois, was the signature event of the decade. This very professional Web site, created and maintained by Julie K. Rose of the University of Virginia, presents the Exposition for today's audiences in a virtual format. This Web site provides a history of the fair, a virtual tour, written reactions by visitors to the fair, the Exposition's historical and cultural legacy, and an extensive bibliographic resource page.

Historical Figures: Presidents of the Era

White House

http://www.whitehouse.gov/WH/glimpse/presidents/html/presidents.html

This site specifically deals with information concerning the presidents of the United States. Managed by the Executive Office staff of the President, citizens and students can obtain full-text inaugural speeches, information about individual Presidential libraries, Presidential First Ladies, and links to other relevant sites.

Ulysses S. Grant, 1869–77

http://www.mscomm.com/~ulysses/page152.html

This is an exceptional and award-winning Web site created by Webmaster Candace Scott. It contains information about Ulysses S. Grant's family history, his early childhood, and his life as private citizen, father, husband, soldier, general, and as president. This is an extremely important historical resource on a very controversial historical figure.

Rutherford B. Hayes, 1877–81

http://www.rbhayes.org/

The Rutherford B. Hayes Presidential Library is the first presidential library in the United States, located in Fremont, Ohio. This Web site provides information on Hayes's service during the Civil War, his personal papers and diaries, and presidential papers. The Hayes Center also contains information on Ohio Civil War soldiers and is sponsored in part by the Ohio Historical Society.

James A. Garfield, 1881

http://www.whitehouse.gov/WH/glimpse/presidents/html/jg20.html

Chester A. Arthur, 1881–85

http://www.whitehouse.gov/WH/glimpse/presidents/html/ca21.html

Grover Cleveland, 1885–89 and 1893–97

http://www.rain.org/~turnpike/grover/Timeline.html

The Grover Cleveland timeline provides a complete picture of Cleveland as

President and private citizen. This site was produced by Josh Smith of Dos Pueblos High School in Santa Barbara, California. Individuals can examine photographs, speeches, family history, and bibliographic sources about Cleveland. This Web site also includes additional links for Cleveland and the tumultuous era in which he lived.

Benjamin Harrison, 1889–93

http://205.185.3.2/presidents/nbk/bios/23pharr.html

One of the more interesting sites concerning the life of Benjamin Harrison is this contribution provided by Harrison Elementary School, Cedar Rapids, Iowa. It provides basic information on the life of President Harrison and a link to William Henry Harrison, this country's ninth president, and his grandfather. The second Web resource is produced by the Grolier Encyclopedia Company. This site offers extensive links and information concerning Benjamin Harrison and his presidency.

William McKinley, 1897–1901

http://www.history.ohio-state.edu/projects/mckinley/

An excellent source for the era of William McKinley is this Web site produced by Ohio State University's History Department. This Web resource Web page is particularly well-suited for students seeking information on Ohio politics, such as Mark Hanna, McKinley's infamous political campaign manager. The site also contains information on McKinley as president, the Spanish–American War of 1898, and political cartoons and photographs of the period.

Creating Industrial America

American Memory

http://lcweb2.loc.gov/ammem

Established by the Library of Congress, this Web site is an excellent research Web source providing search features, printed, film, and photographic indexes on all topics related to American history.

Andrew Carnegie (1835–1919)

http://www.clpgh.org/exhibit/french1.html
http://www.pbs.org/wgbh/pages/amex/carnegie/

Andrew Carnegie: A Tribute to the Reading Blacksmith is an excellent Web site providing information on the true-life rags to riches story of industrialist and philanthropist Andrew Carnegie. Sponsored by the Carnegie Library of Pittsburgh in association with Common Knowledge: Pittsburgh, this ambitious Web site contains photographs and audio links detailing Pittsburgh's history and culture. The second Web resource is titled "The Richest Man in the World: Andrew Carnegie," a companion site for PBS's The American Experience. The site includes extensive materials on Carnegie, his personal philosophies, timelines, and an in-depth analysis of the Homestead Steel Strike of 1892.

John D. Rockefeller (1839–1937)

http://voteview.gsia.cmu.edu/entrejdr.htm

Created and produced by Professor Keith T. Poole, Professor of Politics and Political Economy and Research Director, Carnegie Mellon University, this site demonstrates the capabilities of adopting the Internet for historical instruction. The site details the rise of Rockefeller as an industrialist, the creation of Standard Oil and his role as public philanthropist.

J. Pierpont Morgan (1837–1913)

http://www.jpmorgan.com/CorpInfo/History/overview.html
http://nyyc.org/Heritage%20Series/Morgan.htm

Morgan is perhaps the most admired, hated, and despised figure in American financial history. Heading J.P. Morgan and Company, his firm became the most influential financial center in America, helping to finance the capital needed for the burgeoning post–Civil War American economy. This site, sponsored by the J.P. Morgan Company, provides a brief history of its founder and a history of the firm. The second Web site, sponsored by the New York Yacht Club, showcases J.P. Morgan enjoying one of his many private pursuits.

Industrial Conflict in an Industrializing Age

Haymarket Square (1886)

http://cpl.lib.vic.edu/004chicago/timeline/haymarket.html

The Haymarket Massacre: An Internet Memorial, sponsored by Netizen, is an interesting Web site tracing the events leading up to the Haymarket Square tragedy. This Web resource site contains a chronology, autobiographies, daily life, and the status of Chicago labor in the 1880s.

Homestead, Pennsylvania (1892)

http://trfn.clpgh.org/sihc/1892.html

Sponsored by the Steel Heritage Institute, this excellent Web site traces the history of the Homestead Strike, detailing with it the rise of the American Steel Industry. This Web resource site contains photographs, maps, songs, stories, and online journeys through the steel mills and mill towns of Western Pennsylvania.

The Pullman Palace Car Strike (1894)

http://metalab.unc.edu/spc/articles/5.94.html

This essay, written by author J. Quinn Brisben, chronicles the social and economic background that is associated with the Pullman Palace Car strike. This confrontation typified the nineteenth century's attitudes by business and government toward the presumed threats by organized labor.

Inventors for a New Age

Bell, Alexander Graham (1847–1922)

http://www.fitzgeraldstudio.com/html/bell/default.html
http://www.pbs.org/wgbh/pages/amex/technology/telephone/

This outstanding Web resource site produced by Fitzgerald Studios traces the life of Alexander Graham Bell, inventor of the telephone and speech teacher. The site contains biographical information about Bell, his humanitarian efforts, and his role as inventor. Interestingly the site also contains a QuickTime Movie with directions on downloading this useful utility for those wishing to hear and see Alexander Graham Bell. The second Web resource site is a companion site to the PBS American Experience production titled "Technology in America: The Telephone," an excellent Web source detailing how technology has changed American life and culture.

Edison, Thomas A. (1847–1931)

http://www.tir.com/~quincy/index.html

Thomas Edison's Boyhood Home Page, sponsored and produced by the Port Huron, Michigan Museum of Arts and History, is an excellent start for individuals wanting to know more about what a *New York Times* poll reported was "The Greatest Living American" of his time. This Web site includes Edison's family history, Edison the boy, archaeological searches of his boyhood home, and charming stories surrounding the mythology surrounding Edison's youth.

Sears, Richard Warren (1863–1919)

http://ernie.bgsu.edu/~wgrant/1890s/sears/sears.html

This excellent Web resource site traces the rise of the Sears Roebuck Company and its founder, Richard Warren Sears. Written by Lori Ligget, a Ph.D. candidate in Bowling Green State University's American Culture Studies Program's Web project "America in the 1890s: A Chronology," offers substantial information concerning the impact mass merchandising had on Gilded Age American culture.

Wanamaker, John (1838–1922)

http://www.srmason-sj.org/council/journal/3-mar/lavender.htm

This Web site provides a thorough narrative on the life and times of Philadelphian John Wanamaker, known as "America's Greatest Merchant." Produced by *Scottish Rite Journal*, the site includes photographs and an interesting link to the "Friends of the Wanamaker Organ, Inc." a group interested in preserving the style and substance of the turn-of-the-century department store in all its lavish formats and decorations.

Wright, Frank Lloyd (1867–1959)

http://www.wam.umd.edu/~stwright/FLWr/index.html

Considered one of America's greatest architects, Wright became world renowned for his stunning private residences and dramatic public buildings. This excellent Web resource site provides extensive knowledge of Wright's life, work, and legacy to American architecture.

Literary Writers; Philosophers; Social Activists

Addams, Jane (1860–1935)

http://nlu.nl.edu/ace/Resources/Addams.html

Produced by the Continuing Education Department of Louis-National University, this excellent narrative essay chronicles the life of social reformer Jane Addams. This Web resource site contains an extensive bibliography, a good beginning for those wishing to learn more about this famous settlement-house pioneer.

Anthony, Susan B. (1820–1906)

http://www.graceproducts.com/anthony/life.html

Susan B. Anthony, regarded as the foremost leader in the early women's rights movement in the United States, advocated that women be given the right to vote and stressed the importance of economic independence for women as a means toward emancipation. "In Search of Heroes: The Susan B. Anthony Story," produced by Grace Products Corporation, is an excellent Web resource site, providing information on Susan B. Anthony's life, other women suffragettes, and the history of the American suffrage movement.

Bryan, William Jennings (1860–1925)

http://incolor.inetnebr.com/dennis/populist.shtml

Under the rubric "Populist History," those interested in the charismatic William Jennings Bryan will discover an excellent list of Web resources on "The Great Commoner." The collection includes biographical information, speeches, songs, and links to the motion picture *Inherit the Wind*, based on the Scopes Monkey trial of 1925.

Crane, Stephen (1871–1900)

http://www.geocities.com/Paris/Metro/5014/crane.htm
http://www.americanliterature.com/RBC/RBCINDX.HTML

Crane is best remembered for his works *Maggie: A Girl of the Streets* (1893) and *The Red Badge of Courage* (1895). Two Web sites: one, sponsored by GeoCities, provides a brief biography, excerpts from *Maggie*, and additional links detailing Crane's literary career. The second site, sponsored by American Classics Library, provides an entire online publication of *The Red Badge of Courage*.

Debs, Eugene (1855–1926)

http://douglass.speech.nwu.edu/appr_a82.htm

Eugene Debs, labor organizer and socialist, worked tirelessly on behalf of American laborers. Long a leader of the American Railroad Union, he led the strike against the Pullman Company of Chicago in 1893, resulting in his arrest and imprisonment for union organizing. The Northwestern University School of Speech provides an interesting Web site containing three essays in praise of Debs and his meaning to labor and the socialist movement.

DuBois, W.E.B. (1868–1963)

http://www-unix.oit.umass.edu/~cscpo/db.html

This Web link resource page, produced by Colin S. Covell, a University of Massachusetts political science major is an excellent Web resource for those seeking online information about W.E.B. DuBois. DuBois is considered the leading African-American intellectual of the twentieth century and a man consumed with seeking economic, social, and political justice for African-Americans. He wrote tirelessly about the African diaspora, especially in his book *Souls of Black Folk* (1903).

Jewett, Sarah Orne (1849–1909)

http://sites.unc.edu/storyforms/pointedfirs/

Known as a "regionalist" because her writings captured the flavor of her native New England, Sarah Orne Jewett is most remembered for her *The County of the Pointed Firs* (1896). Produced by Storyforms, Pedagogy, and Digital Composition Group from the Department of English, University of North Carolina, this is an excellent use of online literature complemented by the ability of the reader to interact with the text of Jewett's story.

Jones, Mary Harris (Mother) (1837–1930)

http://www.mojones.com/info/maryharris.html

Mother Jones was a popular labor organizer working on behalf of the United Mine Workers of America. She was a free-ranging spirit speaking out against social and political injustices that she felt were damaging American society.

Muir, John (1838–1914)

http://www.sierraclub.org/john_muir_exhibit/

John Muir became America's first conservationist and activist for the preservation of wildlife and forest areas, in doing so he became revered and reviled for his efforts. This informative Web site explores the life of John Muir and provides extensive links chronicling his life and contributions.

Randolph, A. Philip (1889–1979)

http://www.pbs.org/weta/apr/

This excellent Web resource site is a companion site to the film documentary titled "A. Philip Randolph: For Jobs and Freedom." Randolph is perhaps the foremost civil rights and labor activist of his era, supporting what he called "the common man" and African-American workers in particular.

Turner, Frederick Jackson (1861–1932)

http://www.pbs.org/weta/thewest/wpages/wpgs400/w4turner.htm
http://longman.awl.com/history/primarysource_17_3.htm

The American historian Frederick Jackson Turner presented his "frontier thesis" at the American Historical Association's 1893 meeting, thereby setting the stage for rethinking America's past. Turner's thesis influenced an entire generation of historians, but most importantly how Americans came to view themselves and their past. This first Web site, sponsored by The West Film Project and PBS station WETA, offers a brief overview of Turner's life and impact on American historians; the second site, sponsored by American History Online, presents the entire "frontier thesis" as presented by Turner.

Twain, Mark (1835–1910)

http://etext.lib.virginia.edu/railton/about/mtabout.html

This is a very ambitious work-in-progress Web site organized by Stephen Railton and the University of Virginia Library. The stated goal of "Mark Twain in His Times" is to provide the Web reader the experience of encountering Twain in his own time and place. Featured on the site are online texts, piloting lessons, student projects, archived texts, bibliographies, and featured links about Mark Twain.

Whitman, Walt (1819–92)

http://lcweb2.loc.gov/wwhome.html

Author of *Leaves of Grass* (1855), Whitman is best known for a remarkable collection of observations about American life, history, politics, geography, occupations, and speech. The American Memory Web page is an excellent source for everything concerning the enigmatic Whitman, his life, and writings.

Willard, Francis (1839–98)

http://www.wctu.org/Frances.htm

Francis Willard was another of the dynamic women living and working during the Gilded Age. Long a champion of women's rights, she dedicated her life to elevating the status of women. She was one of the founding members of the Women's Temperance Christian Union. Sponsored by the modern-day WCTU, this informational Web site provides biographical information about Willard, the history of the WCTU, and the 1873 Women's Crusades.

American Expansionism in the Gilded Age: Manifest Destiny and the Spanish American War of 1898

"The World of 1898"

http://lcweb.loc.gov/rr/hispanic/1898/

This Library of Congress Web site titled "The World of 1898" provides excellent source materials, especially documenting the people and places that factored into the fighting of the war.

The Spanish–American War Centennial Web Site

http://www.spanam.simplenet.com

The Spanish–American War Centennial Web site is an ambitious site detailing the military campaigns of American forces fighting the Spanish and American War. This extensive Web resource includes a chronology of the war; bibliographic sources; background of the Cuban Revolution of 1895–98; eyewitness reports written by protagonists of both sides; the role of the American press in promoting the war; music written about the war; and links to events, exhibits, and Rough Rider activities.

Sentenaryo/Centennial: The Philippine Revolution and Philippine-American War

http://www.boondocksnet.com/centennial/index.html

Sentenaryo/Centennial: The Philippine Revolution and Philippine–American War, produced by Syracuse University historian Jim Zwick, is an extensive Web site devoted to understanding the cultural and political impact of the Philippine Revolution and the Philippine–American War. The site includes photographs and essays on a variety of topics relating to the clash of these two cultures.

Topical Issues

African-Americans

http://wimall.com/pullportermu/
http://www.scsra.org/~scsra/library/porter.html
These first two Web resources chronicle the courage of African Americans

ing as Pullman Porters during the heyday of American railroad travel. The third research site provides an extensive list of links devoted to African-American history and culture.

Joplin, Scott (1868–1917)

http://www.lsjunction.com/people/joplin.htm
http://www.scottjoplin.org/

Considered the Father of Ragtime Music, Joplin was a popular figure within the African-American community. Each of these Web sites traces the evolution of Joplin's career and the continuing popularity of ragtime music.

Supreme Court: Plessy v. Ferguson (1896)

http://ernie.bgsu.edu/~wgrant/1890s/plessy/plessy.html

In 1892 Homer Plessy, an African-American, refused to sit in a separate railroad car mandated by the state of Louisiana, which in 1890 adopted a law proclaiming "equal but separate accommodations for the white and colored races." Thomas Zimmerman, of Bowling Green State University, provides analysis of *Plessey v. Ferguson*, noting that the Supreme Court's decision in Plessey to enforce social segregation under the "separate but equal" doctrine of the Constitution withstood scrutiny until the 1954 *Brown v. Board of Education* ruling declared it unconstitutional.

Vaudeville

http://personal.nbnet.nb.ca/muldrew/
http://www.bestwebs.com/vaudeville/

Before television, radio, and movies, there was Vaudeville! The first Web site contains a wealth of information on this popular turn-of-the-century entertainment medium. The second Web site presents an online "live" vaudeville show open twenty-four hours a day!

Asian Americans

http://www.geocities.com/CapitolHill/Senate/7715/ahistory1.html

This very thorough timeline provides pertinent information on the history of Japanese and Chinese immigration to the United States and the cultural, social, political, economic, and legal barriers these individuals have encountered living in American society.

Native Americans

http://ernie.bgsu.edu/~wgrant/1890s/woundedknee/WKIntro.html

Created by Lori Liggett of Bowling Green State University, this descriptive and informative Web resource page details the Wounded Knee Massacre and the developments associated with The Ghost Dance Religion.

THE AGE OF ROOSEVELT

Andrew E. Kersten

METASITES

American Memory

http://lcweb2.loc.gov/ammem

This Web site is maintained by the Library of Congress and ought to be the first site visited for anyone interested in American History.

New Deal Network

http://newdeal.feri.org

The Franklin and Eleanor Roosevelt Institute sponsors this Web site, which is the starting point for all issues, historical figures, and events about the Age of Roosevelt.

HISTORICAL FIGURES

Herbert C. Hoover

President Herbert C. Hoover Presidential Library

http://www.hoover.nara.gov

The Hoover Presidential Library and Museum constructed this Web site that contains information on his presidency, education modules, and research guides to both the Hoover Presidential Papers and the papers of Rose Wilder Land and her mother, Laura Ingalls Wilder. Rose Wilder wrote one of the first biographies of Hoover, published in 1919. This site, which is the best place to start for topics on Hoover, is updated weekly and has links to related sites.

White House—Herbert Hoover

http://www.whitehouse.gov/WH/glimpse/presidents/html/hh31.html

Maintained by the White House staff, this page has biographies of the President and the First Lady, Lou Henry Hoover, with links to the text of President Hoover's inaugural address and to the Hoover Presidential Library.

Huey P. Long

Every Man a King

http://www.ssa.gov./history/huey.html

Constructed by the Social Security Administration, this site contains excerpts from Long's autobiography, *Every Man a King,* published in 1933.

My First Days in the White House

http://www.ssa.gov./history/hueywhouse.html

The Social Security Administration also maintains this page, in which one can find excerpts from all eight chapters of Long's 1935 book, *My First Days in the White House.*

Franklin D. Roosevelt

FDR Cartoon Archive

http://www.nisk.k12.nx.us/FDR

At this award-winning site, constructed by Paul Bachorz of Niskayuna High School in Niskayuna, New York, one can find an extensive collection of over 30,000 FDR cartoons taken from newspapers and magazines during the 1930s and 1940s. There are also links to other Web sites, suggestions for schoolteachers, and Roosevelt's inaugural addresses.

Franklin D. Roosevelt Presidential Library

http://www.academic.marist.edu/fdr

Created by the staff of the Roosevelt Presidential Library, this site provides short biographies of the president and the First Lady. Additionally, the site contains several guides to the collections at the Roosevelt Presidential Library. Increasingly the Library is putting documents online. Now accessible is a collection of several thousand documents from the White House safe files during the Roosevelt years. Finally, there is an exceptional, copyright-free, online photograph database.

White House—FDR

http://www.whitehouse.gov/WH/glimpse/presidents/html/fr32.html

The White House staff maintains this site, which contains short biographies of Franklin and Eleanor Roosevelt. There are links to the texts of FDR's inaugural addresses.

Anna Eleanor Roosevelt

Eleanor Roosevelt Resource Page

http://personalweb.smcvt.edu/smahady/ercover.htm

This is a wonderful place to start any Internet search relating to ER. The site, authored by Sherry S. Mahady, contains biographical and bibliographical information, quotes from scholars and peers, documents from ER's column, newspaper articles, letters from her papers and the National Archives, video clips, and links to other sites with information, pictures, and documents pertaining to Eleanor Roosevelt.

Eleanor Roosevelt Val-Kill Center

http://www.ervk.org

Val-Kill was Eleanor Roosevelt's cottage along the Hudson River. The Val-Kill Center's purpose is "to preserve Eleanor Roosevelt's home as a vibrant living memorial, a center for the exchange of significant ideas and a catalyst for change and for the betterment of the human condition." The Center maintains this page to provide information on ER and some photographs of her. There is an extensive list of useful links to topics and issues concerning Eleanor.

Eleanor Roosevelt: The American Woman

http://www.geocities.com/CollegePark/Library/4142/index.html

Created by Deborah K. Girkin, this excellent site contains extensive biographical and bibliographical information, documents, pictures, cartoons, and links to other sites on ER. Another good place to start a search on Eleanor Roosevelt.

The Great Depression

American Memory: FSA-OWI Photographs

http://lcweb2.loc.gov/ammem/fsowhome.html

American Memory is maintained by the Library of Congress and is a wonderful Web site for all topics in American history and has thousands of primary sources that relate to the Age of Roosevelt. This particular location contains over 50,000 (including 1,600 in color) Farm Security Administration and Office of War Information photographs covering the years 1935 to 1945.

New Deal Network

http://newdeal.feri.org

The New Deal Network, sponsored by the Franklin and Eleanor Roosevelt Institute, maintains this awarding-winning Web site, which is the best place to begin any Internet search for documents, photographs, Web links, modules for teachers, and information on organizations that relate to the Age of Roosevelt.

African Americans and the New Deal

http://newdeal.feri.org/texts/subject.htm

This location is part of the New Deal Network and contains dozens of documents relating to African Americans and the New Deal.

The Shenandoah Chapter of the Civilian Conservation Corps

http://pages.prodigy.com/reunion/ccc.htm

The Shenandoah Chapter of the CCC—an organization of former agency workers, scholars, and interested people—maintains this site, which contains some pictures, stories, poetry, and links to other sites concerning the CCC.

National Association of CCC Alumni

http://www.cccalumni.org

The National Association of CCC Alumni's home page has poems, news articles, periodicals, and useful links to secondary school resources, CCC museums, and other related sites.

Dust Bowl Refugees in California

http://www.best.com/~sfmuseum/hist8/ok.html

The Museum of the City of San Francisco maintains a Web page on California history that has this section on Dust Bowl refugees. It contains primary sources and photographs.

The Voices from the Dust Bowl (American Memory)

http://lcweb2.loc.gov/ammem/afctshtml/tshome.html

This page is a part of American Memory and contains oral histories, photographs, and dozens of other primary documents relating to the Dust Bowl.

New Deal Art in South Carolina

http://people.clemson.edu/~hiotts/index.htm

This online exhibit of New Deal art in South Carolina, maintained by Susan Giaimo Hiott, has art from the state and links to New Deal art in other states, topics about the Age of Roosevelt, and exhibits from other libraries and museums. A visit to this page is worthy even if South Carolinian art is not one's primary topic.

A New Deal for the Arts

http://www.nara.gov/exhall/newdeal/newdeal.html

The National Archives and Records Administration maintains a Web version of this exhibit. The page has several good examples of New Deal art in various forms, including painting, photographs, and posters.

"Scottsboro Boys" Trials

http://www.law.umkc.edu/faculty/projects/ftrials/scottsboro/scottsb.htm

This location is part of the larger Famous American Trials Web site created by Doug Linder. The page on the Scottsboro Boys contains a short history, biographical and bibliographical information, photographs, and trial documents.

Social Security Administration

http://www.ssa.gov/history

The United States Social Security Administration built this page, which contains oral histories, video and audio clips, documents, photographs, brief biographies, and guides to the Social Security Administration archives.

Supreme Court Decisions

http://supct.law.cornell.edu/supct/

The Legal Information Institute and Cornell University sponsor this Supreme Court decisions Web site, which is an excellent place to gain quick access to decisions from the Wagner Act to Japanese Relocation. The site also contains general information on the Supreme Court.

Works Progress (later Projects) Administration (WPA) Folklore Project and Federal Writers Project

http://rs6.loc.gov/wpaintro/wpahome.html

This American Memory site has several thousand WPA folklore and federal writers projects representing over 300 authors from twenty-four states.

WPA's California Folk Music Project

http://lcweb2.loc.gov/ammem/afccchtml/cowhome.html

This American Memory Web site includes sound recordings, still photographs, drawings, and written documents from a variety of European ethnic and English-speaking and Spanish-speaking communities in Northern California. The collection comprises thirty-five hours of folk music recorded in twelve languages representing numerous ethnic groups and 185 musicians. This collection is well-documented and easy to use.

WPA Murals and Artwork from Lane Technical High School Collection

http://www.lanehs.com/art.htm

Maintained by Flora Doody, the director of Lane Technical High School's Artwork Restoration Project, this site has several fine examples of WPA artwork, including eleven frescoes, two oil on canvas murals, an oil on steel fire curtain, two mahogany carved murals, and two concrete cast fountain statues. The site also contains artwork created for the General Motors Exhibition at The Century of Progress, Chicago's World Fair (1933–34).

WORLD WAR II HOME FRONT

German Prisoners of War in Mississippi

http://www2.netdoor.com/~allardma/powcamp2.html

Mike Allard's site has minimal text but some interesting pictures of German prisoners at the Clinton, Mississippi, P.O.W. camp.

Japanese-American Internment (Resource Page for Teachers)

http://www.umass.edu/history/internment.html

The History Institute at the University of Massachusetts at Amherst sponsors this site, which is perhaps the best place to start searching for material on the internment of the Japanese-Americans. Well-organized and with dozens of Web links to documents, pictures, and related camp information, this site, designed for K-12 teachers, provides rich primary sources for classroom curricula.

Japanese-American Internment and San Francisco

http://www.sfmuseum.org/war/evactxt.html

This site, maintained by the Museum of the City of San Francisco, contains dozens of newspaper articles about Japanese-American removal, photographs (including those by Dorothea Lange), contemporary accounts, and related information about internment.

Japanese-American Internment at Harmony

http://Faculty.washington.edu/mudrock

The University of Washington Libraries created this Web page, which contains primary source material, including letters, the camp newspaper, drawings, pictures, and other documents. It is a useful place to begin an Internet search about internment and one should consult the next three entries in order to compare Harmony with other camps.

Japanese-American Internment at Manzanar (National Park)

http://monte.mvhs.srvusd.k12.ca.us/~mleck/man/Default.html

Mark Leck and Doug Lockett maintain the Web page, which has a brief history of Manzanar with a photo gallery. It is a good place to begin work on Manzanar and has a useful list of related links.

Japanese Internment Camps During the Second World War

http://www.lib.utah.edu/spc/photo/9066/9066.htm

This online photograph exhibit, sponsored by the University of Utah Special Collections Department, displays a sampling of the library's collections concerning the internment of Japanese Americans, particularly at the Topaz and Tule Lake camps.

Japanese-American Internment in Arizona

http://www.library.arizona.edu/images/jpamer/wraintro.html

This exhibit, directed by Roger Myers of the University of Arizona, has maps, photographs, primary documents such as the text of Executive Order 9066, and poetry.

NARA Powers of Persuasion

http://www.nara.gov/exhall/powers/powers.html

The National Archives and Records Administration maintains this page, which has thirty-three war posters and one sound file. The page is divided into two categories representing the two psychological approaches used in rallying public support for the war.

Northwestern WWII Propaganda Poster Collection

http://welles.library.nwu.edu/govpub/collections/wwii-posters/

Northwestern University Library's Government Publications division maintains this site. It has a searchable database of 300 wartime posters.

Office of War Information Photographs

http://lcweb2.loc.gov/ammem/fsowhome.html

This site contains thousands of photographs of the home front taken for the Office of War Information during the war years. It is part of the American Memory project maintained by the Library of Congress.

Rhode Island Women During World War II

http://www.stg.brown.edu/projects/WWII_Women/tocCS.html

Students at South Kingstown High School conducted interviews with twenty-six women to document their experiences during World War II.

Rutgers World War II Oral History Project

http://history.rutgers.edu/oralhistory/orlhom.htm

The Rutgers World War II Oral History project was funded by the Rutgers class of 1942 and directed by G. Kurt Piehler. Several dozen oral histories from veterans and civilians are available for download (in Adobe Acrobat format).

San Francisco During World War II

http://www.sfmuseum.org/1906/ww2.html

Yet another site maintained by the Museum of the City of San Francisco. It has information about San Francisco during the war years. Most of the primary sources on this site come from the *San Francisco News*.

THE COLD WAR

Margaret M. Manchester

American Experience: Race for the Superbomb

http://www.pbs.org/wgbh/pages/amex/bomb/

PBS companion site explores a top secret U.S. Cold War program to build a weapon more powerful than the atomic bomb dropped on Japan. This site includes audio clips, a timeline, primary documents, and other educational materials.

The American Experience/Spy in the Sky

http://www.pbs.org/wgbh/pages/amex/u2/u2.html

This companion site to the American Experience episode dealing with the U-2 incident is a good introductory Web site for K-12 students seeking basic information about the U-2 spy cameras, including aerial photographs taken from the stratosphere and schematics of the U-2 planes. Brief biographical sketches of pilots Gary Powers and Kelly Johnson are also provided.

The Avalon Project: Documents in Law, History, and Diplomacy

http://www.yale.edu/lawweb/avalon/coldwar.htm

Maintained by the Yale University Law School, this site contains basic documents relating to: American Foreign Policy 1941–49; the United States Atomic Energy Commission proceedings in the Matter of J. Robert Oppenheimer; The Warsaw Security Pact: May 14, 1955; State Department Papers Relating to the Foreign Relations of the United States Vol. X, Part 1 1958–60; the U-2 Incident: 1960; the RB-47 Airplane Incident: July–September 1960; and the Cuban Missile Crisis.

The Berlin Airlift

http://www.wpafb.af.mil/museum/history/postwwii/ba.htm

This Web site is part of the larger online exhibit entitled, "U.S. Air Force Museum, Post-WWII History Gallery 1946–50s." The focus is primarily military. The site is a good source of information and images of the aircraft used to airlift provisions to the inhabitants of Berlin.

The Berlin Wall

http://userpage.chemie.fu-berlin.de/BIW/wall.html

This Web site is provided by the City of Berlin. It contains a brief background, with information on the construction of the Wall and its fall. The site also contains links to images of the Berlin Wall Memorial, artistic responses to the rise and fall of the Berlin Wall, and links to other sites containing further information.

Chronology of Russian History: The Soviet Period

http://www.departments.bucknell.edu/russian/chrono3.html

The Bucknell University history department maintains this chronology of Soviet history from 1917 until 1991. The chronology contains numerous links to primary and secondary source materials that provide further information and background.

CNN-Cold War

http://cnn.com/SPECIALS/cold.war/

This Web site was created to accompany the twelve-part series on the Cold War airing on CNN in the winter and spring of 1998–99. The Web site is a valuable resource because it provides an extraordinary diversity of materials, including multimedia and audio clips, interactive maps, primary documents, newspaper and journal coverage of the events, and transcripts of interviews that formed the basis for the series.

Cold War Hot Links: Web Resources Relating to the Cold War

http://www.stmartin.edu/~dprice/cold.war.html

David Price, an anthropologist at St. Martin's College in Lacey, Washington, has compiled an impressive list of links to Web sites that contain both primary sources as well as essays and analyses examining the impact of the Cold War on American culture.

Cold War International History Project

http://cwihp.si.edu/default.htm

The Cold War International History Project (CWIHP) Web site was established at the Woodrow Wilson International Center for Scholars in Washington, D.C., in 1991. The project supports the full and prompt release of historical materials by governments on all sides of the Cold War. In addition to Western sources, the project has provided translations of documents from Eastern European archives that have been released since the collapse of communism in the late 1980s. Users may join discussion groups and download issues of the *Bulletin* issued by CWIHP.

The Costs of the Manhattan Project

http://www.brook.edu/FP/PROJECTS/NUCWCOST/MANHATTN.HTM

These estimates were prepared by the Brookings Institute and are part of the larger U.S. Nuclear Weapons Cost Study Project.

The Cuban Missile Crisis

http://www.msstate.edu/Archives/History/Latin_America/crisis.html

Located at the Historical Text Archive at Mississippi State University, this site contains excellent links to primary source materials, as well as a bibliography from the U.S. Army, essays evaluating the significance of the crisis and the continuing "lessons of the past."

The Cuban Missile Crisis

http://www.state.gov/www/about_state/history/kenxi.html

This is the site for Volume XI of *Foreign Relations of the United States*, which is the official U.S. Department of State volume of documents dealing with the Cuban Missile Crisis. The entire volume can be read online or one can read excerpts. A very important source for the official documents dealing with this crisis.

The Cuban Missile Crisis, 1962

http://www.fas.org/irp/imint/cuba.htm

The FAS, the intelligence resource program of the Federation of American Scientists, maintains this metasite. It contains links to online State Department documentation, analysis of Kennedy's advisors, the photographic evidence, transcripts of ExComm deliberations, and photographic evidence of the Soviet presence in Cuba until the 1980s.

The Cuban Missile Crisis, 1962

http://www.seas.gwu.edu/nsarchive/nsa/cuba_mis_cri/cuba_mis_cri.html

This Web site contains a brief historiographical essay, a timeline, and photographs (including aerial views) from the John F. Kennedy Library.

The Cuban Missile Crisis, October 18–29, 1962

http://www.hpol.org/jfk/cuban/

This Web site contains audio files of a set of tape recordings released by the John F. Kennedy Library in October 1996. These recordings were made in the Oval Office. They include President Kennedy's personal recollections of discussions, conversations with his advisors, and meetings with the Joint Chiefs of Staff and members of the president's executive committee. Transcripts of the audio files are included. A rich source of information on the American perspective of the crisis.

Documents Relating to American Foreign Policy: The Cold War

http://www.mtholyoke.edu/acad/intrel/coldwar.htm

The International Relations Program at Mount Holyoke College maintains this Web site. Broken down on a yearly basis from pre-1945 to recent retrospectives on the meaning and significance of the Cold War, this site contains hundreds of links to both primary and secondary source materials—especially useful to students and researchers because of the variety of sources available.

Documents Relating to American Foreign Policy: Cuban Missile Crisis

http://www.mtholyoke.edu/acad/intrel/cuba.htm

This collection of links allows researchers and students access to newspaper coverage of the crisis. The Web site also contains important links to information relating to Soviet and Cuban perspectives on the crisis. Links to essays and books by the most influential historians of this crisis are also provided.

Famous American Trials: Rosenbergs Trial, 1951

http://www.law.umkc.edu/faculty/projects/ftrials/rosenb/ROSENB.HTM

Professor Douglas Linder of the University of Missouri–Kansas City School of Law created this site. The Web site contains links to a wealth of first-hand materials, including excerpts from the trial transcript, the judge's sentencing statement, excerpts from appellate court decisions, images, the Rosenbergs' final letter to their sons, and a link to the Perlin Papers, a collection of about 250,000 pages that relate to the investigation, trial, and execution of Julius and Ethel Rosenberg. The papers were declassified in the 1970s.

Fifty Years from Trinity

http://www.seattletimes.com/trinity/supplement/internet.html

The *Seattle Times* compiled this list of Internet resources relating to the development of the atomic bomb and nuclear energy.

For European Recovery: The Fiftieth Anniversary of the Marshall Plan

http://lcweb.loc.gov/exhibits/marshall/

An excellent online exhibit prepared by the Library of Congress. The site contains primary and secondary source materials. The site also links to materials on the Marshall Plan that were developed by the Koninklijke Bibliotheek (the National Library of the Netherlands), and other European libraries.

Harvard Project on Cold War Studies (HPCWS)

http://www.fas.harvard.edu/~hpcws/

This annotated set of links to sites relating to the study of the Cold War is prepared and maintained by the Davis Center for Russian Studies at Harvard University. The project intends to build on the achievements of the Cold War International History Project and the National Security Archive. The site also contains links to Harvard University's new *Journal of Cold War Studies*.

The History of the Berlin Wall in Text and Pictures

http://members.aol.com/johball/berlinwl.htm

This site was an entry in the Connecticut state competition for National History Day on May 10, 1997. It is a great resource for K-12 students to begin to explore the history of the wall.

The Hungarian Revolution, 1956

http://www.osa.ceu.hu/events/TenYears/Links.htm

Links are provided to both English-language and Hungarian resources, both primary and secondary.

The National Security Archive Home Page

http://www.seas.gwu.edu/nsarchive/

The National Security Archive is an independent nongovernmental research institute and library located at The George Washington University in Washington, D.C. The archive collects and publishes declassified documents acquired through the Freedom of Information Act (FOIA). The archive boasts the world's largest nongovernmental library of declassified documents, including thousands of documents relating to nuclear history, U.S.–Japanese relations, the Cuban Missile Crisis, and other crises of the 1960s and 1970s.

1948: The Alger Hiss Spy Case

http://www.thehistorynet.com/AmericanHistory/articles/1998/0698_cover.htm

This links to a June 1998 *American History* article by James Thomas Gay that examines the Alger Hiss Case and the issues that remain unresolved fifty years later.

Secrets of War

http://www.secretsofwar.com/

This is the companion site to the History Channel twenty-six part documentary series entitled *Sworn to Secrecy: Secrets of War*, which was aired in 1998. The site contains transcripts, links to maps, images, and other information relating to the history of espionage.

A Select Bibliography of the U-2 Incident

http://redbud.lbjlib.utexas.edu/eisenhower/u2.htm

This brief bibliography is located at the Dwight D. Eisenhower Presidential Library.

Senator Joe McCarthy: A Multimedia Celebration

http://webcorp.com/mccarthy/

This archive contains film and audio clips from Senator Joseph McCarthy's speeches and appearances on television.

Soviet Archives Exhibit

http://metalab.unc.edu/expo/soviet.exhibit/entrance.html#tour

The Library of Congress developed this online exhibit. Visitors to this site may browse images of documents from the Soviet archives. The two main sections of the exhibit are the Internal Workings of the Soviet System, and The Soviet Union and The United States. The section on postwar estrangement includes commentary on Soviet perspectives on the Cold War and on the Cuban Missile Crisis.

The U-2 Incident of 1960

http://www.yale.edu/lawweb/avalon/u2.htm

This Web site was developed by the Avalon Project at Yale University. It is a useful starting place to find the basic diplomatic documents, including the exchange of notes between the U.S. and Soviet governments, public statements by State Department officials, and the documentation maintained by the State Department in the Foreign Relations of the United States Series.

The Venona Project

http://www.nsa.gov:8080/docs/venona/venona.html

VENONA was the codename used for the U.S. Signals Intelligence effort to collect and decrypt the text of Soviet KGB and GRU messages from the 1940s. These messages provided extraordinary insight into Soviet attempts to infiltrate the highest levels of the U.S. Government. The National Security Agency has declassified over 3,000 messages related to VENONA and made them available at their home page.

TWENTIETH-CENTURY AMERICAN HISTORY
Scott Merriman and Dennis Trinkle

The American Experience—America 1900

http://www.pbs.org/wgbh/pages/amex/1900/index.html

This site looks at the PBS program of the same title, which detailed what life was like in 1900. The site includes a detailed description of the program, a teacher's guide, and a timeline.

American Memory Collection

http://memory.loc.gov/ammem/ammemhome.html

Over fifty collections and one million items are now online. Collections in twentieth-century history range from Baseball Cards to Voices from the Dust Bowl to Mapping the National Parks. Includes a frequently asked questions section and a "Today in History" section, which has links to related collections and sites. Includes information on future initiatives. A must-see for all interested in American History.

American Temperance and Prohibition

http://www.history.ohio-state.edu/projects/prohibition/

A good overview of the move toward prohibition in America. Presents biographies of key figures and an outline of the developments. Includes tables of data for alcohol consumption and beer production. Also has an excellent collection of cartoons.

Anti-Imperialism in the United States, 1898–1935

http://www.boondocksnet.com/ail98-35.html

This site looks at a variety of issues concerned with American Imperialism in the first third of the twentieth century. Presents many writings, including Rudyard Kipling's *The White Man's Burden* and numerous period cartoons. The U.S. intervention in Haiti and the Philippines, along with many writings on related subjects by William Jennings Bryan, are featured. A good site for both people interested in the period and teachers.

Apollo Lunar Surface Journal

http://www.hq.nasa.gov/office/pao/History/alsj/frame.html

This site examines the lunar landings of the Apollo missions. It includes many photographs and video clips, as well as summaries of the missions, checklists, crew lists, and crew biographies. Also presents summaries of each mission.

Broadcasting in Chicago, 1921–89

http://www.mcs.net/~richsam/home.html

This looks at sixty-eight years of broadcasting in America's Second City. Includes an examination of many of the programs aired in Chicago, including

"Amos n' Andy" and "Fibber McGee and Molly." A virtual tour of the studio facilities is also available.

Coal Mining in the Gilded Age and Progressive Era

http://www.history.ohio-state.edu/projects/Lessons_US/Gilded_Age/ Coal_Mining/default.htm

This site looks at coal mining in the late nineteenth and early twentieth centuries. It includes many pictures and reprints of stories from the period. Contains a discussion of the dangers of coal mining. A good site for those interested in coal mining of the period.

CIA and Assassinations: The Guatemala 1954 documents

http://www.gwu.edu/~nsarchive/NSAEBB/NSAEBB4/index.html

This site reproduces several primary sources dealing with the CIA's involvement in the 1954 coup in Guatemala, including the CIA's plan for assassination. A useful series of documents focusing on the darker side of our nation's past.

Coney Island

http://naid.sppsr.ucla.edu/coneyisland/

An engaging popular culture/history site done by a history buff trained in engineering. It discusses the amusement park, presents articles about its history, includes a timeline, links to related sites, and maps.

Detroit Photos Home Page from the Library of Congress

http://lcweb2.loc.gov/detroit/

This site, part of the American Memory Collection, looks at a collection of 25,000 glass negatives and transparencies. These photos were taken by the Detroit Photographic Company and show life at the turn of the century. Includes information on how to order reprints.

Digger Archives

http://www.bearbytes.com

This site is attempting to present the story of this anarchist counterculture group of the Sixties. Among this group's activities, centered in San Francisco, were street theater and free stores. The site presents the activities of the organization, pictures, and links to current related groups. An interesting look at an interesting group.

The Digital Classroom

http://www.nara.gov/education/

Presents classroom lessons utilizing resources available in the National Archives. Includes a documentary analysis sheet that helps one to analyze and work with documents—a vital resource. Also presents information for educators on how they can participate in summer development workshops. The heart of the site is a set of units—ten on the twentieth century alone—that use primary documents as teaching tools.

Documents from the Women's Liberation Movement

http://scriptorium.lib.duke.edu/wlm/

This site includes a large number of primary source materials on the women's liberation movement. Organized into categories, but one can also search by keyword. Includes links to related resources.

Early Motion Pictures, 1897–1920

http://memory.loc.gov/ammem/papr/ermphome.html

A large collection from the Library of Congress's American Memory Project. An excellent and very engaging site. Includes films of San Francisco around the time of the Great Earthquake and Fire of 1906, and films of New York around the turn of the century.

Edsitement

http://edsitement.neh.fed.us/

A good resource for teachers. Includes a large number of lesson plans for teaching any century of American History by using Web resources. Also provided are simple directions for those unfamiliar with the Web, including a glossary, commentary on the pluses and minuses of the Internet, and "Tips for Better Browsing." A very useful site.

Ellis Island

http://www.i-channel.com/features/ellis/

This site examines all aspects of the immigrant experience of coming through Ellis Island. Includes recipes and audio clips, as well as information on the ongoing Ellis Island Oral History Project. Also contains a historical overview, and information on the journey to America and the inspection process that occurred at Ellis Island.

Famous Trials of the Twentieth Century

http://www.law.umkc.edu/faculty/projects/ftrials/ftrials.htm

This site looks at many famous trials in the twentieth century, including the Rosenbergs, Leopold and Loeb, and the Scottsboro Boys. It also includes a few from before the twentieth century, including the *Amistad* case, the Salem Witch trials, and the Johnson Impeachment. A set of very well-done pages, which are generally very informative.

The Fifties

http://www.fiftiesweb.com/fifties.htm

Slightly celebratory look at the Fifties. Aimed at the Boomer generation (it even includes a claim to be "Boomer Enhanced" and thus have no small print). It includes music, TV, and a list of Burma-Shave slogans. An illuminating example of Fifties culture, though not very analytical.

Films: Research and Resources

http://www.gen.umn.edu/faculty_staff/yahnke/film/Default.htm

This site contains a great deal of resources to learn more about film. It includes a list of the top films of each decade with a commentary, and a list of good recent films. Also included here are a list, in the site author's opinion, of the best fifty-five films of all time, and a discussion of intergenerational issues. Although film is not commonly thought of as traditional history, this is a very good site to visit for anyone who loves the cinema and for those interested in a look at another side of history.

For European Recovery: The Fiftieth Anniversary of the Marshall Plan

http://lcweb.loc.gov/exhibits/marshall/

This site discusses the Marshall Plan, which rebuilt Europe after World War II. It presents a detailed chronology of the plan, and explains the reasoning behind it. It also presents excerpts from the book *The Marshall Plan and the Future of U.S. European Relations*, which contains documents from the twenty-fifth anniversary of the Marshall Plan. Presented by the Library of Congress.

The Emma Goldman Papers

http://sunsite.Berkeley.EDU/Goldman/

A good example of how a Web site can promote both primary research and general learning. This site presents an online exhibit about Goldman—a late nineteenth/early twentieth-century radical—along with a discussion of the holdings of the Emma Goldman papers. Includes examples from the collection, images, and moving pictures, as well as materials that could help students learn about Goldman. A good example of what an archive collection site should look like.

Guide to the Supreme Court

http://www.nytimes.com/library/politics/scotus/index-scotus.html

This site, from the *New York Times*, provides a good overview of the Supreme Court at the present time. Includes a list and short description of the "top ten" cases ever decided by the Court, and articles about the justices currently on the court, as well as excerpts from recent decisions.

A History of the White House

http://www.whitehouse.gov/WH/glimpse/top.html

This site, a subsite of the official White House site, contains biographies of every president, First Lady, and family that has lived in the White House. Also contains a history of the house and a virtual tour.

Kennedy Assassination Home Page

http://mcadams.posc.mu.edu/home.htm

The Kennedy Assassination Home Page is the most balanced and extensive online resource for exploring John F. Kennedy's death. It is maintained by John McAdams, a professor of political science at Marquette University. McAdams's list of links on the Kennedy assassination also offers the best gateway to serious and reliable materials.

Little Rock Central High School Fortieth Anniversary

http://www.centralhigh57.org/1957-58.htm

This site examines the events at Little Rock Central High School in 1957. Provides a timeline of the events concerning the integration and a look at the fortieth anniversary celebration in 1997. Contains pictures and videos.

Lower East Side Tenement Museum

http://www.wnet.org/archive/tenement/

An interesting museum for a Lower East Side tenement in New York City. This building had been sealed off for fifty years and so is exactly the way it was in 1935. The site also presents unique dollhouse diorama dramatizations depicting what life was like at the time, complete with descriptions and explanations. It also includes two QuickTime movies of rooms in the tenements, as they might have been in the 1870s and 1930s.

Mapping Urban Development in San Francisco

http://geo.arc.nasa.gov/esdstaff/william/urban.html

This site provides a "time series animation" of the growth of San Francisco from 1850 to the present. Also discusses the approach used.

National Archives

http://www.nara.gov/

Everything you wanted to know about the National Archives and Records Administration. Includes the National Archives Archival Information Locator (NAIL), which allows you to search for records. Also has an online exhibit hall, with examples of records available at the National Archives, including the Declaration of Independence, portraits of Black Chicago, and gifts given to presidents from Hoover to Clinton. A necessary stop for all wanting to ride the research train. Includes general information on grants, research facilities, records management, and the Federal Register. It must be noted that only a very few, percentage-wise, of NARA's four billion records are online, so this is both a good place to FIND material and to FIND how to FIND material.

NAACP Home Page

http://www.naacp.org/

This site primarily offers information about the current NAACP currently, but it also explores the NAACP's past and the struggles it has been involved in.

National Civil Rights Museum

http://www.midsouth.rr.com/civilrights/

This is the Web site of the National Civil Rights Museum, located in Memphis, Tennessee. The site discusses the museum, gives hours and other basic information, and summarizes the exhibits currently portrayed. Includes an in-depth interactive tour of the museum.

The 1920s: A Nation in Flux

http://www2.idsonline.com/jeff/index.html

A surface account of the decade. It contains a timeline, essays on the major events of the period, and an overview. Also includes links to related events.

Oyez, Oyez, Oyez

http://oyez.nwu.edu/

This site includes hours of audio of arguments before the Supreme Court of the United States. Also includes short biographies of each Supreme Court justice, both past and present, and pictures of the justices. Also, for some justices, it presents links to related resources, transcripts of decisions, and lists of selected cases they participated in.

The Population Bomb

http://www.pbs.org/kqed/population_bomb/

A look at Paul Ehrlich's book *The Population Bomb* and a PBS show on the book. The book's basic argument is that the world's population is exploding at an unsustainable rate, and that more developed countries put an overly large strain on the resource base. This is a favorable look at one of the more impor-tant ecology books of the twentieth century. Includes a population timeline.

Presidential Elections, 1860–1996

http://www.lib.virginia.edu/gic/elections/index.html

Contains popular and electoral returns for every election between 1860 and 1996. Includes links to related sites.

Presidential Libraries

http://www.nara.gov/nara/president/address.html

A very useful site for all doing research concerning twentieth-century presidents. All presidents from Hoover to Bush have presidential libraries, and this site con-tains addresses, phone, fax, and e-mail information, and links to specific sites for each library. Includes a very informative overview of the Presidential Libraries that explains the background of the system and answers basic questions.

Presidential Speeches

http://odur.let.rug.nl/~usa/P/

In addition to presidential speeches, this site includes brief presidential biographies and links to other resources. A good starting point to look for presidential addresses. This site focuses on State of the Union addresses and inaugural addresses.

Project Whistlestop

http://www.whistlestop.org/index.htm

An online examination of President Truman's actions. Includes an examination of the Truman Doctrine, the Marshall Plan, and the Berlin Airlift.

Retro

http://www.retroactive.com/

Web magazine discussing a variety of subjects, including politics, fashion, and music. Includes links to related Web sites and feature articles. Includes a community discussion board, and a vintage postcard depot, and one can send these vintage postcards to a friend.

Redstone Arsenal Historical Information

http://www.redstone.army.mil/history/welcome.html

A site dealing with all aspects of the U.S. Army's aviation and missile command. Includes oral histories, information on specific weapons programs, and chronologies of this command's history. Also presents declassified documents and a history of Werner von Braun.

Jonas Salk, Biography

http://www.achievement.org/autodoc/page/sal0bio-1

The site presents a biography of the developer of the polio vaccine, complete with pictures and the transcript of an oral interview with Salk.

Scopes Monkey Trial

http://www.law.umkc.edu/faculty/projects/ftrials/scopes/scopes.htm

Site relates to the 1925 trial in Dayton, Tennessee of John Scopes for teaching evolution. The trial loosely became the model for *Inherit the Wind*. Includes cartoons, part of the textbook used by John Scopes, and a discussion of *Inherit the Wind*. A very balanced and in-depth look at the case.

The Sixties

http://www.bbhq.com/sixties.htm

This is the sixties section of the Baby Boomer Headquarters. It includes a quiz to test your knowledge of the Sixties, a list of the events of the Sixties, a gallery of Sixties music, and reflections from a Baby Boomer.

The Sixties

http://www.geocities.com/SoHo/Studios/2914/

This is a general site on the Sixties. Includes biographies of some of the leading counterculture figures, quotations, the full text of Martin Luther King's "I Have a Dream" speech, and an in-depth timeline for the decade.

Skylighters

http://www.skylighters.org/

This is the official site of the 225th AAA Searchlight Battalion, and a great starting point for WWII resources. Includes a chronology of WWII, related links, and oral histories. Currently under construction.

The Time 100

http://cgi.pathfinder.com/time/time100/index.html

This is a list of the 100 most influential people of the century, as decided by *Time* magazine. It presents biographies of the 100, with links to related sites.

The Trial of the Century—The Lindbergh Case

http://www.lindberghtrial.com/index.htm

This site reminds us that the O.J. Simpson trial was not the trial of the century. This site presents an outline of the kidnapping and recaps the events of the trial. Includes a timeline to manifest historical context. It contains a wealth of pictures, both of people connected with the trial and with the period. Finally, it discusses what has happened since the trial with some of the main principles involved. Also contains links to related sites.

Trinity Atomic Web Site

http://www.enviroweb.org/enviroissues/nuketesting/index.html

This site presents a history of the development of atomic weapons, mostly focusing on the United States. Includes links to related sites. It presents documents, movies, and quotations, as well as an annotated bibliography.

Votes for Women

http://www.huntington.org/vfw/

A very good and comprehensive site on the women's suffrage movement presented by the Huntington Library. Includes biographies of important individuals and descriptions of the important organizations involved. Also presents a breakdown of the various eras in the movement. This site also appends a long list of related links.

Watergate

http://www.washingtonpost.com/wp-srv/national/longterm/watergate/splash1a.htm

This site, sponsored by the Washington Post, looks at the controversy and scandal that toppled President Richard Nixon. Includes a timeline and an examination of where key figures in the scandal are now. The site also discusses speculation on who "Deep Throat"—a key source for the reporters—was.

Women and Social Movements in the United States, 1830–1930

http://womhist.binghamton.edu/

While not wholly on the twentieth century, this is still a good site to explore for this issue. The co-directors of this project include Kathryn Kish Sklar, and it presents undergraduate and graduate student work, and includes related links. Projects of relevance for the twentieth century include: Workers and Allies in the New York City Shirtwaist Strike, 1909–10, Women's International League for Peace and Freedom, and Right-Wing Attacks, 1923–31. An interesting example of student work posted to the Web.

Writers and Their Works

http://www.pitt.edu/~englweb/writers.html

This examines some of the top nonfiction writers of the postwar era. Writers profiled include Hunter Thompson, Truman Capote, and Joan Didion. Includes links to related sites.

WOMEN'S HISTORY

Jone Johnson

4,000 Years of Women in Science

http://www.astr.ua.edu/4000WS/4000WS.html

This large collection of names, many with biographies, is ordered by field of study as well as alphabetically and in a timeline.

9,000 Years of Anatolian Woman

http://www.turknet.com/ninethousand/ninethousand1.html

Gunsel Renda's online illustrated exhibit, telling women's story on this peninsula from ancient times to modern Turkey.

Ninety-Six Years of Women in the Olympics

http://www.feminist.org/fmf/graphics/intro.html

History of women's sports plus great women athletes.

About.com Women's History

http://womenshistory.about.com

Site includes Web links on women's history topics, original articles, index of news stories on women's history, index of recent book reviews, women's quotes, an online forum, and occasional chats.

African-American Women

http://scriptorium.lib.duke.edu/collections/african-american-women.html

Manuscripts and texts from African-American women, focusing on the slave experience.

African-American Women Writers of the Nineteenth Century

http://digital.nypl.org/schomburg/writers_aa19/

The New York Public Library's index of online books by and about African-American women. Search by author, title, or category.

Amazon City Museum of Women in Science and Technology

http://www.amazoncity.com/technology/museum/index.html

Biographies of some famous women in science and technology.

American Women's History: A Research Guide

http://frank.mtsu.edu/~kmiddlet/history/women.html

This rich and well-updated resource includes bibliographies of print and Internet materials, helpful information for researchers, a subject index to research sources, and links to electronic discussion lists.

Anthony, Susan B.: Anthony's Rochester Home

http://www.susanbanthonyhouse.org/

Site includes information on this home, now a National Historic Landmark, and biographical information on one of the best-known American women.

Bible Passages on Women

gopher://dept.english.upenn.edu/11/Courses/Lynch3/Bible

Mostly Christian New Testament, some Hebrew Scriptures: passages on the role and status of women.

Biographies of Women Mathematicians

http://www.agnesscott.edu/lriddle/women/women.htm

Agnes Scott College students have written this large collection of biographies.

Celebration of Women Writers

http://www.cs.cmu.edu/People/mmbt/women/writers.html

Extensive collection of links to biographies and online books by women writers. Includes many international writers. Names and birth/death years for authors whose works and biography are not (yet?) online.

Civil War Women

http://odyssey.lib.duke.edu/collections/civil-war-women.html

Online primary sources for studying the lives of women during the American Civil War.

Diotoma: Materials for the Study of Women and Gender in the Ancient World

http://www.uky.edu/ArtsSciences/Classics/gender.html

One of the Web's best examples of how to make resources available online. Extensive range of topics. Primary sources, some in translation and some graphic images. Secondary sources include essays from a variety of other sites. Includes Biblical studies.

Distinguished Women of Past and Present

http://www.netsrq.com/~dbois/

Danuta Bois's collection of biographies of women. The biographies are generally short and basic. Includes searches by name and field of endeavor. Most biographies include a short bibliography for more information.

Documents from the Women's Liberation Movement

http://scriptorium.lib.duke.edu/wlm/

Texts and scanned images and documents from the 1969–74 U.S. Women's Liberation Movement. Flyers, pamphlets, and booklets provide a view into that energetic period of women's history.

Early Women Masters in Buddhism, Taoism, Shinto, and Zen

http://pages.nyu.edu/~sw4/RaihaiWomen.html

Essays and links for more information on women in Asian religions, focusing on China, Japan, and Tibet.

Early Music Women Composers

http://music.acu.edu/www/iawm/pages/

Sarah Whitworth's excellent site includes information on women composers and illustrations by contemporary women artists. Includes links and discography.

The Emancipation of Women 1750–1920

http://www.spartacus.schoolnet.co.uk/resource.htm

Hypertext site covering the history in Britain of women's rights. Biographies, short essays on related topics, bibliography, portraits.

Encyclopedia of Women's History

http://www.teleport.com/~megaines/women.html

By and for K-12 students, this collection of biographies was a school's project in women's history. (No longer associated with the school of its origin, and apparently no longer being updated.)

Famous American Women

http://www.plgrm.com/history/women/

A helpful index to notable women—no content here, just helpful formatted search engine links.

Feminist Collections: Quarterly of Women's Studies Resources

http://www.library.wisc.edu/libraries/WomensStudies/fcmain.htm

Online essays often include Web site reviews and information on how to study women's issues using Web resources.

First Ladies

http://www.firstladies.org/

Bibliographies and portraits of the wives of American presidents.

First Ladies of the United States of America

http://www2.whitehouse.gov/WH/glimpse/firstladies/html/firstladies.html

Part of the White House Web site, this collection includes biographies and portraits.

Gage, Matilda Joslyn

http://www.pinn.net/~sunshine/gage/mjg.html

Web site with biography and other information on this nineteenth century women's rights leader (and mother-in-law of *Wizard of Oz* author Frank Baum).

Gifts of Speech

http://gos.sbc.edu/

Archives of women's speeches that have influenced history or by famous women.

Godey's Lady's Book Online

http://www.history.rochster.edu/godeys

Godey's Lady's Book was a nineteenth century popular women's magazine whose articles and fashions helped shape the middle class American woman. A good resource for fashions, lifestyle research, and the articles and poetry.

Guide to Uncovering Women's History in Archival Collections

http://www.lib.utsa.edu/Archives/links.htm

A geographical listing of libraries with archival collections relating to women's history. Heavy on the United States, but also includes international collections, mostly in English-speaking countries.

H-Minerva

http://www.h-net.msu.edu/~minerva/

Focused on the study of women and war and women in the military in many eras. Site hosts a moderated discussion list, archives of discussions, conference and call-for-papers announcements, and book reviews.

H-Women

http://www.h-net.msu.edu/~women/

Directed to researchers, teachers, and librarians, this site hosts a moderated discussion list, archives of women's history syllabi, book reviews, bibliographies, and discussion threads.

Hawaii Women's Heritage

http://www.soc.hawaii.edu/hwhp/

Exhibits on the life of women in the history of Hawaii.

Hearts at Home: Southern Women in the Civil War

http://www.lib.virginia.edu/exhibits/hearts/

Images of manuscripts, letters, journals, and other documents showing the many aspects of life for Southern women. Includes topics from music, poetry, and religion to slavery, hard times, and war work.

Herstory: An Exhibition

http://library.usask.ca/herstory/

English and French site, honoring the history of Canadian women.

History of Ladies Magazines

http://www.workhouse.com/girls/american_lady/index.html

Women's magazines in the nineteenth and twentieth century targeted interests in fashion and the home. This series of pages (click on the image of the lady) include a timeline, images, and discussion of the history of these magazines.

History of the Suffrage Movement

http://www.rochester.edu/SBA/hisindx.html

The University of Rochester—near the site of the 1848 Seneca Falls Convention—with a history of women's suffrage in America, including a bibliography and links.

Images of Women in Prints from the Renaissance to the Present

http://www.lib.virginia.edu/dic/bayly/women/docs/home.html

Walk through an online exhibit from the Bayly Art Museum, and experience how women have been seen in history, through prints and contemporary writing.

Indiatime Women

http://www.indiatime.com/women/women.htm

Biographies of women in India's history as well as contemporary Indian women.

International Alliance for Women in Music Home Page

http://music.acu.edu/www/iawm/

Resources for women in music. Includes extensive modern resources and links to resources on historical women composers.

Jewish Women's Archive

http://www.jwa.org/main.htm

Current and archived exhibits, including photographs, essays, and transcriptions of letters and other primary sources.

Kassandra Project: Visionary German Women Around 1800

http://www.reed.edu/~ccampbel/tkp/

Bibliography and webliography, most notably of Karoline von Günderrode.

Legacy: Women in Religion

http://www.gtu.edu/Centers/cwr/legacy.html

Changes monthly: women's contributions to religious history.

Lesbian History Project

http://www-lib.usc.edu/~retter/main.html

Annotated links to print and Web resources for studying lesbian history. Many eras represented; also includes links for studying lesbians of color.

Living the Legacy: The Women's Rights Movement, 1848–1998

http://www.legacy98.org/

This site was designed for the 150th anniversary of the Women's Rights Convention at Seneca Falls, New York. The resources on the site are still valuable—with teaching and activism ideas, and an overview of 150 years of women's rights.

Madam C.J. Walker (1867–1919)

http://www.madamcjwalker.com/

Biography and photos of an African-American millionaire, inventor, and social activist.

Matrix: Resources for the Study of Women's Religious Communities

http://matrix.divinity.yale.edu/MatrixWebData/matrix.html

Profiles of individuals and communities ("monasticon"), an image library, a glossary, an index of secondary sources, and a bibliography. The search routine can be frustrating without a table of contents of the individual items.

Medieval Women

http://www.georgetown.edu/labyrinth/subjects/women/women.html

Georgetown's Labyrinth project lists key links for researching medieval women, including Hildegard of Bingen, Joan of Arc, and Julian of Norwich. Also points to good bibliographies.

Medieval Women Web Sites

http://www.library.wisc.edu/libraries/WomensStudies/fc/fcwebho.htm

Cynthia Ho, Amelia Washburn, and Tim Gauthier suggest and review key Web sites for studying medieval women's history.

National Museum of Women's History

http://www.nmwh.org

New U.S. women's history project presents online exhibits while working toward building its own. First exhibit: Political Culture and the Imagery of American Suffrage.

National Women's Hall of Fame

http://www.greatwomen.org/

This Seneca Falls, New York, museum Web site honors a woman each month and includes information on visiting the museum, a history of the museum, classroom educational activities, and an online catalog of books and gifts.

National Women's History Project

http://www.nwhp.org/

The organization behind Women's History Month, this site focuses on support for education on women's history, particularly at the middle and high school levels. Includes an online catalog of educational and promotional materials.

New York Public Library: Women's Studies/History Research Guide

http://web.nypl.org/research/chss/grd/resguides/womhist.html

A list of books available at the New York Public Library (and, usually, other libraries as well) on topics in women's history.

The Ninety-Nines

http://www.ninety-nines.org/bios.html

Women in aviation, including astronauts. Includes the story of thirteen women who qualified as American astronauts but were denied positions.

Notable Women Ancestors

http://www.rootsweb.com/~nwa/

Genealogical information on researching women ancestors. Site includes contributed essays on women, both famous and not.

Notable Women with Liberal Religious Connections

http://www.geocities.com/Wellesley/Garden/1101/

List of women with Unitarian, Universalist, Ethical Culture, and Free Religion connections, plus an annotated bibliography for those doing research on the topic.

The Shadow Story of the Millennium

http://www.nytimes.com/library/magazine/millennium/m2/index.html

Articles, images, audio, and forums: key issues in women's history in the last 1,000 years.

Social Studies: Women's History

http://www.socialstudies.com/c/@0/Pages/womenindex.html

Products, mostly for purchase, for teaching women's history from kindergarten through 12th grade. Some essays and some curriculum units (with reproducible master) are available without charge on the site.

Sources for Women's Studies in the Methodist Archives

http://rylibweb.man.ac.uk/data1/dg/methodist/methfem.html

A bibliographic essay on women in Methodist history.

Suffragists Oral History Project

http://library.berkeley.edu/BANC/ROHO/ohonline/suffragists.html

Online transcripts of interviews with twelve leaders and participants in the

U.S. Suffrage movement. Taped in the 1970s, it is now available for study of the Suffrage movement and its activists.

University Press Associates: Women's Studies

http://www.lexis-nexis.com/cispubs/guides/womens_studies/womens.htm

These guides to manuscript collections and other resources each detail historical information on aspects of women's history.

Victorian Women Writers Project

http://www.indiana.edu/~letrs/vwwp/vwwp-links.html

Links to journals, online projects on individual authors or related topics, syllabi, and related information.

Voice of the Shuttle: Gender Studies

http://vos.ucsb.edu/shuttle/gender.html

Extensive Webliography, including much of current interest as well as historical.

Votes for Women: Selections from the National American Woman Suffrage Association Collection, 1848–1921

http://lcweb2.loc.gov/ammem/naw/nawshome.html

From the U.S. Library of Congress, letters and other writings plus images from the collection donated by Carrie Chapman Catt.

What Did You Do In the War, Grandma?

http://www.stg.brown.edu/projects/WWII_Women/tocCS.html

High school students' oral history project, documenting women's roles in World War II. Excellent both as an information resource and as a model for a student project in women's history.

What Is Women's Studies?

http://www-unix.umbc.edu/~korenman/wmst/whatis.html

Introduction to the topic and its breadth of coverage.

What's New in Women's History?

http://xroads.virginia.edu/g/DRBR/gordon.html

Linda Gordon, women's historian, on the history and purpose of women's history.

The Witching Hours

http://www.goth.net/~shanmonster/witch/index.html

Resources on the witch-craze of Europe, 1100–1700 C.E.

Women and Social Movements in the United States, 1830–1930

http://womhist.binghamton.edu

The history of women in the United States is connected to the history of the social movements they founded and in which women developed and applied leadership skills. Student essays on a broad range of topics.

Women Come to the Front

http://lcweb.loc.gov/exhibits/wcf/wcf0001.html

Women journalists and photographers at the warfront in World War II. Primary sources—including newspaper and magazine articles and photographs—from the U.S. Library of Congress.

Women in America, 1820–1842

http://xroads.virginia.edu/~hyper/detoc/fem/home.htm

Selections from writings (letters, journals, books) of notable European travelers to early nineteenth-century America, excerpted to highlight their observations on women's lives.

Women in World History Curriculum

http://home.earthlink.net/~womenwhist/

Commercial site; extensive collection of curriculum materials on women in world history. Some sampler lesson plans free, and the essays and other materials will interest many researchers who are not teachers.

Women Mathematicians

http://www.agnesscott.edu/lriddle/women/women.htm

More than 100 biographies, with bibliographies of print and Web resources. Many have photographs.

Women Nobel Laureates

http://www.almaz.com/nobel/women.html

Women who have won the Nobel Prize for their contributions to science, peace, and literature.

Women of Africa Resources

http://www.lawrence.edu/fac/BRADLEYC/war.html

Bibliographies, links to essays, articles, and other material on African women, contemporary and historically.

Women Veterans

http://userpages.aug.com/captbarb/

"Captain Critical" presents a large collection of online material on women in the military. The site documents the role of women in American wars from the Revolution through today's news.

Women Writers of the Middle Ages

http://www.millersv.edu/~english/homepage/duncan/medfem/medfem.html

Biographies, primary sources in translation, essays, and other secondary sources on women's lives in the Middle Ages, bibliographies, and links to more sites. Author: Bonnie Duncan of Millersville University.

Women's Heritage

http://www.womensheritage.org/herstory/

Issues in the American struggle for women's rights, including the abolitionist connection and a contrast of white women's rights with Iroquois women's rights in 1848.

Women's History Resource Center

http://www.gale.com/schools/resrcs/womenhst/bios.htm

Gale Group, publishers of materials for libraries, presents an online sampler including more than eighty biographies of women.

Women's International Center

http://www.wic.org/

Web home of the Living Legacy award, with an extensive index of biographies, birthdate calendar, quotations, and basic overviews of women's history.

Women's Internet Information Network

http://www.undelete.org/

Irene Stuber's site, including more than 20,000 profiles of notable women.

Women's Legal History Biography Project

http://www.stanford.edu/group/WLHP

Biographies of more than 100 women lawyers and judges in American history.

Women's Life in Greece and Rome

http://www.uky.edu/ArtsSciences/Classics/wlgr/wlgr-privatelife.html

Documents, in translation, show the life of somen in ancient Greece and Rome.

Women's Studies Programs, Departments and Research Centers

http://research.umbc.edu/~korenman/wmst/programs.html

From the University of Maryland–Baltimore County, Joan Korenman's extensive list of women's studies programs—about half the list is programs in the United States, and the other half in other countries. Includes links to several other lists of such programs.

WORLD HISTORY

David Koeller

In choosing Web sites for the study of world history, I have focused on sites that are global or interregional in scope and especially those that focus on the interactions among regions of the world. I have not listed sites for individual regions, cultures, or countries. For those resources, look elsewhere in this book.

METASITES

NM's Creative Impulse

http://history.evansville.net/index.html

This is one of, if not the best, metasite for world history resources. While it is concerned mostly with the histories of various cultures, rather than with their interactions, this site provides links to many important resources on the Web. Maintained by Nancy Mantz for Harrison High School, Evansville, Indiana and for the University of Evansville. Of special note are the links for cultural resources, such as poetry, music, and drama, rather than just politics, religion, or philosophy.

World Culture

http://sun.kent.wednet.edu/curriculum/soc_studies/text/gr7.html

Maintained by Diana Eggers of the Kent School District, Kent, Washington, this site provides links to material for a seventh-grade world cultures course. The geographic distribution is quite good—it even includes material for Australia and Polynesia.

The World History and Information Links Page

http://www.historyoftheworld.com/

While strictly speaking this is not a world history site, it is a metasite that lists the nations of the world alphabetically and then provides links to Web sites related to those nations. Not all of the Web sites linked are historical, but it does provide a handy resource for investigating a particular nation or for developing a more comparative project.

The World History Compass

http://www.SchillerComputing.com/whc/index.htm

Like the "World History and Information Links Page," this is not, strictly speaking, a world history Web site since it is organized by region and nation, rather than interregionally or globally. Nevertheless, this metasite has such an extensive collection of links on such a wide range of subjects that anyone teaching or studying world history will find it useful. The site is maintained by Schiller Computing and serves as a way to draw customers to their online bookstore.

World History Links

http://www.milan.k12.in.us/ss10.htm

A metasite that features links to hundreds of Web sites. The links are organized to correspond to the Glencoe *World History, the Human Experience* textbook. It is maintained by the Milan, Indiana Community School Corporation.

ORGANIZATIONS AND JOURNALS

The *Journal of World-Systems Research*

http://csf.colorado.edu/wsystems/jwsr.html

The *Journal of World-Systems Research* is an electronic journal distributed free over the Internet. As the name suggests, it is "dedicated to scholarly research on the modern world-system and earlier, smaller intersocietal networks." World-system theory is one of the important approaches to the study of world history, and this Web site and journal are an important resource for learning about the latest scholarship in this field.

National Center for History in the Schools

http://www.sscnet.ucla.edu/nchs/

The National Center for History in the Schools has developed standards for World History in Grades 5–12. This site provides an online version of those standards. In addition, the Center also has samples from its sourcebook, *Bring History Alive!*, to help teachers meet these standards.

New England Regional History Association

http://www.hartford-hwp.com/nerwha/docs/mcneill.html

In addition to news of the association, this site is of interest for the collection of conference papers, including papers by William McNeil, H. Haines Brown, and others.

Studies in the World History of Slavery, Abolition, and Emancipation

http://www.h-net.msu.edu/~slavery/

This is an electronic journal for the global study of slavery. Edited by Patrick Manning, Northeastern University, and John Saillant, Massachusetts Institute of Technology.

United Nations Organization

http://www.un.org/

For those interested in world history, this Web site is particularly useful for its online databases and document collections. These include the United Nations Treaty Collection, social indicators for the nations of the world and official documents of the General Assembly, Security Council, and Secretary-General.

The World History Association

http://www.hartford-hwp.com/WHA/

The official Web site of the World History Association, the leading organization for world historians. It contains a series of links to many of the resources listed here, as well as a series of links to teaching resources, including course syllabi.

The World History Center at Northeastern University

http://www.whc.neu.edu/

The World History Center at Northeastern University is a "uniquely comprehensive institution, supporting basic and applied research, curriculum development, and institutional growth in world history." As a result of this broad mission, the center's Web site is an important resource for the study of world history. Among the resources are a series of bibliographies for secondary, college, and graduate study in history, reviews of world history textbooks, and the course syllabi used by the instructors at the center.

Teacher Resources

Dr. Silvestri's World History Resources

http://www.ancientworld.simplenet.com/

This site was designed for use in a ninth-grade world history course. The site consists of the instructor's lecture notes and supporting materials. As of this moment, the supporting material is still largely under construction. The lecture notes, however, are complete and provide some useful information. The graphics and layout of the page are quite well done.

H-World Home Page

http://www.h-net.msu.edu/~world/

This is the Web site for the H-World online discussion group. This discussion group, sponsored by the National Endowment for the Humanities and Michigan State University, has among its members leaders in the field of world history. This site is both an archive of the group's discussions and a resource for world historians. A search engine is available. Besides the discussion archives, the site includes course syllabi, bibliographies, and reviews of recent scholarship and teaching aids.

Introduction to World History

http://columbus.andrew.cmu.edu/projects/World_History/

This is the Web site for the World History course taught by Peter Stearns at Carnegie-Mellon University. Professor Stearns was one of the pioneers in the field of world history instruction and his textbook is still very popular. However, if you are already familiar with Stearns's text, you will not find much new here.

The World History Reader

http://www.wsu.edu:8080/~wldciv/world_civ_reader/

An advertisement for a now out-of-print world history reader, this site nevertheless has some useful excerpts from primary sources. The editor of the anthology is Paul Brians of Washington State University. While the translator is often mentioned by name, we are given little other information about the source of the translation. Many of the sources are taken from older translations, but some appear to have been done specifically for this analogy.

WORLD HISTORY TO BROWSE

BBC Online: Modern World History

http://www.bbc.co.uk/education/modern/

A very impressive site. To fully use the site's resources, you must have a Shockwave-enabled browser.

Fleet Gazelle

http://www.ojo.com/

Fleet Gazelle publishes a number of educational CD-ROMs and has three Web sites to advertise them. The first—and most relevant for the study of world history—is cultures.com, which features several short multimedia pieces mostly on pre-urban societies. The second, MesoWeb, is dedicated to the study of MesoAmerican cultures. Finally, MythWeb is devoted to Greek Mythology, but has some resources for teaching mythology. All three sites feature impressive graphics, animations, and extensive teacher guides.

The Gateway to World History

http://www.hartford-hwp.com/gateway/index.html

This is one of three sites maintained by Haines Brown. While not as extensive as some of the other metasites, it is well-integrated into the following two Web sites: World History Archives and Images from History.

World History Archives

http://www.hartford-hwp.com/archives/

This is the second site administered by Haines Brown. This archive centers on secondary sources for contemporary world history, mostly from the perspective of the left.

Images from History

http://www.hartford-hwp.com/image_archive/index.html

This is the third site in Haines Brown's series of world history resources on the Web. Originally housed in Hartford with his other two sites, this site is now housed in the University of Alabama and administered by Ed Kujawski. This is perhaps the most generally useful of the three sites. The images cover a much broader range of history both chronologically and geographically. Most are of quite good quality.

Hyper History

http://hyperhistory.com/online_n2/History_n2/a.html

This site shows the real potential for the Internet for teaching and studying history. The site consists of an image-mapped chronology of world history from prehistory to the present. The events listed on the chronology are then hyperlinked to a very brief description of the event. It is very good for visualizing the temporal relations between events in different parts of the world.

Twentieth-Century World History

http://www.cybe.edu.on.ca/hwt/

There are some brief overview essays on various topics for the course followed by a series of links to Internet resources. It was developed for use in Toronto District Schools for use in teaching advanced placement twentieth-century world history. It is maintained by Alan Kirkwood-Zahara. The site begins with a very useful guide to using the Internet and to evaluating Internet resources.

WebChron: The Web Chronology Project

http://www.northpark.edu/acad/history/WebChron/index.html

While there are many Web sites of chronologies, WebChron is unique in that it attempts to present a global chronology, that it uses hyperlinks to "nest" more detailed chronologies "inside" more general chronologies and that it describes many of the events using student-written articles. This "nesting" allows one to get a sense of how one period relates to another and how events in one region of the world correspond to events in other regions of the world. Because the articles are student projects their quality is uneven, but many are excellent.

Women in World History Curriculum

http://home.earthlink.net/~womenwhist/index.html

Developed by Lynn Reese to promote her "Women in World History Curriculum," for which this site is an advertisement, it provides some very useful resources for teaching about women in world history. Especially impressive is a page devoted to the role of women in the industrial revolution that shows—through the use of primary source material—the differences and inequities of the roles of men and women. On the other hand, the material on Confucianism and China should be used with caution. It consists of some "Confucius Says" snippets from various sources that are presented without context.

World Cultures: An Internet Classroom and Anthology

http://www.wsu.edu:8080/%7Edee/WORLD.HTM

One is first struck by the very impressive graphic presentation at this site. Then one is pleasantly surprised that the content is as good as the presentation. Developed by Richard Hooker of Washington State University for a course for first-year college students, the site integrates a world cultures text, written principally by Hooker, with primary source readings and links to other Web resources. While very impressive in its treatment of the cultures represented, the focus of the course and of the site is the development of these, not on their interaction. Nevertheless, this site is quite impressive.

AGRICULTURAL HISTORY AND RURAL STUDIES
Leo E. Landis

Agricultural Engineering Historic Landmarks

http://asae.org/awards/histcomm.html

The American Society of Agricultural Engineers has designated a number of significant places and machines, and this site includes summaries of these landmarks.

Agricultural History

http://www.public.iastate.edu/~history_info/aghistry.htm

This is the site for the editorial office of the academic journal *Agricultural History*. The site is updated quarterly and contains selected book reviews from the current and past volumes.

Agripedia Glossary

http://frost.ca.uky.edu/agripedia/glosfram.htm
http://frost.ca.uky.edu/agripedia/agrimain.htm (main site)

This is a good glossary of agricultural terminology for novices. These sites are part of a larger agriculture site developed by the University of Kentucky. (The glossary appears to have some navigation problems with the menu buttons in the upper frame.)

American Local History Network—Agriculture

http://www.rootsquest.com/~amhisnet/topic/ag.html

This site presents an extensive list of links related to agricultural history. The organization is exhaustive, but loosely arranged, and not all links are current.

Appleton's *Cyclopedia* of Applied Mechanics

http://www.history.rochester.edu/appleton/a/agmac-m.html

A limited online version of Appleton's *Cyclopedia* from the late nineteenth century is presented here, and the links offer primary source descriptions and images of selected agricultural machinery.

Books of The Kansas Collection

http://www.ukans.edu/carrie/kancoll/books

The site includes a number of public domain full-text documents relevant to agriculture of the Midwest and Great Plains.

Breeds of Livestock, Oklahoma State University Department of Animal Science

http://www.ansi.okstate.edu/breeds/

This site is based out of the Oklahoma State University's Animal Science Department. It contains a directory of common breeds of livestock in the United States, including historical background and images.

Directory of Rural Studies Scholars and Educators

http://www.nal.usda.gov/ric/ricpubs/scholars.html

Though not updated since the mid-1990s, this page is an excellent listing of more than 800 scholars with interests in American agriculture and rural studies. The site contains a subject and regional directory at the conclusion of the page.

"The Farmer's Wife"—"Frontline"

http://www.pbs.org/wgbh/pages/frontline/shows/farmerswife/

This "Frontline" program explored the life of the Boeschkoetter family and their struggle to maintain their marriage and their Nebraska farm in the late 1990s. The site contains a number of links related to American agricultural issues in the late twentieth century.

Glidden's Patent Application for Barbed Wire

http://www.nara.gov/education/teaching/glidden/wire.html

Part of the National Archives' initiative "Teaching With Documents," this site blends the history of technology and agricultural history in order to correlate with National Education Standards.

A History of American Agriculture, 1776–1990

http://www.usda.gov/history2/back.htm

This site, an online version of a U.S. Department of Agriculture poster, has been updated through the 1990s. The topics include milestones from U.S. agricultural history in the following categories: Economic Cycles, Farm Economy, Farmers and the Land, Farm Machinery and Technology, Crops and Livestock, Transportation, Agricultural Trade and Development, Life on the Farm, Farm Organizations and Movements, Agricultural Education and Extension, and Government Programs and Policy.

McCormick–International Harvester Company Collection

http://www.shsw.wisc.edu/archives/ihc/index.html

Nicely designed, though somewhat light on content, this site offers an introduction to one of the more significant archival collections for American agriculture.

National Agricultural Library

http://www.nalusda.gov/speccoll/

The National Agricultural Library holds volumes of significant materials. The Web site provides information on the research collections and visitor information. The Special Collections page and the homestead and steward links hold a selection of images.

North Carolina Agricultural History

http://www.agr.state.nc.us/stats/history/history.htm

One of the best, and maybe the only, state agricultural history on the Web. This site offers an excellent overview of agriculture in the upper American South, although it has little flexibility in navigation.

The Northern Great Plains, 1880–1920: Images from the Fred Hultstrand and F. A. Pazandak Photograph Collections

http://lcweb2.loc.gov/ammem/award97/ndfahtml/

The collections on this site offer unparalleled photographic documentation of rural life in North Dakota. The holdings are from the Institute for Regional Studies at North Dakota State University. The site is now part of the American Memory Project of the Library of Congress. The pages contain about 900 photographs, are well-designed, and load quickly. Visitors can also explore links that contain background and bibliographic information.

The Rice Museum, Georgetown, South Carolina

http://www.ego.net/us/sc/myr/rice/

An informative Web site on an oft-ignored American agricultural crop. The site contains a brief history of rice culture in the Low Country and a bibliography on Low Country life.

A Rural Studies Bibliography—U.S. Department of Agriculture

http://www.nal.usda.gov/ric/ricpubs/ruralbib.html

An online version of a 1994 publication from the USDA, the site is an extensive bibliography of 216 sources compiled by the National Rural Studies Committee. The citations are annotated and range from classics in agricultural history such as Paul Gates's *The Farmer's Age: Agriculture, 1815–1860* to sociological studies of rural America.

"Surviving the Dust Bowl—The American Experience"

http://www.pbs.org/wgbh/pages/amex/dustbowl/about.html

The Web site for the PBS program "American Experience." The site contains audio oral histories, teacher's guides, bibliographies, and other resources for educators.

Smithsonian: Agriculture and Horticulture

http://www.si.edu/resource/faq/nmah/agriculture.htm

A brief collection of links related to agriculture and horticulture hosted by the Smithsonian Institution.

"Troublesome Creek: A Midwestern Challenge—The American Experience"

http://www.pbs.org/wgbh/pages/amex/trouble/about.html

The Web site for this Sundance Film Festival award-winning documentary, which was broadcast on the PBS program "American Experience." The site contains photographs dating to the late nineteenth century and lesson plans for educators based on the program.

University of Saskatchewan, College of Agriculture— "History of Agriculture"

http://pine.usask.ca/cofa/displays/college/plains/history.html

A Canadian site from the University of Saskatchewan that offers a brief timeline and narrative for agriculture on the Canadian prairie.

HISTORY OF SCIENCE

Kalpana Shankar

GENERAL DIRECTORIES AND INDEXES

E-mail Forums and Web Sites

http://www.shef.ac.uk/~psysc/hpsss.html

This Web site, maintained by the library at the Center for Psychotherapeutic Studies at Sheffield University in the United Kingdom, contains subscription information for a number of listservs in the history of science, science as culture, and science, technology, and society studies. There are also several listservs listed that pertain to the history and philosophy of the social sciences. The rest of the page contains many Web sites of interest, but they are not well-organized or annotated.

History of Science on the World Wide Web

http://www.ou.edu/cas/hsci/rel-site.htm

This Web site is the work of the History of Science department at the University of Oklahoma. It contains links to many of the other resources listed here, as well as more libraries, archives, and research centers of note. However, there is no annotation or order to the list—apart from some very general top-level categories—but the list is small enough to scroll through. This site is useful for the number of links to subject indexes on the history of various scientific disciplines.

Horus' Web Links to History Resources

http://www.ucr.edu/h-gig/horuslinks.html

Horus is maintained and sponsored by the faculty of the University of California–Riverside's history department. The areas of specialization to date include history of science, technology, medicine, mathematics, public health, and technology. Numerous subdivisions within each category contain links to online texts, academic departments, and collections of resources. One weakness of this Web site is the lack of annotation. However, this is another good place to begin research.

H-MED-SCI-TECH

H-MED-SCI-TECH is a moderated and active listserv on any aspect of history of science, medicine, and technology. To subscribe to the History of Medicine, Science, and Technology listserv, send subscription information to: http://www.h-net.msu.edu/~smt/.

Internet History of Science Sourcebook

http://www.fordham.edu/halsall/science/sciencesbook.html#Islam

This page and other Internet History sourcebooks have been created and are maintained by Paul Halsall of Fordham University. Organized chronologically, Halsall provides teachers with links to public domain texts, commentaries, and other Web sites. His sections on Greco-Roman scientific philosophy and culture, science in Latin Christendom, and Islamic science are particularly strong; non-Western scientific topics are not well-represented, and there is little annotation. Nevertheless, this is a useful resource for undergraduate educators.

WWW Virtual Library History of Science, Technology, and Medicine

http://www.asap.unimelb.edu.au/hstm/hstm_ove.htm

Australian Tim Sherratt maintains this Virtual Library, online since 1994. One can access the categorized sites alphabetically or by scientific discipline, geographical region, and kind of resources (listserv, archive, etc.). The Web sites are briefly rated for depth, content, and design and often contain a brief editor's note. However, there is no indication of the audience for each Web site. Another weakness is a lack of resources on international areas of scientific history, apart from China, Australia, and Canada. However, this is a good place to begin one's research.

HISTORY OF ASTRONOMY

The Galileo Project

http://es.rice.edu:80/ES/humsoc/Galileo/

The Galileo Project is a hypertext source of information on the life and work of Galileo Galilei (1564–1642) and the science of his time. The project is supported by the Office of the Vice President of Computing of Rice University, and it represents the collective efforts of Drs. Albert Van Helden and Elizabeth Burr and their students.

The History of Astronomy Home Page

http://www.astro.uni-bonn.de/~pbrosche/astoria.html

This is the most extensive metasite for the history of astronomy. It is maintained on behalf of Commission 41 (History of Astronomy) of the International Astronomical Union and the Working Group for the History of Astronomy in the Astronomische Gesellschaft.

HISTORY OF BIOLOGY

CADUCEUS-L

CADUCEUS-L is a moderated electronic discussion list that provides a forum for exchanging information on any aspect of the history of the health sciences. To subscribe: Send the command sub caduceus-l [your name] to listproc@list.ab.umd.edu.

History of Biomedicine

http://www.mic.ki.se/History.html

This site, maintained at the Karolinska Institute in Sweden, is extremely thorough. Links are divided by categories, including extensive sections on traditional Indian, Chinese, and Islamic biomedicine. There are also links to resources on ethnobotany and pharmacognosy. Many of the links are extremely general (links to the Mahabharata, for example). The site does not have a search feature.

History of Medicine Division of National Library of Medicine

http://www.nlm.nih.gov/hmd/hmd.html

The National Library of Medicine, a division of the National Institutes of Health, maintains this Web site. The most important resource is HISTLINE, NLM's bibliographic index to literature published since 1965 in the history of medicine and related topics. It currently contains about 150,000 citations and is updated weekly. Another major resource is the searchable database of nearly 60,000 images from the print and photo collection of the Division. These images are digitized, but one can order high-resolution prints from the Division.

Natural History Caucus, Special Libraries Association

http://www.lib.washington.edu/sla/

The home page of the SLA Natural History Caucus is aimed at special librarians working in natural history museums and repositories, but there are useful resources for the historian as well. There is a hyperlinked, alphabetical list of natural history libraries around the world. However, these are not annotated. There is a similar list of natural history museums around the world, which is organized by geographical region. There are also hyperlinked lists of annotated bibliographies and other resources that are oriented to scientists.

HISTORY OF CHEMISTRY

CHEM-HIST

CHEM-HIST seeks to promote information and communication among historians of chemistry and of the chemical industry. To join send mail to MAISER@LISTSERV.NGATE.UNI-REGENSBURG.DE with the following command in the body of your message: subscribe CHEM-HIST.

Classic Papers in Chemistry

http://dbhs.wvusd.k12.ca.us/Chem-History/Classic-Papers-Menu.html

This Web site is maintained by ChemTeam and John L. Park, a high school chemistry teacher. Although many of the chemistry resources are aimed at educators and students, the Classic Papers section contains a growing list of historical works in chemistry (mostly excerpted). Unfortunately, it is not clear which papers have been excerpted and which sections have been removed.

Selected Classic Papers from the History of Chemistry

http://maple.lemoyne.edu/~giunta/papers.html

This page, maintained by Carmen Giunta at Le Moyne College, is a companion Web page to John Park's Classic Papers in Chemistry page listed above. There are more papers (although some links point to the ChemTeam site) and more annotations. The papers are divided by subject category, but there is no searchable index. Guinta notes when papers are excerpted. This Web site contains an extensive collection of papers, but there are some links that are unique to the ChemTeam Web site and are not cross-linked here.

HISTORY OF GEOLOGY

GeoClio: Webserver for the History of Geology and the Geosciences

http://geoclio.st.usm.edu/

This Web site has been in existence since the fall of 1995 and was created at the University of Southern Mississippi with the assistance of a grant from the National Science Foundation. The list of links is small and not annotated. Many of the links listed are quite broadly historical or scientific, but contain some resources of relevance to the history of geology.

HISTORY OF MATHEMATICS

L-MATH

L-MATH is a mailing list on the history and philosophy of mathematics and probability. To subscribe, send a message to l-math-request@math.uio.no.

The MacTutor History of Mathematics Archive

http://www-history.mcs.st-and.ac.uk/~history/index.html

This searchable Web site, maintained at the University of St. Andrews in Scotland, contains biographies of mathematicians of note (accessible chronologically or alphabetically), images, references, information on Famous Curves, bibliographies, and links to other resources. The generally informal tone of the site and the lack of primary references make this site more suitable for teaching purposes than for research.

Women in Mathematics

http://www.scottlan.edu/lriddle/women/women.htm

This Web site is part of an ongoing project of mathematics students at Agnes Scott College in Atlanta, Georgia. This resource is best for teachers and students in K-12. The biographical essays are fairly brief and contain some references and photographs.

HISTORY OF THE PHYSICAL SCIENCES

AIP Center for History of Physics

http://www.aip.org/history/

The American Institute of Physics has had a long history of promoting study of the history of physics. Their semiannual newsletter since 1994 is online and contains articles, announcements, reports on archival materials, bibliographies, and funding and conference opportunities. The Niels Bohr Library catalog, aids to finding various archival collections, the Emilio Segrè Visual Archives photo collection catalog, online exhibits, and an extensive list of related links make this collection useful to scholars, teachers, and others.

Contributions of Twentieth-Century Women to Physics

http://www.physics.ucla.edu/~cwp/

Sponsored by the American Physical Society, this Web site is maintained by physicist Dr. Nina Byers at the University of California–Los Angeles. The site contains a searchable archive of biographies, indexed by subfields of physics. The research for the biographies is verified by working physicists around the world. The information may be more useful as an educational tool than as a research tool, as there are almost no links to primary resources or mention of archival collections related to each scientist.

History of Oceanic and Atmospheric Science Locator

http://www.lib.noaa.gov/docs/windandsea4.html#HistoryOceanic

Although this site is only part of a much larger Web page, there are no other metasites that deal with this subject. The page points to biographical information and other National Oceanic and Atmospheric Administration resources. The resources that are mentioned are not hyperlinked, however.

Map History/ History of Cartography

http://www.ihrinfo.ac.uk/maps

Tony Campbell, the map librarian at the British Museum in London, maintains this exceptional Web site. It is an extensive and extremely well-organized collection of resources for both the scholar and the amateur. It contains links to both paper and electronic resources, including reference books, map listservs, grants, societies, and commercial venues. This list is not searchable, however.

National Oceanic and Atmospheric Administration History

http://www.history.noaa.gov/

This site makes available many of the historical resources of the National Oceanic and Atmospheric Administration. The site contains a catalog (with low-resolution images that can be printed to a plotter in higher resolution) of the entire map and chart collection of the Office of Coast Survey, as well as biographical sketches of important persons (these were drawn from official newsletters), an extensive photo library, and stories and poems.

HISTORY OF PSYCHOLOGY

History and Philosophy of Psychology Web Resources

http://www.yorku.ca/dept/psych/orgs/resource.htm

This site is maintained by Christopher D. Green at York University in Canada and is shared by several divisions of the American Psychological Association, the Canadian Psychological Association, and other international professional organizations. It contains links to relevant professional organizations, archives and manuscript collections, full-text documents, and translated versions of important texts and papers in psychology. The classic papers section is searchable by keyword, but the rest of the site is not.

Resource Guide: History of Psychology

http://www.slu.edu/colleges/AS/PSY/510Guide.html

This library guide was compiled by Miriam E. Joseph of the University of St.

Louis. It is a good resource for students and teachers interested in the history of psychology. It contains annotations to relevant and useful books, reference works, overviews, journals, citation indexes, manuscript collections, and Web sites.

MISCELLANEOUS SCIENCE RESOURCES

Catalog of the Scientific Community in the Sixteenth and Seventeenth Centuries

http://es.rice.edu/ES/humsoc/Galileo/Catalog/catalog.html

This catalog, compiled by the late Dr. Richard S. Westfall of the Department of History and Philosophy of Science at Indiana University, contains extensive biographical profiles of sixteenth- and seventeenth-century scientific personalities. The database can be searched by any of twenty fields, including means of support, religion, and nationality. In addition to biographical information, Dr. Westfall included known references to the scientist. One shortcoming is that there is no way to browse the list of scientists.

The Faces of Science: African Americans in the Sciences

http://www.lib.lsu.edu/lib/chem/display/faces.html

This Web site is maintained by the Louisiana State University Libraries group. In addition to biographical profiles of numerous African-American scientists, inventors, and doctors, the Web site also contains links to electronic conferences on this topic, historical data on doctoral degrees awarded to African-Americans, and bibliographies. This site is probably best suited to teachers, both university and K-12, who are interested in the historical role of African Americans in science.

The Medieval Science Page

http://members.aol.com/mcnelis/medsci_index.html

The Web site is maintained by James McNelis, the editor-in-chief of *Envoi: A Review Journal of Medieval Literature.* Although the list does not appear to have been updated in several months, the site contains a large amount of information. Annotated links are organized by topic and include links to scholarly listservs and other materials. The list is not searchable, but instead is organized in linear fashion. Included are links to full-text documents and classic texts.

WISE: Archives of Women in Science and Engineering

http://www.lib.iastate.edu/spcl/wise/miss.html

This Web site is the informational page of Iowa State's collection of records and papers of women in science, one of the largest in the United States. Although there are some K-12 resources, virtual exhibits, and bibliographies, this Web site is primarily useful for its collection list.

INTERNATIONAL HISTORY OF SCIENCE AND MEDICINE

ASAPWeb: Australian Science Archives Project

http://www.asap.unimelb.edu.au/

ASAP is an organization that is working to identify and preserve scientific records of enduring value, both those from the past and those that are being created today. One feature on the Web site is *Bright Sparcs*, a searchable database of biographical information on Australian scientists in history. Where appropriate, there are links to information on archival repositories that house information on the scientist. Other important resources include a biographical and bibliographic database of Australian physicists to 1945, and information on Australian archival repositories.

Canada Wide Health and Medical Archives Information Network

http://www.fis.utoronto.ca/research/ams/chmain/

The Network, which maintains this Web site, is a nonprofit reference and referral center serving researchers, archivists, and custodians of Canadian health care collections. They will assist in finding sources of information and records. The site contains a list of Internet resources and contact information.

Chi Med: History of Chinese Medicine Web Page

http://spider.albion.edu/fac/hist/chimed/

This Web site is maintained at Albion College. In addition to an international list of scholars working in the field, this Web site has links to numerous online resources. bibliographies. syllabi. conference and grant listings. and research institutions. The Web site is still fairly small, but growing. There is also subscription information for a listserv devoted to junior faculty and graduate students researching this area.

WWW Virtual Guide to the History of Russian and Soviet Science and Technology

http://web.mit.edu/slava/guide

This guide was established and is maintained by Dr. Slava Gerovitch, a lecturer in the Science, Technology, and Society program at MIT. There is an extensive list of archival collections, journals, scholars, relevant Russian institutions, and course syllabi. The site is fairly easy to navigate, but does not have search capability. This unique site would be useful for both research and teaching.

HISTORY OF TECHNOLOGY

Eric G. Swedin

METASITES

History of Technology Resources Available on the Internet via Internet Connections for Engineering (ICE)

http://www.englib.cornell.edu/ice/lists/historytechnology/historytechnology.html

List of history of technology sites, including e-mail lists, and a short bibliography; provided by the Internet Connections for Engineering project at Cornell University.

H-GIG Technology

http://www.ucr.edu/h-gig/hist-science/techn.html

One of the finest collections of history of technology links on the web. Produced by the Department of History at University of California–Riverside.

Media History Project

http://www.mediahistory.com/

The site's slogan is "promoting the study of media history from petroglyphs to pixels." Includes an extensive timeline and well-organized links to related sites.

Technology History

http://www.refstar.com/techhist/index.html

An "annotated collection of links" to Web sites in the history of technology, "including little-known subsites buried on many well-known commercial sites."

World History Compass, History of Science, Medicine, and Technology

http://www.lexiconn.com/lis/schcomp/whl/science.htm#Technology

Contains a short catalog of history of technology sites.

WWW Virtual Library for the History of Science, Technology, and Medicine

http://www.asap.unimelb.edu.au/hstm/hstm_technology.htm

Excellent list of links to other history of technology sites, including summaries of each site.

WWW Virtual Library for the History of Science, Technology, and Medicine (Biographical Sources)

http://www.asap.unimelb.edu.au/hstm/hstm_bio.htm

Links to online biographies of many important scholars, scientists, engineers, and inventors.

GENERAL SITES

A-Bomb WWW Museum

http://www.csi.ad.jp/ABOMB/

An activist site based in Japan, with English and Japanese versions.

All About The Internet: History of the Internet

http://www.isoc.org/internet-history/

Sponsored by the Internet Society (ISOC); includes many links to documents and other sites concerning the founding of the Internet. Includes a historical narrative written by the founders of the Internet themselves.

Ancient Metallurgy Research Group

http://www.brad.ac.uk/acad/archsci/depart/resgrp/amrg/amrginfo.html

Part of the Department of Archaeological Sciences at the University of Bradford, this site describes the group's efforts and provides links to other archaeometallurgy sites.

Aquae Urbis Romae: The Waters of the City of Rome

http://www.iath.virginia.edu/waters/

Created by the Institute for Advanced Technology in the Humanities at the University of Virginia, this cartographic study uses graphics, QuickTime movies, and interactive maps to survey the 2,800-year history of water in Rome. Includes a timeline and bibliography. This ambitious site is currently incomplete.

Charles Babbage Institute of Computer History

http://www.cbi.umn.edu/

Based at the University of Minnesota, the Institute is an archive for the history of computing that also sponsors research in the field. Some excellent sections illuminate various aspects of computing. An extensive list of "sites related to the history of information processing" is also provided.

Alexander Graham Bell's Path to the Telephone

http://jefferson.village.virginia.edu/albell/homepage.html

Describes Bell's invention of the telephone; includes reproductions of Bell's lab notebooks in the form of images and transcripts.

Caltech Archives

http://www.caltech.edu/archives/

Archives of the California Institute of Technology, including descriptions of manuscript holdings and an online archive of 3,000 photographs and other visual materials.

Centre for the History of Defense Electronics

http://chide.museum.org.uk/

Sponsored by the School of Conservation Sciences at Bournemouth University in the United Kingdom. This virtual museum contains narratives, exhibit photos, and links to similar sites.

Discovery Online, Feature Stories—The Unkindest Cut

http://www.discovery.com/stories/history/panama/panama.html

Discovery Channel often creates Web sites to supplement the material in their television programs. This site features the building of the Panama Canal, including an interactive timeline, audio recordings, and videos.

Firearms History

http://www.btinternet.com/~rrnotes/firearms/index.htm

Includes primary documents on the history of firearms and links to similar sites.

General Electric Archives

http://www.gec.com/ah1.htm

Ambitious site that plans to trace the history of the General Electric Company from its roots three hundred years ago to the present. Currently contains a centenary tribute to Guglielmo Marconi and a virtual tour of some of the artifacts in the archives.

Hagley Museum and Library

http://www.hagley.lib.de.us/

Web site for the Wilmington, Delaware museum and library. Hagley's "mission is to promote the understanding of American business and technological history."

Henry Ford Museum and Greenfield Village

http://www.hfmgv.org/

This site has received many Web awards for its comprehensive content and is a worthy companion to the impressive museum and village in Dearborn, Michigan. It includes inventor biographies, many pictures, and a virtual tour of the museum.

The Hiroshima Project

http://err.org/akke/HiroshimaProject/

Well-organized comprehensive examination of Hiroshima from different perspectives, with numerous links to other Web sites. Includes photographs, original sources, and analysis.

History of Australian Science and Technology

http://www.asap.unimelb.edu.au/hast/asaphast.htm

Starting point for exploring the Australian contributions to science and technology.

The History of Chemical Engineering

http://www.cems.umn.edu/~aiche_ug/history/h_intro.html

Overview of chemical engineering, which moves from "its conceptual origins in Great Britain, subsequent struggle for survival in the United States, and concludes with a cornucopia of contributions made in this Century." Includes a lengthy timeline, numerous graphs, and a large bibliography.

History of Computing

http://ei.cs.vt.edu/~history/

Large collection of primary materials related to the history of computing.

ICOHTEC: International Committee for the History of Technology

http://www.icohtec.org/

The international equivalent to the American-dominated Society for the History of Technology (SHOT). Includes the full text of newsletters and the tables of contents to *Icon*, the Committee's annual journal.

Inventure Place: National Inventors Hall of Fame

http://www.invent.org/

Contains dozens of short biographies of different inductees into the National Inventors Hall of Fame, located in Akron, Ohio. Various programs and exhibits are also described.

Issues in Science and Technology Home Page

http://www.nap.edu/issues/

Web site for the *Issues in Science and Technology* quarterly, "published by the Cecil and Ida Green Center for the Study of Science and Society at the University of Texas at Dallas in cooperation with the National Academy of Sciences." The site includes the full content of back issues.

Jerome and Dorothy Lemelson Center for the Study of Invention and Innovation

http://www.si.edu/lemelson/index.html

The Lemelson Center is part of the Smithsonian Institution's National Museum of American History. By sponsoring research and education, the Center seeks to "foster an appreciation for the central role invention and innovation play in the history of the United States." Extensive site with a featured inventor on the home page.

The Museum of Science and Industry in Manchester

http://www.msim.org.uk/

Web site for the museum, located in Manchester, England. Includes hands-on games and extensive information on the exhibitions and resources of the museum.

NASA History Office

http://www.hq.nasa.gov/office/pao/History/history.html

Comprehensive history of the National Aeronautics and Space Administration, including a catalog of publications, a timeline, a reference guide, and links to other sites.

Oral History on Space, Science, and Technology

http://www.nasm.edu/NASMDOCS/DSH/ohp-introduction.html

Excellent example of providing primary historical material on the Web. This NASA site contains the complete transcripts of "over 850 hours of oral history interviews with more than two hundred interviewees" involved in the space industry from World War II to the present. A summary and a table of contents are provided for each interview.

Psychology of Invention

http://hawaii.cogsci.uiuc.edu/invent/invention.html

By examining the invention of the airplane and telephone, this site explores the psychology behind the practice of inventing. Includes extensive text, diagrams, short videos, bibliography, and links to similar sites.

Science and Technology in the Making

http://sloan.stanford.edu/

An ambitious effort, funded by the Alfred P. Sloan Foundation, to "establish a network of history of technology Web sites." The five completed projects are: History of Electric Vehicle Owners and Drivers, History of Human Computer Interaction, History of the Invention of Polymerase Chain Reaction, History of the New York City Blackouts of 1965 and 1977, and History of Scheme Z and the Building of the Boston Central Artery. Includes primary and secondary material.

SHOT: The Society for the History of Technology

http://shot.press.jhu.edu/associations/shot/index.html

Official site of the leading history of technology academic organization. Includes sample syllabi, an archive of society newsletters, job opportunities, and other announcements.

STS Links

http://www2.ncsu.edu/ncsu/chass/mds/stslinks.html

Large list of links provided by the North Carolina State Program on Science, Technology, and Society.

Technology and Culture

http://shot.press.jhu.edu/associations/shot/tc.html

The journal of the Society for the History of Technology (SHOT). Includes notes for contributors, sample articles, the current journal index, and subscription information.

Technology Review

http://www.techreview.com/

Web site for MIT's "Magazine of Innovation," including sample articles from each issue. The magazine often publishes articles of historical interest.

"To Fly is Everything..."

http://hawaii.cogsci.uiuc.edu/invent/airplanes.html

This comprehensive site is a "A Virtual Museum covering the Invention of the Airplane."

Totalizator (Totalisator) History—A World's First

http://www.ozE-mail.com.au/~bconlon/

A patriotic ode to Australian inventor Sir George Julius, who in 1913 invented the automatic totalisator, an early form of mechanical computer.

Eli Whitney Armory Site

http://www.yale.edu/ewhitney/

Extensive report by Yale University on the continuing archeological excavations at the site of Eli Whitney's arms factory.

Whole Cloth: Discovering Science and Technology Through American Textile History

http://www.si.edu/lemelson/centerpieces/whole_cloth

Extensive site developed by the Society for the History of Technology (SHOT) and the Lemelson Center of the Smithsonian Institution to assist teachers in American survey courses. Both high school and college instructors will find a wealth of information. Among the instruction modules are such topics as Early Industrialization, True Colors, and Synthetic Fibers. Lesson plans, documents, glossaries, bibliographies, and sample essays are included. A model to emulate of how to create an instructional site offering curriculum materials.

Robert C. Williams American Museum of Papermaking

http://www.ipst.edu/amp/

Includes a virtual tour of the Atlanta, Georgia museum that covers the entire history of papermaking.

JEWISH HOLOCAUST STUDIES
Solomon Davidoff

AMCHA

http://www.amcha.org/

AMCHA is the support organization of Israeli centers for Holocaust survivors and the children of survivors.

Anne Frank Online

http://www.annefrank.com/

The site for the Anne Frank Center USA, with educational information for teachers and students, information on their traveling exhibit and activities at the Center.

Anne Frank House

http://www.annefrank.nl/

The Web site for the Anne Frank House, this site gives viewing information, exhibition information, a keyword and book list, and information and photos of her famous diary.

Bulgarian Jews During World War II

http://www.b-info.com/places/Bulgaria/Jewish/

An archive of articles, letters, and other documents that attempts to explain the experience of Jews in Bulgaria, and why not a single Bulgarian Jew was deported to the Nazi death camps during World War II. Also includes a bibliography and link section.

Cybrary of the Holocaust

http://remember.org

An impressive resource for both teachers and students of the Jewish Holocaust. This site includes a wide variety of both text and artwork, including discussion forums, eyewitness accounts, poetry, photos, and bibliographies, with all contents donated by users/participants.

The Desert Holocaust Memorial

http://www.palmsprings.com/points/holocaust/

A photo and information page for a memorial site in Rancho Mirage, California, that has an impressive number of Holocaust-related links.

The Forgotten Camps

http://www2.3dresearch.com/~June/Vincent/Camps/CampsEngl.html

These extensive sites are devoted to several of the lesser known concentration camps, work camps, police camps, transit camps, and similar facilities, created by Vincent Chatel, son of a survivor, and Chuck Ferree, a witness and camp liberator. Also accessible in a French version.

H-Holocaust

http://www.h-net.msu.edu/~holoweb/

The Web location for the Humanities and Social Science Online Initiative's

Holocaust discussion list. Includes an opportunity to join the list, as well as scholarly reviews, academic announcements, course syllabi, and an entire log of H-Holocaust messages.

Holocaust Education Forum

http://www.kqed.org/cell/school/socialstudies/holocaust/index.html

A premier site for teachers, including a vast array of connections, links, resources, and information for teaching about the Holocaust.

Holocaust Guide

http://holocaust.miningco.com/mbody.htm

Hosted by Jennifer Rosenberg on Miningco, this site includes a wide variety of links, a chat room, a photographic tour of Theresienstadt, a book club discussion, newsletter, and more.

Holocaust: Non-Jewish Victims of the Holocaust

http://www.holocaustforgotten.com/

A site dedicated and devoted to the over five million people, other than Jews, who were slaughtered during the Holocaust.

The Holocaust History Project

http://www.holocaust-history.org/

An archive of documents, photographs, recordings, book reproductions, and essays regarding the Holocaust, with a focus on direct refutation of Holocaust denial.

Holocaust Memorial Center

http://www.holocaustcenter.com/

The first American Holocaust Memorial site, the site for this museum/archive in West Bloomfield, Michigan contains exhibits, an archive of documents and artifacts, and an oral history archive. An interesting addition is the Lifechance exhibit, an interactive role-playing scenario wherein you make choices, and find if you would have lived or died during the Holocaust.

Holocaust Pictures Exhibition

http://www.fmv.ulg.ac.be/schmitz/holocaust.html

A collection of thirty-seven photos with documentation and commentary. Also available in French.

The Holocaust Ring

http://www.webring.org/cgi-bin/webring?ring=shoah&list

A list of Web pages that all contribute to Holocaust understanding, study, research, or dynamics.

Holocaust Teacher Resource Center

http://www.Holocaust-trc.org/

Sponsored by the Holocaust Education Foundation, this site offers lesson plans, curricula, essays and publications, bibliographies, and a vast array of information and locations for those intending to teach about the Holocaust.

Holocaust Understanding and Prevention

http://idt.net/~kimel19

Informative site, recommended by The History Channel, created by Holocaust survivor Alexander Kimel. Contains a wide variety of documents, memoirs, and poetry by Holocaust survivors, as well as an online magazine on Holocaust issues. Contains an excellent collection of links to other sites.

KZ Mauthausen-GUSEN Info-Pages

http://linz.orf.at/orf/gusen/

An archive of documentation and information about the Mauthausen-GUSEN death camps, considered the worst of all the camps that existed.

L'Chaim: A Holocaust Web Project

http://www.charm.net:80/%7Erbennett/l'chaim.html

Another educational site project, containing a virtual tour of Dachau, a glossary, and a link section, as well as two photo essays and the story of survivor Ingrid Griffin.

Louisiana Holocaust Survivors

http://www.tulane.edu/%7Eso-inst/laholsur.html

With space contributed by The Southern Institute for Education and Research, this is a Web-based archive of the stories of Louisiana residents who survived the Holocaust.

Mauthausen Concentration Camp Memorial

http://www.mauthausen-memorial.gv.at/engl/index.html

Web site for the Mauthausen concentration camp memorial. Contains documentation and information about the camp.

National Museum at the Concentration Camp of Lublin-Majdanek

http://www.lublin.pol.pl/majdanek/english.html

An online collection of information concerning the Lublin-Majdanek concentration camp, including photos and files on labor, conditions, the building of the camp, its liberation, and other related materials.

The Nizkor Project

http://www.nizkor.org/

The Nizkor Project Web site is the home page of an international multimedia project, spearheaded by Canada-based archivist Ken McVay (http://veritas.nizkor.org/~kmcvay/), that aims to counter those who deny the Holocaust. It is an extremely well-documented and rich resource, containing over four thousand documents, and is the world's largest collection of Holocaust-related materials online.

Rescuers Bibliography

http://www.cs.cmu.edu/afs/cs.cmu.edu/user/mmbt/www/rescuers.html

A bibliography of works in English that discuss the lives and actions of rescuers during the Holocaust.

To Save A Life: Stories of Jewish Rescue

http://www.humboldt.edu/~rescuers/

The text from a previously unpublished work by Ellen Land-Weber that tells the stories of nine Jews who were rescued from the Holocaust and of the six people who helped to save them.

The Simon Wiesenthal Center Online

http://www.wiesenthal.com/

The Simon Wiesenthal Center in Los Angeles is dedicated to chronicling the history of human rights and the Holocaust. The Center's online site contains exhibits, glossaries, articles, information on the center's activities, and more.

Survivors of the SHOAH Visual History Foundation

http://www.vhf.org/

Founded by Steven Spielberg in 1994, this nonprofit foundation is dedicated to videotaping and archiving interviews of Holocaust survivors all over the world, using the latest technology. The site offers information on the project, repositories, and production status.

Teaching The Holocaust

http://www.socialstudies.com/c/@c0kc44xusXy6Y/Pages/holo.html

A collection of links to resources and materials for teaching about the Holocaust.

Teaching the Holocaust Through Stamps, Pictures, and Text

http://mofetsrv.mofet.macam98.ac.il/~ochayo/einvert.htm

An interdisciplinary computer-based resource for teaching about the Holocaust through stamps, pictures, texts, and paintings by children who were in the Holocaust. Offers a complete teacher's guide, dictionary, and teaching unit, and is also available in a Hebrew version.

The United States Holocaust Museum

http://www.ushmm.org/

The official site of the United States Holocaust Museum. Offers information on exhibits and activities of the museum, as well as an array of documents and contact information. The museum is a memorial to everyone who perished in the Holocaust, and focuses on photographic and cinematic exhibits.

The Wolf Lewkowicz Collection

http://web.mit.edu/maz/wolf/

The Wolf Lewkowicz Collection is made up of 178 letters translated into English (the original Yiddish is also available) from a man in Poland to his nephew in the United States, written between 1922 and 1939. Lewkowicz was later sent to Treblinka, where he died. Photos and sound recordings are also available. A list of names and a chronology of the letters is included to help researchers.

Women and the Holocaust: A Cyberspace of Their Own

http://www.interlog.com/~mighty/

A collection of essays, tributes, bibliographies, poetry, and personal reflections that focus on women's experiences during the Holocaust.

Yad Vashem: The Holocaust Martyrs and Heroes Remembrance Authority

http://www.yad-vashem.org.il/

Yad Vashem is the Jerusalem-based Holocaust memorial established in 1953. The site consists of online exhibits, information about the center and its research, calls for papers, their vast collection of publications (now available online), and more.

LEGAL, CIVIL LIBERTIES, AND CIVIL RIGHTS HISTORY

Richard P. Mulcahy

LAW

Guide to Legal History Resources on the Web

http://www.law.utexas.edu/rare/legalhis.htm

Maintained by the Jamail Center for Legal Research of the University of Texas's Tarlton Law Library, this site is probably the single most comprehensive guide to legal history resources available on the World Wide Web. Because of this, the site should be a first stop for all students and scholars doing research in this field.

The site is divided into five subject headings: General Sources, Court Records, Academic Libraries, Research Libraries, and Full-Text Sources. Each section is figuratively a treasure trove of information. For example, in the General Studies section, the user can choose from a host of various sites ranging from the Ames Foundation to Roman law. The same thorough and methodical approach is plainly evident in the other sections. Particularly helpful are the annotations that appear with each listing. These give a basic description of the individual sites and what they contain. Well-organized and thoughtfully laid out, this site is most highly recommended.

Connections

http://www.law.pitt.edu/hibbitts/connect.htm

Connections is maintained through the University of Pittsburgh's School of Law. It is designed primarily for use by law students, and so contains a section dealing with estate and trust law. However, it also features sections dealing with American Legal History, Ancient Law, and English Legal History. Of these three, Ancient Law is by far the largest, with American Legal History running a distant second.

Under American Legal History, interested students can access such diverse items as decisions of the United States Supreme Court, slave narratives, and a chronology of the Salem Witch Trials. The Ancient Law section provides access to the Code of Hammurabi, the Cicero Home Page, the Athenian Constitution, and other similar works. Because of this, the site is not only useful to historians, but classicists as well. Finally, the site is linked to various law journals currently available on the World Wide Web.

The Bill of Rights—National Archives

http://www.nara.gov/exhall/charters/billrights/

This is a subsection of a much larger site established by the National Archives. The site's purpose is to make important documents in America's legal history available to both students and educators. The Bill of Rights section features a full transcription of the Preamble to the Constitution, as well as the Bill of Rights itself and later amendments. In addition, the site also features informational items, such as the article "A More Perfect Union," which gives an overview of the Constitutional Convention. The site is informative and well thought out.

The Amistad Case—The National Archives

http://www.nara.gov/education/teaching/amistad/home.html

This site is also a subsection of the site maintained by the National Archives, and deals with the Amistad case. Although it too is well laid out, it is less informative that the site covered above. While offering some excellent graphics, such as a high-resolution image of the first page of John Quincy Adams's handwritten petition for *certiorari* (in preparation of his case for the Supreme Court), it does not currently provide the full texts of the documents involved. This problem aside, it is an interesting site, and well worth viewing.

Famous American Trials

http://www.law.umkc.edu/faculty/projects/ftrials/ftrials.htm

Without exaggeration, this is one of the most extensive and informative sites on the World Wide Web dealing specifically with American court cases. The site is maintained by the University of Missouri–Kansas City School of Law, and is associated with its Famous Trials seminar. It offers detailed coverage of eight major cases, including Leopold and Loeb, the Scopes Monkey Trial, the Rosenberg case, and the Amistad case. Four additional sections are currently under construction, including the Chicago Seven Trial and the My-Lai Court Martial.

Civil Liberties

The Literature and Culture of the American 1950s

http://dept.english.upenn.edu/~afilreis/50s/home.html

Maintained through the University of Pennsylvania's Department of English, this site is a clearinghouse for information on America in the 1950s, with special reference to McCarthyism and the Cold War. Stated simply, this site offers an "embarrassment of riches."

Webcorp Multimedia

http://webcorp.com/mccarthy/

Unlike the sites covered above, which provide access to text and still graphics, this site offers audio and video clips of some of the major figures of the McCarthy era. Included on the list are Senator Joseph R. McCarthy himself, President Dwight David Eisenhower, and (then) Vice President Richard Nixon. The video the site features consists of clips from such famous television events as Nixon's "Checkers" speech and the Army McCarthy hearings of 1954. Here, the viewer can see and hear candidate Nixon deny that his wife Pat has a mink coat, but owns a "respectable Republican cloth coat" instead. This site manages to be both amusing and informative.

The American Radicalism Collection

http://www.lib.msu.edu/spc/digital/radicalism/index.htm

Maintained by Michigan State University, this site offers access to digital reproductions of various writings and pamphlets dealing with American radicalism. With this, each of the titles contained in the site is part of the public domain. Arranged both topically and alphabetically, the subject matters covered include the Hollywood Ten, the Scottsboro Boys, the Rosenberg Case, the Sacco-Vanzetti Case, and others. Although the quality of the individual selections varies widely, each is valuable by providing insight to the time it was written, as well the mentality of the audience it was attempting to reach.

LeftWatch

http://www.leftwatch.com

Covering McCarthyism, as well as more recent political events, this site works from a conservative point of view. Its purpose is to allow conservatives the opportunity to present their side of the story and to dispel certain left-liberal mythologies. Aside from the factual and bibliographic material the site offers, its greatest contribution is its effective presentation of what must be considered alternative opinions of the matters discussed here.

Paul Robeson Centennial

http://www.founders.howard.edu/robeson.htm

Interest in Paul Robeson by Left Watch and other more friendly groups was sparked by the fact that April 9, 1998 was his centennial birthday. Regardless of his failings, Robeson forced this nation to look at and reassess its attitudes about race relations. His importance to both the areas of civil liberties and civil rights are undeniable. With this in mind, Howard University Libraries has established a site dedicated to Paul Robeson and his work. Essentially a clearinghouse, the site provides the user with an extensive series of links to other sites dealing with everything from his films to his personal papers. For anyone interested in getting information on Paul Robeson from the World Wide Web, this is the place to start.

Civil Rights

American Association for Affirmative Action

http://www.auaa.org

This site was created and is maintained by the American Association for Affirmative Action. Although affirmative action is a contemporary matter, the site offers a library of full-text primary documents dealing with race relations.

MILITARY HISTORY

Mark Gellis

GENERAL RESOURCES

African-American Military History

http://www.coax.net/people/lwf/aa_mh.htm

Bennie J. McRae, Jr. has provided this valuable set of indices to links on the history of Black Americans during armed conflict—from the Revolution to the Vietnam War—as part of his "Lest We Forget" project.

Air Force Historical Research Agency

http://www.au.af.mil/au/afhra/

The United States Air Force's historical agency provides links to various resources on military aviation history.

American History: Wars of the Twentieth Century

http://www.geocities.com/Athens/Academy/6617/wars.html

A short but useful index of military history sites on the Internet.

American Merchant Marine

http://www.USMM.org/

The home page of the United States Merchant Marine includes extensive resources on the history of merchant marine efforts during wartime.

Article Index

http://www.thehistorynet.com/general/articleindex.htm

Historynet's article index features more than five hundred online articles, many of them dealing with various aspects of military history.

The Center of Military History

http://www.army.mil/cmh-pg/

The United States Army's Center of Military History provides access to a large number of resources, including a large number of online articles, photographs, and artwork. In addition, one can view and order from the Center's extensive catalog of publications on military history.

Department of Defense Dictionary of Military Terms

http://www.dtic.mil/doctrine/jel/doddict/
An online dictionary of military terminology.

Fighter Tactics Academy

http://www.saunalahti.fi/~fta/
A detailed site providing information on modern military aircraft and the history of their development. The site also includes a large number of links to related sites.

History, Reference, and Preservation

http://www.usni.org/hrp/hrp.html
Historical and reference links at the United States Naval Institute's Web site.

Homework Center: Wars and World History

http://www.multnomah.lib.or.us/lib/homework/warwldhc.html
The Homework Center, developed by the Multnomah County Library, provides an index of sites oriented around the needs of students learning about military history.

Military Data Resource

http://www.militarydataresource.com/
A large index of military-related sites on the World Wide Web.

The Military History Collections of the New York Public Library

http://www.nypl.org/research/chss/subguides/milhist/home.html
Information on special collections held by the New York Public Library.

Navy Historical Center

http://www.history.navy.mil/
The United States Navy provides this page as a starting point leading to a very

large number of links related to naval history. Links include everything from underwater archeology and information about available research grants to online encyclopedias of naval history and navy ships.

Redstone Arsenal Historical Information

http://www.redstone.army.mil/history/welcome.html

An index to many military history sites, many of them dedicated to the role of missilery in military history.

Twentieth-Century Documents

http://www.yale.edu/lawweb/avalon/20th.htm

Part of the Avalon Project at the Yale University Law School, this index provides links to many online copies of historical documents related to the conflicts of the twentieth century.

United States Naval and Shipbuilding Museum

http://www.uss-salem.org/

This is one of the best Internet sites in the world for those interested in modern naval warfare. The site includes the *World Navies Today* page, which provides detailed information on virtually every navy in the world, including the Russian and Chinese navies.

War, Peace and Security WWW Server

http://www.cfcsc.dnd.ca/index.html

This Canadian site, provided by the Information Resource Centre at the Canadian Forces College, offers an extensive list of resources on past and current conflicts and modern armed forces.

Weapons and Warfare on the Web

http://www.seanet.com/~gtate/members.htm

A useful index of links to sites covering military history, military statistics, and military technology.

CONFLICTS AT THE TURN OF THE CENTURY

Border Revolution

http://ac.acusd.edu/History/projects/border/page01.html

An illustrated online explication of the Mexican Revolution.

The Philippine-American War

http://home.ican.net/~fjzwick/centennial/war.html

Jim Zwick has developed a number of Web-based projects on Imperialism and related subjects. Here he provides a list of articles and other documents related to the fighting in the Philippines at the turn of the century.

South African War Virtual Library

http://www.uq.net.au/~zzrwotto/open.html

Historian Robert Wotton has developed an extensive virtual archive that contains research data related to the Second South African War (1899–1902).

The Spanish-American War

http://home.ican.net/~fjzwick/centennial/spanam.html

A partner site to Jim Zwick's *The Philippine–American War*, this site provides links to articles and documents related to the conflict between Spain and America.

WORLD WAR I AND ITS AFTERMATH

The Australian Light Horse Association

http://www.lighthorse.org.au/

This site contains both historical and current information on famous Australian regiments and battles during the Boer War and World War I.

The First World War

http://www.spartacus.schoolnet.co.uk/FWWtitle.html

Spartacus, an educational publishing company, is committed to providing free informational resources for the Internet community. Here, they have developed an extensive and illustrated hypertext encyclopedia dedicated to World War I.

The History of the Battle of the Somme

http://www.somme.com/

Created by the combined efforts of a publishing company, a military collectibles company, and the official magazine of the Royal Artillery Association, this is a detailed online discussion of one of the most costly battles of the twentieth century. It offers a variety of multimedia resources and links to other World War I sites.

The Russian Civil War

http://mars.acnet.wnec.edu/~grempel/courses/stalin/lectures/CivilWar.html

One of several lectures placed online by Professor Gerhard Rempel, this one outlines the events of the Russian Civil War that followed the 1917 Revolution.

World War I

http://www.msstate.edu/Archives/History/USA/WWI/ww1.html

Part of the Historical Text Archives Project at Mississippi State University, this page provides links to articles and multimedia resources about World War I, including a detailed examination of the effects of World War I on smaller European powers and Arabs.

The World War I Document Archive

http://www.lib.byu.edu/~rdh/wwi/

Developed by scholars at Brigham Young University, this page provides links to a wide range of historical documents related to World War I, ranging from treaties and government proclamations to personal memoirs. The site also includes a biographical dictionary and an image archive.

World War I: Trenches on the Web

http://www.worldwar1.com/

Another Web site providing extensive links to historical documents and multimedia files.

THE SPANISH CIVIL WAR

Bibliography of Specific Wars: The Spanish Civil War

http://chomsky.arts.adelaide.edu.au/person/DHart/ResponsesToWar/
Bibliography/SpecificWars/20thC/SpanishCivilWar.html

Historian David M. Hart has developed an online bibliography of sources related to the Spanish Civil War.

Spanish Civil War

http://ac.acusd.edu/History/WW2Timeline/Prelude07.html

Part of a larger project on the history of World War II, this site contains a timeline and links to an image archive.

The Spanish Revolution and Civil War

http://www.geocities.com/CapitolHill/9820/

Eugene W. Plawiuk's site offers an index of Web resources related to the Spanish Civil War

WORLD WAR II

Achtung Panzer

http://www.achtungpanzer.com/panzer.htm

One of many enthusiast sites dedicated to German armor. This one features many illustrations, tables of technical data, and a large number of links to other World War II sites.

Atrocities of the Japanese Imperial Army

http://www.hep.upenn.edu/~naoki/jia/index.html

A useful index on the various war crimes committed by the Japanese during the Second World War.

The Battle of Britain Historical Society

http://www.bobsoc.demon.co.uk/

A detailed site dedicated to the aerial battle over Great Britain in 1940.

The Control Tower: World War II Aviation Links

http://members.aol.com/zeno303/Pages/World_War_II_Aviation_Link.html

An extensive index of World Wide Web sites on World War II aviation.

Dad's War: Finding and Telling Your Father's World War II Story

http://members.aol.com/dadswar/index.htm

If you can tolerate the small promotional effort for his works on writing personal history, Wes Johnson has done a service with this index of personal histories and initial instructions on writing your own history for a family member who served in World War II (and, by extension, any war).

East Anglia: The Air War

http://www.stable.demon.co.uk/

Contains a series of informative essays with illustrations concerning various air forces and the aircraft flown during the Second World War. The site also provides an excellent index of links to related Web pages and a bibliography of print reference works.

Enola Gay Perspectives

http://www.glue.umd.edu/~enola/hist/history.html

Carolyn McCracken's site is a short but useful hypertext history and timeline of the war in the Pacific.

504th World War II Home Page

http://www.geocities.com/~the504thpir/index.html

An example of the many sites dedicated to military units, this one chronicles the experiences of the 504th Parachute Infantry Regiment during World War II.

German Armed Forces in World War II

http://www.uwm.edu/People/jpipes/start.html

A detailed Web site developed by a graduate student at the University of Wisconsin at Milwaukee covering "the history of the units and formations of the various military, paramilitary and auxiliary forces from 1933–45." Includes discussions of various battles and a bibliography of nearly five hundred titles.

Guadalcanal Online

http://www.geocities.com/Heartland/Plains/6672/canal_index.html

Detailed discussion of the first major American offensive in the war in the Pacific.

Hyperwar: A Hypertext History of the Second World War

http://metalab.unc.edu/hyperwar/

A linked anthology of articles related to the Second World War, many of them discussing specific battles in detail, along with links to other sources.

Imperial Japanese Navy Page

http://www.skypoint.com/members/jbp/kaigun.htm

Enthusiast Jon Parshall has created a detailed index to links about the Japanese Navy during the Second World War, including detailed histories of individual vessels.

The Luftwaffe Home Page

http://home4.inet.tele.dk/mholm/index.htm

This site provides data on the Luftwaffe and an index of links to Luftwaffe-related Web pages.

A Marine Diary: My Experiences on Guadalcanal

http://www.gnt.net/~jrube/indx2.html

Entries from the diary of a Marine who served at Guadalcanal, with a large set of links to related World War II resources on the Internet.

Marines at Midway

http://metalab.unc.edu/hyperwar/USMC/USMC-M-Midway.html

Part of the Hyperwar project, this is a detailed illustrated examination of the Battle of Midway, written by Lieutenant Colonel R.D. Heinl, Jr., USMC.

Naval Air War in the Pacific

http://www.ixpres.com/ag1caf/navalwar/

Photos and paintings of American air combat during World War II.

Normandy: 1944

http://normandy.eb.com/

Encyclopedia Britannica's multimedia examination of the Normandy invasion.

Pacific War

http://hyperion.advanced.org/18106/

An online anthology of articles about the war in the Pacific.

A People at War

http://www.nara.gov/exhall/people/people.html

This site presents an online exhibition by the National Archives. It includes a brief discussion of events leading up to the war and links to related sites. Focuses much more on the people who served than on a traditional history of the war.

Red Steel

http://www.algonet.se/~toriert/

Enthusiast Thorleif Olsson's extensive Web site on Russian tanks and armored vehicles.

Return to Midway

http://www.nationalgeographic.com/features/98/midway/

National Geographic has created this multimedia site featuring images and streaming video of the wrecks of the carriers sunk at the Battle of Midway.

U-Boat Net

http://uboat.net/

A comprehensive study of the German U-boat, including maps, technology, and profiles on more than 1,100 German submarines employed during World War II.

What Did You Do in the War, Grandma?

http://www.stg.brown.edu/projects/WWII_Women/tocCS.html

An oral history of Rhode Island Women during World War II, written by students in the Honors English Program at South Kingstown High School, this site not only provides information about lesser known aspects of the war, but also provides a good model of action for teachers interested in using the Internet for class projects.

The Women's Army Corps

http://www.army.mil/cmh-pg/WAC.HTM

The United States Army has developed this online article about the Women's Army Corps during World War II.

The World at War

http://www.euronet.nl/users/wilfried/ww2/ww2.htm

Wilfried Braakhuis has created an extremely detailed timeline of the war, with illustrations, statistics, and a very large number of links, organized by relevant dates. This graphic-intensive site takes a while to load, but is worth looking at.

World War II in Europe

http://www.historyplace.com/worldwar2/timeline/ww2time.htm

Part of The History Place, a large Web site dedicated to assisting students and educators, this is a World War II timeline with links to illustrations and short articles on specific events.

World War II on the Web

http://www.bunt.com/~mconrad/links.htm

An index to more than four hundred Web sites concerned with the Second World War, many of them highly specialized.

The World War II Sounds and Pictures Page

http://www.earthstation1.com/wwii.html

Sounds, video, and images of many items related to World War II. The site includes aircraft, warships, propaganda posters, and other assorted images.

World War II Resources

http://metalab.unc.edu/pha/index.html

An extensive collection of historical documents from the Second World War based at the University of North Carolina–Chapel Hill.

World War II Seminar

http://ac.acusd.edu/History/classes/ww2/175.html

Class materials for a World War II history course from the University of San Diego, including an extended bibliography and fifteen timelines created by students.

World War II Timeline

http://ac.acusd.edu/History/WW2Timeline/start.html

A fairly good general timeline for World War II. Includes a very valuable list of additional links. Also has a number of interesting pictures, maps, documents, and a good bibliography. Includes some student pages. A first-rate site by Steve Schoenherr of the University of San Diego's History Department.

THE KOREAN WAR

Fiftieth Anniversary of the Korean War

http://www.tcsaz.com/koreanwar.html

A site commemorating the fiftieth anniversary of the Korean War presented by Tanner Publishing, a small press specializing in history. It includes a timeline of the war, personal accounts of the war, and links to related sites. Also lists related organizations and gives veterans a chance to have their personal accounts published.

Korea

http://tlc.ai.org/korea.htm

This educational site on Korea features an index of links to Web sites on the Korean War.

The Korean War

http://www.homeusers.prestel.co.uk/simonides/links/wars/korea/korea.html

An index of Web sites related to the Korean War.

The Korean War Museum

http://www.theforgottenvictory.org./

This home page provides an index of links to Internet sites on the Korean War. It also provides information on the museum and its newsletter.

The Korean War Project

http://www.koreanwar.org/html/home_page.html

An index to a large set of links (particularly in the "Reference" section), including other Web sites, articles, images, and maps.

The Korean War Veteran Association

http://www.kwva.org/

This organizational home page provides information on and for veterans of the Korean War.

THE VIETNAM WAR

The American Experience—Vietnam

http://www.pbs.org/wgbh/pages/amex/vietnam/index.html

This site was developed to accompany the PBS program *Vietnam: A Television History*. It includes a "who's who," a list of acronyms, maps, a bibliography, primary source material, and transcripts of the program. The site also presents a video clip of the program and information on how to purchase a video.

Documents Relating to the Vietnam War

http://www.mtholyoke.edu/acad/intrel/vietnam.htm

This site contains a large number of primary and secondary source materials relating to the Vietnam War. It includes letters from Presidents of the United States, transcripts of TV interviews, and other documents relating to the war.

Images of My War

http://www.ionet.net/~uheller/vnbktoc.shtml

One of many personal accounts of Vietnam veterans, this one is a detailed autobiography of a U.S. Army Ranger, focusing on his experiences during the conflict.

U.S. POW/MIAs in Southeast Asia

http://www.wtvi.com/wesley/powmia/powmia.html

An index of online resources related to P.O.W./M.I.A. issues.

Vietnam War Internet Project

http://www.lbjlib.utexas.edu/shwv/vwiphome.html

This online project, housed on the Lyndon Baines Johnson Library Web server at the University of Texas, provides links to an extensive list of resources, including bibliographies, images, personal memoirs, documents related to the war, and a complete archive of the Soc.History.War.Vietnam newsgroup.

Vietnam War Bibliography

http://hubcap.clemson.edu/~eemoise/bibliography.html

Professor Edwin Moïse of Clemson University has developed a large bibliography of print sources and other sources on the Vietnam conflict.

The Wars for Vietnam

http://students.vassar.edu/~vietnam/

This site, developed at Vassar College, provides a historical overview of the war, with links to historical documents and other Vietnam-related Web pages.

OTHER COLD WAR RESOURCES

Captain Vitalj Burda's "Foxtrot" Class Submarine

http://www.wtj.com/artdocs/u-475.htm

An online photo essay touring a Cold War weapon, a Soviet Foxtrot-class diesel submarine.

Cold War Hot Links

http://www.stmartin.edu/~dprice/cold.war.html

Professor David Price offers a detailed index of Web resources—mostly articles, but some multimedia—on the leading figures and events of the Cold War.

THE ISRAELI–ARAB WARS

The Battle of Latakia

http://www.usa.pipeline.com/~albatros/latakia.htm

An online article discussing the historic naval battle—the first involving missile boats—between Israeli and Syrian forces, in 1973.

History of the Israeli Defense Force

http://www.idf.il/English/HISTORY/history.htm

Detailed historical essays by the Israeli Defense Force outlining the activities of the IDF during the War of Independence, the Six Day War, and other operations.

Israel

gopher://gopher.umsl.edu:70/11/library/govdocs/armyahbs/aahb6

An Army Area Handbook on Israel, this online book covers the various Israeli–Arab conflicts.

Timeline for the History of Judaism

http://www.us-israel.org/jsource/History/timeline.html

This timeline, part of a larger Web site designed to assist students of Jewish history and culture, also serves as a chronologically arranged index of links to online essays and other sites related to the Israeli–Arab conflicts of the twentieth century.

THE FALKLANDS WAR

Falklands: Fifteen Years On

http://www.thenews.co.uk/news/falklands/menu.htm

This site, developed by an online Portsmouth newspaper, covers a wide range of aspects of the war, including a timeline and a large number of short articles and photographs.

The Falklands Island Conflict

http://met.open.ac.uk/group/cpv/falkland.htm

This site features a data library on military vessels and aircraft, a QuickTime video library, and links to other Falklands-related sites.

THE GULF WAR

Desert-Storm.com

http://www.desert-storm.com/

An index of sites related to operations Desert Shield, Desert Storm, and Desert Fox.

Operation Desert Storm

http://www.fas.org/man/dod-101/ops/desert_storm.htm

This site provides a brief summary of the Gulf War and an extensive set of links to articles about the conflict and other military resources.

Persian Gulf War/Operation Desert Storm

http://www.msstate.edu/Archives/History/USA/GulfWar/gulf.html

Another historical site from Mississippi State University, this page offers a list of documents related to the Gulf War, including the diaries of an Israeli woman and an Iraqi soldier.

Fog of War

http://www.washingtonpost.com/wp-srv/inatl/longterm/fogofwar/fogofwar.htm

An extensive set of resources on the Gulf War developed by the Washington Post, including government documents, images, and video clips.

Ronald A. Hoskinson's Gulf War Photo Gallery

http://users.aol.com/andyhosk/gwmain.htm

Images and a detailed personal account from a field artillery captain who served in the Gulf War.

807th MASH: Operation Desert Shield and Operation Desert Storm

http://www.iglou.com/law/mash.htm

An online account of the experiences of a mobile army surgical hospital's staff during the Gulf War.

OTHER RECENT CONFLICTS

The 1971 India–Pakistan War

http://freeindia.org/1971war/

A detailed online history, from an Indian perspective, of the short but brutal conflict between India and Pakistan in 1971.

Operation Urgent Fury

http://www.specialoperations.com/grenada.html

This site provides links to Web sites related to the American invasion of Grenada, including a detailed discussion of SEAL operations during the invasion, a bibliography of printed sources, and a video clip of Ronald Reagan announcing the invasion.

Artillery and Counterinsurgency: The Soviet Experience in Afghanistan

http://call.army.mil/call/fmso/fmsopubs/issues/arty/arty.htm

An online monograph from the United States Army on the Soviet invasion of Afghanistan.

The Soviet War in Afghanistan: History and Harbinger of Future War?

http://call.army.mil/call/fmso/fmsopubs/issues/waraf.htm

Another Army monograph discussing the Soviet invasion of Afghanistan.

Operation JUST CAUSE

http://www.army.mil/cmh-pg/documents/panama/just.htm

Supplemental documents from the U.S. Army on Operation Just Cause.

Operation Just Cause: Lessons Learned

http://call.army.mil/CALL/NEWSLTRS/90-9/9091toc.htm

Online book written by the U.S. Army on Operation Just Cause.

The Somalia Intervention

http://www.users.interport.net/~mmaren/interventionx.html

An index of Web sites and online articles on United Nations intervention in Somalia.

ORGANIZATIONS AND OTHER MILITARY HISTORY SITES

The Battleship Page

http://www.battleship.org/

This page is hosted by the Iowa Class Preservation Association—a nonprofit organization dedicated to preserving this aspect of America's heritage—and provides links to a large number of pages related to the role of the battleship in modern military history.

Institute for the Advanced Study of Information Warfare

http://www.psycom.net/iwar.1.html

Provides links to sites and articles related to the gathering and use of information in warfare.

Military Aircraft Database

http://www.csd.uwo.ca/~pettypi/elevon/gustin_military/

An online encyclopedia dedicated to past and present military aircraft of the world.

Military Woman Home Page

http://www.MilitaryWoman.org/homepage.htm

An index of resources related to issues facing women who serve in the military or who are married to those who serve. Useful for those investigating the history of private lives.

The South African Military History Society

http://rapidttp.com/milhist/

Home page for the organization with various links, including a journal with some online articles related to the Boer War and other subjects.

Three-Four-Nine: The Ultimate Reference for the Ultimate F-16 Enthusiast

http://allserv.rug.ac.be/~svhastel/

A remarkably detailed online encyclopedia dedicated to the F-16 Falcon, one of the most widely exported combat aircraft in the world.

United States Commission on Military History

http://www.uscmh.org/

An organizational home page including links to membership, bibliography, and related sites.

PSYCHOHISTORY

Lloyd deMause

The Institute for Psychohistory

http://www.psychohistory.com

A rich 250-page site of complete articles and book chapters on psychohistory, the study of historical motivations. Includes articles from *The Journal of Psychohistory*, chapters of the book *Childhood and History* by Lloyd deMause, a twenty-five-year subject index to *The Journal of Psychohistory*, and links to psychohistorical sites.

The International Psychohistorical Association

http://www.geocities.com/Athens/Acropolis/8623

The activities of the International Psychohistorical Association, its yearly convention, and an outline of the profession of psychohistory.

Psychohistory Discussion Listserv Resource List

http://sooth.com/ph/

Archives and resources of a discussion list on psychohistory, a bulletin board and chat room intended as a resource for individuals studying psychohistory, and a forum for scholarly discussions. Includes daily discussions of the psychological approach to current political and social events, group fantasies, past and present, the history of childhood, and bibliographic resources. You can actually subscribe to the discussion group by sending an empty e-mail message to PH-L-subscribe@sooth.com.

HISTORIOGRAPHY: THE HISTORY OF HISTORY

Guido Abbattista

METASITES AND GENERAL HISTORICAL METHODOLOGY

Historiology

http://www.cannylink.com/historyhistoriology.htm

A short index of sites on historical methodology at the Cannylink Internet Guide.

History and Historiography, Carnegie Mellon University

http://eng.hss.cmu.edu/history/

A valuable collection of links to historical resources.

The History Index at the University of Kansas

http://www.ukans.edu/history/VL/

This site provides an extensive list of links to historical sites on all the relevant subdivisions of historical research.

Voice of the Shuttle

http://humanitas.ucsb.edu/shuttle/history.html#historiography.

On the history page of this well-known metaindex, under the category "Historiography," there is a choice for the best sites of historiographical interest.

Yahoo: Index of History Resources

http://www.indiantrailonline.com/history.htm

This enumerates several sites of historical interest: It is worth browsing in search of materials of a more definitely historiographical-methodological character.

ELECTRONIC LIBRARIES AND HISTORIOGRAPHICAL TEXTS

American Hypertexts

http://xroads.virginia.edu/~HYPER/hypertex.html

A large collection of textual resources on American history, including *The Federalist Papers*, Tocqueville's *Democracy in America*, and works by Francis Parkman and Frederick Jackson Turner.

Aragonese Historiography

http://eng.hss.cmu.edu/history/aragonese-historiography.txt

An essay online on the essentials of Aragonese historiography, this resource is part of the English Server at the Carnegie Mellon University.

CHPE—Centre d'histoire de la pensée économique— Bibliothèque virtuelle de la pensée économique

http://panoramix.univ-paris1.fr/CHPE/textes.html

Located at the Université de Paris–I, this virtual library gives access to rich materials on the history of economic thought, as well as the history of historiography and methodology in modern Europe—for example, texts by Giovanni Botero, Matthew Hale, Lord Bolingbroke, Jean-Jacques Rousseau, Adam Ferguson, Thomas Malthus, Frederic Maitland, and Benedetto Croce.

Eliohs—Electronic Library of Modern Historiography

http://www.unifi.it/riviste/eliohs/index.html

An electronic and virtual library of texts concerning modern (mainly seventeenth- to eighteenth-century) historiography, philosophy of history, and methodology. This is the only resource born out of a project expressly devoted to the history of historiography, and it led to the creation of the electronic journal *Cromohs* (see page 388). Its catalogue includes electronic editions of historical, methodological, and philosophico-historical works from the sixteenth to the twentieth century produced by Eliohs, and includes links to texts of the same kind electronically published elsewhere on the Net.

Fernand Braudel Center

http://fbc.binghamton.edu/

The French historian Fernand Braudel made a profound impact on how historians view and practice their discipline. He played a leading role in the articulation of social history and interdisciplinary studies. This Web site at the Binghamton University, State University of New York, provides a wealth of resources relating to Braudel. Among the members of its scientific board is Immanuel Wallerstein.

Gallica (Bibliothèque Nationale de France)

http://gallica.bnf.fr/

The French national library offers online versions of many nineteenth-century French historians' most important works.

The Internet Classics Archive at the Massachusetts Institute of Technology

http://classics.mit.edu/index.html

Offers full texts of works by such Greek, Jewish, Roman, and Persian historians as Herodotus, Thucydides, StraboXenophon, Josephus, Plutarch, Julius Caesar, Livy, Tacitus, Firdousi, and Lao-tze. Texts are not in their original language, but are translated into English They are available for free downloading in text-only format. This site has been on the Internet since 1994, and is sponsored in part by the MIT Program in Writing and Humanistic Studies.

The Scriptorium: Center for Christian Studies

http://www.scriptorium.org/~Scriptorium/Home.html

The Scriptorium: Center for Christian Antiquities is a nonsectarian research center working in conjunction with The Van Kampen Foundation, and serves as the repository for The Van Kampen Collection of ancient artifacts, manuscripts, and rare printed materials. The collection consists primarily of biblical texts in all representative forms and is supplemented by secondary resources and the personal library of Eberhard Nestle, a leading nineteenth-century German biblical scholar. The Scriptorium sponsors various academic initiatives reflecting the faculty's commitment to public education, scholarly research, and innovative pedagogy.

Crusade Historiography

http://www.uni-heidelberg.de/subject/hd/fak7/hist/o1/logs/mt/
t7/940901-051/

Anybody concerned with historical narratives of the Crusades? At this Web location it is possible to read a series of mails belonging to a thread of discussion on the theme of Crusade historiography. More mails on different aspects of the history of historiography, methodology, and philosophy of history (for example: philosophies of history and contemporary historical research on the Middle Ages; definitions of "Medieval") can be read retrospectively at the same site under the URL http://www.uni-heidelberg.de/subject/hd/fak7/hist/o1/logs/mt/t7/

The Historian Underground—Making History Relevant for Life

http://www.geocities.com/SoHo/Cafe/8579/under.htm

A voice from outside the academic world. This site is designed to give voice to views about the object of history that challenge the normal aims of the historian's craft. It is based on the presupposition that normal academic historical method has lost touch with the importance of history for people's lives. This site's editors, therefore, are attempting to gather some articles to challenge traditional ways of thinking and stir up a bit of controversy. These pages go deep into an examination of the relation of history, philosophy, and even a little literature, as well as evaluating education and its role.

Historians and Philosophers

http://www.corvinia.org/history/histphil.html

This is a site by P. Rasmussen consisting of a biographical dictionary of historians (and philosophers) from ancient times to the contemporary age (arranged in four sections: ancient, medieval, early modern, and modern period), in the form of original or linked biographical profiles, (sometimes) bibliography, and external links to electronic editions of main works. The biographies are not written according to a uniform project and are very unequal in content and value. A useful reference site for history of historiography, but still heavily under construction.

The Hume Archives

http://www.utm.edu/research/hume/

This very important site, maintained by Jim Fieser, includes Hume's writings, commentaries, eighteenth-century reviews of Hume's works, and early biographies. Available are also some writings by the Scottish philosopher documenting his ideas on history and his historical treatment of such subjects as man's religious sentiments.

Internet Public Library Online Texts

http://readroom.ipl.org/bin/ipl/ipl.books-idx.pl?type=deweystem&q1=901.

Classic texts of interest for the methodology of history and general views of the historical process are present in this remarkable electronic library at the University of Michigan. Among the collection are writings by Francis Bacon, John Milton, James Dunbar, John Millar, Constantin-François Volney, T. B. Macaulay, Charles Babbage, Edwin Seligman, Antonio Labriola, Joel Salit, and Charles Kingsley.

Labyrinth

http://www.georgetown.edu/labyrinth/

This project from Georgetown University hosts a selection of contemporary sources on Medieval history arranged on a linguistic basis. Attention: each Labyrinth Library section (e.g., "Auctores et fontes") does not give direct access to digital editions, but is just a small choice of external sites loosely referring to several European areas of medieval history. Among these you may happen to find important electronic editions of relevant sources, but frequently one may be disappointed to be offered heterogeneous links not critically selected.

Liber Liber

http://www.liberliber.it/biblioteca/index.htm

An excellent multidisciplinary searchable collection of mainly Italian, but also foreign texts, books, articles, documents, theses, and reviews available all over the world. Every text is accompanied by information about the author and his production and a small introduction. Works by Italian early-modern and modern historians can be found here, like Dino Compagni, Giovanni Villani. Niccolò Machiavelli, Francesco Guicciardini, Giambattista Vico, Vincenzo Cuoco, Francesco de Sanctis, Antonio Labriola. This is part of Progetto Manuzio and is hosted at the University of Milan.

Philosophy of History Archive

http://www.nsu.ru/filf/pha/

This Russian site introduces itself as follows: "The International Philosophy of History Archive (PHA) administered by Prof. Nikolai S. Rozov is a Web node that indexes links and materials related to the Philosophy of History and Theoretical History (PH&TH) on the Internet. It aims to serve those whose research interests include the rational theoretical explanatory approaches to World History and Modernity, the scientific predictions of global future trends, and the application of philosophical and scientific research results to Global Praxis." It contains a list of internal and external links to e-texts and sites related to philosophy of history and theoretical history.

Giambattista Vico Home Page

http://www.connix.com/~gapinton/

This site, maintained by Giorgio A. Pinton, offers a biography and chronology of the life of one of the most important eighteenth-century European philosophers of history and bibliographies relating to his major works.

Voltaire, Oeuvres Diverses

http://perso.wanadoo.fr/dboudin/Voltind.htm

In this electronic library of works by Voltaire, some historical works are also included.

Voltaire Page

http://res2.geocities.com/Athens/7308/

A site compiled by F. DeVenuto and expressly devoted to one of the most outstanding Enlightenment historians, with links to related sites.

Voltaire Society of America: Web Sites on Voltaire

http://humanities.uchicago.edu/homes/VSA/Websites.html

More sites on the great Enlightenment philosopher and historian.

World History Archives

http://www.hartford-hwp.com/archives/10/index.html

World Historiography is a selection of materials proposed by Hartford Web Publishing. This site hosts a collection of essays, excerpts from classics of historiography, messages, dialogues, shorter essays on interpretative aspects of world history (e.g., peculiarity of world history, Eurocentrism, the limits and divisions of history, world-systems approach). This material has been mainly selected from the H-NET list for World History. It is an interesting proposition of ideas and insights expressed through the medium of a discussion list.

ELECTRONIC JOURNALS

Cromohs

http://www.unifi.it/riviste/cromohs/

This is an electronic journal, founded in 1995, and expressly devoted to the history, theory, and methodology of historiography. It publishes in yearly issues original articles, review essays, and short reviews. Among its services there are a very useful current bibliography of monographs and periodical literature and a list of relevant events. It was born as both a journal and an electronic library of sources. The library, called Eliohs (q.v.), has grown so much as to acquire a distinct identity. Chief editors and initiators of both *Cromohs* and Eliohs are Guido Abbattista and Rolando Minuti.

Histos—The Electronic Journal of Ancient Historiography

http://www.dur.ac.uk/Classics/histos/about.html

This journal, founded in 1997, is published at the Durham Classics Department and contains articles, essays, reviews, notices on research projects, and conferences on any aspect of ancient historiography.

Reviews in American History

http://muse.jhu.edu/journals/reviews_in_american_history/toc/rahv026.html

An invaluable tool for an up-to-date survey of contemporary historiographical production and debates both on general theoretical and methodological topics and in particular on American history research.

PRINT JOURNALS WITH WEB SITES

History and Theory

http://www.historyandtheory.org/

This is the site of the well-known journal of historical methodology and philosophy of history established in 1960, which represents the main reference for contemporary research and debate on these topics.

Storia della Storiografia

http://www.cisi.unito.it/stor/home.htm

Storia della Storiografia—History of Historiography—Histoire de l'Historiographie—Geschichte der Geschichtsschreibung is a journal founded in 1982 by the International Commission for the History of Historiography and publishes, in four languages, articles on all relevant aspects of the history and theory of historiography and the historical profession. Its Web site provides general information on the journal's activity and complete indexes of past, current, and forthcoming issues with an archive of contributors.

Teaching History: A Journal of Methods

http://www.emporia.edu/socsci/journal/main.htm

This is the Web site of a journal whose aim is to give general information and indexes of current and past issues. Designed for history teachers at all levels who wish to read about, or contribute to, innovative methods of teaching history, it is edited by Samuel Dicks and maintained by Michael Handley at the Division of Social Sciences of Emporia State University.

DIDACTIC RESOURCES

Internet Modern History Sourcebook—Studying History

http://www.fordham.edu/halsall/mod/modsbook.html
http://www.fordham.edu/halsall/mod/modsbook01.html

An outstanding, first-rate didactic project devoted to a full presentation of the problem of historiographical research, knowledge, and methodology—and of theories of history in the modern age—with excerpts from primary sources and a rich library of essays, pages of important works on the subject, and lectures, being collectively a large anthology of class materials. Many of these materials are not locally produced, but just linked on the Net.

National Standards for World History

http://www.iac.net/~pfilio/part1.html

The electronic text of one of the most controversial documents on the reform of history teaching in the United States.

Ten Commandments of Good Historical Writing

http://www.bluffton.edu/~schlabachg/courses/10commnd.htm

This site, by Theron F. Schlabach, contains a list of practical commonsense (but at times controvertible) suggestions from a teacher to beginners or amateurs—interesting nonetheless as representative of an opinion on what a historian-to-be's work ought to be. Better to weigh than really consider them as mandatory commandments.

HISTORICAL POPULATION DATABASES

Gunnar Thorvaldsen

INTRODUCTION

Population databases contain information on the inhabitants of a certain region—most notably whole countries—enabling users to do statistical studies or find information on individuals or groups of persons. Some data sets are statistical—typically the number of men and women, or the number of births or deaths, based on censuses, ministerial records or longitudinal population registers. The tables or data extracts requested can be stored in static formats or created dynamically to the user's specifications on the basis of individual level information in a database interacting with specially designed software. Alternatively or complementary, such microdata may be presented for downloading or inspection online. Historical population databases often contain contemporary data, but we have omitted from this overview those mostly containing data sets assembled during the last couple of decades.

Metapage: Historical Microdata around the World

http://www.sv.uit.no/seksjon/rhd/nhdc/micro.htm

The main section of this page lists links to significant sites with information on the individual level, e.g., transcriptions from censuses or church records. "Significant" excludes sites with data stemming from individual research projects. Some of these are listed in an auxiliary section called "other databases for historical research." The metapage is maintained by The Norwegian Historical Data Centre at The University of Tromsø in Norway.

The Canadian Families Project

http://web.uvic.ca/hrd/cfp/

The project team is completing a five-percent national sample of the 1901 Census of Canada employing the same methods for sampling and standardization as the Integrated Public Use Microdata Series (IPUMS) project in the United States. No data sets are presently available online, but the nationally representative sample with 50,943 dwellings and 265,286 persons will be made available to researchers as a public use sample in 2001. The Canadian Families Project is based at the University of Victoria, but is a collaborative research project by eleven scholars in five Canadian universities.

Census Data for the United States 1790–1970

http://fisher.lib.virginia.edu/census/

The statistical data presented here describe the people and the economy of the United States for each state and county based on all the decennial censuses from 1790 to 1970. The data sets were provided by the Inter-university Consortium for Political and Social Research (ICPSR), and can be browsed online with software provided by The Instructional Computing Group of Harvard University.

The Danish Demographic Database

http://ddd.sa.dk/ddd2.htm

Here the 1787–1911 censuses for selected districts in Denmark and the Danish emigrant database for 1868–1900 can be searched free of charge for information on individuals and their families. The latter database is considered to be more complete than the U.S. immigration registers. This site is a cooperative effort of the Danish Data Archives, the Danish Emigration Archives, and the Centre of Microfilming in the Danish Provincial Archives.

The Demographic Data Base

http://www.ddb.umu.se/DDB/eng/index.htm

The DDB holds transcripts of nineteenth-century catechismal records for seven selected parishes and three regions in Sweden. A demonstration sample can be searched free of charge via the Internet, but researchers must contact the DDB to order data extracts. Historical population statistics for Swedish localities and provinces are also available. The DDB is a permanent part of Umeå University and cooperates closely with its Centre for Population Studies.

The Digital Archive

http://www.hist.uib.no/arkivverket/index-en.htm

The National Archives of Norway have made major parts of the 1865 and 1900 censuses available for online data retrieval via the Internet, together with various other kinds of source material, such as emigration records and probate registers. The University of Bergen hosts the databases, also making available the 1801 census for all of Norway. Some statistical functions, like filtering and cross tabulations, are available for the censuses.

The Historical Sample of the Netherlands

http://www.iisg.nl/~hsn/

This site presents a longitudinal and representative sample of about 80,000 people born in the Netherlands during the period 1812–1922, built on information from certificates of births, deaths, and marriages, records from the population registers, and other historical sources. Occupations, locations, etc., have been encoded for statistical analyses. A provisional data set from the Utrecht pilot project can be ordered at a nominal price. The database is hosted by The International Institute of Social History in Amsterdam.

The History Data Service

http://hds.essex.ac.uk/homepage.stm

The HDS aims to take into custody data sets from historical projects and provide possibilities for reuse in future research. The organization provides access to manuscript census records, primarily the 1881 census of Great Britain. At present no data sets are available online, but the register of archival holdings can be searched in the database Biron. The HDS is located at and integrated with The Data Archive at the University of Essex, which is the national social science data archive for the United Kingdom.

IPUMS: Integrated Public Use Microdata Series

http://www.ipums.umn.edu/

The IPUMS project integrates representative samples from thirteen U.S. censuses covering the period 1850 to 1990 in the world's largest historical database (currently IPUMS-98). The samples enable researchers to study the American population by combining variables such as race or occupation on the individual or household level. Sample densities vary from one in 760 (1900 census) to one in twenty (1980 and 1990 censuses), the aim being to have at least one percent samples for every census. With the exception of group quarters, the entire household is kept intact when sampling. For 1970 to 1990 there exist several samples based on different densities and strategies. Two nominative censuses are not available: the 1890 census returns were burned in a fire, and for 1930 data entry is pending.

While the samples stem from different sources, the IPUMS project has molded them into the same form, using record and variable formats with a uniform layout, so that, e.g., occupational coding schemes are compatible over the whole series of censuses. A number of auxiliary variables make explicit the location of family members such as fathers and mothers within the household. The original work with the census returns, the data entry process, and the IPUMS group's data integration are documented in three volumes, the content of which is available for inspection or downloading in Acrobat Reader format via the Web pages. The entire samples (25GB uncompressed) can be downloaded individually via FTP. A better method is to use the online data extraction system via the button "Get IPUMS data" to order subsets of whatever censuses, sample densities, variables, and geographic areas are of interest in a particular research project. Afterward the tailor-made data set can be downloaded free of charge.

Genealogists should be warned that samples from after 1920 contain no names, and that earlier samples, having a density of one percent or less, give little chance of identifying particular individuals. IPUMS is based in the Department of History at the University of Minnesota.

IREP: L'Institut interuniversitaire de recherches sur les populations

http://infoserv.uqac.uquebec.ca/irep/bienvenu.htm (in French)

The Interuniversity Institute for Population Research bases much of its activities on the database BALSAC, mainly containing parish records for parts of the Quebec Province from 1838 up to 1971. Various other records, e.g., economic or cultural, have been added to the relational database for specific research purposes. In order to protect privacy and economize resources, the data sets are only made available to researchers after an evaluation of the ethical character and scientific significance of each project. The IREP now consists of researchers from seven universities and other institutions in Quebec, mainly dealing with demographic and genetic aspects of the population's history.

The Norwegian Historical Data Centre

http://www.isv.uit.no/seksjon/rhd/indexeng.htm

The NHDC computerizes historical microdata such as censuses and ministerial records from selected municipalities. Full-text and encoded versions are available as books, on microfiche, as computer files, and on the Web for research, teaching, and genealogical purposes. Significant parts of the 1865, 1875, and 1900 censuses are available free of charge for retrieval via an interactive HTML interface. Another major data set available in this way is the 1886 tax assessment list covering all registered Norwegian farms and farmers. Encoded individual level versions of the censuses can be ordered for downloading into major statistical packages. Upon application, the NHDC will computerize historical material from the original sources for research projects meeting certain standards. The Norwegian Historical Data Centre is a permanent part of the University of Tromsø.

The Research Archive (Forskningsarkivet)

http://www.foark.umu.se/

This is another part of Umeå University holding various types of archival resources. Most notably, significant parts of the 1890 census for Sweden are searchable through a Web interface. There is currently only a Swedish version of these pages.

The Stockholm Historical Database

http://www.ssa.stockholm.se/texter/shd.htm

This database covers the central parts of the Swedish capital during the period 1878 to 1926, with records on each move made by the inhabitants. It is probably the best resource in the world for studying historic gross migration longitudinally. There is no online interface, and the Web page is in Swedish only, so Agneta.Geschwind@ssa.stockholm.se should be contacted for further information, e.g., on their CD-ROM and microfiche products.

HISTORIC PRESERVATION AND CONSERVATION

Charlene Mires

Preserve/Net

http://www.preservenet.cornell.edu

Incorporating the Preserve/Net Information Service and the Preserve/Net Law Service, this site at Cornell University includes extensive links to preservation organizations, education programs, conferences and events, and job and internship opportunities. The Law Service offers texts of major state and federal preservation legislation and models for preservation ordinances. This is also the host site for the Guide to the African-American Heritage Preservation Foundation Inc. (http://www.preservenet.cornell.edu/aahpf/homepage.htm).

National Center for Preservation Technology and Training

http://www.ncptt.nps.gov

This project within the National Park Service includes an extensive, annotated database of online resources in archaeology, history, historic architecture and landscapes, and conservation of materials and objects. The database includes links for subscribing to listservs related to preservation and conservation.

Advisory Council on Historic Preservation

http://www.achp.gov

Created by the independent federal agency that advises the president and Congress on historic preservation issues, this site offers links to historic preservation officers throughout the United States and information about the National Historic Preservation Act of 1966.

The American Institute for Conservation of Historic and Artistic Works

http://sul-server-2.stanford.edu/aic

This organization of professional conservators shares its expertise on how to care for prized possessions from paintings and photographs to home videotapes. The site also offers advice on how to locate and select a professional conservator.

Built in America: Historic American Buildings Survey/ Historic American Engineering Record, 1933–Present

http://memory.loc.gov/ammem/hhhtml/hhhome.html

As part of its American Memory project, the Library of Congress has begun digitizing the vast documentation of American architecture, engineering, and design collected by the Historic American Buildings Survey and the Historic American Engineering Record. As the records go online, they can be searched by keyword, subject, and geographic area.

Conservation Online

http://palimpsest.stanford.edu

From Stanford University Libraries, this site has information on a wide range of conservation topics of interest to libraries and their users, including digital imaging and the conservation and use of electronic records.

Council on Library and Information Resources

http://www.clir.org/home.html

Offers online publications related to current issues in the preservation of library materials.

Heritage Conservation and Historic Preservation

http://home.vicnet.net.au/~conserv/hp-hc.htm

The State Library of Victoria in Australia has assembled this online library about conservation issues. International in scope, the many topics addressed by articles and accompanying Web links include information about caring for cultural objects such as books and paper, film and photography, and sound and magnetic materials.

Keeping Our Word: Preserving Information Across the Ages

http://www.lib.uiowa.edu/ref/exhibit

This virtual version of an exhibit by the University of Iowa Libraries addresses the issues of preserving materials from cave paintings and clay tablets to electronic media. The exhibit includes links for doing further research on preservation issues.

National Archives and Records Administration

http://www.nara.gov/nara/preserva

From the experts at the National Archives, this site provides information about preserving documents and photographs.

National Center for Heritage Development

http://www.nchd.org

Dedicated to developing heritage initiatives throughout the United States, this nonprofit organization offers information about joining its coalition and links to projects such as the American Heritage Rivers Initiative.

National Park Service Links to the Past

http://www.cr.nps.gov

A site of great scope and depth, this project of the National Park Service is the place to start for information about visiting historic sites throughout the national parks system, teaching with historic places, and becoming involved with historic sites as a national parks volunteer. Online exhibits cover topics such as the life of Frederick Douglass and camp life at Gettysburg, and virtual tours take Web visitors to historic places in Detroit, Seattle, and other regions of the country. The site also serves as the gateway to programs such as Tools for Teaching (http://www.cr.nps.gov/toolsfor.htm), the Historic American Buildings Survey/Historic American Engineering Record (http://www.cr.nps.gov/habshaer), and the National Register of Historic Places (http://www.cr.nps.gov/nr).

National Preservation Institute

http://www.npi.org

This organization offers online registration for its numerous training seminars in historic preservation and cultural resources management.

National Trust for Historic Preservation

http://www.nthp.org

This private, nonprofit organization dedicated to saving historic buildings, neighborhoods, and landscapes offers a site with information about the group's mission and many projects, including its annual list of the nation's most endangered places. A link to its *Preservation* magazine offers tables of contents, book reviews, and excerpts from some other features of the magazine. A link to the National Trust's Main Street Center (http://www.mainst.org), which works to revitalize historic and traditional commercial areas, provides information about the history and preservation of Main Street communities and advice for organizing a Main Street revitalization project.

Northern States Conservation Center

http://www.collectioncare.org

Numerous articles about the management and preservation of museum collections, including advice about museums' use of the World Wide Web, are offered here by Northern States Conservation Center of Saint Paul, Minnesota.

Research Libraries Group (RLG) DigiNews

http://www.rlg.org/preserv/diginews

Online newsletter by the Research Libraries Group, focusing on preservation through digital imaging.

The Society of Architectural Historians

http://www.sah.org

This organization's collection of Internet resources includes links to collections of images of historic buildings.

State Historic Preservation Legislation Database

http://www.ncsl.org/programs/arts/statehist_intro.htm

The National Conference of State Legislatures offers this database of state legislation and constitution articles governing historic sites, archaeological sites and materials, and significant unmarked burial sites.

World Heritage

http://www.unesco.org/whc/nwhc/pages/home/pages/homepage.htm

Home page for the UNESCO project that encourages the preservation of cultural and natural heritage sites around the world. This site includes information about more than five hundred World Heritage sites, including those considered endangered.

World Monuments Fund

http://www.worldmonuments.org

The site of this private, nonprofit organization working to safeguard works of art and architecture includes information about the fund's international list of 100 most endangered sites.

LIVING HISTORY AND HISTORIC REENACTMENT

Bambi L. Dingman

METASITES

Living History

http://www.jaxnet.com/~ahrendt/livhist.htm

A great index of Web sites related to historical research, sutlers and suppliers, and living history sites, sorted by time period.

Living History Online

http://www.LivingHistoryOnline.com

An online magazine that serves as a reference source for all historical periods, this site contains excellent articles, an events calendar, bibliographies, and a search capability.

Reenactment and Living History Web

http://www.access.digex.net/~bdboyle/reenact/reenact.html

A large listing of regimental Web sites, sutlers and equipment suppliers, recipes, tips, and other useful information for reenactors.

Reenactor's WebMall

http://rampages.onramp.net/~lawsonda/mall/

A comprehensive source for reenacting information, including a sutler's list, arranged by time period.

The UK Register of Reenactment Web Sites

http://www.compulink.co.uk/~novar/listings.htm

Links to general suppliers and craftsmen, historical information, online reenactment information, and societies that recreate the time period 1600–1900.

U.S. Regular Army Reenacting Unit Directory

http://www.halcyon.com/strandjr/Regs.html

A huge index of reenacting units, sorted by time period. Some organizations have links to their Web pages, while others have e-mail contact information.

World Wide Register of Reenactment and Living History Societies

http://nuntius.ukc.ac.uk/SU/Societies/deBec/Welcome

This register contains contact information for living history units around the globe, with a brief description of each.

GENERAL SITES

22nd Alabama Infantry, Company D

http://www.geocities.com/~bobjones/22ndalinf.htm

A nice example of a company home page with a regimental history, online documents, and reenacting information.

ALHFAM—Association for Living History, Farm, and Agricultural Museums

http://www.alhfam.org/

Home of the Association for Living History, Farm, and Agricultural Museums. The association's Web page has conference information, employment classifieds for living history specialists, planning tips for living history sites, and extensive links to living history organizations throughout the world.

The Alliance of Early American Interpreters

http://members.xoom.com/AEAI/index.html

The Alliance of Early American Interpreters is dedicated to recreating the lives of civilian colonists in America in the period 1750–90. Their Web site has membership information, an events calendar, recipes, and related sites.

The American Civil War

http://users.iamdigex.net/bdboyle/cw.html

A comprehensive index of Civil War sites on the Web, categorized by area of interest. Topics include bibliographies, reenacting groups, battlefields and historic sites, flags, movies, diaries, etc.

American Civil War Historical Reenactment Society

http://www.worldchat.com/public/acwhrs

Dedicated to honoring the role Canadians played in the American Civil War. Their Web page has membership information, an events schedule, information about period music, and links to related sites.

American Longrifle Association

http://www.meridiantc.com/alra/

A period trekking group and umbrella organization spanning the years 1750–1850. A calendar of events can be found online, and also photographs and a bibliography.

Angelcynn

http://www.geocities.com/Athens/2471/index.html

All content is related to Anglo-Saxon living history representing the period 400–900 A.D., clothing and appearance of the early Christian Anglo-Saxons, weapons and armor, history, and related links.

The Arte of Defense

http://jan.ucc.nau.edu/~wew/fencing.html

An interesting page related to the art of fencing and swordplay. Topics include period masters, terminology, types of blades, and links to other fencing sites on the Web.

14th Brooklyn New York State Militia International Reenacting Organization

http://www.geocities.com/Athens/Agean/7862

Recreating the persona of the men and women of the original 14th Brooklyn. The company Web site has information on enlistment, uniforms, company history, and reenacting.

Buckskins and Black Powder

http://www.geocities.com/Yosemite/Gorge/7186/index.htm

This excellent site has links to a variety of black powder and buckskinning sites on the Web. Also includes information about black powder clubs, the fur trade era, and recreating history.

Butler's Rangers

http://iaw.on.ca/~awoolley/brang/brang.html

This corps of Rangers served in the American Revolution and is recreated at living history events today. Information about the Rangers, both past and present, can be found on this site, as well as historical source material and other information.

C & D Jarnagin Company

http://www.jarnaginco.com/

A provider of fine wares for the period 1750 through 1865, with a full complement of uniforms and equipment for American troops.

California Historical Group

http://www.primenet/~chgww/

A photo gallery, upcoming events, stories, and links to groups portraying German, Russian, American, and British troops during World War II.

Camp Chase Gazette

http://www.cybergate.net/%7Ecivilwar/

A well-known publication devoted to American Civil War recreation. The online edition contains informative articles, a virtual roster of Civil War reenactors, upcoming events, and other relevant information.

Camp Life

http://www.cr.nps.gov/csd/gettex/

Gettysburg National Park holds the largest Civil War collection in the National Park System, with more than 40,000 catalogued items. A unique aspect of the collection is that many of the pieces are common everyday items that allow us a glimpse into the lives of the soldiers who owned them. Now part of the collection can be viewed online in this virtual museum of photographs and artifacts devoted to everyday camp life.

Castle Keep Ltd.

http://www.reenact.com

Living history information and supplies for reenactors, categorized by period of interest, from Medieval times to the twentieth century.

Seventeenth-Century Reenacting and English Civil War Living History Resources

http://www.lukehistory.com/resources/index.html

Full-text versions of period pamphlets, blackletter ballads, letters, and articles about seventeenth-century culture.

The Civil War Artillery Page

http://www.cwartillery.org/artillery.html

Information about organization and drill, weapons, ammunition, equipment, history, and reenactment of field and foot artillery units of the American Civil War.

Civil War Sailor and Marine Magazine Association

http://members.aol.com/CWSMMA/index.html

This organization teaches and shares the story of the American Civil War naval conflict by organizing micro-events. Some battles include rebuilt ironclads and full-size sailing ships. Membership information can be found online.

Clothing of the Ancient Celts

http://www47.pair.com/lindo/Textiles_Page.htm

The primary focus of this Web page is on prehistoric and classical Celtic culture and costuming, with a wealth of information about hair, jewelry, dyes, textiles, and links to other Celtic sites.

Compagnie Franche de la Marine du Detroit

http://www.richnet.net/~kamoore/

A volunteer living history interpretation organization devoted to all Detroit impressions, including marine, militia, Native American, and civilian, c. 1754–60. Their company Web page has original and current unit history.

Company of Saint George

http://www.chronique.com/george.htm

This site fosters the spirit of chivalry by portraying a tournament company of the fourteenth and fifteenth centuries. Ceremony information, upcoming events, and a discussion about the role of historic interpreters can be found at this site.

Coon 'n Crockett Muzzleloaders

http://www.coon-n-crockett.org/

This page is loaded with information about the club, the muzzleloading hobby, photos, upcoming events, and more!

The Costume Page

http://members.aol.com/nebula5/tcpsupp.html

This is the definitive source for costuming information on the Web, conveniently sorted by period of interest. Links to costume suppliers, accessories, and patterns for every time period.

The Costumer's Manifesto

http://www.costumes.org/pages/pagesindex.htm

Another great resource for costume and historical costume information, organized by area of interest.

Digital History Ltd.

http://digitalhistory.org

A comprehensive site for everything related to the French and Indian War, including well-written accounts of the battles, forts, and participants, as well as links to groups that are currently recreating colonial North American history.

Elizabethan Period Costumes

http://www.renfaire.com/Costume/index.html

A complete source of information on Elizabethan clothing, patterns, and footwear.

English Renaissance Reenactment Home Page

http://www.webcom.com/st_mike/

Anyone interested in English Renaissance reenacting will want to look here for information on upcoming events, groups, clothing, literature, medicine, and more!

Fall Creek Sutlers

http://fcsutler.com/

Supplies for Civil War reenactors and Victorian era enthusiasts.

Flintlock FAQ

http://www.aye.net/~bspen/flintlockfaq.html

A beginners's guide to flintlock shooting.

Florida Spanish-American War Reenactors

http://www.rhickox.simplenet.com/saw1898.htm

Reenactors of the Spanish-American War of 1898 can find uniform and equipment requirements, a list of suppliers, and related reenactment organizations on this page, as well as a list of museums with Spanish-American War exhibits, a monthly newsletter, and the 1898 *Illustrated Manual of Arms*.

French and Indian War Magazine Online

http://members.aol.com/fiwar/home.html

An electronic magazine that will interest French and Indian War reenactors. This informative site has a great listing of reenactment groups and other topics related to the war, such as British and French forts, music, and clothing.

GI Journal

http://www.militaria.com

Articles of interest to WWI and WWII reenactors and links to division Web pages, reproduction uniforms, and military history magazines.

Great War Militaria

http://www.greatwar.com/

An online catalogue of books, clothing, and equipment from French, British, German, and U.S. soldiers of WWI.

The Gunfighter Zone

http://www.gunfighter.com

A Web site for reenactors of the Old West and Cowboy Action Shooting groups, with links to discussion boards, suppliers, books, magazines, and informative articles.

Historic Arms and Armour

http://www.historicenterprises.com/arms_and_armour/index.html

Specializes in highly accurate handmade replicas of museum pieces. Although it is a commercial site, there is also a great deal of historical information and interesting photos of their work.

The Historical Maritime Society

http://www.btinternet.com/~pjehome/hms.htm

Recreates life in the British Navy from 1793 to 1815 (Napoleonic War Period).

Historical Reenactors

http://novaroma.org/via_romana/reenactments/index.html

Costuming information, reenactment guidelines, and a listing of reenactment groups portraying military and civilian life during the Roman era, compiled and presented by Nova Roma, an organization dedicated to the study and restoration of Ancient Roman culture.

Hudson's Bay Company Digital Collection

http://collections.ic.gc.ca/hbc/hbcen.htm

A digital collection of artifacts from the fur trade era, presented by the Manitoba Museum of Man and Nature.

19th Indiana Volunteer Infantry, Company A

http://www.19thindiana.com

Civil War reenactors and nineteenth-century civilian impressionists. Their Web page has an event schedule, company newsletter, and historical information.

49th Indiana Volunteer Infantry, Company F

http://www.intersource.com/~bjohnson/49th.html

A great company home page with a history of the 49th Indiana and a lot of information related to reenacting the American Civil War.

Jas. Townsend & Son

http://www.jastown.com/

A mail order company specializing in historic clothing, camp gear, tents, books, music, knives, tomahawks, oak kegs, and other assorted items for the period 1750–1840.

1st Kansas Volunteer Infantry and Kansas Women's Relief Corps

http://www.firstkansas.org/

Another great company Web page.

King & Country

http://www.wgn.net/~kngcntry/index.html

Makers of British and American uniforms for WWII reenactors.

King's Arms Press and Bindery

http://www.kingspress.com/

Specialized reprints of eighteenth-century books and pamphlets, including drill books and regulations, as well as military treatises.

Knighthood, Chivalry, and Tournaments Resource Library

http://www.chronique.com/

Information on books, battle accounts, codes of conduct, and more! Also includes a lengthy index of sites related to chivalry, armor, and reenactment groups.

Le Poulet Gauche

http://www.lepg.org/

A compendium of information on the history, daily life, and culture of sixteenth-century France. Le Poulet Gauche was formed by a group of Bostonians who recreated a sixteenth-century alehouse. Their Web site offers information on food, drink, gaming, clothing, fencing, tradesmen, and suppliers.

Links to the Past

http://www.cr.nps.gov/colherit.htm

An amazing Web page from the National Park Service with online archives for many historic sites, as well as battle summaries, battlefield information, national landmarks, online exhibits, and much more!

28th Massachusetts Volunteer Infantry, Companies A, C, & H

http://www.28thmass.org/

A well-designed Web page with information for historical research and reenacting.

Medieval and Renaissance Games Home Page

http://www.inmet.com/~justin/game-hist.html

This site provides an excellent source of information on everything related to games in the Medieval and Renaissance periods, including rules, bibliographies of period game sources, a history of card games, children's games, and a selection of vendors.

Medieval/Renaissance Food Home Page

http://www.pbm.com/~lindahl/food.html

A comprehensive site containing recipes, primary sources, clip art, medieval cooking articles, and food publications.

The Mifflin Guard

http://www.voicenet.com/~fieldhdj/mifflin.html

An umbrella organization with membership in the mid-Atlantic region. Members have an active interest in the American Civil War and portray Federal soldiers or Mifflin Guard Civilians. This page has links to member units, Civil War bands, and preservation efforts.

Milieux: The Costume Site

http://www.milieux.com/costume/

A comprehensive list of links to costuming sites with diversified themes, such as Medieval costuming, armor, Civil War uniforms, colonial garb, and modern accessories.

Morningside Books

http://www.morningsidebooks.com

Noted for their Civil War collection and as a recognized dealer of Don Troiani artwork.

Mountain Men and the Fur Trade

http://www.xmission.com/~drudy/amm.html

A bibliography, gallery of artwork, an archive of trade records, and links to Web sites related to the fur trade era.

National Muzzle Loading Rifle Association

http://www.nmlra.org

A complete source of information for pre-1840 Rendezvous. The NMLRA sponsors shoots, rendezvous, and territorial matches.

National Renaissance Faire Directory

http://Renaissance-Faire.com/Locations.htm

A listing of Renaissance Faires around the country with links to Web pages and event information.

NetSerf

http://itassrva.cpit.cua.edu/netserf/

A huge index arranged by subject matter and with links to all things Medieval–including religion, culture, art, literature, etc.

Nevada Civil War Volunteers

http://www.netcom.com/~baugh1/index.html

Participation in living history events throughout Northern Nevada. Web page has an events schedule and recommended equipment list.

1st New York Regiment of Engineers

http://www.jaxnet.com/~ahrendt/1stny.htm

This Web site has pictures of some original unit officers in carte-de-visite (CDV) format, historical papers, period surveying lessons, and other useful information.

47th New York State Volunteers, 'Washington Grays'

http://www.awod.com/gallery/probono/cwchas/47ny.html

A Federal reenacting unit. Their Web page has an extensive unit history and reenactment information.

5th New York Volunteer Infantry, Company A, Duryée's Zouaves

http://www.zouave.org/

An excellent company Web page with a detailed history, roster, and extensive photo gallery.

North/South Alliance

http://www.nsalliance.org/

Information on the First Confederate and First Federal Divisions in the American Civil War and a five-year event listing.

The Northwest Territory Alliance

http://www.netins.net/showcase/nwta/main.html

This group strives to recreate the lifestyle, culture, and arts of the Revolutionary War era with an accurate representation of uniforms, weaponry, and battlefield tactics. This Web site offers forms and documents useful to reenactors, an event schedule, a chronology of events in the War for Independence, pattern lists, publications, and more!

Now That I'm Here, What Do I Do?

http://www.access.digex.net/~bdboyle/reenact/ssc.html

An extremely well-written article by Susan Lyons Hughes and presented at the Southern Civilians Conference in 1997. Ms. Hughes offers an insightful look at female and civilian reenacting and discusses key aspects of historical interpretation. Anyone who reenacts, or is interested in reenacting, should read this wonderful article!

Oakhill Enterprises

http://www.frontiernet.net./~oakhill

Guns, clothing, and accessories for the period 1640–1840.

The Patriots of Fort McHenry

http://www.bcpl.lib.md.us/~etowner/patriots.html

This organization hopes to preserve the historical legacy of the patriots who defended Baltimore in 1814. Fort McHenry is best known as the scene of the battle Francis Scott Key witnessed and wrote about in the "Star Spangled Banner."

114th Pennsylvania Volunteer Infantry, Company A, "Collis' Zouaves"

http://www.concentric.net/~sthutch/114th.html

A nice regimental history, photographs, and reenactment information.

Plimoth Plantation

http://www.plimoth.org/museum/Pilgrim_Village/1627.htm

Plimoth Plantation's Pilgrim Village brings to life the Plymouth of 1627. This Web site has plenty of information about the village and also includes educational information for reenactors. This is a wonderful source of information for anyone who wishes to interpret in the first person.

Pre-1840's Buckskinning

http://www.geocities.com/Yosemite/2839/index.html

Contains a lengthy list of rendezvous groups around the United States, publications, trader events, and buckskinning classifieds.

Proper Elizabethan Accents

http://www.resort.com/~banshee/Faire/Language/index.html

Pronunciation guide, drills, and vocabulary to perfect your accent for the Faire.

Rationed Fashion

http://www.geocities.com/Sotto/Coffeehouse/6727/rationed_fashion.html

American fashion during WWII with style descriptions, designers, images, and sources.

Reenactor Net

http://www.reenactor.net/

A list of links to reenactor Web sites, categorized by time period.

Reenactors Page

http://www2.tsixroads.com/~rodbond/reenacting.html

This Web site offers photos, history, trivia, event reviews, and related links for reenactors and Civil War enthusiasts.

Regia Anglorum

http://www.regia.org

A society with a vast number of resources available for portraying the British people as they were 100 years before the Norman conquest. Their Web site has membership and contact information.

64th Regiment of Foot

http://www.cvco.org/sigs/reg64/index.html

Members of the 64th Regiment portray British infantry soldiers from the Revolutionary War era. Their Web page has information on the British army, regimental colors, the Brown Bess, women and the army, and plenty of primary reference material.

Renaissance Faire Overview

http://www.resort.com/~banshee/Faire/General/faire.html

An introduction to attending Faires and a description of what to expect.

Renaissance Magazine

http://www.renaissancemagazine.com

Well-known to reenactors as an informative print magazine, the online version is packed with useful information as well. Enjoy past features on books, music, movies, and products, or link to related Web sites.

The Rolls Ethereal

http://www.inmet.com/~justin/rolls.html

This is an online directory for members of the Society for Creative Anachronism, with hundreds of searchable listings.

Roman Life

http://www.dl.ket.org/latin1/things/romanlife/index.html

This site contains historical information on Roman life and directions for making your own Roman-style costumes.

Roman Orgy

http://www.home.ch/~spaw1087.orgy/

An excellent site with information about the art of Roman cooking, recipes, historical documents, and links to related sites.

The 42nd Royal Highland Regiment, "The Black Watch"

http://www.lib.purdue.edu/%7Epsmith/XLII/home.html

This well-designed site is a terrific source of information on period music, dancing, uniforms, and everything related to the Black Watch of the late 1700s in North America.

SCA Music and Dance Home Page

http://www.pbm.com/~lindahl/music_and_dance.html

Links to primary sources, articles, and sound files related to Renaissance music and dance.

SCRIBE's History Archives

http://www.faire.net/SCRIBE/archives/History.Htm

These pages contain hundreds of text files related to the history of the Renaissance and the Middle Ages. You will find listings of Faire participants, guilds, groups, song lyrics, and events around the country. Images and articles related to period crafts such as Celtic knotwork, heraldic crests, brewing, cooking, blacksmithing, and textiles can also be found at this site.

Second Panzer Division

http://members.aol.com/gruppen/panzer.htm

The largest and best equipped German reenacting unit in North America. Their Web site has information about equipment and tactics, a bibliography, and links to WWII reenactors.

Shadows of the Past

http://www.sptddog.com/sotp.html

This organization's guide to reenacting the Old West, with articles, historical resources, photographs, literature, and links to related sites.

Society for Creative Anachronism (SCA)

http://www.sca.org/

Dedicated to researching and recreating pre-seventeenth-century European history. This site has a huge amount of information on topics related to Medieval history, including official documents, events, art of combat, and more.

1st South Carolina Artillery, C.S.A

http://www.awod.com/gallery/probono/cwchas/1scart.html

Reenacts the history of the men who manned the artillery of the Confederate defenses of the South Carolina coast during the American Civil War. Their Web site has history, photos, and a bibliography.

A Stitch Out of Time

http://ourworld.compuserve.com/homepages/Wymarc/master1.htm

Medieval embroidery techniques for the ninth to sixteenth centuries.

Trans-Mississippi Rifles Infantry

http://members.aol.com/rlhtmr

Portrays both Union and Confederate soldiers. This Web site has membership information, an events listing, and extensive links to Civil War reenacting groups.

Trev's Rendezvous Down Under

http://www.geocities.com/Yosemite/Trails/1878/

This site has contact information for many groups who only have e-mail, as well as to organizations that are already on the Internet.

U.S. Civil War Center

http://www.cwc.lsu.edu/

The Civil War Center is an attempt to index all of the Civil War sites on the Web. There are links to national parks, battlefields, roundtables, reenacting groups, events, and much more! This should be one of your first stops if you are interested in recreating the American Civil War!

4th U.S. Infantry Regiment, Company C

http://www.halcyon.com/strandjr/4thUS_INF

Information about Civil War arms and equipment, regimental insignia, and the Army of the Potomac.

The Victorian Lady and Gentleman

http://www.dstylus.com/victorianlady/default.html

An online guide to women's roles during the Civil War, with helpful tips for creating a better female impression.

The Viking Home Page

http://www.control.chalmers.se/vikings/indexframe.html

Reenactors and organizations interested in Viking culture will want to bookmark this page, which has information about sagas, eddas, runes, Viking ships, culture, exhibitions, and links to groups that are interpreting this time period.

42nd Virginia Volunteer Infantry

http://www.erols.com/va42nd/present.html

A helpful introduction to reenacting, an authenticity code, reference room, and related information.

Welcome to Fort Erie and the War of 1812

http://www.iaw.on.ca/~jsek/

Great information about the Fort Erie siege and the War of 1812 reenactment units.

White Oak Society, Inc.

http://www.whiteoak.org/

This Web site has a wealth of information about Rendezvous and the Fur Trade Era, from interpreters who portray authentic characters of the eighteenth century.

World War I Trenches on the Web

http://www.worldwar1.com/index.html

A compendium of information for the World War I reenactor. This history of The Great War has a reference library, WWI poster reproductions, interesting articles, and reenactor photographs.

WWW Rendezvous

http://www.rendezvous.home.mindspring.com/

A comprehensive source of information for mountain men, buckskinners, and muzzleloaders! Includes a huge worldwide e-mail directory, a list of sutlers, and a wealth of reference material.

GENEALOGY

Samuel Dicks

INTRODUCTION

Genealogists have created many Internet sites and other research tools that are also of use to biographers, social historians, military historians, and others. Many sources can be accessed only by visiting a location, or arranging for a local researcher. Nevertheless, the Internet makes it easy to find out the kinds of materials available before a trip is planned, make contact with others working on the same family lines, discover many sources not easily accessed any other way, and, in some cases, obtain genealogical information by the Internet or by mail.

Not included in the following list are the local libraries in major urban areas that have collections, not only of their own region, but for all parts of the world. Many libraries have their holdings listed on the Internet. Smaller local or college libraries may also have holdings peculiar to their region or to ethnic groups dominant in their area. These are generally identified in various state and local sites, and in sites familiar to reference librarians. One Web site for libraries online is http://sunsite.berkeley.edu/Libweb/.

LDS Family History Library Online

http://familysearch.org/

The most important event of 1999 for genealogists was the world's largest genealogy library, operated by the Mormon Church, going online with portions of its collection. Go to "Browse" to see the various categories available. The International Genealogical Index (IGI), with its vital records, is especially useful. Many Family History Centers, generally in local LDS churches, continue to provide assistance, especially for those items not online.

Cyndi's List of Genealogy Sites on the Internet

http://www.cyndislist.com/

Cyndi Howells's list is the best known, most comprehensive, and most useful of all Internet genealogy sites. It has over 40,000 links to states, counties, provinces, countries, military sites, ethnic groups, and many other sites too numerous to note. The United States is listed alphabetically near the bottom (many Americans bookmark it separately), where there are links to the detailed sites for each of the states. Browse through this site slowly over many days. There is a great deal more here worth exploring. Items not available in other sites noted below will most likely be found here.

RootsWeb

http://www.rootsweb.com/

RootsWeb is the oldest and largest genealogy site. It includes the RootsWeb Surname List or RSL (http://rsl.rootsweb.com/cgi-bin/rslsql.cgi), which connects people internationally who are pursuing the same surnames—this list is considered not only helpful, but essential, for making important connections in genealogy. The localities or regions of the surnames, other surnames being pursued by the same researcher, and e-mail connections are among the features provided on this international bulletin board. Many other Web sites are included on RootsWeb—especially note the list of resources in each state available on the State-by-State Site (http://www.rootsweb.com/roots-l/usa.html#Statelist).

The U.S. GenWeb Project

http://www.usgenweb.org/index.html

The U.S. GenWeb Project is one of the most useful sites for quickly accessing states and counties. Manned by volunteers, this site provides a map (or, if you prefer, a table). Click on the state desired, and then the county desired. Also note other projects and links.

Ancestry.com

http://www.ancestry.com/main.htm

Ancestry.com is a highly popular low-cost subscription library of genealogical sources and references. Additions are free for the first ten days, and many sites are permanently free. The free sites include several noted columnists, genealogy lessons, and many other items. There are over eight hundred databases for subscribers, including the Periodical Source Index (PERSI), a genealogy index listing over 1.1 million searchable genealogy periodical articles at the Allen County Public Library of Ft. Wayne, Indiana. Available both to subscribers and guests is the SSDI or Social Security Death Index (http://www.ancestry.com/ssdi/advanced.htm), which lists over sixty million names and provides excellent instructions in order to maximize use. Ancestry also has an outstanding free daily newsletter that notes new sites, links, and other useful information.

State Historical Societies and Archives

http://www.ohiohistory.org/textonly/links/arch_hs.html

Most states have a state historical society and a state archive. The historical society will probably include microfilm copies of newspapers and census records, early state and county histories, and other publications relating to state and local history, as well as privately donated manuscripts. A state archive is ordinarily the custodian of state government papers, some of which are of interest to the genealogist. In some states the state archive and state historical society are a single institution, usually in the state capital. In other states they are separate organizations and may even be in different cities. Certain holdings of interest to genealogists may also be in a state library. This Ohio Historical Society page provides links to these institutions in forty-four states. For comparable institutions in the other six states (Idaho, Mississippi, Nebraska, New Mexico, Oklahoma, and Wyoming) see one of the previous sites.

The Genealogy Page: National Archives and Records Administration

http://www.nara.gov/genealogy/genindex.html

NARA is one of the most "user-friendly" sites provided by the federal government. Census schedules, immigration and naturalization records, ship passenger records, military and military pension records, and American Indian records are among the sources most commonly used by genealogists. Many of the microfilmed materials—including the census schedules and military pension indexes—are also in the thirteen regional branches of NARA. (The branches may also be accessed from this site.) This site provides information on the holdings in each regional branch and how one may receive copies of materials or additional information. Among the useful links from this site are Clues in Census Records, 1850–1920 (http://www.nara.gov/genealogy/cenclues.html) and "The Soundex Machine" (http://www.nara.gov/genealogy/soundex/soundex.html). Soundex is a system originally developed in the 1930s for Social Security applicants who were born before birth certificates were common and who needed to prove their date of birth for benefits. It provides a code that takes into account different spellings, and acts as an index to most Census Schedules since 1880.

The Genealogical Database Index

http://www.gentree.com/

This index contains links to all known searchable databases on the Web. Sites devoted to a family are not included unless a database is available for searching. This file may take a considerable time to load. Scroll to the end for a note on the methods of accessing this file.

The Surname Web

http://surnameweb.org/

This smaller site may provide surname connections that were not on RootsWeb. It also provides a number of other useful links.

U.S. Surname Distribution

http://www.hamrick.com/names/index.html

The 1850, 1880, and 1920 U.S. Census, and 1990s phone books are used to show the distribution of surnames by states at these four different times. Use the arrow next to the "Display" button and go to "All Periods" for quick comparisons. Hamrick software also has programs to facilitate the use of photographs in compiling a genealogy.

GENERAL SITES

African-American Genealogy: Christine's Genealogy Web Site

http://ccharity.com/

This provides information and links to most other sites that deal African-American genealogy. Also see the African-American page on Cyndi's List (http://www.CyndisList.com/african.htm).

The Cherokee Genealogy Page

http://www.io.com/~crberry/CherokeeGenealogy/links.html

This detailed Web site also has many links to other Native-American genealogy sites, and to other sites useful to historians. For Native Americans also see
Cyndi's List (http://www.CyndisList.com/native.htm).

Information for Genealogists

http://www.pro.gov.uk/genealogy

The British Public Record Office provides information and links for those
researching families from the British Isles. Go to "Resources for Genealogists" to access numerous other links. See Cyndi's page, above, for additional
United Kingdom links and for other parts of the world.

The Commonwealth War Graves Commission

http://www.cwgc.org/

Personal and service details of the 1.7 million soldiers of the British Commonwealth who died in World War I or World War II. Also includes civilian
casualties and other information.

Federation of East European Family History Societies (FEEFHS)

http://feefhs.org/

A basic Web site for Central and Eastern European countries, including Switzerland and Germany, as well as much of Eastern Europe. Indexes connect
with related Web sites from all parts of the world.

JewishGen

http://www.jewishgen.org/

JewishGen is the primary Internet source for all those engaged in Jewish genealogy. It connects with numerous databases, including JewishGen Family
Finder, which connects people searching the same ancestral towns and surnames. Missing Identity (http://www.jewishgen.org/missing-identity/) is a recent addition for locating Holocaust survivors.

Vital Records: United States

http://vitalrec.com/index.html

Provides information on how to obtain birth, marriage, divorce, and death records in the United States. It also has links to sources for many other countries.

International Black Sheep Society of Genealogists

http://homepages.rootsweb.com/~blksheep/

An organization for those with horse-thieves or other scoundrels among their ancestors, the site has many interesting stories and useful links.

Family Tree Maker Online

http://www.familytreemaker.com/

Broderbund's Family Tree Maker has one of the largest software programs for genealogists. It also provides much free information on its Web site.

The 10,000 Year Calendar

http://calendarhome.com/tyc/

This is a site of great practical use to historians and genealogists. A calendar for any month of any year desired, along with information on calendar changes, Mayan and Chinese calendars, and much more are provided here.

The Civil War Soldiers and Sailors System

http://www.itd.nps.gov/cwss/

The National Park Service—in conjunction with the National Archives and Records Administration, the Genealogical Society of Utah (LDS Church), the Federation of Genealogical Societies, the United Daughters of the Confederacy, and numerous other military and genealogy organizations—is developing a computerized database of all soldiers and sailors of the Civil War. The United States Colored Troops list is complete: (http://www.itd.nps.gov/cwss/usct.html). Meanwhile many lists are also available on various state and county sites.

Korean War and Vietnam War Casualties

http://www.nara.gov/nara/electronic/kcashr.html
http://www.nara.gov/nara/electronic/vcasal.html

The National Archives has a list by state of casualties of the Korean War and of the Vietnam War.

STATE HISTORICAL SOCIETIES

Scott Merriman and Dennis Trinkle

Arizona Historical Society
http://www.pima.com/tahs.htm

Australian Historical Association
http://www.unimelb.edu.au/infoserv/aha/

California Historical Society, San Francisco
http://www.calhist.org/

Canada's National History Society
http://www.historysociety.ca/

The Georgia Historical Society
http://www.georgiahistory.com/

The Hawaiian Historical Society
http://www.hawaiianhistory.org/index.html

Idaho State Historical Society
http://www.state.id.us/ishs/index/html

Historical Society and Archives (Montana)
http://nris.msl.mt.gov/otherlib/hist.html

Indiana Historical Society
http://www.indianahistory.org/

Illinois State Historical Society
http://alexia.lis.uiuc.edu/~sorensen/hist.html

The Kansas State Historical Society
http://www.kshs.org/

Maryland Historical Trust
http://www2.ari.net/mdshpo

Massachusetts Historical Society
http://masshist.org

Michigan Historical Center
http://www.sos.state.mi.us/history/history.html

Minnesota Historical Society
http://www.mnhs.org/

Nevada Historical Society
http://dmla.clan.lib.nv.us/docs/museums/lv/vegas.htm

New Hampshire Historical Society
http://www.nhhistory.org/index.html

The Ohio Historical Society
http://www.ohiohistory.org/

South Carolina Historical Society
http://www.historic.com/schs/index.html

Texas Historical Commission
http://www.thc.state.tx.us/

Texas State Historical Association
http://www.dla.utexas.edu/texhist/

State Historical Society of Iowa
http://www.culturalaffairs.org/shsi/index.html

State Historical Society of Wisconsin, Archives Division
http://www.shsw.wisc.edu/

The Utah State Historical Society, 1897–1972
http://history.utah.org/

HISTORY BOOKS ON THE INTERNET
Susanna Betzel

The Internet has brought about one of the greatest changes—and advances—in the out-of-print/rare book trade in decades. With the advent of Internet search networks—which can search the inventories of thousands of dealers worldwide in seconds—it has suddenly become far easier to hunt down that elusive out-of-print (or, for that matter, in-print) book, and to compare prices among dealers offering it. The following networks are leaders in the field:

Advanced Book Exchange

http://www.abebooks.com

Used, out-of-print, and rare books. Especially recommended.

Amazon.com

http://www.amazon.com

New books. Also does searches for rare books.

Antiqbook

http://www.antiqbook.com/

Has a larger percentage of rare/antiquarian book dealers, especially European.

Barnes and Noble

http://www.barnesandnoble.com/

New books. Also does searches for rare books.

Bibliocity

http://www.bibliocity.com/

Used, out-of-print, and rare.

Bibliofind

http://www.bibliofind.com

Used, out-of-print, and rare. Especially recommended; the fastest and most efficient of the networks.

Yourbooks

http://www.yourbooks.com

A small used/out-of-print network. Anyone may register without charge to offer books for sale.

Bookfinder

http://www.bookfinder.com

Simultaneously searches most of the above networks and displays the results on a single page. Bookfinder also searches the in-print databases at Amazon.com and Powell's Books (see page 432).

Books and Book Collecting

http://www.trussel.com/f_books.htm

This is a fabulously useful site for all facets of out-of-print book buying and collecting, including SetMaker, a free search/sell forum for odd volumes from multivolume sets. BookSeek links to the online catalogues of many dealers who are not members of the large networks, and has direct links to major library catalogues, the search networks, and many large individual book dealers worldwide who have their own searchable sites.

INDIVIDUAL BOOK DEALERS

The following is just a sampling of book dealers and bookstores worldwide who specialize in history books (new, remaindered, and/or out-of-print) or who have strong history sections, and who have a presence on the Internet, either as members of one of the networks or with their own Web sites and online catalogues.

Note:**Credit cards: AE=American Express; D=Discover; MC=MasterCard; V=Visa

Academy Book Store, Inc.

E-mail: staff@academy-bookstore.com
Web site: http://www.academy-bookstore.com

Specialty: General History, American, European, Medieval/Renaissance, Scholarly. Number of history books: 5,000. Founded 1977. Credit cards: AE MC V. Location: USA.

Alden Books, Inc.

E-mail: aldenbks@cdt.infi.net
Web site: http://www.aldenbooks.com

Karen and Steve Deutsch and Maria and Charles Melchioris. Specialty: General History, Scholarly. Number of history books: 2,500. Credit cards: AE MC V. Location: USA.

Antiquariat Hohmann

E-mail: antiquariat-hohmann@t-online.de

Wilhelm Hohmann. Specialty: Economic and Business History. Number of history books: 5,000. Fifty percent of total stock is history books. Credit cards: No; foreign checks accepted. Location: Germany

Archer's Used and Rare Books, Inc.

E-mail: archers@megsinet.net

Paul Bauer. Specialty: General History, Americana. Number of history books: 1,000. Founded 1986. Credit cards: MC V. Location: USA.

The Avid Reader Used and Rare Books, Inc.

E-mail: avid@avidreader.com
Web site: http://www.avidreader.com

Barry Jones. Specialty: General, American, Scholarly, American Regional, Southern, Genealogy. Number of history books: 15,000. Fifty percent of total stock is history books. Credit cards: D MC V. Location: USA.

Beulahland Books

E-mail: beulahland@coslink.net

William Tompkins. Specialty: General History. Number of history books: 4,000. Founded 1980. Credit cards: D MC V. Location: USA.

Book CloseOuts Inc.

E-mail: als@bookcloseouts.com
Web site: http://www.bookcloseouts.com

Al Siebring, Customer Service. Specialty: General History. Number of history books: 3,000. Founded 1982. Credit cards: MC V. Location: USA.

Book House in Dinkytown

E-mail: bookhous@pro-ns.net

Kristen Eide-Tollefson. Specialty: General History. Number of history books: "40 cases." Founded 1976. Credit cards: AE D MC V; foreign checks accepted. Location: USA.

Books Unlimited

E-mail: otierney@booksunlimited.com
Web site: http://www.booksunlimited.com

Joseph, Barbara, and Owen Tierney. Specialty: General History, American. Number of history books: 10,000. Founded 1988. Credit cards: D MC V. Location: USA.

Boston Book Warehouse

E-mail: booksrus@bellsouth.net
Web site: http://www.bostonbookwarehouse.com (under construction)

Specialty: General History, Military, American. Number of history books: 10,000. Credit cards: MC V. Location: USA.

Calhoun Book Store

E-mail: calhounbk@aol.com

Virginia Lou Seay. Specialty: General History, University Press. Number of history books: 6,000. Founded 1961. Credit cards: No; foreign checks accepted w/surcharge. Location: USA.

Chameleon

E-mail: afrank9@ibm.net (may change)
Web site: http://www.abebooks.com/home/chameleon/

Alan D. Frank. Specialty: General History, Native and Western American, African, African American, History of Medicine, Art History. Number of history books: 8,000. Credit cards: MC V. Location: USA.

Clifton Books

E-mail: jhodgk9942@aol.com
Web site: http://www.bibliofind.com/cliftonbooks.html

John Hodgkins. Specialty: General History, British History Since 1600. Number of history books: 4,500 listed on the Web; 25,000 in stock. All of the stock is history books. Founded 1969. Credit cards: AE MC V Access; U.S. dollars and checks accepted. Location: UK.

Comenius-Antiquariat

E-mail: shess@access.ch
Web site: http://www.comenius-antiquariat.com

Samuel Hess and Joerg Zoller. Specialty: General History, Swiss, Social, Anarchism. Number of history books: 6,000. Credit cards: MC V; foreign checks accepted w/surcharge. Location: Switzerland.

Ed Conroy, Bookseller

E-mail: edconroy@wizvax.net

Edward Conroy. Specialty: Russian, Military, Political/Social Science, University Press. Number of history books: 36,000; Ninety percent of total stock is history books. Founded 1987. Credit cards: MC V; U.S. and British checks accepted. Location: USA.

D.K. Publishers/Distributors Ltd.

E-mail: dkpd@del3.vsnl.net.in
Web site: http://www.dkpdindia.com

Parmil Mittal. Specialty: Asian. Number of history books: 7,000. Founded 1974. Credit cards: No; foreign checks accepted. Location: India.

Editions

E-mail: nleditions@aol.comWeb site: http://www.nleditions.com

Norman and Joan Levine. Specialty: General History. Number of history books: 20,000. Founded 1948. Credit cards: D MC V. Location: USA.

Expatriate Bookshop of Denmark

E-mail: expatbks@post11.tele.dk
Web site: pending

John Jackson. Specialty: General History, South Asia. Number of history books: 2,000. Credit cards: No; foreign checks accepted. Location: Denmark.

Franklin's Old Book Shop

E-mail: oldbooks@usit.net
Web site: http://www.bibliocity.com/search/fobs

Ed Franklin. Specialty: General History. Number of history books: 4,000. Credit cards: yes. Location: USA.

Great Northwest Bookstore

E-mail: gnw@greatnorthwestbooks.com
Web site: http://www.greatnorthwestbooks.com

Phil Wikelun, John Henley, and Grace Pastine. Specialty: General, American West, Prehistory. Number of history books: 85,000; Fifty percent of total stock is history books. Founded 1977. Credit cards: AE D MC V; foreign checks accepted. Location: USA.

Greenfield Books

E-mail: greenfld@escape.ca
Web site: http://www.escape.ca/~greenfld

Specialty: General History, Military, Nautical, Canadian, Polar Exploration. Number of history books: 8,000. Credit cards: AE MC V; U.S. and Canadian checks accepted. Location: Canada.

Ground Zero Books, Ltd.

E-mail: gzbooksltd@aol.com

R. Alan Lewis. Specialty: Military History, World Wars, Vietnam, American Civil War. Number of history books: 50,000. Founded 1978 and operated by trained historians. Entire stock is military history books. Credit cards: AE D MC V. Location: USA.

Gutenberg Holdings

E-mail: gutenbrg@ziplink.net
Web site: http://gutenbergholdings.com

Rhett Moran. Specialty: General History, American. Number of history books: 13,000. Credit cards: AE D MC V. Location: USA.

Peter J. Hadley Bookseller

E-mail: books@hadley.co.uk
Web site: http://www.hadley.co.uk

Peter J. Hadley. Specialty: General History, English History. Number of history books: 1,200; fifty percent of total stock is history books. Founded 1984. Credit cards: MC V Switch; checks in U.S. dollars accepted. Location: UK.

Caroline Hartley Books

E-mail: Hartleybk@clara.net

Caroline Hartley. Specialty: General History, British. Number of history books: 3,500. Founded 1983. Credit cards: MC V. Location: UK.

History To Go

E-mail: old_stuff@bigfoot.com
Web site: pending

Lance Sprung. Specialty: Historic Documents, Letters, Autographs, Signed Books, Newspapers, Broadsides, Manuscripts, Diaries, from the Middle Ages to the present. Number of documents: about 3,500. Not a book dealer per se, but certainly of interest to historians; Entire stock is historical items. Plans to issue catalogues. Credit cards: MC V (in shop only). Location: USA

R.R. Knott Bookseller

E-mail: rrknott@cyberus.ca
Web site: http://www.cyberus.ca/~rrknott

R.R. Knott. Specialty: Medieval, Canadian, Military, Ancient. Number of history books: 6,000; fifty percent of total stock is history books. Founded 1980. Credit cards: MC V; foreign checks accepted. Location: Canada.

Labyrinth Books

E-mail: books@labyrinthbooks.com
Web site: http://www.labyrinthbooks.com/

Specialty: General History, Scholarly/University Press. Number of history books: Thousands—new and remaindered. Credit cards: AE MC V. Location: USA.

David M. Lesser, Fine Antiquarian Books LLC

E-mail: dmlesser@lesserbooks.com
Web site: http://www.lesserbooks.com

David Lesser. Specialty: Americana. Number of history books: 10,000; Ninety-five percent of total stock is history books. Credit cards: MC V. Location: USA.

McDermott Books

E-mail: mcdermottbooks@gdinet.com

Patrick McDermott. Specialty: General History. Number of history books: 10,000. Credit cards: D MC V. Location: USA.

O and I Books

E-mail: oibooks@sprint.ca
Web site: http://www.oibooks.com

Juan M. Ormaechea. Specialty: General History, Hispanic. Number of history books: 1,000. Credit cards: V; checks accepted in all major currencies. Location: Canada.

The Old Bookroom

E-mail: books@OldBookroom.com
Web site: http://www.OldBookroom.com

Sally and Barbara Burdon. Specialty: Asia, Africa, Middle East, Australia. Number of history books: 15,000. Founded 1969. Credit cards: AE MC V Diners. Location: Australia.

The Owl at the Bridge

E-mail: owlbridge@home.com

Samuel and Penelope Hough. Specialty: General History, Medieval, Italian Renaissance. Number of history books: 4,000. Founded 1981. Credit cards: MC V; foreign checks accepted w/surcharge. Location: USA.

Parmer Books

E-mail: parmerbook@aol.com
Web site: http://www.bibliocity.com/search/Pa
or http://www.abaa-booknet.com/usa/parmer/

Jean Marie Parmer. Specialty: Voyages, Exploration, Discovery, Western Americana. Number of history books: 3,000; Ninety-five percent of total stock is history books. Founded 1983. Credit cards: yes; foreign checks accepted w/ surcharge. Location: USA.

The Personal Navigator

E-mail: persnav@shore.net
Web site: http://www1.shore.net/~persnav/books1.htm

Samuel W. Coulbourn. Specialty: American, Nineteenth-Century Diaries, Journals, and Autograph Books. Number of history books: 500. Credit cards: MC V. Location: USA.

Mark Post, Bookseller

E-mail: markpost@att.net

Mark Post. Specialty: American, European, Medieval, Colonial Africa, Historical Fiction. Number of history books: 1,200. Credit cards: MC V. Location: USA.

Powell's Books

E-mail: powelischicago@MSN.com
Web site: http://www.powells.com/

Specialty: General Scholarly. Number of history books: Probably in the tens of thousands; Powell's is a vast warehouse dealer of remaindered and out-of-print university press books. Credit cards: yes. Location: USA.

Prairie Reader Bookstore

E-mail: praireader@ctos.com

Hans Knoop. Specialty: General History, Western U.S., U.S. Presidents, Colorado History. Number of history books: 15,000; fifty percent of total stock is history books. Credit cards: AE D MC V. Location: USA.

Priceless Books

E-mail: priceless@net66.com
Web site: http://www.abebooks.com/home/priceless

William Thornhill, Michael Vaillancourt, and Leslie Troutman. Specialty: General History. Number of history books: 3,000. Credit cards: D MC V. Location: USA.

John William Pye Rare Books

E-mail: pyebooks@tiac.net

John William Pye. Specialty: Ancient, Ancient Egypt, Egyptology. Number of history books: 3,000; Ninety percent of total stock is history books. Credit cards: MC V. Location: USA.

Gaston Renard Fine and Rare Books (Books Australasia)

E-mail: booksaus@ozE-mail.com.au
Web site: http://bibliocity.com/dealers/renard

Julien Renard. Specialty: General, Australian, Pacific Rim, Exploration/Discovery/Voyages. Number of history books: 10,000. Founded 1945. Credit cards: AE MC V Bankcard; checks accepted in Australian$, US$, British sterling. Location: Australia.

Richard Owen Roberts Booksellers and Publishers

E-mail: roberts@safeplace.net
Web site: http://www.abebooks.com/home/RORoberts/

Richard Owen Roberts. Specialty: General History, Church History. Number of history books: 15,000. Founded 1961. Credit cards: MC V. Location: USA.

Serendipity Books

E-mail: serendip@merriweb.com.au
Web site: http://www.merriweb.com.au/serendip

Ilonka and David McGill. Specialty: Australia, the Pacific, Southeast Asia, University Press/Academic Books. Number of history books: 11,000; fifty percent of total stock is history books. Founded 1974. Credit cards: AE MC V Bankcard; US and British checks accepted w/surcharge for conversion. Location: Australia.

Seven Mountains Books

E-mail: usedbook@vicon.net
Web site: http://www.abebooks.com/home/zeppelin

Elaine Meder and Fred Ramsey. Specialty: General History, British, British Commonwealth, American Presidential, Russian/Soviet. Number of history books: 10,000. Founded 1974. Credit cards: AE D MC V. Location: USA.

Neil Shillington—Bookseller

E-mail: neilsbks@bellsouth.net

Neil Shillington. Specialty: European, American, Historical Biography, Jewish, History Related to Theology. Number of history books: 3,000. Founded 1980. Credit cards: pending; foreign checks accepted. Location: USA.

Strand Book Store, Inc.

E-mail: strand@strandbooks.com

Specialty: General History. Number of history books: 30,000. No searchable Web site or online catalogue, and not a member of a network, but as the largest used book store in New York City, the Strand cannot be ignored. Credit cards: AE MC V. Location: USA.

Naomi Symes Books

E-mail: naomi@symes.demon.co.uk
Web site: http://www.symes.demon.co.uk/

Naomi Symes. Specialty: Social History, Women's History, British, Victorian, Eighteenth Century. Number of history books: 1,200. Credit cards: MC V; foreign checks accepted w/surcharge for conversion. Location: UK.

Time and Again Books

E-mail: mcurtis@inetport.com
Web site: http://www.abebooks.com/home/mcurtis

Michael S. Curtis. Specialty: American. Number of history books: 2,000. Credit cards: yes. Location: USA.

Tomes of Glory Books

E-mail: ppodolick@aol.com

Web site: http://www.abe.com/home/tmsfglry

Phillip A. Podolick. Specialty: Military, American, American Civil War. Number of history books: 7,500; Ninety percent of total stock is history books. Credit cards: AE MC V. Location: USA.

Tricolor Books

E-mail: tricolor@mhonline.net

Web site: http://www.angelfire.com/ny/tricolorbks

Susanna Betzel. Specialty: French History, Eighteenth/Nineteenth-Century British and European History, French Revolution. Number of history books: 3,000; entire stock is history books. Credit cards: No; foreign checks accepted with a three dollar surcharge for conversion. Location: USA.

Triple A Books

E-mail: tripleabks@aol.com

Web site: http://www.abebooks.com.home.aaaalways

David A. Katz. Specialty: American, Russian, American Presidential Biography. Number of history books: 8,000; seventy-five percent of total stock is history books. Credit cards: MC V. Location: USA.

Valley Books

E-mail: orders@valleybooks.com

Web site: http://www.valleybooks.com

Lawrence and Charmagne Pruner. Specialty: General History, New England. Number of history books: 4,000. Founded 1975. Credit cards: AE MC V. Location: USA.

Vintage Books

E-mail: vintageb@teleport.com

Web site: http://www.vintage-books.com

B. Milner. Specialty: General History, Regional (Washington State), History Of Crime, Transportation History, Sports History. Number of history books: 10,000. Founded 1975. Credit cards: AE D MC V. Location: USA.

Volk and Iiams, Booksellers

E-mail: christ@vibooks.com
Web site: http://www.abebooks.com/home/vibooks/
or http://www.bibliofind.com/vibooks.html

Christine Volk and Shep Iiams. Specialty: African American, Women's. Number of history books: 3,000. Credit cards: MC V. Location: USA.

Winghale Books

E-mail: winghale@enterprise.net
Web site: pending

Irwin and Hilary Johnston. Specialty: European, American, British, Classical, Medieval (all scholarly). Number of history books: 10,000; Self-described as the leading dealer in academic history books in the UK. Founded 1985. Issues snailmail catalogues. Credit cards: AE MC V; US checks accepted w/surcharge. Location: UK.

Wolf's Head Books

E-mail: wolfhead@aug.com
Web site: http://wolfsheadbooks.com

Harvey Wolf and Barbara Nailler. Specialty: Americana, Military, Florida, American Civil War, World War I and II. Number of history books: 10,000. Founded 1980. Credit cards: AE D MC V. Location: USA.

Woodland Park Bookstore

E-mail: woodbook@lex.infi.net
Web site: http://www.woodbook.com

Diana Turnbull. Specialty: General History. Number of history books: 12,000; Fifty percent of total stock is history books. Founded 1985. Credit cards: yes; foreign checks accepted. Location: USA.

Xerxes Fine and Rare Books and Documents

E-mail: catra@xerxesbooks.com
Web site: http://xerxesbooks.com

Carol Travis. Specialty: General History. Number of history books: 2,500. Founded 1980. Credit cards: AE MC V. Location: USA.

HISTORICAL ASSOCIATIONS AND ORGANIZATIONS

Scott Merriman and Dennis Trinkle

Nearly every existing scholarly association and organization now has a Web presence, and one could fill a book simply by listing them all. Those sites listed below represent the largest societies and the best gateways. Through the following Web pages, one can quickly and efficiently access the many society pages.

Scholarly Societies Project

http://www.lib.uwaterloo.ca/society/overview.html

This site is the best gateway to scholarly society Web pages. The database can be searched by keyword, subject area, name, founding date, and a variety of other modes. It is the work of the University of Waterloo library and is updated frequently.

The American Association for History and Computing

http://www.theaahc.org/

The American Association for History and Computing (AAHC) is dedicated to the reasonable and productive marriage of history and computer technology. To support and promote these goals, the AAHC sponsors a number of activities, including an annual meeting, an electronic journal—the *Journal of the American Association for History and Computing* (*JAHC*)—a continuing publication series, and a variety of summer workshops.

American Association for State and Local History

http://www.aaslh.org

This site contains links to many state and local history organizations.

American Council of Learned Societies

http://www.acls.org/jshome.htm

The American Council of Learned Societies (ACLS) is a private nonprofit federation of sixty-one national scholarly organizations. The mission of the ACLS, as set forth in its constitution, is to "advance humanistic studies in all fields of learning in the Humanities and the related social sciences and to maintain and strengthen relations among the national societies devoted to such studies." Their Web pages contain information on fellowship and grant opportunities, links to constituent societies and other humanities and social science resources, and selected ACLS publications.

The American Historical Association

http://www.theaha.org/

This is the oldest and largest organization of historians in America.

Association for Living Historical Farms and Agricultural Museums

http://www.alhfam.org/

ALHFAM is the museum organization for those involved in living historical farms, agricultural museums, outdoor museums of history and folklife, and those museums that use "living history" programming.

Center for History and New Media

http://chnm.gmu.edu/

Located at George Mason University, this group works to explore the promise of history in the electronic age.

National Coordinating Committee for the Promotion of History

http://www.h-net.msu.edu/~ncc/

This committee is composed of members from more than fifty historical associations and is dedicated to the support of historical research and instruction. The site is a large clearinghouse for information. It allows subscription to the H-Net discussion list that distributes the *NCC Newsletter*.

Organization of American Historians

http://www.indiana.edu/~oah

The OAH is the largest scholarly society devoted to American history. It comprises a membership of more than 12,000 professionals and scholars from around the world interested in the American past. Their Web site includes membership information and access to many resources and association publications, including the *Journal of American History*, the *OAH Newsletter*, and the *Magazine of History*.

MAPS AND IMAGE COLLECTIONS
Mary K. Mannix

MAPS—METASITES

Cartography—Calendar of Exhibitions

http://users.supernet.com/pages/jdocktor/exhibit.html

The Washington (D.C.) Map Society, a group of map historians and aficionados, maintains a calendar of cartographic exhibits, and when these exhibits have an accompanying Web site, or are a Web site, the link is provided in the description. A quick way to access present exhibitions.

Historical Map Web Sites

http://www.lib.utexas.edu/Libs/PCL/Map_collection/map_sites/ hist_sites.html

A product of the Perry–Castañeda Library (University of Texas–Austin), this gateway identifies nearly 200 links to digitized maps, map collections, and map exhibits. The links are generally arranged by continent, with separate divisions for the Middle East and Russia. Astronomical maps are also included. The destination is given for the vast majority of links.

Maps and Cartography Resources Page

http://dizzy.libary.arizona.edu/users/mount/maps.html

Compiled by Jack D. Mount, a librarian at the University of Arizona, this metasite is an alphabetical list, based on the title of the site, to over 100 sites pertaining to maps and cartography. Convenient and easy to navigate.

Mercator's Resources and World Links

http://www.mercatormag.com/links.html

Mercator's World, The Magazine of Maps, Exploration, and Discovery, is a bimonthly print journal with a Web presence. This page supplies links to sites considered to be of interest to their readers. The links are arranged into twenty-five subject areas. Those subject headings of potential interest to map researchers include libraries and collections, atlases, cartography, and museums. Identified in the list are the titles of the sites or the point of destination, the URLs, and sometimes a descriptive sentence.

Odden's Bookmarks

http://oddens.geog.uu.nl/index/html

An exceptional, if not remarkable, site compiled by Roelof P. Oddens, the head map curator of the Map Collection of the Faculty of Geographical Sciences, Utrecht University. This is a very large metasite providing links to all things cartographic—probably the field's most all-encompassing site. As of January 1999, the site reports to consist of nearly 6,250 links, with over 180 pointing to map collections, and 1,000 to electronic map resources.

MAPS—EXHIBITS AND COLLECTIONS

Color Landform Atlas of the United States

http://fermi.jhuapl.edu/states

Ray Sterner, an employee of The Johns Hopkins University Applied Physics Lab, developed and maintains this site, which provides access to a variety of topographic maps of the United States, arranged by state. Among the maps offered are shaded relief maps, county maps, and the U.S. portion of the 1895 *Rand McNally Atlas of the World*. An accompanying list of "other map users"—individuals who have utilized the maps Sterner provides here—is a great source of examples of interesting map projects. Many of the links are accompanied by a descriptive sentence.

Contents.html

http://ccmail.sunysb.edu/libmap/contents.htm

The virtual exhibit "Long Island Maps and Their Makers" has been assembled by David Yehling Allen, a map librarian at SUNY–Stony Brook. Access is provided here to the maps that illustrate his book of the same name. The maps have been arranged chronologically. Also included are the book's introductory chapter and instructions on downloading a Long Island Cartobibliography. The maps are well-identified and the institutions that hold the original are given.

1895 Atlas Title Page

http://www.livgenmi.com/1895.htm

This site, the work of genealogist Pam Rietsch, provides access to the United States portion of an 1895 world atlas. Arranged by state, this site also makes available the city and town data for the period. This data includes the population, the county, the area of the state where the jurisdiction can be found, and whether or not there was a post office, a railroad, or an express office. County maps are also included. The county maps have been enhanced for visibility.

Exhibitions: Maps

http://www.bl.uk/exhibitions/maps/

"The Earth and the Heavens, The Art of the Mapmaker": This British Library site presents six maps, drawn from a much larger nonvirtual collection. Stemming from the first century A.D. to the mid-nineteenth century, these artifacts trace the history of Western mapmaking. Also included is a list for further reading.

Exploring the West from Monticello: Home

http://www.lib.virginia.edu/exhibits/lewis_clark/home.html

This is an electronic edition of a 1995 exhibit held at the University of Virginia, subtitled "A Perspective in Maps from Columbus to Lewis and Clark." The majority of artifacts shown are held by UVA. The focus of the exhibit is "the evolution of cartographic knowledge of North America up through the time that Lewis and Clark set out." Seventy items, including navigational tools, are displayed. An excellent exhibit/exhibit catalog. Included are a bibliography and links to related resources.

Greenwood's Map of London 1827

http://www.bathspa.ac.uk/greenwood/home.html

An excellent site that provides access to a single map. It is the product of the compelling interest of one individual, Mark Annand. Along with the map, the site includes a list of place names from the map, a chronology and history of the map, a bibliography, and a discussion on the project itself. Even if you have no interest in London or the time period, this is an example of a site well done.

Map Collections Home Page

http://lcweb2.loc.gov/ammem/gmdhtml/gmdhome.html

The Library of Congress's American Memory program includes a section on maps, a sampling of the materials held by the LC's Geography and Map Division. This page is divided into seven sections—Cities and Towns, Conservation and Environment, Discovery and Exploration, Immigration and Settlement (which includes Maps of Liberia, 1830–1870), Military Battles and Campaigns, Transportation and Communication, and General Maps. The maps are searchable by keyword, subject, creator, location, and title. Maps can also be downloaded.

Map Machine@nationalgeographic.com

http://www.nationalgeographic.com/maps/

This useful, and fun, site provides access to contemporary electronic maps of the world, both physical and political. It is a point and click resource. The accompanying text is from the 1995 National Geographic Atlas of the World. The site's list of "Map Resources" is worthwhile.

MapHist Illustration Pages

http://www.maphist.nl/ill/inhand.html

MapHist is a major listserv for map historians. As of January 1999, there were more than 800 reported members. This site does not provide access to a map or map collection or to a map exhibit, but it does display maps that were discussed on the list, along with the original message relating to the map. Many of these maps were posted to aid in identification. An interesting site, with interesting text, written by individuals schooled in the field. The archive is maintained for approximately a year.

Maps and Gazetteers for Genealogy Research at Ancestry.com

http://www.ancestry.com/ancestry/maps.asp

Ancestry, a leading genealogical publishing house, both in print and on the Web, issues a daily electronic newsletter. A feature of the "Daily News" is the map of the day. An archive of such maps can be found via Ancestry's home page. The maps can be conveniently searched alphabetically, in a single list, or by category. A wide variety of time periods and themes is offered.

The Perry–Castañeda Library Map Collection

http://www.lib.utexas.edu/Libs/PCL/Map_collection/Map_collection.html

This excellent site presents 2,400 digitized contemporary and historic maps for the United States and the World from the holdings of the University of Texas–Austin's Perry–Castañeda Library. A collection strength is governmental maps—CIA, National Park, and USGS. Maps originally found in books have also been included. Maps can be searched by locale and U.S. maps also can be queried by historical period. The 100 "U.S. Historical City Maps" should be noted.

Rare Map Collection

http://scarlett.libs.uga.edu/darchive/hargrett/maps/maps.html

Eight hundred or so maps are held by the Hargrett Rare Books and Manuscripts Library at the University of Georgia. They have all been digitized and approximately twenty percent are available to the general public through this Web site. They span four centuries and can generally be accessed by time period. Transportation, including railroad and canal maps, is another category. A collection strength appears to be, naturally enough, the southern United States.

Table of Contents—Library of Congress Geography and Maps

http://lcweb.loc.gov/rr/geogmap/guide

The Library of Congress's Geography and Map Division has the world's largest cartographic collection, numbering over 4.5 million. Thus, an illustrated guide to that representative collection is also a guide to the development of maps of the world. The nearly seventy maps included in the illustration cut across space and time. The section "Concordance of Images" provides quick access to the images.

University of Arizona Library Map Collection: Maps of the Pimeria

http://dizzy.library.arizona.edu/branches/spc/set/pimeria/intro.html

Jack D. Mount, a science reference librarian at the University of Arizona, has curated an exhibit of twenty-nine maps all from the collection of the University of Arizona Library. They cover four decades of mapping, from the sixteenth century through the nineteenth, of the area of today's southwestern Arizona once referred to as the territory of Pimeria.

IMAGES—METASITES

Australian National University Art History Top Level Menu Page

http://rubens.anu.edu.au/

A resource of the Australian National University, the site provides access to a wide variety of images useful to historians and art historians. It should be noted, however, that it is a site that requires registration and charges for access for many of its visual materials. Generally divided by art periods, there are a wide variety of search options. It is possible within each division to search by medium, by artist, or by country. Includes good documentation. Also included are images of Canberra and ANU. A variety of price ranges are available and it could well be worth the investment for some researchers.

The Daguerreian Society: Links

http://www.daguerre.org/resource/links.html

This page, compiled by the Daguerrian Society, provides very useful links to individual daguerreotypes, collections, and exhibits. A page off of it provides access to many useful sites relating to other aspects of the history of photography and to other image sites. An excellent starting point for anyone interested in photography.

Digitizing Medieval Manuscripts; Colloquium Index Page

http://medieval.mse.jhu.edu

This home page for a digitization initiative at The Johns Hopkins University provides links to exhibits and collections of medieval manuscripts.

Massachusetts Institute of Technology: Rotch Visual Collections: Exploring Image Collections on the Internet Resources at MIT and Beyond

http://libraries.mit.edu/rvc/imgcolls/imgcol1.html

The home page for MIT's Rotch Visual Collections provides a useful arrangement of links to image collections relating to archaeology, architecture, urban design, and related fields of study. The section dealing with anthropology and archaeology is of special interest.

NM's Creative Impulse: The Artist's View of World History and Western Civilization

http://history.evansville.net/index.html

This is one of, if not the best, metasites for visual resources in world history. Maintained by Nancy Mantz for Harrison High School, Evansville, Indiana and for the University of Evansville, it contains a rich collection of links to cultural resources, such as paintings, poetry, music, and drama, rather than just politics, religions, or philosophy.

PhotArchipelago

http://www.city-gallery.com/resource/pa/photoarch.html

An excellent gateway compiled by William Allen of the Arkansas State University Art Department and Steve Knoblock, developer of another photographic history Web resource, City Gallery. It is a well-constructed group of links relating to pre-1950 photography. The goal is to bring together the best. The links are divided into categories, for browsing, such as Institutions, Noteworthy Exhibits, and Online Collections.

IMAGES—EXHIBITS AND COLLECTIONS

Alfred Eisenstaedt

http://pathfinder.com/Life/eisie/eisie.html

This *Life* magazine site, "Life Remembers Eisie: Over 50 Years of Putting Our Lives in Pictures," features the work of Alfred Eisenstaedt, one of the twentieth century's most well-known photojournalists, perhaps best remembered as the photographer of the V-J Day kiss photograph. During his career, he was responsible for over eighty of *Life*'s well-known covers. This site provides access to all these covers, running from the 1930s to the 1970s. Each cover is identified. *Life*'s home page also provides access to all of the covers of Life from 1936–72, the period when *Life* was a weekly. It is possible to search for the covers by date, subject, and photographer.

American Memory Collections: All Collections

http://memory.loc.gov/ammem/amtitle.html

The tremendous "American Memory" is the product of the National Digital Library Project of the Library of Congress. This site allows access to an incredible number of primary source materials, in a variety of media. Cataloging records are included. The variety of offerings include: baseball cards, Civil War photographs, broadsides, daguerreotypes, and Historic American Buildings Survey/Historical American Engineering Record photographs. The list goes on. This site should be visited by anyone interested in U.S. history or the history of photography.

Berenice Abbott

http://www.nypl.org/research/chss/spe/art/photo/abbottex/abbott.html

This exhibit, "Changing New York 1935–38," is one of a number of useful photo collections available through the digital collections of the New York Public Library. Abbott's images, all exterior shots, document the life of one of the world's major cities. It should be noted that these are Federal Works Progress Administration photographs.

The Bill Douglas Center: Tour of the Collection

http://www.ex.ac.uk/bill.douglas/contents.html

This center at the University of Exeter is dedicated to popular culture. Its site provides access to prints, printed ephemera, and tools relating to the "prehistory of cinema"—the optical entertainments that came before motion pictures, such as the Panorama and the Magic Lantern. Also included in this tour are cinema images from sheet music covers, comic books, and artifacts relating to Charlie Chaplin and Disney, two sources of durable popular culture iconography.

City-Gallery.com—Popular History of Photography and Genealogy

http://www.city-gallery.com

This site has its roots in the genealogical research of a single individual. The goal is to attempt to draw together genealogists and photohistorians. It is an interesting site that provides access to a number of online exhibits. Of special interest to genealogists is the digital album, where family photos can be posted. The major emphasis of the site is studio photography. City Gallery also serves as the home page of the PhotoGenerations listserv and includes a gallery for images posted for discussion on the list.

Clearwater Public Library: Local History

http://public.lib.ci.clearwater.fl.us/cpl/lochist.html

This site is a fine example of the types of visual resources often held by local history collections, no matter their size: photographs, postcards, illustrated school annuals, and illustrated promotional publications and how these resources can be put to use. Although a small site, it is still noteworthy for the amount of descriptive information—about both the subject of the image and the image itself—that it provides. Images come not only from the Public Library, but also from the Clearwater Historical Society.

Currently on Exhibit at the Mudd Library

http://www.princeton.edu/~mudd/exhibit/

This site, a virtual version of Princeton's Seeley G. Mudd Manuscript Library exhibit "Reflections on Photographing Princeton," not only provides a visual history for the University, but also shows how almost any photography collection is useful to illustrate the history of the medium. The images included in the collection are the work of professional photographers as well as students. Interesting connections are made between photographs and the growth of science at the university.

The Daguerreotype: The Daguerreian Society Home Page

http://www.daguerre.org/home.html

An exceptional site, the home page for this photohistorical group offers exhibits on this early nineteenth-century photographic medium, the first practical photograph—the daguerreotype. Exhibits of daguerreotypes from institutional holdings and those in the hands of private collectors—as well as contemporary examples—are included, each largely with very informative text. Also available at this site are reprints of nineteenth-century articles relating to daguerreotypes, many of which are illustrated. This site not only provides a great deal of information on the history of photography, but also is of interest to those studying nineteenth-century life.

George Eastman House: Photograph Collections

http://www.eastman.org/9_colphoto/9_index.html

While the Eastman House does not provide online access to their collections, they do provide a very small, yet wonderful, representative sample of their daguerreotypes, nineteenth-century British and French photography on paper, and American nineteenth-century holdings.

Historic Photograph—Home Page

http://royal.okanagan.bc.ca/histphoto/index.html

Part of an inter-institutional project, Living Landscapes, documenting the human and natural history of the Thompson/Okanagan region of south central British Columbia (Canada). Material is drawn together from the collections of the Kelowna Museum, the Historic O'Keefe Ranch, the En'Owkin Center, and the Okanagan Center Museum. Largely spanning the years from 1900 through World War II, these images document multiple facets of life in the area during that time. This site has good documentation and is searchable using Library of Congress subject headings.

Images from the History of Medicine

http://wwwihm.nlm.nih.gov/

An exceptional site providing access to nearly 60,000 images from the collection of the National Library of Medicine's History of Medicine Division, one of the premier history of medicine collections. A variety of media is included. The site has excellent search capabilities. It should not be considered to be only for those with an interest in the history of medicine.

The Lester S. Levy Sheet Music Collection—Home Page

http://levysheetmusic.mse.jhu.edu

Special Collections, Milton S. Eisenhower Library, of The Johns Hopkins University provides access to a wide selection of the over 29,000 pieces found in their Levy Collection. Those pieces over seventy-five years old are included in the site. The strong Levy Collection spans the years 1780–1960. Besides searching by keyword or subject heading, it is possible to browse the "cover art" through thirty-eight topical categories, such as patriotic songs, sports, schools, and transportation.

Massachusetts Institute of Technology: Rotch Visual Collections

http://libraries.mit.edu/rvc/

This home page of MIT's Rotch Library provides to the public at large access to two image collections useful for art history, architectural history, and historic preservation—the "Aga Khan Visual Archives" and the "Kidder-Smith Collection of American Architecture." The Aga Khan Visual Archives provides access to a wide variety of contemporary photographs of standing examples of Islamic Architecture. G.E. Kidder Smith was a prominent mid-twentieth-century architectural historian. MIT holds a collection of 3,400 of his slides. Those slides dealing with New England buildings have been placed on this site. It is reported that other areas will be added to the site in the future.

Museum of the City of New York—Currier and Ives

http://www.mcny.org/currier.htm

The Harry T. Peters Collection of the Museum of the City of New York is reported to be the most complete set of Currier and Ives prints. The images digitized here not only show examples of the works of these well-known lithographers, but present images that have come to represent the popular view of nineteenth-century America. Nearly eighty prints are shown here, arranged into nine categories, including "Happy Family," "American Country Life," and "Progress of the Century."

Museum of the City of New York—Prints and Photographs Collection

http://www.mcny.org/prints.htm

This site, under "Exhibitions" and "Collections," provides access to a variety of media (photographs, printed ephemera, architectural drawings, and photos of artifacts) that document the City of New York, both past and present. Included in the featured exhibits are parades, circuses, New Amsterdam, the Irish, and a Settlement Program in Harlem. A unique feature of the page is "The Talk of the Town: Rea Irvin of The New Yorker," which contains selections of cover art.

The National Archives Online

http://www.nara.gov/exhall/exhibits.html

This site provides access to selections from a number of National Archives and Records Administration (NARA) collections. Included in the offerings are "Portrait of Black Chicago" (1970s work of Pulitzer Prize winner John H. White), "When Nixon Met Elvis" (rumored to be the Archives' most requested image), a collection of panoramic photographs, and images from varied media relating to New Deal art projects.

New York Public Library Digital Schomburg Images of African Americans from the Nineteenth Century

http://digital.nypl.org/schomburg/images_aa19/

A mission of the Schomburg Center for Research in Black Culture of the New York Public Library is to document the life and history of peoples of African descent throughout the world. This excellent site provides access to a variety of visual media that do just that. It is possible to search the site by category (such as the Civil War, Politics, and Genre) and also by keyword. Good documentation is provided with the images.

Osher Map Library: Exhibitions on the Web

http://www.usm.maine.edu/~maps/web_exhibit.html

The University of Southern Maine's Osher Map Library and Smith Center for Cartographic Education holds a varied and rich collection. The Center maintains a Web page of their electronic exhibit catalogs. Impressively, their exhibits cover a wide variety of topics, and among the exhibits accessible here are "Maps of Spain from the Enggass Collection," "Africa: A Continent Revealed," and "Jerusalem 3000: Three Millennia of History."

Photography: Archive@nationalgeographic.com

http://www.nationalgeographic.com/photography/archive/index.html

Visions Galleries is a series of exhibits of the work of National Geographic photographers (twenty, at the time of this writing). Each exhibit consists of twelve or so images, along with an interview with the photographer and, at times, comments by a National Geographic editor. The photographers' subjects cut across a wide variety of topics, as would be expected—i.e. African-American cowboys, the rain forests of Malaysia, Times Square, and the celebration of Halloween.

The Photograph Collection

http://gowest.coalliance.org/index.html

This dedicated Photography Collection of the Western History/Genealogy Department at Denver Public Library provides access to 50,000 images, with more in the works, from the Library's collection of 600,000 images. It serves as an important source of primary material documenting the West of the last two centuries. Special mention should be made of the Native American images, which are affiliated with the LC American Memory project. This site is well-documented and searchable using Library of Congress methods.

Powers of Persuasion—Poster Art of World War II

http://www.nara.gov/education/teaching/posters/poster.html

Part of the National Archives and Records Administration's "Digital Classroom" program, this very useful site not only makes available ten posters, but also supplies a lesson plan and a "Poster Analysis Worksheet."

The Samuel Putnam Avery Collection

http://www.nypl.org/research/chss/spe/art/print/collections/avery/avery.htm

This site provides access to sixteen prints from the New York Public Library's Avery collection, developed by its donor, an art dealer, to document the art of the second half of the nineteenth century. Out of a collection of 17,775 prints of some of the major artists of the day are accessible here: Goya, Whistler, Cassett, and Manet, for example.

Small Town, Black Lives

http://www.blacktowns.org

This excellent exhibit, "Small Towns, Black Lives: African-American Communities in Southern New Jersey," is an outgrowth of Wendel A. White's art-documentary project. The site makes use of contemporary and historical photographs, printed ephemera, documents, maps, and RealVideo. Access is available on the site through the names of the towns, as well as by certain individuals. A wonderful use of the WWW to create a documentary of a particular place and its peoples.

Stokes Collection of American Historical Prints

http://www.nypl.org/research/chss/spe/art/print/stokes/stokes.htm

From the New York Public Library, this site provides access to sixteen historic prints of the United States. This site includes sixteenth and seventeenth-century prints. It has useful views of early America. Includes a short bibliography for further investigation.

Temple of Liberty: Building the Capitol for a New Nation

http://lcweb.loc.gov/exhibits/us.capitol/s0.html

This exhibit includes prints, architectural drawings, plans, and plats that relate to the building and expansion of the Capitol Building and also to the history of Washington, D.C.

They Still Draw Pictures

http://orpheus-1.ucsd.edu/speccoll/tsdp/

An exceptional, unique site that provides access to a collection of children's drawings from the Southworth Spanish Civil War Collection, Mandeville Special Collections Library, University of California–San Diego. This collection, over 600 drawings, all available here, were created during the Spanish Civil War by Spanish schoolchildren in Spain and in French refugee centers. Each image is captioned with whatever notes can be found on the front and back of the drawing. The age of the artist is provided, as is the city where they were located, and the school. A wonderful collection and a wonderful site.

UCR—California Museum of Photography

http://www.cmp.ucr.edu/

This site provides access to both certain portions of the institution's collections and to their exhibitions. A collection strength is the Keystone View Collection, glass-plated negatives for stereographs, spanning the years 1890–1935. Twenty-five of these images are on display. Red/blue (3-D) glasses will give the experience of using a stereograph viewer. At this point twenty-one different exhibits are viewable and cut across a variety of topics: burlesque, Cambodian Prison Camps, Los Angeles of 1910, California's surf culture, and the vanity portrait—hand-tinted photographs sold door to door.

United Nations Photos

http://www.un.org/av/photo

This site provides access to a number of exhibits developed from the large collection of photographs held by the United Nations. "Visits to Countries" consists of contemporary photographs arranged by countries constituting a sampling of the areas where the UN works. The "UN Pictorial History" is essentially arranged by decade, and presents a quick visual history of the twentieth century. "Special Exhibits" is a series of thematic exhibits, some only contemporary photographs—e.g., landmines, the year of the older person—but historic images are included in exhibits on the human rights and peacekeeping over the UN's fifty years.

Virtual Greenbelt

http://www.otal.umd.edu/~vg

This site is affiliated with a house museum in Greenbelt, Maryland, a New Deal planned community. The "Photograph Album" provides ordinary images that depict the everyday life of this middle-class white community at mid-century. Sports, school, birthday parties, holiday celebrations, and vernacular structures, such as gas stations, are all shown. "Selected Artifacts" provides photographs of many ordinary household tools. This site provides strong visual documentation for a period perhaps too recent to be considered truly "historic" through photographs that would perhaps be considered too mundane by some to be worthy of study.

Welcome to The American Museum of Photography

http://www.photographymuseum.com/

This Web site allows access to the large private photographic collection of William B. Becker, which concentrates on the first seventy-five years of photography, stopping at World War I. There are presently seven exhibits up, based on different formats (i.e., *Carte-de-Visite*) and subjects/themes. Each exhibit has a brief introductory essay. Special note should be made of the exhibit "Of Bricks & Light: Architectural Photographs 1845–1915." This exhibit of over thirty images not only cuts across time, but also spans the globe. It should be of value to those interested in the built environment.

Frank Lloyd Wright: Designs for an American Landscape, 1922–1932

http://lcweb.loc.gov/exhibits/flw/flw.html

This exhibit features architectural drawing and plans by Wright from a number of holders.

Women Come to the Front

http://lcweb.loc.gov/exhibits/wcf/wcf0001.html

This Library of Congress exhibit, with the explanatory subtitle "Journalists, Photographers, and Broadcasters During World War II," features the work of women photojournalists, thus documenting not only the war, but also the medium and the changing role of women in the twentieth century. The women featured in the exhibit are Therese Bonney, Toni Frissell, Marvin Breckinridge Patterson, Clare Boothe Luce, Janet Flanner, Esther Bubley, Dorothea Lange, and May Craig.

RESOURCES FOR TEACHERS OF HISTORY: K-12 AND COLLEGE

Stephen Kneeshaw

METASITES

Academic Info

http://www.academicinfo.net/table.html

Academic Info is a subject directory designed for college-level use that provides both annotated listings of Internet sites and gateways to specialized materials. The site offers metaindexes, general directories, and teaching materials to serve needs at many academic levels. Especially useful is the section on U.S. history—Academic Info United States History at http://www.academicinfo.net/histus.html—with an annotated directory of Internet resources in American history.

Index of Resources for Historians

http://www.ukans.edu/history

Maintained by the University of Kansas and "Lehrstuhl für altere Deutsche" at the University of Regensburg in Germany, the Index of Resources for Historians is an exceptional metasite, with more than 3,000 connections arranged alphabetically by subject and name. There are no annotations, but subject breakdowns make this an easily usable site. The list emphasizes college and university-level history, but some sites are geared specifically to K-12 audiences. Designed originally as a lynx site accessible by telnet, with text rather than graphics, the index is effective with text-to-speech and text-to-braille, making it friendly to the visually handicapped.

Lesson Plans and Resources for Social Studies Teachers

http://www.csun.edu/~hcedu013/index.html

This site, maintained by Marty Levine in secondary education at California State University–Northridge, should be the first gateway accessed by elementary and secondary history teachers who want to sample the wealth of the World Wide Web. A clickable table of contents on the opening page leads to nine areas such as "Lesson Plans and Teaching Strategies," "Other Social Studies Resources" (including government and museum sites), "Teaching Current Events," and "Newsgroups and Mailing Lists." The lengthy lists of links are alphabetized and annotated for a quick reading of contents.

THE BEST SITES—TEN FROM THE LIST

American Memory

http://rs6.loc.gov

The rich collections of the Library of Congress come to life in words and pictures in American Memory. This rapidly growing site, now with forty-two collections online, includes documents, maps, photos and prints, motion pictures, and sound recordings. An easy-to-use search engine and a list of entries alphabetized by both keywords and titles provide entry to topics ranging from "baseball cards, Civil War photographs, and the conservation movement (one of my favorites) to presidents and first ladies, the Spanish-American War, and "Voices from the Dust Bowl."

The Digital Classroom

http://www.nara.gov/education

The Digital Classroom, from the National Archives and Records Administration (NARA), encourages teachers at all levels to use documents in their classrooms. This is NARA's complement to American Memory from the Library of Congress. The site delivers documentary materials from the National Archives, lesson plans, and suggested methods for teaching with primary documents. The topics already available online span a wide range, from the *Amistad* case to the Zimmerman Telegram to FDR's "court-packing" scheme. NARA also provides a reproducible set of document analysis worksheets for written documents, photographs, cartoons, posters, maps, artifacts, sound recordings, and motion pictures that history teachers will find easy to use and attractive to their students.

Digital Librarian: A Librarian's Choice of the Best of the Web—History

http://www.servtech.com/~mvail/history.html

Self-described as "a librarian's choice of the best of the Web" (and run by Margaret Vail Anderson of Cortland, New York), the Digital Librarian covers virtually every academic discipline, many of which are linked to the History page. This site provides an entry point for such diverse topics as the ancient world, genealogy, Judaica, Latin America, the Middle East, and women's resources. For elementary teachers, there are useful connections to children's literature and resources. Lists are alphabetized and annotated briefly, but there is no internal search mechanism.

History Matters

http://historymatters.gmu.edu

Designed for secondary and college teachers in American history, History Matters combines the efforts of the American Social History Project at the City University of New York and the Center for History and New Media at George Mason University. With an express "focus on the lives of ordinary Americans," this site offers teaching materials, first-person documents, interactive exercises, electronic essays, "syllabus central," and threaded discussions on teaching history. The current focus is on the years 1876–1946, but eventually the site will grow to cover all of the American experience. A keyword search option allows users easy access to materials in the site.

History/Social Studies Web Site for K-12 Teachers

http://www.execpc.com/~dboals/boals.html

As the name suggests, this site focuses on the needs of K-12 classroom teachers in locating and using the resources of the Internet. A clickable table opens a wide range of topics, including K-12 resources, archeology, genealogy, geography, American history, and non-Western history. This site provides a gateway to some 600 locations, including lesson, commercial, project, and general sites. The one downside is that the lists are not alphabetized, although they do provide brief but useful annotations.

Learning Space—Washington Social Studies Home Page

http://www.learningspace.org/socialstudies

The Learning Space provides many links specific to a single state, here Washington, but the site has great value for all history teachers, with links for history, geography, museums, Holocaust resources, K-12 education, and much more. Each connection provides lengthy alphabetized and annotated lists of Web sites for history teachers at all levels everywhere.

Kathy Schrock's Guide for Educators

http://www.capecod.net/schrockguide

Maintained by Kathy Schrock, technology coordinator for the Dennis–Yarmouth Regional School District in Massachusetts, this is one of the best-known Web sites for educators. This "categorized list of sites on the Internet," which is updated daily, covers the whole span of academic subjects. Clicking the link for history and social studies opens connections to American and World History as well as "general history and social studies sites." The site also provides links to several search engines, bulletin board ideas, and critical evaluation tools.

SCORE History–Social Science Resources

http://www2.rims.k12.ca.us/score/index.html

This site, designed primarily for K-12 teachers, comes from Schools of California Online Resources for Education (SCORE). Links include resources and lessons by grade level, resources by theme and topic, virtual projects and field trips, and more. Although one objective of SCORE is to link WWW resources to California's curriculum, this site will be useful to teachers in all states. All of the materials have been evaluated and rated on a 1–5 scale by a team of educators, assuring some quality control in such areas as accuracy, grade appropriateness, depth, and variety.

Studying and Teaching History

http://www.tntech.edu/www/acad/hist/study.html

This fine Web site from Tennessee Technological University aims to create a database of syllabi and suggestions for history teachers and students. Currently available are study guides for history classes from several universities, reference works, guides for research and writing, and links for oral history, maps and A-V materials, portfolios, living history and reenactments, studying and teaching history at K–12 levels, and graduate schools.

Teaching History: A Journal of Methods

http://www.emporia.edu/socsci/journal/main.htm

Designed and maintained at Emporia State University by the publication team for the journal *Teaching History,* this site reflects the main objective of the journal: to provide teachers at all academic levels "with the best and newest teaching ideas for their classrooms." Besides information on the journal, this site provides links to a rich list of resources in ten history-related categories, from American and World History to genealogy, maps, writing and editing, and teaching resources.

HISTORY AND SOCIAL STUDIES ORGANIZATIONS

American Historical Association

http://www.theaha.org

The home page for the American Historical Association provides information on the AHA and more than 100 affiliated societies, selected articles from the newsletter *Perspectives,* a calendar of historical events, and "a primer" on how the AHA serves K-12 teachers in history.

H-NCC—National Coordinating Committee for the Promotion of History

http://www.h-net.msu.edu/~ncc

Run through the H-Net group out of Michigan State University, H-NCC is "the official electronic voice" of the National Coordinating Committee for the Promotion of History, which supports history and historians in the political circles of Washington, D.C. and the American states. Included at the site is a connection to past issues of *Washington Updates* that describe the work of NCC and its lobbying successes. A keyword search mechanism allows easy use of materials in the H-NCC site.

National Council for History Education

http://www.history.org/nche

The NCHE Web site is more useful than many organizational sites because it goes well beyond descriptions of NCHE and its programs. For example, "History Links" sends a user to a diverse mix of sites: Web sites for historical organizations; history education sites; links of interest to social studies educators; and repositories of primary sources, which gets promoted as "a listing of over 3,000 Web sites...for the research scholar."

NCSS Online—National Council for the Social Studies

http://www.ncss.org

NCSS Online offers Web-based information services for the National Council for the Social Studies, the largest "umbrella organization" for social studies educators. This site promotes NCSS, which is to be expected, but it also provides links for professional development, standards and curriculum, and teaching resources.

Organization of American Historians

http://www.indiana.edu/~oah

The Organization of American Historians is the premier professional association for United States history. But beyond its service to college and university teachers and researchers, OAH serves precollegiate history teachers through such means as the OAH Magazine of History and outreach programs, which are described at this site. A link to "History Teaching Units" introduces lesson plans for grades 6-12 based on primary documents developed by the OAH in concert with the National Center for History in the Schools at UCLA.

Society for History Education—The History Teacher

http://www.csulb.edu/~agunns/relprm/tht01.html

This site, now under construction, will feature the Society for History Education, which publishes *The History Teacher.* The two entities will be linked together through the Web server at California State University at Long Beach, where the journal is housed.

WWW RESOURCES FOR HISTORY TEACHERS

AskERIC Virtual Library

http://ericir.syr.edu/virtual

The AskERIC Virtual Library archives hundreds of lesson plans in a variety of disciplines, informational guides on topics of interest to K-12 educators, links to the searchable databases of ERIC Digests (brief reports on educational issues), information on using the Internet in the classroom, and links to other Internet sites. Under both American and World history. AskERIC offers descriptive and adaptable lesson plans for grades 1-12.

The Avalon Project: Documents in Law, History, and Government

http://www.yale.edu/lawweb/avalon/avalon.htm

History teachers frequently use documents to enrich lesson plans and illustrate key ideas. The Avalon Project from the Yale Law School provides connections to a wealth of documents from before the eighteenth century through the twentieth century. An alphabetic author and title list for all documents in the collection and a search engine within the project make this a user-friendly Web site that is accessible to all grade levels.

Awesome Library—K-12 Education Directory

http://www.neat-schoolhouse.org/awesome.html

Awesome Library "for teachers, students, and parents" gives users links to all teaching fields. Under the social studies link, you can click into history and lesson plans or make connections to more specialized history-related fields such as current events, ecology, holidays, and multicultural resources.

Association for Academic Computing: WWW Services for Historians

http://grid.let.rug.nl/ach/hist.html

This Web site delivers an eclectic mix of links for topics such as general historical sites and computing in the humanities to e-magazines. Based in the Netherlands, this site provides links to many countries (alphabetical by continents) on a wide range of topics. The suggestions are quite diverse. For example, in the list of sites in the United States, you can link to such disparate individuals as Anne Frank, Emma Goldman, and John Muir.

Biographical Dictionary

http://www.s9.com/biography

Biographical Dictionary offers biographies of more than 25,000 men and women "who have shaped our world from ancient times to the present." Users can search the list by names, birth or death years, professions, literary and artistic works, and other keywords, making these men and women easily accessible for students and teachers.

Biography.Com

http://www.biography.com

This Web site is the gateway to the popular Arts and Entertainment television series "Biography." The Biography.com Store currently stocks more than 1,500 videos that have run on the cable network. For teachers who use videos to supplement class presentations, this site will be quite valuable.

Center for International Higher Education

http://www.bc.edu/bc_org/avp/soe/cihe/Center.html

This site contains information about the Center for International Higher Education—at Boston College—and the activities of the center. In addition, there are discussions of teaching, links to educational sites, and access to International Higher Education, a newsletter published by the center.

Chronicle of Higher Education

http://chronicle.merit.edu/index.html

This Web site provides online access to some of the materials delivered in print each week by the *Chronicle of Higher Education.* The clickable links include topics such as today's news in education, information technology, government and politics, grants, and job announcements.

CIT Infobits

http://www.unc.edu/cit/infobits/infobits.html

CIT Infobits is an electronic service of the University of North Carolina–Chapel Hill that provides brief notes on information technology and instructional technology sources. Besides the summaries, the site gives links to Web resources mentioned in the summaries and brief book notes. Subscriptions to CIT Infobits are free.

Clip Art Resources for History

http:/library.hilton.kzn.school.za/history/history.htm

For teachers who use clip art and art images to enrich their teaching materials—Web pages, lectures, handouts, overhead, and such—this site will be extremely valuable. The site, which is maintained by Hilton College in South Africa, provides a clickable map to access clip art image search engines, directories of clip art sites, and clip art sites. There is also an alphabetized category list of clip art and icons.

CLNET History Resources

http://latino.sscnet.ucla.edu/research/history.html

This Web site from UCLA provides a gateway (with annotations) to more than thirty sites on Chicano/a and Latino/a history. The diverse resources list links the user to topics such as historical documents, "Hispanics in the American Revolution," the Chicano movement in history, and the Mexican-American civil rights movement in the United States.

Core Documents of U.S. Democracy

http://www.access.gpo.gov/su_docs/dpos/coredocs.html

This Web site from the Government Printing Office delivers more than the title suggests. Beyond such "core documents" as the Declaration of Independence, Constitution and Bill of Rights, and Supreme Court decisions, users get a statistical abstract of the United States, a weekly compilation of presidential documents, and more. This site will be useful for history teachers who bring current events into their classrooms.

Documents for the Study of American History

http://history.cc.ukans.edu/carrie/docs/amdocs_index.html

This Web site, managed at the University of Kansas, provides users with one of the richest lists of documents on American history available on the Web. The documents range from Columbus's letter to Ferdinand and Isabella in 1494 to Bill Clinton's inaugural address in 1993. The list is strongest in the eighteenth and twentieth centuries, but the whole of U.S. history gets good coverage. This kind of Web site removes the need to buy documents collections for the classroom when such good materials are available at a click.

Dolly and Buster's K-4 Main Page

http://www.concentric.net/~terrapin/index.html

For teachers at lower grade levels, Dolly and Buster is a good place to start looking for ideas for the classroom. Users will find everything from lesson plans and classroom activities to teacher tips, information on specific topics, and a teacher e-mail idea exchange. Each site provides more links "to an almost infinite amount of educational resources." The front page also includes a "classroom jump page" as a starting point for K-4 students using the Web, promising "safe, educational, fun links."

EDTECH

http://h-net.msu.edu/~edweb

EDTECH is one of several H-Net-sponsored discussion lists. This site contains an archive of all past messages from the EDTECH group and links to other educational technology sites.

Encyclopedia of Women's History

http://www.teleport.com/~megaines/women.html

This Web site, "written by and for the K-12 community," publishes biographies of historical and contemporary women written by elementary and secondary students. There is a useful alphabetized index of entries and links to "further research" and to other collections on women.

Folkmusic.dot.org

http://www.folkmusic.org

Folkmusic.dot.org links users to "the human resources in the folk and acoustic music community." For teachers who want to include music resources in their history curriculum, this site includes biographies, discographies, pictures, lyrics, and sound bytes.

FREE: Federal Resources for Educational Excellence

http://www.ed.gov/free/index.html

FREE is the result of a "partnership" of teachers and federal agencies to develop Internet-based learning modules and learning communities. The agencies include the CIA, FBI, National Park Service, Library of Congress (American Memory), NARA (Digital Classroom), the White House, and others. A "site map" provides connections to various topic areas, including the social studies. Topics are arranged alphabetically with the sponsoring agency identified. There are no annotations, but the descriptive titles give good direction for users.

Helping Your Child Learn History

http://ericps.ed.uiuc.edu/npin/respair/texts/helping/history/
helphist.htm#TableOfContents

This Web site, aimed primarily at parents, offers suggestions to bring history to life for young children, especially ages four through eleven. The suggestions, of course, are equally pertinent for lower-grade teachers. Topics include "History Education Begins at Home" (e.g., "history is a habit"), "History as

Story" (e.g., "cooking up history), and "History as Time" (e.g., "put time in a bottle"). The original print version of Helping Your Child Learn History came from the U.S. Department of Education; the University of Illinois prepared this electronic version.

The History Channel

http://www.historychannel.com

This Web site provides an easy gateway into the video materials that play on the cable network, The History Channel. "The History Store" is the place to order videos, but this is more than just a commercial site. "Traveler" introduces historic sites and "Great Speeches" provides clips of "the words that changed the world," from such diverse characters as Franklin D. Roosevelt, Malcolm X, and Martin Luther King Jr. to Babe Ruth and Casey Stengel. Classroom materials are available online to accompany videos, including vocabulary terms, discussion questions, and extended activities.

History Departments around the World

http://chnm.gmu.edu/history/depts

Maintained by George Mason University, this site provides an index of links to all history departments around the world that have an online presence. An in-site search engine allows a search for departments inside or outside the United States or a searcher can browse the entire list.

History Happens

http://www.ushistory.com

History Happens is a commercial site that advertises and sells music video materials for the classroom. With a self-description that this model mirrors the old ABC television series "School House Rocks," History Happens says its primary audience is teachers and parents of children ages eight to fifteen.

The History Net: Where History Lives on the Web

http://www.thehistorynet.com

When you first look at The History Net, with its clickable list of historical times and topics along the edge, you might think it is just another history Web site. In fact, its major role is to provide links to published articles on the times and topics, using journals such as *Civil War Times*, *Military History*, *Vietnam*, *British Heritage*, *Wild West*, and *American History*. For an interesting sidebar, The History Net also provides a link to materials on "alternate history," that is the history that might have been if events had run differently.

The History Place

http://www.historyplace.com/index.html

The History Place provides a variety of links that will be useful to history teachers, especially at the secondary level. At this point, the site emphasizes American history, but there are some strong sections on Hitler and the Holocaust, with an annotated bibliography on Hitler's Germany. Other European topics are listed "in progress." Users will find timelines (e.g., the Civil War through quotations), photographs, and "points of view," which are reviews and reflections from established writers and historians. The site also offers an annotated list of "Great History Videos."

History on Public Television

http://www.current.org/hi1.html

Drawing from *Current,* a biweekly newspaper on public television and radio in the United States, this site provides a guide to history programming on PBS, access to stories from back issues of *Current,* and links to various media sites. Teachers will find useful materials to supplement classroom videos that aired originally on PBS.

H-Net Teaching

http://www.h-net.msu.edu/teaching

H-Net Teaching provides a gateway to an extensive number of sites on teaching maintained by the H-Net system (Humanities and Social Science Online) out of Michigan State University. Each of these sites includes edited, threaded discussions on topics of interest to list subscribers, and archives, complete with search mechanisms, on previous discussions. H-Net Teaching includes the following:

H-AfrTeach

Teaching African history and studies.

H-High-School

Teaching high school history and social studies (an indispensable site for secondary history teachers).

H-Mmedia

High-Tech teaching, multimedia, CD-ROM.

H-Survey

Teaching United States history survey courses (a "must-see" site for college American survey teachers).

H-Teach

Teaching history at all levels (my personal favorite of the H-Net sites, with enlightening discussions on a wide range of important topics for history teachers).

H-W-Civ

Teaching Western Civilization courses (a companion to H-Survey).

Humanist Discussion Group

http://www.princeton.edu/~mccarty/humanist/humanist.html

This site is an international electronic seminar on the application of computers and computer technology to the humanities. The efforts of the discussion group, including editing and archiving, are directed by several universities in the United States and the United Kingdom.

IBM K-12 Education

http://www.solutions.ibm.com/k12

This site, designed and maintained by IBM, does much more than promote the products designed and sold by "Big Blue." Users will find links to various social studies topics, such as American history, baseball, holidays, inventions, maps and mapping, Native Americans, and multicultural education, as well as teacher resources.

InterActive Teacher

http://interactiveteacher.com

This site provides an online forum, with articles and multimedia presentations related to teaching in general. Overall, it has minimal value for history teachers except for a fine list of links to museums around the world, which can become the source for virtual field trips for students.

Internet Archive of Texts and Documents

http://history.hanover.edu/texts.html

This Internet archive from Hanover College delivers a variety of primary texts and documents on United States and European history, all from the public domain. The site promises additions on Latin America, Africa, the Middle East, and Asia. Some of the documents come through the Hanover Historical Texts Project; some others arrive via links to other repositories.

Internet for Educators: History and Social Studies Resources

http://www.speakeasy.org/educators/history.html

This site provides a large database of links for K-12 teachers in history, with a clickable chart that allows easy moves into other disciplines, some of which have value in the history classroom, such as arts resources and diversity resources. The list of sites now available in history is small but useful.

InforMNs Internet for Minnesota Schools

http://informns.k12.mn.us

Here is another site designed with the needs of teachers in a state. (Here Minnesota is the primary focus.) But as with the Learning Space (Washington) and SCORE (California) sites (described above), InforMNs delivers information and links useful to a much wider audience. The site also allows quick jumps to search engines, metasearch engines, subject directories, and topical directories through a link to TIES (i.e., Technology and Information Educational Services).

Internet Modern History Sourcebook: History and Music

http://www.fordham.edu/halsall/mod/modmusic.html

As this site notes, it does not provide a history of music. Instead, this section of the Internet Modern History Sourcebook links the user to musical texts and sounds (lyrics and/or music) that illustrate selected topics and times in modern history. Some songs get "streamed" over the Internet through RealAudio. Times run from the Reformation into Modern Europe, while topics include such themes as nineteenth-century nationalism and imperialism. The United States gets some play, but most materials apply to European history.

K–12 History on the Internet Resource Guide

http://www.xs4all.nl/~swanson/history

This K-12 site, run by two teachers from the Netherlands, provides a series of valuable links for history teachers. Clicking on "general information sources," users enter into a section called "charting the unknown" where a variety of navigational tools and information resources introduce connections to history-related sites around the world.

The Library in the Sky

http://www.nwrel.org/sky/index.html

Run by the Northwest Regional Educational Laboratory in Portland Oregon, the Library in the Sky offers more than 6,300 links to educational resources for teachers, librarians, students, and parents, in every field of study. History and the social studies get enough attention to make this a useful site for the K-12 community.

Multimedia/Hypermedia

http://eng.hss.cmu.edu/multimedia

This site offers a sizable collection of media and hypertext materials run through the English Server at Carnegie Mellon University and other servers across the Internet. Users will find a good selection of multimedia materials, including ASCII art, audio, public-domain clip art, hypermedia, maps, soundtracks, and videos (using QuickTime technology).

National Center for History in the Schools

http://www.sscnet.ucla.edu/nchs

The National Center for History in the Schools, located at UCLA, publishes online the National Standards for United States History, K-4 and 5-12, the National Standards for World History, and the Revised Standards for History. In addition, "Bring History Alive" introduces sourcebooks for U.S. and World history, grades 5-12, with more than 1,200 activities arranged by grade level and keyed to the revised standards.

Northwest Ohio Computer Association

http://www.nwoca.ohio.gov/www/default.html

The NWOCA home page links users to search engines and subject areas, including history and social studies. Included here are links to government, news and media, and educational sites. With some topics, world history for example, NWOCA highlights "featured topics" and describes lesson plans from teachers and classroom projects from students.

Online Courses: The Portal to Higher Education on the Web

http://www.newpromise.com

This commercial site provides a comprehensive list of links to online courses in history and other subject areas, plus a search mechanism to help users locate online courses by either category or institution.

ParkNet National Park Service

http://www.nps.gov

The National Park Service, through ParkNet, delivers one of the best Web sites run and maintained by a U.S. government agency. "Links to the Past" sends users to "tools for teaching" (archeology, historic landscapes, structures, and more) and "teaching with historic places" (which gets a full description below). "Visit Your Parks" opens links for all NPS properties. Some of these—Olympic National Park in Washington state for example—have expanded Web sites that provide attractive resources for teachers, such as lesson plans to pick up and use with ease.

Presidential Letters U.S. Postal Service

http://www.usps.gov/letters/volume2/pres-main.html

Organized by the U.S. Postal Service, this site provides—what else?—a series of letters that show the "hopes, dreams, [and] passions" of America's executive leaders. With letters from fifteen different presidents, running from Washington to Reagan, the purpose is "to humanize the men we have chosen to lead our nation." These letters will provide nice supplements for lectures, class projects, and research assignments, especially for secondary level courses.

Project Gutenberg

http://www.promo.net/pg

One of the best known early WWW sites, Project Gutenberg provides a wealth of "fine literature digitally re-published" to bring hundreds of classic works in world history and literature into the classroom as electronic texts at the click of a mouse. An in-site search engine allows users to find e-texts by checking alphabetical lists of authors and titles, which can be downloaded via FTP or the Web.

Smithsonian Institution Social Studies Lesson Plans

http://educate.si.edu/lessons/lists/sslist.html

The Smithsonian Institution, by reputation, is a storehouse for artifacts in American and World history. This site allows users to tap into the assets of the Smithsonian to find lesson plans in several disciplines, including social studies. This is a developing site that promises to enrich our teaching across the span and scope of history. For an example of the melding of objects and stories, one plan now available focuses on the Bering Sea Eskimo people. Others offer in-depth looks at historical Africa and Japan.

Social Studies Resources

http://www.kent.wednet.edu/curriculum/soc_studies/soc_studies.html

This Web site from the Kent School District in Washington state provides a variety of lesson plans in all disciplines, including social studies, where teachers can make connections in history, state history, family history, and more. The lesson plans are broken into grade levels K-3, 4-6, junior high, and high school, which makes them easy to identify and introduce. The resources area—with outline lessons, project ideas, and mini-lessons—includes separate sections for every grade level K-12.

Social Studies School Service

http://catalog.socialstudies.com

This commercial site advertises the wares of the Social Studies School Service in Culver City California. Here users can bypass printed catalogs to locate and order CD-ROMs, laser disks, maps and globes, videos, simulations, and reproducibles, as well as books. Different mechanisms allow searches by grade level, by reading levels, or by author, title, and subject.

SyllabusWeb

http://www.syllabus.com

This site, produced by *Syllabus* magazine, contains articles and information on the application of electronic technologies in education. Subscription information (*Syllabus* is available free by mail) is available, along with related links and a search engine that allows easy access to the archives of SyllabusWeb.

Teachers Helping Teachers

http://www.pacificnet.net/~mandel/index.html

Teachers Helping Teachers opened in 1995 under the direction of Scott Mandel, a middle school English and history teacher in Pacoima, California, who updates the site each week during the school year. Now with more than one million hits testimony to its value for teachers, the site provides lesson plans (all submitted by teachers) for K-12 grade levels. Many of these plans are easily adaptable to a variety of teaching situations. Other useful sections include a teacher chat room and links to educational resources on the Web that have been alphabetized by subject.

Teaching with Historic Places

http://www.cr.nps.gov/nr/twhp/home.html

This site, run through the National Park Service, focuses on the teaching opportunities presented by properties on the National Register of Historic Places. The purpose is to "enliven" the teaching of history by moving students beyond textbooks and helping them "connect history to their own lives." The NPS provides lesson plans, education kits, and workshops to facilitate the integration of historic places into the curriculum.

Teachnet.Com

http://www.teachnet.com

Opening with the "brainstorm of the day"—actually several ideas introduced in one paragraph each—this attractive site packages a mix of materials and ideas that teachers will enjoy and use. Some of the more useful links are "lesson ideas," "teacher-2-teacher," and "how-to" ideas that include everything from classroom decor to classroom management.

THOMAS

http://thomas.loc.gov/

Thomas bills itself as "legislative information on the Internet." It is certainly that and much more. Run through the Library of Congress, Thomas follows the work of the United States Senate and House of Representatives, providing summaries, status reports, and full texts of legislation in the Congress. The site also provides directories for members of Congress, making it a critical tool for teachers who use current events in their classrooms.

UCLA's Social Sciences Division

http://www.sscnet.ucla.edu

The UCLA Social Sciences Web site is a fine starting point for social studies links. It contains connections to social science departments, institutes, and resources at UCLA. By working through several layers in some program descriptions—notably the American Indian Studies Center—users will get to a series of useful links to other WWW resources.

United States Department of Education

http://www.ed.gov

This is the official home page of the U.S. Department of Education. It is a good place to learn about federal educational initiatives, and it contains links to related sites, e.g., FREE (described on page 462). Those who are interested also can find a variety of policy documents online at this site.

United States Distance Learning Association

http://www.usdla.org

This is the online presence of the U.S. Distance Learning Association. It contains information about the organization and links to distance learning resources from pre-K through higher education.

Web66: A K-12 World Wide Web Project

http://web66.coled.umn.edu

For most teachers the greatest value of Web66 is its ability to link users to most American elementary and secondary schools with a WWW presence, encouraging all kinds of exchanges between teachers across cities, states, and regions. Web66 also provides access to Mustang, a "Web cruising vehicle" to help teacher "cruise" rather than "surf" the Web. And the site provides links to many WWW resources in history and social studies that make it particularly suited to the needs of history teachers.

Words and Deeds in American History

http://lcweb2.loc.gov/ammem/mcchtml/corhome.html

Here is one more site from the Library of Congress. Actually an offshoot of American Memory (described on page 454), Words and Deeds gives a condensed collection of manuscript materials (with some ninety "representative documents") that can enrich the teaching and study of history. The LOC has provided a detailed description to accompany each document and links to other resources in the library's collection that relate to the documents.

DISCUSSION GROUPS
Keith C. Trinkle

Discussion groups are one of the most beneficial and useful resources on the Internet. Many organizations and associations now sponsor lists for their fields, and the number of lists is climbing rapidly. There is also a large consortium sponsoring history discussion lists called H-Net—the Humanities Online Initiative. H-Net is funded by the National Endowment for the Humanities and Michigan State University. It supports more than one hundred discussion groups covering a wide range of historical topics. The list below outlines the major discussion lists, but there also are hundreds of smaller, less active groups that are not listed. The best online guide to these lists is The Directory of Scholarly and Professional E-Conferences at http://n2h2.com/KOVACS/.

As mentioned in Chapter One, you must subscribe to a discussion list to participate. To subscribe, it is necessary to send what is called a "subscribe message" to the address listed below. A subscribe message contains simply the text listed below followed by your full name. An example would be:

Subscribe H-France Michael Garrison

Chapter One describes subscribing to discussion lists in more detail. The following information gives the addresses of the listservers to which subscription messages should be sent.

H-NET LISTS

For the following lists, send a subscribe message to

LISTSERV@H-NET.MSU.EDU

EDTECH, Educational Technology
H-Africa, African history
H-Afro-Am, African-American Studies
H-AfrTeach, Teaching African History and Studies
H-AHC, Association for History and Computing

H-Albion, British and Irish history
H-AmIndian, American Indian History and Culture
H-AmRel, American religious history
H-AmStdy, American studies
H-Antisemitism, Antisemitism
H-ANZAU, History of Aotearoa / New Zealand and Australia
H-Appalachia, Appalachian History and Studies
H-ASEH, Environmental History
H-Asia, Asian studies and history
H-California, History and Culture of California
H-Canada, Canadian history and studies
H-Childhood, History of Childhood and Youth
H-CivWar, American Civil War
H-CLC, Comparative literature and computing
H-Demog, Demographic history
H-Diplo, Diplomatic history, international affairs
H-Ethnic, Ethnic, immigration, and emigration studies
H-Film, Scholarly studies and uses of media
H-Frauen-L, Women and Gender in Early Modern Europe
H-GAGCS, German-American and German-Canadian Studies
H-German, German history
H-Grad, Graduate student topics
H-High-S, Teaching high school history/social studies
H-Holocaust, Holocaust Studies
H-Ideas, Intellectual History
H-Indiana, Indiana History and Culture
H-Islamart, History of Islamic Art and Architecture
H-Italy, Italian History and Culture
H-ItAm, Italian-American History and Culture
H-Japan, Japanese History and Culture
H-Judaic, Judaica and Jewish history
H-Labor, Labor history
H-LatAm, Latin American history
H-Law, Legal and constitutional history
H-LIS, History of Library and Information Science
H-Local, State and local history and museums
H-Mac, Macintosh users
H-Michigan, History and Culture of Michigan
H-Mideast-Medieval, The Islamic Lands of the Medieval Period
H-Minerva, Women in War and Women and War
H-MMedia, Discussions of multimedia teaching
H-NCC, The National Coordinating Committee for the Promotion of History

H-NEXA, The Science-Humanities Convergence Forum
H-Nilas, Nature in Legend and Story
H-Ohio, History and Culture of the State of Ohio
H-OIEAHC, Colonial and Early American History
H-Oralhist, Studies Related to Oral History
H-PCAACA, Popular Culture and American Culture Association
H-Radhist, History, Theory, Politics from a Radical Perspective
H-Review, Book reviews
H-Rhetor, History of rhetoric and communications
H-Rural, Rural and agricultural history
H-Russia, Russian history
H-SAE, European anthropology
H-SAfrica, South African History
H-SAWH, Women and Gender in the U.S. South
H-Sci-Med-Tech, History of Science, Medicine, and Technology
H-SEASIA, South East Asia
H-SHEAR, Early American Republic
H-SHGAPE, American Gilded Age and Progressive Era
H-Skand, Scandinavian History
H-South, American South
H-Survey, Teaching United States Survey Courses
H-State, Discussions of the welfare state
H-Teach, Teaching college history
H-Teachpol, Teaching Political Science (Post-secondary)
H-Texas, History and Culture of Texas
H-Turk, Turkish Studies
H-Women, Women's history
H-World, World history
H-UCLEA, Labor Studies
H-Urban, Urban History
H-US-Japan, U.S.-Japan Relations
H-USA, International Study of the USA
H-War, Military History
H-W-Civ, Teaching Western Civilization
H-West, United States West, frontiers
H-West-Africa, West African History and Culture
Habsburg, Austro-Hungarian Empire
Jhistory, List for Discussion of History of Journalism and Mass Communication

For the list below, send a subscribe message to listserv@ksuvm.ksu.edu

H-Pol, United States Political History

For the following lists, a subscribe message should be sent to

listserv@vm.cc.purdue.edu

H-France, French history

For H-Mexico, send a subscribe message to h-mexico@servidor.unam.mx

H-MEXICO, Mexican history and studies

For the lists below, send a subscribe message to lists@eh.net

EH.DISC, Economic history extended discussion
EH.Eastbloc, Economic history of Eastern Europe
EH.Macro, Macroeconomic history, business cycles
EH.NEWS, Economic history news, announcements
EH.RES, Economic history short research notes and queries
EH.Teach, Teaching economic history
H-Business, Business history
HES, History of economics/economic thought

Other Discussion Lists:

AERA-F, Educational history and historiography
Send a "subscribe AERA-F" message to listserv@lists.asu.edu

AEROSP-L, Aeronautical and aerospace history
Send a "subscribe AEROSP-L" message to listserv@sivm.si.edu

AMERCATH, History of American Catholicism
Send a "subscribe AMERCATH" message to listserv@lsv.uky.edu

ANCIEN-L, Ancient history
Send a "suscribe ANCIEN-L" message to listserv@listserv.louisville.edu

ASTR-L, Theater history
Send a "subscribe ASTR-L" message to listserv@postoffice.cso.uiuc.edu

AZTLAN, Pre-Columbian history
Send a "sub AZTLAN" message to listserv@listserv.louisville.edu

C18-L, Eighteenth-century interdisciplinary studies
Send a "subscribe C18-L" message to listserv@lists.psu.edu

CHEIRON, Society for the History of the Social and Behavioral Sciences
Send a "subscribe CHEIRON" message to listserv@yorku.ca

EARLYSCIENCE-L, History of Science Society, Early Science Interest Group
Send a "subscribe EARLYSCIENCE-L" message to listserv@listserv.vt.edu

ELIAS-I, Figurational studies in social science, history and psychology
Send a "subscribe ELIAS-I" message to listserv@nic.surfnet.nl

ETHNOHIS, Ethnology and history
Send a "subscribe ETHNOHIS" message to listserv@nic.surfnet.nl

HASTRO-L, History of astronomy
Send a "subscribe HASTRO-L" message to listserv@wvnvm.wvnet.edu

HISTORY-OF-GEOG, History of geography & geographical thought
Send a "subscribe HISTORY-OF-GEOG" message to listserv@lsv.uky.edu

HISLAW-L, Legal history
Send a "subscribe HISLAW-L" message to listserv@listserv.louisville.edu

HOPOS-L, History of the philosophy of science
Send a "subscribe HOPOS-L" message to listserv@listserv.nd.edu

HPSST-L, History and philosophy of science and science teaching
Send a "subscribe HPSST-L" message to listserv@post.queensu.ca

HTECH-L, History of technology
Send a "subscribe HTECH-L" message to listserv@sivm.si.edu

INDIAN-ROOTS-L, Native American history and genealogy discussion
Send a "subscribe INDIAN-ROOTS-L" message to listserv@listserv.
indiana.edu

ISLAM-L, History of Islam
Send a "subscribe ISLAM-L" message to listserv@listserv.louisville.edu

KYROOTS, Kentucky Genealogy & History Discussions
Send a "subscribe KYROOTS" message to Listserv@lsv.uky.edu

MEDART-L, Medieval art history
Send a "subscribe MEDART-L" message to listserv@listserv.utoronto.ca

MEH, Media History
Send a "subscribe MEH" message to listserv@frodo.carfax.co.uk

MENA-H, History of the Middle East and North Africa
Send a "subscribe MENA-H" message to Listserv@listserv.louisville.edu

NORTHEAST-ROOTS, Genealogy and history in the New England area
Send a "subscribe NORTHEAST-ROOTS" message to Listserv@listserv.indiana.edu

PSYHX, Psychology History Archive
Send a "subscribe PSYHX" message to listserv@maelstrom.stjohns.edu

PHILOFHI, Philosophy of history
Send a "subscribe PHILOFHI-L" message to listserv@yorku.ca

PUBLHIST, Public history
Send a "subscribe PUBLHIST" message to listserv@listserv.iupui.edu

RENAIS-L, Renaissance history
Send a "subscribe RENAIS-L" message to listserv@listserv.louisville.edu

RUSHIST, Russian history
Send a "subscribe SAH-L" message to listserv@VM.USC.EDU

SHARP-L, Society for the History of Authorship, Reading, and Publishing
Send a "subscribe SHARP-L" message to listserv@listserv.indiana.edu

SISTER-L, History of female Catholic religious
Send a "subscribe SISTER-L" message to listserv@listserv.syr.edu

SLAVERY, History of slavery
Send a "subscribe SLAVERY" message to listserv@listserv.uh.edu

SOCHIS-L, Social History of Medicine
Send a "subscribe SOCHIS-L" message to listserv@webber.oup.co.uk

SPORTHIST, Sports history
Send a "subscribe SPORTHIST" message to listserv@pdomain.uwindsor.ca

STUDIUM, University history
Send a "subscribe STUDIUM" message to listserv@cc1.kuleuven.ac.be

TAMHA, Teaching American history
Send a "subscribe TAMHA" message to listserv@lists.wayne.edu

WHIRL, Women's history in rhetoric and language
Send a "subscribe WHIRL" message to listserv@lists.psu.edu

WOMENSHISTORYFORUM, Women's history
Send a "subscribe WOMENSHISTORYFORUM" message to listserv@ashp.listserv.cuny.edu

---

NEWSGROUPS (USENET GROUPS)
Keith C. Trinkle

Like discussion lists, newsgroups are an interesting and enjoyable way to engage in a discussion or learn about your favorite historical topics. The addresses of newsgroups are simple to remember. They are the name of the group plus the tag news://. For example, to have your browser bring up the soc.history.living group, you would type news://soc.history.living. A complete list of the more than ten thousand newsgroups is accessible online at:

UseNet News Groups: Comprehensive Directory
http://www.tile.net/tile/news/index.html

The following groups are likely to be of particular interest to readers of *The History Highway 2000*:

alt.history.abe-lincoln
alt.history.ancient-worlds
alt.history.californian-controversy
alt.history.colonial
alt.history.costuming
alt.history.exile
alt.history.future
alt.history.living - History and reenactments.
alt.history.ocean-liners.titanic - The history of oceanliners.
alt.history.punitive.expedition
alt.history.richard-iii
alt.history.what-if - What-if scenarios in history.
soc.college - A general forum on college issues.
soc.college.teaching-asst - Issues affecting TAs.
soc.history - A wide array of historical topics.

soc.history.living - Living history and reenactment.
soc.history.medieval - Medieval topics.
soc.history.moderated - All aspects of history.
soc.history.science - History of science.
soc.history.war - All wars and military history.
soc.history.war.misc - Military history.
soc.history.war.us-civil-war - Aspects of the U.S. Civil War.
soc.history.war.vietnam - The Vietnam War.
soc.history.war.world-war-ii - World War II and the Holocaust.
soc.libraries - Library issues.

ELECTRONIC JOURNALS
Todd Larson and Dennis Trinkle

DIRECTORIES

The History Journals Guide

http://www.crispinius.com/nfh2/zeitschriften/hjg-start.html

This guide is compiled by Stefan Blaschke of the German Nachrichtendienst für HistorikerInnen (News Service for Historians Project). It includes a comprehensive listing of print and electronic journals. Blaschke updates the section on e-journals frequently, and it is the best starting point for efficiently locating online history journals.

NewJour

http://gort.ucsd.edu/newjour/

NewJour is a frequently updated database that lists new online journals and their addresses as they appear. It is a place to watch for new journals on topics that interest you.

Project Muse

http://muse.jhu.edu/

Project Muse is the National Endowment for the Humanities–sponsored project to make the Johns Hopkins Journals available online. At present, the full texts of more than forty journals in the humanities and sciences are online, including *Eighteenth-Century Studies, Bulletin of the History of Medicine, French Historical Studies, Modernism/Modernity, New Literary History,* and *Reviews in American History.* Access to the full-text issues is limited to those affiliated with subscribed institutions, but bibliographic material and tables of contents are freely accessible for all the journals.

Scholarly Journals Distributed Via the World-Wide Web

http://info.lib.uh.edu/wj/webjour.html

This directory provides links to established Web-based scholarly journals that offer access to English language article files without requiring user registration or fees.

E-JOURNALS

Arachnion: A Journal of Literature and Ancient History on the Web

http://www.cisi.unito.it/arachne/arachne.html

Published in Italy at the University of Bologna, *Arachnion* is an online journal that features articles and forums on the ancient world. There are also announcements and many useful links to related sites.

The Bryn Mawr Classical Review

http://ccat.sas.upenn.edu/bmcr

The Bryn Mawr Classical Review is a monthly journal published jointly by Bryn Mawr College and the University of Pennsylvania. It contains reviews of books on Greek and Latin literature and history and has occasional notices (e.g., about conferences). It has an excellent archive of past articles and reviews that is searchable by author, reviewer, or book title. Located only in Gopher (nongraphic) format, it has been online since 1990, and like its sister publication *The Bryn Mawr Medieval Review*, there are plans to put it on the World Wide Web.

The Medieval Review

http://www.hti.umich.edu/b/bmr/tmr.html

The Bryn Mawr Medieval Review is based at the Medieval Institute at Western Michigan University in conjunction with Bryn Mawr College. It publishes timely reviews of current work in all areas of medieval studies, a field it interprets as broadly as possible (chronologically, geographically, and culturally). The editorial board consists of influential scholars in the field, including Patrick Geary (UCLA) and Robert Stacey (University of Washington).

Chronicon

http://www.ucc.ie/chronicon/

Chronicon is an electronic journal of international history published by the Department of History at University College, Cork, Ireland. It is published annually and is freely available on the Internet. Each volume appears at the start of the calendar year and remains open for that year. As new articles are received they are added to the current volume.

Classics Ireland

http://www.ucd.ie/~classics/ClassIre95.html

Classics Ireland is the official journal of the Classical Association of Ireland and publishes articles and reviews on the Classics, ancient history, and archaeology. Like *Chronicon*, it appears as an annual register.

Clio En Afrique: L'histoire africaine en langue française

http://newsup.univ-mrs.fr/~wclio-af/

Clio en Afrique is a French-language journal dedicated to African history. It is published triennially under the auspices of the Université de Provence African Studies program.

Comitatus: A Journal of Medieval and Renaissance Studies

http://www.humnet.ucla.edu/humnet/cmrs/publications/comitatus/comitatu.htm

Published under the auspices of the UCLA Center for Medieval and Renaissance Studies, *Comitatus* is devoted to publishing articles by new scholars, either working toward doctoral degrees or having completed such work within the previous three years. It also maintains a tradition of gathering work from across disciplines, with a special interest in articles that have an interdisciplinary scope.

The Concord Review

http://www.tcr.org/

The Concord Review was founded in March 1987 to recognize and to publish exemplary history essays by high school students in the English-speaking world. With the thirty-sixth issue (Spring 1999), 407 research papers have been published from authors in thirty-seven states and twenty-four other countries. As of September 1998, *The Concord Review* remains the only quarterly journal in the world to publish the academic work of secondary students.

Connections: American History and Culture in an International Perspective

http://www.indiana.edu/~oah/connections/

Connections is an international announcements newsletter distributed monthly on e-mail and quarterly in print to over 100 countries. The newsletter is supported by the Organization of American Historians and provides a concise digest of information for students, scholars, and professionals who wish to develop international contacts with others interested in the transnational study of American history and culture.

Cromohs: Cyber Review of Modern Historiography

http://www.unifi.it/riviste/cromohs/

Cromohs is the first electronic review of history of modern historiography and its aim is the establishment of a particularly effective on-line resource for studies and research relating to modern historical culture (historiography, erudition, philosophies of history, methodologies of historical research, and didactics of history). The term "modern historical culture" is intended to refer to a period from the end of fifteenth century to the contemporary age, the assumption being that the links between this period and our times are an important element in determining a consciousness and a cultural and civic responsibility for men of letters, and particularly for historians, that ought not to be neglected.

Electronic Antiquity: Communicating the Classics

http://scholar.lib.vt.edu/ejournals/ElAnt/

This is a monthly newsletter published out of the University of Tasmania, Australia that deals with ancient history and archaeology. It is a refereed, international journal that publishes scholarly articles and reviews, as well as "kite-flying" papers seeking feedback and items of interest (announcements of conferences, and vacant positions) to the wider Classics community.

Electronic Journal of Australian and New Zealand History

http://www.jcu.edu.au/aff/history/home.htm

The Electronic Journal of Australian and New Zealand History is an initiative of the School of Humanities, James Cook University, the Centre for Cross-Cultural Research, Australian National University, and the Tasmanian School of Nursing, University of Tasmania.

Electronic Newsletter for the History of Astronomy

http://aibn91.astro.uni-bonn.de/~pbrosche/aa/enha/

The Electronic Newsletter for the History of Astronomy is published monthly by the Working Group for the History of Astronomy.

Essays in History

http://etext.lib.virginia.edu/journals/EH/

Essays in History is a refereed journal published annually for the past thirty-five years by graduate students of the Corcoran Department of History at the University of Virginia. On-line since 1994, it now appears only in electronic form. Each issue has approximately six to eight scholarly journal articles in a wide variety of fields.

49th Parallel: An Interdisciplinary Journal of North American Studies

http://artsweb.bham.ac.uk/49thparallel/

49th Parallel is a quarterly electronic journal published by the Department of American and Canadian Studies at the University of Birmingham, England. The journal aims to promote interdisciplinary study of the North American continent in the nineteenth and twentieth centuries. The editors seek contributions from disciplines including history, politics, international relations, cultural studies, literature, cultural geography, media studies, and sociology. It is run by postgraduate students, and aims to promote the work of postgraduates alongside that of more established scholars.

Heritage Post Interactive

http://heritage.excite.sfu.ca/hpost_e/ipost1/editors_desk/default.html

Published in full color in a tabloid-size format, the bilingual *Heritage Post* tells stories from Canada's past and raises questions about issues in Canadian history. Stories in the *Post* are suggested by commemorative stamps from Canada Post Corporation and Heritage Minutes, one-minute dramatizations that appear on television and in movie theaters. The Web site presents the full contents of the print journal.

Intermarium: The Online Journal of East Central European Postwar History and Politics

http://www.columbia.edu/cu/sipa/REGIONAL/ECE/intermar.html

Intermarium provides an electronic medium for noteworthy scholarship and provocative thinking about the history and politics of Central and Eastern Europe following World War II. The journal is meant to broaden the discourse on aspects of national histories that are undergoing change thanks to the availability of new documentation from recently opened archives. Its name, Intermarium, reflects East Central Europe's geographic location between the seas: Baltic, Adriatic, and Black. It is a project of the Institute of Political Studies of the Polish Academy of Sciences and Columbia University's Institute on East Central Europe.

IOUDAIOS Review

http://listserv.lehigh.edu/lists/ioudaios-review/

IOUDAIOS Review is a quarterly journal for professional scholars of early Judaism and related fields and was spawned by the listserv discussion group IOUDAIOS-L. It is primarily intended to serve professional scholars of early Judaism and related fields, so some knowledge of classical Hebrew and Hellenistic Greek is assumed. It is intended to disseminate information on conferences and publish reviews of pertinent literature. There is an archive of all past issues with a fully cross-referenced bibliographic index. There is also a guide that gives instructions for contributors and supplies transliteration tables for Greek and Hebrew text.

Journal of the Association for History and Computing

http://mcel.pacificu.edu/JAHC/jahcindex.htm

This journal is sponsored by the American Association for History and Computing. The AAHC aspires to promote and develop interest in the use of computers in all types of historical study at every level, in both teaching and research. The journal is intended for a general audience of teachers, students, and researchers interested in the application of computers in historical studies. The journal will keep readers abreast of the latest developments in the field. In addition to articles dealing with the creative application of computers to particular problems in history, we will also be reviewing relevant research in the field, appropriate software, and related Internet resources. It will be published quarterly, though individual issues will be continually updated for a period of one year via interactive devices before being archived. Those wishing to be notified by e-mail as each volume of the journal is published can contact kdvorak@BGNet.bgsu.edu and in the subject heading enter: "Notification JAHC."

The Journal for Multimedia History

http://www.albany.edu/jmmh/

The *JMMH* is supported by the University at Albany–SUNY history department. The journal is dedicated to presenting and reviewing historical scholarship focusing on all periods and all nations.

Journal of Online Genealogy

http://www.onlinegenealogy.com/

The *Journal of Online Genealogy* carries articles and notices intended to help the genealogical community.

Journal of World-Systems Research

http://csf.Colorado.EDU:80/wsystems/jwsr.html

The *Journal of World-Systems Research* is an electronic journal dedicated to scholarly research on the modern world-system and earlier, smaller intersocietal networks. It is intentionally interdisciplinary in focus. *JWSR* is published under the sponsorship of the Program in Comparative International Development in the Sociology Department at Johns Hopkins University.

KMT: A Modern Journal of Ancient Egypt

http://www.egyptology.com/kmt/

Created in 1990, *KMT* is an English-language journal published quarterly in Egypt. The title of the journal *KMT* is an abbreviation of Kemet, meaning black country, which is what the ancient Egyptians called their homeland. Readers can find the full text of *KMT*'s articles, announcements, reports, and reviews online.

Media History Monographs

http://www.scripps.ohiou.edu/mediahistory/mhminfo.htm

Media History Monographs (*MHM*) is a quarterly online journal devoted to publishing historical scholarly works that are too long for regular journal articles and too short for books. All articles are peer-reviewed and all methodologies are welcome. *Media History Monographs* was created to accommodate the increased study of history in the field of mass communications. The journal is sponsored by the cooperative efforts of the School of Journalism at Ohio University and the Mass Communication Department at Emory and Henry College.

MERGER: Newsletter of the Migration and Ethnic Relations Group for European Research

http://www.ercomer.org/merger/index.html

As its title indicates, *MERGER* is the newsletter for the Migration and Ethnic Relations Group for European Research. It is published three times a year, and the online version contains the full text of the newsletter.

Old World Archaeology Newsletter

http://www.wesleyan.edu/classics/OWAN.html

The *Old World Archaeology Newsletter* (*OWAN*) is published three times a year by the Department of Classical Studies at Wesleyan University, Middletown, Connecticut.

Orientalia Ab Argentina

http://www.geocities.com/Athens/Troy/9742/orabarg.html

Orientalia Ab Argentina is an electronic Journal devoted to the historical and interdisciplinary studies on the Ancient Near East. It is edited by Bernardo Gandulla, Co-Director of Argentina's Team in Tel Gerisa Archaeological Project.

Perspectives Online

http://chnm.gmu.edu/aha/persp/index.html

Perspectives Online is the electronic newsletter of the American Historical Association. It is published monthly except during the summer recess.

Postmodern Culture Journal

http://ernie.bgsu.edu/~swilbur/PMC_MOO.html

Postmodern Culture is an interdisciplinary e-journal produced under the auspices of the University of Virginia and the Institute for Advanced Technology in the Humanities. Unlike other journals, it is published and revised in a free-flowing and experimental manner. It contains articles, musings, and other types of imaginative scholarly exchange. A truly postmodern journal of cultural studies.

Renaissance Forum

http://www.hull.ac.uk/Hull/EL_Web/renforum/

Renaissance Forum is an interdisciplinary refereed journal. It specializes in early-modern English literary and historical scholarship and in the critical methodologies of these fields. The journal is published biannually by an editorial board based in the Departments of English and History at the University of Hull.

Slavic Review

http://www.econ.uiuc.edu/~slavrev/

Published quarterly by the University of Pennsylvania's Center for Eastern European and Russian Scholars, *The Slavic Review* has been online since 1994, making it one of the first Internet journals.

Southern Register

http://www.olemiss.edu/depts/south/index.html

The Southern Register is the official newsletter of the Center for the Study of Southern Culture at the University of Mississippi. Published four times a year, the online version contains the full contents of the print journal, including articles, reviews, forums, and announcements.

Time and Writing

http://www-azc.uam.mx/tye/indice-in.html

Time and Writing is dedicated to Mexican history and is produced by the Universidad Autónoma Metropolitana.

War Times Journal

http://www.wtj.com/

The *WTJ* is a popular journal devoted to all areas of military history.

LIBRARIES

Laura Winninghoff

Library of Congress

http://www.loc.gov

Arguably one of this country's premier collections, the Library of Congress collects in all areas *except* medicine and technical agriculture. Items are in many formats (books, periodicals, maps, music, prints, photographs, recorded sound, and videos), and most items are available through interlibrary loan. On the Web site, one can search the library's holdings, including some links to digitized materials, but the catalog is only available limited hours:

> Monday–Friday: 4:40 a.m.–9:30 p.m.
> Saturday: 8:00 a.m.–5:00 p.m.
> Sunday: 11:35 a.m.–5:00 p.m.
> (all times Eastern)

When searching, there are two options: a word search or a browse. Browsing is a much more general search, and most records used in this type of search are available at any time (Monday–Friday), as they give an indication of the library's holdings in a certain area but not call numbers for specific works. A word search is more specific and only available during the hours stated above, and the types of materials one can search are also limited (e.g., most pre-1975 *cataloged* items are not available). Note: all inquiries by author, title, and Boolean searches for subject, name, series, notes, etc. are considered "word" searches.

The library also makes available its *experimental* search system, which only has ten percent of the library's holdings entered. Two major improvements over the current catalog are the possibility of browsing a shelf (or section) without being in the library and performing a search for "related" materials. This latter improvement is a very good way to determine the correct Library of Congress Subject Heading (LCSH) once you have narrowed your topic. These Subject Headings are the basis of entry in most library catalogs, and are not always intuitive terms or phrases.

American Memory: Historical Collections of the National Digital Library

http://memory.loc.gov/ammem/ammemhome.html

The American Memory Collection is the collective term for those items deemed by the Library of Congress to be important to the cultural history of the United States. The level of cataloging varies with the collection and depends partly on the format, its age, and its acquisition date. Most collections are searchable and many have finding aids such as subject and author lists.

The Center for Research Libraries

http://wwwcrl.uchicago.edu OR telnet crlcatalog.uchicago.edu (login as "guest" at prompt)

The Center for Research Libraries is a consortium of college and university libraries from all over the United States. The Center holds materials deemed by many libraries to be important but too obscure to take up valuable shelf space in their own institution. Through membership in the CRL, libraries take advantage of these materials and their patrons have fairly quick access to them. Currently, ninety-eight percent of the nearly five million entries in the CRL's catalog are available online, including books, newspapers, serials, microforms, archival collections, and other research materials. There is a handbook on the Web page describing, in greater detail, the holdings in certain areas; a name authority file is also available.

The Newberry Library

http://www.newberry.org/virtua/english/virtua-basic.html

The Newberry is slowly adding to its Web-based catalog, but currently only fifteen percent of collections are searchable. Where available, OCLC has the complete holdings of the Newberry already as part of their database. Bibliographic guides are available on the Web site for beginning researchers.

The Bancroft Library (UC–Berkley)

http://sunsite2.berkeley.edu/oac/

Provides access to the Bancroft Library's collections, via the Online Archive of California, including access to UC–Berkeley Finding Aids and the California Heritage Digital Image Access Database.

The Beinecke Library (Yale's Rare Books and Manuscripts Library)

http://webpac.library.yale.edu/webpac/orbis.htm

Searchable through ORBIS, Yale's online catalog.

The Lilly Library

http://www.indiana.edu/~liblilly/lillyhome.html

At present, the Lilly Library's online resources include searchable indexes of the manuscript collections, Chapbook collection, and French Revolution documents. The library's holdings are searchable via Indiana University's catalog, IUCAT (telnet infogate.ucs.indiana.edu. Login as "guest," and when prompted enter IUCAT). This is a command-driven catalog.

The Hagley Library

http://205.128.217.50/libinfo.htm

The Hagley Museum and library's focus is American Business and Technological History. As of this writing, their catalog is under construction.

The Public Records Office–UK

http://www.pro.gov.uk/finding/catalogue/default.htm

At present, the catalogue only contains references to selected policy records of twentieth-century British government departments.

The Library Company of Philadelphia

http://www.librarycompany.org/catalogFrameset.html

Founded in 1731 by Benjamin Franklin, the Library Company of Philadelphia has over half a million items covering American History and culture from the seventeenth to the nineteenth century. The online catalog, WolfPAC, currently has about twenty percent of the collection included, with more added daily. However, this online catalog also includes records from the Union catalog of the Philadelphia Area Consortium of Special Collections Libraries (PACSCL): the Academy of Natural Sciences, the Balch Institute for Ethnic Studies, Saint Charles Borromeo Seminary, and the Philadelphia Museum of Art. Joining in the near future are the Rosenbach Museum and Library, the Presbyterian Historical Society, the Athenaeum, and the Historical Society of Pennsylvania. Several other PACSCL member libraries have, or will soon have, catalogs available through the PACSCL Web site, or through their individual institution's Web site. These include the American Philosophical Society, the Free Library of Philadelphia, the University of Pennsylvania, Winterthur, The Hagley Museum and Library, Temple University, The College of Physicians of Philadelphia, the Wagner Free Institute of Science, Bryn Mawr, Haverford, and Swarthmore.

The New York Public Library

http://catnyp.nypl.org/

CATNYP is the online catalog of the Research Libraries of The New York Public Library. This catalog includes materials added to the collections after 1971, as well as some materials acquired before 1971. At this time, however, the best place to search the Libraries' holdings is the 800-volume *Dictionary Catalog of the Research Libraries*, published by G.K. Hall. Copies of this catalog are available at many research institutions and all NYPL Research libraries. There is a link on the Web page to a global list of libraries that own a copy of the *Catalog*.

OhioLink

http://www.ohiolink.edu

This is the communal catalog for all libraries (public, private, college, and university) in Ohio.

OPAC97 at the British Library

http://opac97.bl.uk/

OPAC97 provides access to the major catalogs of the British Library in London and Boston Spa. Presently, individual collections have separate catalogs, but all can be searched using the form given on the Web page. The collections include humanities, social science, hard science, technology, and business collections cataloged from 1975 to the present; all music cataloged from 1980 to the present; and all reference materials cataloged before 1975 (including the archives and materials of the former India Office and colonial Africa). In the older reference materials, please note that the "D-" before items means the original was destroyed during WWII and has since been replaced. Finally, all serials from 1700 to the present are included in the catalog. Hours of operation: Monday–Saturday 4 a.m.–midnight (GMT).

OLIS-Oxford's Bodleian Library

telnet://library.ox.ac.uk

Without a password from Oxford you may not search any other Oxford library (although all are listed). This is a command-driven search, and most materials are available for interlibrary loan.

The Getty Research Institute for the History of Art and the Humanities

http://opac.pub.getty.edu

Collections include Western art, archaeology, and architecture from the Bronze Age to the present, with a special strength in French, German, Russian, Italian, and American avant garde materials. There are also extensive collections on the conservation of cultural heritage and historic preservation. Also included is an unparalleled auction catalog collection with more than 110,000 volumes of materials from the late seventeenth century to the present. Included in the Special Collections are artists' journals and sketchbooks, albums, architectural drawings, early guidebooks, emblem books, prints, and drawings. The Getty collection's strengths are in Futurism, Dada, Surrealism, the Bauhaus, Russian Constructivism, and Fluxus. Many items from the research library are available for interlibrary loan.

EuroDocs: Primary Historical Documents from Western Europe

http://www.lib.byu.edu/~rdh/eurodocs/

Compiled by Richard Hacken, a librarian at Brigham Young University, this list of links connects to Western European (mainly primary) historical documents that are transcribed, reproduced, and, in some cases, translated.

The National Library of China

http://www.nlc.gov.cn/etext.htm

Non-Chinese-speaking visitors to this site submit questions to librarians, who then search for the information. This site is best if you have a specific question or request, and the catalog is searchable if your computer registers Chinese characters—and if you can read them.

Bibliothèque Nationale de France

http://www.bnf.fr/web-bnf/catalog/index.htm

Catalog of the French National Library, in French, with an English gateway under construction. The above link is to the summary page for all four catalogs, including GALLICA—an effort to chronicle nineteenth-century France through digitized images and sound.

Oriental Institute (the University of Chicago) Research Archives

http://www-oi.uchicago.edu/OI/DEPT/RA/ABZU/ABZU.HTML

This is a guide to resources for the study of the Ancient Near East available on the Internet, compiled and updated by Charles E. Jones, research archivist at the Oriental Institute's Research Archives, consisting of primary and secondary indexes of information.

Labriola National American Indian Data Center at Arizona State University

http://www.asu.edu/lib/archives/labriola.htm

The Labriola National American Indian Data Center, part of the ASU Libraries, brings together current and historic information on government, culture, religion and worldview, social life and customs, tribal history, and information on individuals from the United States, Canada, and Sonora and Chihuahua, Mexico. All materials held by the Center are searchable via ASU's online catalog (http://catalog.lib.asu.edu/).

Univeristy of Oklahoma Western History Collection

http://www-lib.ou.edu/depts/west/index.htm

This collection's aim is to provide opportunities for research into the development of the Trans-Mississippi West and Native American cultures. Catalog information for many of the materials within the Western History Collections may be accessed through the University of Oklahoma Libraries online catalog, OLIN. Catalog information for Western History Collections material is divided as follows: choose "OU Catalog" from the Libraries menu to search for books held by the Western History Collections, or choose "Archives" from the Libraries menu to search for manuscript and photo collections of the Western History Collections.

The Schlesinger Library, Radcliffe College

(Searchable via Harvard's online catalog at telnet://hollis.harvard.edu)

The Schlesinger Library is the foremost library on the history of women in America. Its holdings of audiovisual materials, books, ephemera, manuscripts, oral histories, periodicals, and photographs document the social history of women in the United States, primarily during the nineteenth and twentieth centuries.

Schomburg Center for Research in Black Culture

http://www.nypl.org/research/sc/sc.html
(holdings searchable via CATNYP, the New York Public Library catalog, http://catnyp.nypl.org)

The Schomburg Center for Research in Black Culture is a national research library devoted to collecting, preserving, and providing access to resources documenting the experiences of peoples of African descent throughout the world. The Center provides access to—and professional reference assistance in—the use of its collections to the scholarly community and the general public through five research divisions. The Center's collections include art objects, audio and video tapes, books, manuscripts, motion picture films, newspapers, periodicals, photographs, prints, recorded music discs, and sheet music.

The Kinsey Institute for Research in Sex, Gender, and Reproduction

http://www.indiana.edu/~kinsey/

(Collections searchable via KICAT, at telnet infogate.ucs.indiana.edu. Login as "guest" and when prompted to choose a catalog, type KICAT.)

KICAT does not contain records for all items in the library, nor does it contain records for the Institute's art and archival collections. Records are continually being added to the online catalog as part of the library's retrospective conversion project. Information on other materials is available only through onsite finding aids and published book catalogs (citations available on the Web site). For help in using the library's holdings of sex-related magazines, films and videos, newspapers and tabloids, pulp fiction, and books still cataloged in Dr. Kinsey's system of categories, users must consult with library staff. Records for these materials will be entered into the online catalog as quickly as legal restrictions and resources permit. Until then, access is limited to information available through in-house files, lists, and databases. E-mail libknsy@indiana.edu or call (812) 855-3058 for more information about the library.

Top Ten Research Libraries in the United States*

1. Harvard University
telnet://hollis.harvard.edu
Excellent instructions on searching strategies for HOLLIS and other command-driven search systems are available at http://www.radcliffe.edu/schles/libcolls/search/index.htm

2. Yale University
http://webpac.library.yale.edu/webpac/orbis.htm
ORBIS is available in a Web-based or telnet platform, with links to either appearing on this page.

3. University of Illinois at Urbana–Champaign
http://www.library.uiuc.edu/
This gateway provides access to search systems for library materials and serials. The catalog is, as of this writing, telnet accessible, with an experimental Web catalog available for users as well.

4. University of Texas at Austin
http://dpweb1.dp.utexas.edu/lib/utnetcat/

5. University of Michigan
http://www.lib.umich.edu/libhome/mirlyn/mirlynpage.html

6. University of California at Berkley
http://www.lib.berkeley.edu/Catalogs/guide.html
UC–Berkley has four options in searching its collections—and this page lists all four, along with a chart indicating which system to use for specific searches. Pathfinder is the Berkley-specific catalog, MELVYL (Web or telnet) contains the holdings of all nine campus libraries of the University of California, and GLADIS is the technical services catalog.

7. Columbia University

http://www.columbia.edu/cu/libraries/indexes/resource_type_10.html

CLIO (Columbia Libraries Information Online) and all other New York City area libraries have links on this page. Please be aware that each library at Columbia has its own catalog (e.g., Law School, Medical School, Teacher's College), necessitating many searches to get a complete picture of the holdings on most subjects.

8. Stanford University

http://www-sul.stanford.edu/search/socii/

Socrates II, the Web-based catalog for Stanford, is only available to those with a Stanford ID. The general public can, however, access the older, telnet-based and command-driven Socrates from this page.

9. University of California at Los Angeles

http://www.library.ucla.edu/

10. The University of Chicago

http://webpac.lib.uchicago.edu/

Digest of Education Statistics, U.S. Department of Education. National Center for Education Statistics, 1997, 464, table 417.

ARCHIVES AND MANUSCRIPT COLLECTIONS

Susan Ferentinos

INFORMATION FOR RESEARCHERS

Primary historical research can be intimidating for the beginner. The following sites provide background for new researchers and will help to make the structure of archives seem less daunting.

Introduction to Archives

http://www.umich.edu/~bhl/bhl/refhome/refintro.htm

This essay, part of the Web site of the Bentley Historical Library of the University of Michigan, details the ways in which archives differ from libraries in their collecting focus and their organization.

Primary Sources Research Colloquium

http://www.library.yale.edu/ref/err/primsrcs.htm

Designed to complement a Yale University course in primary research, this site supplies introductory information on using primary documents in historical research. It discusses various types of sources and supplies definitions of words such as *records, collection, finding aids,* and *manuscripts.* Although some parts of the site deal specifically with Yale University resources, overall it contains valuable resources for beginning researchers.

SAMCC Personal Preservation Tips

http://www.sacto.org/dwntwn/history/PTips.htm

The Sacramento Archives and Museum Collection Center (SAMCC) has compiled this list of preservation tips for individuals wishing to preserve their personal documents for posterity. The suggestions are fairly basic, and thus can be accomplished with minimal effort. They also serve as recommendations for the proper handling of material in archives during research.

Using Archives: A Practical Guide for Researchers

http://www.archives.ca/www/svcs/english/using.html

Maintained by the National Archives of Canada, this online essay is geared toward first-time users of archives. It discusses research strategies, what to expect from an archive, and how to locate desired material.

INFORMATION FOR ARCHIVISTS

For those interested in learning more about the profession of collecting, organizing, and preserving historical documents, the following sites are good starting points.

Archives of the Archivist Listserv

http://listserv.muohio.edu/archives/archives.html

This page offers information on the major archivist listserv. Through links, visitors may join the list, review past postings, and search the listserv's archives for specific topics or authors.

Conservation OnLine (CoOL)

http://palimpsest.stanford.edu/

Maintained by Stanford University Libraries, Conservation OnLine (CoOL) is a clearinghouse of information on the conservation of manuscript material. Visitors can access online articles on a wide range of conservation topics, such as pest infestation or digital imaging. Lists of conservation professionals and organizations throughout the world (though mostly in English-speaking countries) are also provided, and the entire site is searchable.

Encoded Archival Description (EAD) Official Web Site

http://lcweb.loc.gov/ead/

Encoded Archival Description (EAD) promises to make collection finding aids widely available on the Web. The Library of Congress maintains the EAD Official Web Site, which contains an introduction to the format, relevant links, and updates on the development of the process.

So You Want to Be an Archivist: A Student's Guide

http://www.wam.umd.edu/~maxwell/690.htm

This individually maintained site provides an introduction to the archival profession that is concise and easy to read. Geared toward the reader contemplating a career in archiving, this site explains archivists' basic duties, types of employment available, educational requirements, and salary expectations. It also lists suggestions for further reading and links to sites with job postings and employment information.

Society of American Archivists (SAA)

http://www.archivists.org/

The Society of American Archivists (SAA) is the major American professional organization for archivists. Its Web site provides information on the organization, as well as position papers, job postings, and a list of SAA publications.

Resources for Archivists

http://www.archives.state.ut.us/referenc/archive.htm

The Utah State Archives sponsors this metasite providing links to pages on topics of interest to archivists. Sections include Archival Education, Grant Writing, Preservation and Conservation, and Software for Archives.

ARCHIVES, MANUSCRIPTS, AND SPECIAL COLLECTIONS

With such a wealth of historic documents available, it can be difficult to know where to begin. The following list, arranged by general topic, includes information on locating sources, along with the Web sites of repositories particularly well-known in their area of specialty. The majority of repositories affiliated with larger institutions (such as universities or national government) now enable connection to catalog searching through their Web sites; however, a significant portion of collections have not been electronically cataloged. Researchers should contact the reference staff of the repository to ensure that they have not missed valuable sources.

The institutions in North America and Western Europe generally maintain more sophisticated Web sites than those in other regions of the world. In an effort to be inclusive of multiple historical fields, I have included sites from throughout the world that are distinctive within their region, though they may appear somewhat basic to North American eyes. All sites are in English unless otherwise noted.

METASITES—MULTINATIONAL (LISTS FOR A SPECIFIC COUNTRY OR GENRE ARE LOCATED UNDER THE APPROPRIATE SUBHEADING)

Archives Web: National Archives on the Web

http://www.archiefnet.nl

National archives generally contain the records of a country's national government and thus are good starting points for locating information on a given country. This site lists links to national archives around the world.

Gabriel: National Libraries of Europe

http://www.konbib.nl/gabriel/en/countries.html

This site provides address, phone number, major collections, operating hours, and mission for the national libraries of over thirty-five nations in Eastern and Western Europe. It also provides links to the individual servers of each library.

Links to Archives Sites in the Commonwealth

http://www.comnet.mt/acarm/arcdir.html

This list contains links to select manuscript repositories in the British Commonwealth. The following countries are included: Ghana, Namibia, South Africa, Zambia, Hong Kong, Malaysia, Singapore, Canada, Bahamas, Australia, New Zealand, and the United Kingdom.

Repositories of Primary Sources

http://www.uidaho.edu/special-collections/Other.Repositories.html

The University of Idaho maintains this listing of over *three thousand* repositories throughout the world. It is as close to a comprehensive list as is available, and using the links on this site is one of the quickest ways to locate a specific library. The list is arranged by region and also includes a section of links to additional lists.

AFRICA

Africa Research Central: A Clearinghouse of African Primary Sources

http://africa-research.csusb.edu/

Africa Research Central provides information on manuscript repositories with holdings of Africana. African, European, and North American libraries are included. For African repositories, the site lists contact information, use restrictions, Web address, and published inventories for each institution, though some of the data is incomplete. For European and North American repositories, the site provides direct links to home pages. The clearinghouse also offers information on the preservation crisis facing manuscripts in Africa.

ANC (African National Congress) Archives

http://www.ufh.ac.za/collections/anc.htm

Currently the ruling party in South Africa, the ANC (African National Congress) has spent most of its history protesting white domination in South Africa. The ANC Archives contains both the official records of the organization and the personal papers of many of its members. Its Web site offers descriptions of its collections, a timeline of ANC activity, and links to other sites about the organization's history and current activities.

Electronic Journal of *Africana Bibliography*

http://www.lib.uiowa.edu/proj/ejab/1/

This issue of *Africana Bibliography* carries the subtitle: Guides, Collections, and Ancillary Materials to African Archival Resources in the United States. It provides a bibliography of archival resources on the history of Africa that are available in the United States through print or microfilm. Selections are grouped by country, region, and language. The site is similar to a print resource, in that it provides few hypertext links.

National Archives of Nigeria, Enugu Branch

http://www2.hu-berlin.de/inside/orient/nae/index.htm

The Enugu Branch of the National Archives of Nigeria has mounted many of its finding aids onto this site. Visitors can access guides and indices for the archives' major collections, along with introductions to the material and to the aspects of Nigerian history the documents cover.

AFRICAN AMERICANS

Amistad Research Center

http://www.tulane.edu/~amistad/

The Amistad Research Center, an independent library housed at Tulane University, holds one of the preeminent groupings of manuscript material pertaining to African-American history. The center's mission is to enable the study of ethnic history and culture and race relations in the United States, and about ninety percent of its materials pertain to African Americans. Amistad's Web site contains lists of manuscript collections, arranged both alphabetically and by major subject, a description of its small collection of African-American art, a list of exhibits (though none are currently online), and bibliographies on the Harlem Renaissance and the *Amistad* slave ship incident. The site devotes an entire section to the *Amistad* case; it includes historical essays as well as descriptions of the center's resources on this topic.

Moorland-Spingarn Research Center, Howard University

http://www.founders.howard.edu/moorland-spingarn/

The Moorland-Spingarn is a research center devoted to the study of people of African descent in Africa and North America, with a particular emphasis on black "families, organizations, institutions, social and religious consciousness, and the continuing struggle for civil rights and human justice." Its manuscripts department reflects this mission with its offering of oral history projects, personal and organizational papers, special music collection, and prints. The center's Web site provides brief biographies of interviewees in the Black Military History oral history project, digital samples of historic photographs, descriptions of manuscript holdings, and a special bibliography of library resources in African-American women's history.

Schomburg Center for Research in Black Culture

http://www.nypl.org/research/sc/sc.html

The Web site of the Schomburg, a research branch of the New York Public Library (NYPL), carries many of the features of its parent organization's site: multiple digital resources, clear logistical information, and an extensive description of its holdings. The center is devoted to the study of the African experience throughout the world, and its strength lies in twentieth-century history, literature, and the performing arts. Its site provides access to online exhibits, a "multimedia sampler" (utilizing video and sound technology), and digitized examples of its holdings. For more information on its digital resources, see the NYPL entry in the Digital Collections section below.

ASIA AND THE PACIFIC

Diplomatic Records Office—Japan

http://www.mofa.go.jp/about/hq/record/

The Diplomatic Records Office maintains the records of Japan's Ministry of Foreign Affairs. It contains material on Japanese foreign relations in the nineteenth and twentieth centuries, though some valuable records were destroyed during World War II. The Web site contains lists of documents recently made available to researchers, along with a description of the library's major holdings.

Directory of Archives in Australia

http://www.asap.unimelb.edu.au/asa/directory/

Maintained by the Australian Society of Archivists, this site offers contact information, hours, collecting focus, and Web links to the major repositories of Australia. Visitors can search the site by subject.

National Archives of Singapore

http://www.museum.org.sg/nas/nas.html

Singapore's National Archives has a wide collection of materials documenting this country's heritage. They include oral histories, photographs, and public records. The site contains information on the holdings, as well as samples
of material held in the collections.

EUROPE—EASTERN

Archives of Yugoslavia

http://www.gov.yu/arhiv/

This repository houses government records and some personal collections pertaining to the Federal Republic of Yugoslavia from its founding in 1918 to the
present. The site provides information on visiting the archives and the collections held. It also houses a small electronic exhibit of thirteen documents, including the Declaration of Corfu (1917) and maps showing the country in 1917
and 1996. In addition, visitors can link to a speech by Prime Minister Momir
Bulatovic at the ceremony to celebrate the eightieth anniversary of the founding
of Yugoslavia, in which he details the complicated history of this republic.

Levéltárak (Archives)—Hungary

http://www.lib.uni-miskolc.hu/lib/archive/kapcsolat/ukanIndex/h4levtar.htm

This site provides a list of archives in Hungary; however, this page and most
of the archival sites it links to are in Hungarian, with no translation available.

National Library of the Czech Republic

http://www.nkp.cz

The Czech National Library traces its beginnings to 1348 and houses stores of
national historic treasures. In addition to the manuscripts collection detailing
Czech history, the library owns ancient Asian, Roman, and Greek writings,
rare books, and an incunabula collection of nearly four thousand items (incunabula are books created during the early years of printing, generally before 1501). A project is currently under way to digitize highlights from the
library's manuscript holdings; however, the results are available only on CD-
ROM. The Web site contains more information on this effort.

Slavic and East European Collections at UC–Berkeley

http://www.lib.berkeley.edu/Collections/Slavic/collect.html

The University of California–Berkeley collects widely in materials on Slavic and East European countries, including the former Soviet Union. Included in the Special Collections department is an array of modern (post-1989) independent Russian periodicals, an extensive arrangement of materials from the Czech Republics, and information pertaining to writers and literature in these countries.

Slovene Archives

http://www.pokarh-mb.si/today.html

This site provides a listing of archives in the Republic of Slovenia. For each institution that does not have its own Web site, the Slovene Archives site gives contact information along with a preliminary description of its collections. The site supplies links to those repositories that maintain their own Web pages. While the Slovene Archives page is in English, some of the links go to pages in Slovene.

State Archives—Poland

http://ciuw.warman.net.pl/alf/archiwa/index.eng.html

This site not only details the holdings of the Polish State Archives, it also answers FAQs about Polish archives in general, as well as listing links to other Polish repositories. While the main pages of the site have been translated into English, some links from the main page lead to information only available in Polish.

EUROPE—WESTERN

Archives in Germany

http://www.bawue.de/~hanacek/info/earchive.htm

The bulk of this site is in German; however, the initial page is in English and provides a glossary of German words frequently used on the subsequent pages (as well as on other German archival sites). The home page also provides a list of German archives, divided by type (church, state, private, etc.). Following the link on a particular repository leads to a page (in German) providing introductory information on the institution.

ARCHIESPA: Directorio de Archivos de España

http://www.uc3m.es/uc3m/serv/ARC/archiespa/principa.html

ARCHIESPA is a metasite providing links to hundreds of resources on archives in Spain. Links are available to various archives, Spanish archival organizations, online articles about Spain's repositories, digital manuscripts, directories to other libraries in Europe, and links to additional lists of resources. Users should be aware that this site does lack some currency, and so some links are no longer accurate. The site is in Spanish.

ARCHON: Archives Online—United Kingdom

http://www.hmc.gov.uk/archon/noframes.htm

ARCHON is a clearinghouse of information for users of British archives and manuscripts. It offers a list, with links, of all repositories in the United Kingdom, along with information on British history and resources for those in both the history and archival professions. The site also contains a special section on British genealogy.

Bodleian Library, Oxford University—United Kingdom

http://www.rsl.ox.ac.uk/

One of the most famous libraries in the world, the Bodleian houses an extensive array of Western manuscripts, reaching back into ancient times. The library's Web site allows access to multiple catalogs of holdings, lists of subject guides, and general library information.

Bundesarchiv—Germany

http://www.bundesarchiv.de/index.html

Visitors to the National Archives of Germany Web site can access a timeline of the library's history, descriptions and indexes of its major holdings, and a list of the library's publications. The site is entirely in German.

Les Centres de Ressources Documentaires—France

http://mistral.culture.fr/culture/sedocum/ceresdoc.htm

This list, maintained by the French Ministry of Culture, provides access to the major repositories of France. The libraries are grouped by subject area, and users can access data regarding hours of operation, address, major holdings, and library history. The site is completely in French.

LARGO: Libraries and Archives Research Guide Online— London

http://pitcairn.lib.uci.edu/largo/largo/largo.html

LARGO is a project of the University of California–Irvine library that serves as a clearinghouse of information for repositories in the London area. The site provides an index that lists the institutions holding material on a given subject. Information is provided on each of the participating libraries, along with links to the individual repository Web sites. For those libraries without their own sites, LARGO provides more details, such as operating hours and access information. There is a special section that discusses planning a research trip to London.

Libro, Archivos y Bibliotecas—Spain

http://www.mcu.es/lab/archivos/index.html

Spain's Ministry of Education and Culture maintains this site, which provides an overview of state libraries and archives. Users can search a bibliography of Spanish archives, access information on specific repositories, or read a general description on the organization and policies of the libraries within this system. The site is in Spanish.

LATIN AMERICA

Bancroft Collection—Latin Americana

http://library.berkeley.edu/BANC/banccoll/latin.html

The Bancroft library at the University of California–Berkeley collects extensively in Latin American history, primarily Mexico, Central America, and the U.S. borderlands. The emphases include contemporary and historical Mesoamerican indigenous cultures, the Spanish colonial period (1492–1821), and the United States border region. The original manuscript material is supplemented by microfilm of manuscripts held by other institutions, such as the Archivo General de Indias (Spain), the Archivo General de la Nación (Mexico), the Archivo Historico Nacional (Spain), and the U.S. Department of State.

Benson Latin American Collection, University of Texas– Austin

http://www.lib.utexas.edu/Libs/Benson/benson.html

The Benson Collection contains over two million pages of manuscripts on Mexico, Central America, the Caribbean, South America, and the American

Southwest during the period it was part of Mexico and the Spanish Empire. In addition, it houses one of the largest collections of secondary material on this region. A series of archival collection descriptions, bibliographies, and online exhibits are available at the bottom of the library's home page, after an extensive list of databases.

Biblioteca Nacional de Mexico

http://biblional.bibliog.unam.mx/bib01.html

This site gives visitors background on Mexico's National Library, as well as some information on its holdings. The repository owns over two million items, including rare books and manuscripts, all of which pertain to Mexican history. Currently, this site is available only in Spanish.

H-LatAm Archives

http://h-net2.msu.edu/~latam/archives/

The H-Net listserv for Latin American History maintains this resource of information on archives in Latin America. Researchers who have visited a repository complete an extensive questionnaire, which is then posted to this site. Details include contact information, access requirements, information on collections, descriptions of the facilities, and tips for visiting the repository, such as nearby hotels, restaurants, and public transportation. Users of the site should be aware, however, that some of the descriptions are two or three years old, and so might be outdated.

Latin American Library—Tulane University

http://www.tulane.edu/~latinlib/lalhome.html

Tulane's Latin American Library is comprised of both secondary and primary sources, as well as an extensive collection of Latin American rare books. Primary sources include historical newspapers, photographs, and manuscripts. This site contains information on the library's holdings, summaries of recent Latin American exhibits, a bibliography of dissertation research, and links to related sites.

MILITARY HISTORY AND PEACE COLLECTIONS

Hoover Institution: Library and Archives

http://www-hoover.stanford.edu/homepage/library.html

The Hoover Institution of War, Revolution, and Peace at Stanford University boasts collections from throughout the world. The library has particularly strong holdings on the Chinese Revolution, the Russian Revolution, the Nazis, and Italian fascism. At its Web site, visitors can read descriptions of the institute's holdings, historical essays on the collections, bibliographies, and further information about the Hoover Institution. Links to related sites are also available.

Swarthmore College Peace Collection

http://www.swarthmore.edu/Library/peace/

This research archives, collects, and maintains materials pertaining to nongovernmental efforts toward peace. Its holdings include manuscripts, periodicals, and extensive ephemera (such as posters, flyers, and buttons). This site provides collection descriptions, subject guides, online exhibits, and resources for the further study of peace movements.

Virginia Military Institute (VMI) Archives

http://www.vmi.edu/~archtml/index.html

The Virginia Military Institute has extensive holdings on United States military history in the nineteenth and twentieth centuries. The Web site provides genealogy information on VMI alumni, as well as a page devoted entirely to the archives' Civil War collections. Textual transcriptions of some of the Civil War material is available through this page.

RUSSIA AND THE FORMER SOVIET UNION

ArcheoBiblioBase: Archives in Russia

http://www.iisg.nl/~abb/

This English-language resource provides information on Russian archives. The material is divided into three sections: federal archives (administered by the Rosarkhiv), major federal agencies that maintain their own records, and local state archives in Moscow and St. Petersburg. Under each category are lists of archives with contact information, previous names, major holdings, and the titles of any recently published (post-1991) guides.

National Library of Russia

http://www.nlr.ru/hp_rnb/booklet/ten1.htm

This repository owns copies of every publication produced in Russia. In addition, it houses collections of Greek writings from the early Christian era, European codices (handwritten books) and manuscripts, and Eastern texts illustrating the development of writing in that region.

Archives in Ukraine

http://www.sabre.org/huri/abbukr/

Like ArcheoBiblioBase mentioned above, this site offers logistical information to researchers. Visitors can learn contact information, previous names, major holdings, and recently published guides for the six current national-level state archives under the Main Archival Administration of the Cabinet of Ministers of Ukraine; local state archives in Kiev and Lvov; and the two major library manuscript repositories under the National Academy of Sciences of Ukraine.

Estonian Historical Archives

http://www.eha.ee/frames/ing-archives.htm

Previously the Estonian Central State Archives, the Estonian Historical Archives houses documents from Estonia's history, including the eras of Swedish rule, Soviet affiliation, and independent statehood. Its home page offers an essay on the history of the archives, as well as information for researchers planning to visit the repository. An English-language version of the site is available.

National Library of Lithuania

http://www.lnb.lt

The National Library of Lithuania houses a variety of sources beyond those of the government. Personal manuscripts comprise the bulk of its holdings. It also offers substantial material covering religious history and a collection of handwritten newspapers spanning four centuries. Its Web site offers news of upcoming library events and exhibits, collection inventories, and a searchable catalog of holdings.

RELIGION

Department of Special Collections, University of Chicago

http://www.lib.uchicago.edu/e/spcl

Religious studies, particularly Christianity, stands as a particular collecting focus of the University of Chicago. The school's manuscript collection consists of numerous New Testament texts (dating to as early as the second century A.D.), medieval religious manuscripts, and the records of modern religious organizations. The library's rare books division supplements the manuscripts and consists of multiple religious book collections. From the collections's Web site, visitors can access detailed descriptions, a bibliography of printed collection guides, links to related sites, and information and catalogs for previous and forthcoming exhibits.

Yale Divinity Library

http://www.library.yale.edu/div/divhome.htm

This Web page allows access to a wealth of information regarding the research of Christianity. It contains a research guide and online tutorials on library resources, as well as descriptions of the library's holdings. An "Ad Hoc Digital Library" enables users to search for online documents, though some are restricted to Yale users. The Special Collections branch of the library, accessible from the main page, has particular strength in the history of Protestant missionary work.

SEXUALITY

Archiv für Sexualwissenschaft/Archive for Sexology

http://www.rki.de/GESUND/ARCHIV/HOME.HTM

This institute contains numerous resources for the study of sexuality and the history of sexology. The bulk of the materials pertain to Europe and the United States. Its Web site provides articles on the history of sexology, samples from the collection, syllabi for graduate and undergraduate courses, and descriptions of the collections.

Kinsey Institute for Research in Sex, Gender, and Reproduction

http://www.indiana.edu/~kinsey/

Dr. Alfred C. Kinsey gained worldwide attention in the 1940s with the publication of his controversial book *Sexual Behavior in the Human Male*. The Kinsey Institute, which he founded, continues his work by facilitating the study of human sexuality. The library houses materials in numerous formats (including manuscripts, periodicals, photographs, and artifacts) from throughout the world, ranging in date from 3200 B.C. to the present. The institute is not open to the general public, and researchers must gain approval to access the materials; the necessary steps for doing this are described on the Web site.

The site also offers essays describing the life of Dr. Kinsey, the often colorful history of the institute, and the library's holdings. In addition, it gives information on exhibits (with links to some online catalogs), a catalog of publications, a photographic history, and links to other sexology sites.

Rare Books and Manuscripts, Cornell University

http://rmc.library.cornell.edu/Default.htm

Cornell University's Sexuality Collection seeks to document historical shifts in attitudes toward sexuality. It has particular strengths in gay and lesbian history and in the politics of pornography. Its Web site, accessible through the Rare Books and Manuscripts home page, contains a detailed description of its holdings.

UNITED STATES

Congressional Collections at Archival Repositories

http://www.lib.udel.edu/ud/spec/c_clctns.html

While the National Archives holds the collections of many members of Congress, other collections are scattered throughout the United States in various repositories. The University of Delaware has compiled this list of the locations of congressional collections to aid researchers in finding the material they require. Many names on the list contain links to biographical essays or collection descriptions maintained by the holding institution.

National Archives and Records Administration (NARA)

http://www.nara.gov/

This extensive site contains something for every historian interested in U.S. history. An online exhibit hall provides access to digitized collections; the Digital Classroom supplies lesson plans and teaching strategies for a variety of age levels; a genealogy page discusses the family history resources available both at the National Archives and elsewhere on the Web. Online versions of Federal Register publications are available, and the professional development section offers information to archivists and records managers. Of course, all of this is in addition to the more expected features, such as a searchable catalog and collection descriptions. For more information on NARA's online documents, see the Digital Collections section on page 513.

National Union Catalog for Manuscripts Collections (NUCMC) Home Page

http://lcweb.loc.gov/coll/nucmc/nucmc.html

This online version of the National Union Catalog for Manuscripts Collections (NUCMC) allows users to search for manuscript material located throughout the United States. Users enter a subject or keyword, and NUCMC returns a list of relevant collections and their locations. This database is a useful starting point for archival research.

Presidential Libraries

http://www.nara.gov/nara/president/

At this site, the National Archives and Records Administration provides contact information and Web links to all of the U.S. presidential libraries, along with an overview of the presidential library system.

Special Collections in the Library of Congress

http://lcweb.loc.gov/spcoll/

The special collections division of the Library of Congress maintains rare and one-of-a-kind pieces of the nation's history. A selected guide to these collections comprises its Web site. Visitors can search under a variety of parameters to locate items of interest to them. Descriptions of all collections on the site are available, and many collections also offer digitized samples of their contents.

State Archives and Historical Societies

http://www.ohiohistory.org/textonly/links/arch_hs.html

In the United States, state archives provide access to the records of that state's government, and state historical societies normally contain collections of historical manuscripts pertaining to state history. This page, part of the Ohio Historical Society Web site, provides links to state archives and historical societies in the United States.

UNITED STATES IMMIGRATION HISTORY

Arizona State University Archives and Manuscripts

http://www.asu.edu/lib/archives/dampage.htm

Arizona State University owns an extensive Chicano Research collection, which documents the experience of Mexican Americans through books, newspapers, periodicals, photographs, manuscripts, and ephemera. The archives and manuscripts Web site offers information on these holdings, access to an online exhibit of Chicano history, and links to related sites.

California Ethnic and Multicultural Archives (CEMA)

http://www.library.ucsb.edu/speccoll/cema/

The University of California–Santa Barbara administers this repository devoted to documenting the history of African Americans, Latinos, Asian Americans and Native Americans in California. CEMA's Web site houses lists of collections, along with explanatory essays detailing the historical significance of each major manuscript group. The archives' collecting policy is also accessible, so researchers can quickly ascertain the relevance of the library's holdings to their work.

Immigration History Research Center

http://www1.umn.edu/ihrc/

The Immigration History Research Center (IHRC) of the University of Minnesota maintains this Web site providing information on its holdings and mission. The collection focus is on American immigration and ethnic history, particularly as it pertains to groups from Eastern, Central, Southern Europe and the Near East—those most involved in the immigration wave of the late nineteenth and early twentieth centuries. The site provides advice to genealogical researchers, collection descriptions, and an online catalog of publications distributed by the IHRC.

WOMEN

Duke Women's Archives and Special Collections

http://scriptorium.lib.duke.edu/women/

The women's archives at Duke University have a broad collecting focus that includes political activities, labor, Southern writers, religion, and education. The bulk of the materials pertain to women in the United States, though other countries are represented. The archives' Web site is part of Duke's award-winning Scriptorium site. Through it, researchers can access online versions of many holdings and fifteen Web-based bibliographies on topics pertaining to women's history. A list of links to digital collections on women's history is also available (http://scriptorium.lib.duke.edu/women/article.html). For more information on Duke's digital collections, see page 513.

Guide to Uncovering Women's History in Archival Collections

http://www.lib.utsa.edu/Archives/links.htm

The Archives for Research on Women and Gender, at the University of Texas–San Antonio, has compiled a state-by-state listing of repositories with online descriptions of their women's history collections on the web. The list is annotated and provides a hyperlink to each institution's home page.

Schlesinger Library, Radcliffe College

http://www.radcliffe.edu/schles/

The Arthur and Elizabeth Schlesinger Library on the History of Women in America is one of the most well-respected libraries on its topic in the world. As such, it is an excellent starting point for researchers. Examples of the manuscript collections include the personal papers of Charlotte Perkins Gilman, Betty Friedan, and Harriet Beecher Stowe. Visitors to its Web site will find descriptions of the Schlesinger's collections, along with no fewer than eighteen bibliographies on various aspects of women's history, from Women in Science to culinary resources.

DIGITAL COLLECTIONS

The World Wide Web has created the opportunity to share history with a wider audience, and more and more repositories are rising to the challenge by digitizing selections of primary documents and making them available through the Internet. The following list is comprised of prime examples of the potential of the Web to open archives to an ever wider array of people. The sites below contain extensive collections of digitized documents and/or particularly well-curated online exhibits. The sites are in English unless otherwise noted.

METASITES

Library Exhibits on the Web

http://www.sil.si.edu/SILPublications/Online-Exhibitions/
online-exhibitions-frames.htm

The University of Houston Special Collections Department maintains this list of links to online exhibits curated by libraries. Only exhibits containing digital images and textual descriptions are included, and the majority have a historical theme. The list is arranged alphabetically by exhibit title and includes a special section of newly added selections. Each entry includes the name of the institution curating the exhibit.

Library of Congress Grant

http://www.ameritech.com/community/loc/index.html

Ameritech and the Library of Congress have joined together to grant funds to repositories digitizing rare Americana material in their collections. The highlights and summaries of yearly award winners provide descriptions and—as the projects are completed—links to each collection. This site is a useful source of ongoing information on quality digital collections, but visitors should be aware that, because many projects have only recently received the necessary funding, not all descriptions currently link to projects.

Other Digital Image Sites (DL SunSITE)

http://sunsite.berkeley.edu/Collections/otherimage.html

Dozens of digital imaging projects are available through this list maintained by the Berkeley SunSITE (see page 515). By following the links, users can access digitized photos, maps, sheet music, and manuscripts. It is a nice starting point for the visually inclined researcher.

Other Digital Text Sites (DL SunSITE)

http://sunsite.berkeley.edu/Collections/othertext.html

Part of the Berkeley SunSITE (see page 515), this list links users to dozens of digital text collections on the World Wide Web. It covers multiple topics, and thus is a good site for historians who draw on other disciplines, such as literature, in their research.

SITES

American Memory from the Library of Congress

http://lcweb2.loc.gov/ammem/ammemhome.html

The American Memory Web site contains online versions of photographs, documents, sound recordings, and motion pictures from the Library of Congress Americana collection. Currently, over forty collections comprise the site, which is searchable and updated frequently. It is one of the largest digital archives projects currently available.

Berkeley Digital Library SunSITE

http://sunsite.berkeley.edu/

This site offers both digital collections of archival material and resources for the development of such collections. The Catalogs and Indexes pages lists databases for finding historical documents, while the Collections section links to primary documents available for perusal on the Web.

Columbia University Digital Library Collection

http://www.columbia.edu/cu/libraries/digital/

Columbia University has clearly made an effort to make library resources available through the World Wide Web. This site provides access to various projects, including online versions of classics in political thought, and online journals. Finding Aids for the library's major manuscripts collections are also available, as are digital copies of dozens of medieval and Renaissance manuscripts, spanning from the eighth to the sixteenth centuries.

Digital Images from the American Radicalism Collection

http://www.lib.msu.edu/spc/digital/radicalism/

The special collections division of the Michigan State University Library has digitized items from its American Radicalism Collection and made them available through this site. The purpose of this collection is to document the history of political radicalism on both the right and the left. The bulk of the collection chronicles the development of the left in the twentieth-century United States. Examples include items from Students for a Democratic Society (SDS), the American Indian Movement (AIM), the Hollywood Ten, and the Scottsboro Boys. Selections from the Ku Klux Klan of the 1920s and 1930s serve as an example of the library's holdings on the radical right.

Enluminures de la Bibliothèque Municipale de Lyon—France

http://www.bm-lyon.fr/F.HTM/sgbi.htm

The Municipal Library of Lyon, France has digitized over three thousand illuminated manuscripts and made them accessible through this gateway, and there are plans to eventually add three times this amount. Visitors can view electronic reproductions of this material, ranging from the fifth century to the Renaissance, but unfortunately no transcriptions are provided. The site itself is in French and the majority of the texts are in Latin, French, and Greek, though the fine illustration on the manuscripts requires no translation.

GALLICA—France

http://gallica.bnf.fr/

This endeavor of the Bibliotheque Nationale de France aims to digitize major contributions to French history and culture. The project's current focus is on documents of the nineteenth century. To date, over two thousand documents have been added, and these include text, prints, audio, and video. This site is entirely in French.

Lopez Martin Collection of Maps and Manuscripts

http://www.ukans.edu/carrie/ms_room/martin_coll/welcome.html

This site, part of the Carrie Full-Text Electronic Library (http://www.ukans.edu/carrie/carrie_main.html) at the University of Kansas, contains information on early modern Spain and the Netherlands. It contains transcripts of documents from the sixteenth century, digitized images of Dutch maps, an exhibit, and a list of links to other online resources for this period.

Making of America (MOA)

http://www.umdl.umich.edu/moa/

The Making of America (MOA) project at the University of Michigan provides the texts of 1,600 books and 50,000 journal articles published in the United States between 1830 and 1900. The collection includes proscriptive literature, religious tracts, and writings in the then-emerging fields of education and psychology. Users can access the material through specific searches or by browsing lists of holdings.

MOA Journal Collection

http://moa.cit.cornell.edu/MOA/moa-main_page.html

In conjunction with the Making of America site maintained at the University of Michigan (see above), Cornell University offers a satellite site featuring articles from twenty-four additional nineteenth-century journals. In the near future, Cornell plans to add the texts of over a hundred books to this site as well.

National Library of Medicine, History of Medicine Division

http://www.nlm.nih.gov/hmd/

In addition to offering information on the National Library of Medicine's special collections and access to the library's online catalog, this site provides a wealth of online images. It offers ten online exhibits, from Frankenstein to Islamic medical arts. The division also maintains a searchable database of digital images on the history of medicine, so that visitors can access selections on their particular interests.

National Archives and Records Administration (NARA) Online Exhibit Hall

http://www.nara.gov/exhall/exhibits.html

The Online Exhibit Hall of NARA offers numerous exhibits on United States history, as well as showcasing individual documents of great import. Two exhibits deal with different aspects of World War II, and "When Nixon Met Elvis" contains documents and photos surrounding this odd event, which occurred in 1970. The "American Originals" exhibit provides access to documents of our nation's most moving events, such as the police blotter listing President Lincoln's assassination and the 1868 treaty with the Sioux Indian Nation. Additional digital documents can be accessed from NARA's home page (http://www.nara.gov), and its Digital Classroom section is a leader in the effort to bring primary documents into the nation's classrooms via the Internet.

New York Public Library (NYPL) Digital Library Collections

http://digital.nypl.org/

The Digital Library Collections provide a glimpse of the rich offerings available from the New York Public Library. Users can access over a dozen online exhibits covering topics from seventeenth-century European tobacco culture to Depression-era New York City. The Digital Schomburg section of the site provides online documentation of nineteenth-century African Americans. Of particular interest is the Digital Library's collaborative projects, which list resources from multiple archives. Currently, these projects cover the history of dance and the history of women, marriage, and the law.

Prints and Photographs: An Illustrated Guide

http://lcweb.loc.gov/coll/print/guide/

The Library of Congress maintains this rich resource of prints and photographs in its collections. The guide is divided into six thematic chapters: An American Gallery; Pictorial Journalism; Politics and Propaganda; Architecture, Design, and Engineering; American Landscape and Cityscape; and The World at Large. Each section offers an introduction to the theme and images that illustrate the topic. Each image is accompanied by annotations describing its significance. The site includes a chronology of the library's acquisition of substantial print and photograph collections.

Rare Book, Manuscript, and Special Collection Library at Duke University

http://scriptorium.lib.duke.edu/

This site showcases Duke's award-winning Digital Scriptorium, an online collection of historical items from the library's holdings. The documents are accompanied by informational essays providing historical context, transcriptions (where applicable), and links to related information. The scriptorium's selections reflect the strengths of the library: African Americans, women, advertising, and music. Much of Duke's impressive papyrus collection is also represented.

San Diego Historical Society

http://edweb.sdsu.edu/SDHS/HistSoc.html

In addition to the usual information on upcoming events and operating hours, the San Diego Historical Society provides an extensive array of historical information on their Web site. Visitors can peruse online exhibits covering topics as varied as quilts, labor history, and local sports. The society has also digitized many historical postcards and compiled numerous photographs and informational articles, particularly on the Panama-California Exposition (1915–16) and the California Pacific Exposition (1935–36). Finally, visitors can listen to excerpts from oral history interviews in the society's collections.

SCETI (Schoenberg Center for Electronic Text and Image), University of Pennsylvania

http://www.library.upenn.edu/etext/

The Schoenberg Center for Electronic Text and Image (SCETI) allows access to digital versions of selected images and documents from the University of Pennsylvania Special Collections. The site hosts multiple online exhibits, plus an assortment of texts reflecting the library's strengths in South Asian manuscripts; sheet music; cookbooks; diaries; and artifacts about science, the occult, and religion.

Suffragists Oral History Project

http://library.berkeley.edu/BANC/ROHO/ohonline/suffragists.html

At this site, visitors can access transcripts of oral history interviews with leaders of the United States suffrage movement, which fought to obtain women's access to the vote. In addition, the site contains a special section entitled "The Suffragists: From Tea-Parties to Prison," containing interviews with more "rank and file" activists from this movement.

Tesoros de los Archivos Estatales de España (Treasures of the State Archives of Spain)

http://cvc.cervantes.es/obref/arnac/

In recent years, Spain has taken a leading role in digitizing important documents from its history so that the original paper versions may be preserved. The Archivo General de Indias, the repository of materials on Spain's activities in the New World, has received particular attention for its efforts in this area. Unfortunately, the bulk of this digitized material is not available on the World Wide Web. However, historians can view a few samples at this site, which describes the project and offers "treasures" from six of Spain's archives. The site is in Spanish. Visitors should be aware that in order to move beyond thumbnail versions of the documents, they should click "Alta resolución" at the bottom of each page.

University of Michigan Papyrus Collection

http://www.lib.umich.edu/pap/

The University of Michigan owns the largest collection of ancient papyri in the United States, and this site marks an effort to make some of it available online. The majority of texts date from the third century B.C. to the eighth century A.D. and are in Greek. Though a browser that supports the Cyrillic alphabet is required to view the papyri, all users can access online exhibits relating to the collection.

SPECIAL COLLECTIONS
Susan Tschabrun

METASITES

Archives in the World

http://www.unesco.org/webworld/public_domain/archives_world.html

Not nearly as complete as Terry Abraham's *Repositories of Primary Sources* (page 520), this UNESCO site is worth knowing about for the important role UNESCO plays in helping archives around the world. This listing of links covers archives in Europe, North America, Latin America, and Asia and the Pacific, as well as international archival organizations, professional associations, archival training, international cooperation, and Internet resources.

ARCHON: Archives Online

http://www.hmc.gov.uk/archon/archon.htm

The main gateway to repositories with manuscript material for British history, ARCHON is a key British resource for both archivists and researchers. The site is maintained by the Royal Commission on Historical Manuscripts. Researchers will be most interested in the British *National Register of Archives (NRA) at www.hmc.gov.uk/nra/nra.html*. The NRA leads researchers to a wide variety of manuscript collections, including papers of individuals of note, estates, local authorities, and societies, located both inside and outside the United Kingdom. Users may search the indexes by name of individual or corporate body, type of corporate body, and place name.

Repositories of Primary Sources

http://www.uidaho.edu/special-collections/Other.Repositories.html

With over 3,100 links, this Web site is by far the most complete listing of Web sites for actual (not virtual) archives and special collections departments. Updated frequently by Terry Abraham of the University of Idaho, the site arranges its links by geographical region (continent, country, state or province). *Additional Lists* is a good jumping off point for other archive and special collections metasites.

RLIN AMC Search Form

http://lcweb.loc.gov/z3950/gateway.html

This important search gateway will lead the researcher to descriptions of holdings for a large number of manuscript and archival repositories, predominantly, but not exclusively, in the United States. Select from one of three straightforward, fill-in-the-blank-style search forms. This electronic catalog derives from the print source, the *National Union Catalog of Manuscript Collections*, a project of the Library of Congress. Check the "List of RLIN Library Identifiers" on the search forms to see a list of the participating institutions.

www.archivesinfo.net

http://www.archivesinfo.net

Originating out of a University of London Masters project by Simon Wilson, this site—mainly targeted at archivists—provides two important listings of archival links useful to researchers: *UK Archival Repositories on the Internet* and *Overseas Archival Repositories on the Internet.* One of the best features of these lists is the annotations prepared by the site's author that briefly indicate each site's contents.

GENERAL SITES

Africa Research Central: A Clearinghouse of African Primary Sources

http://africa-research.csusb.edu

A collaboration between a history professor and an academic librarian at California State University–San Bernardino, this site assists researchers in locating often scarce information about archives, libraries, and museums with primary source collections related to Africa. The site focuses on repositories in Africa, but also provides information for those in Europe and North America. An important mission of the site is to alert researchers to the preservation crisis under way in many countries in Africa and indicate ways to help.

American Memory: Historical Collections for the National Digital Library

http://memory.loc.gov/ammem/

The forty-two multimedia collections of digitized documents, photographs, recorded sound, moving pictures, and text selected from the Library of Congress's vast Americana holdings cover topics as diverse as twentieth-century architectural design and ballroom dancing. The collections may be searched by keyword, or browsed by titles, topics, or collection type. A fun spinoff is *Today in History*, which presents people, facts, and events associated with the current day's date. Finally, educators are particularly targeted in the *Learning Page,* with activities, lesson ideas, and other information to help teachers use the primary source material at American Memory in their classrooms.

Annuaire des archives et des bibliothèque nationales, des bibliothèque parlementaires et des centres nationaux d'information scientifique et technique de la Francophonie

http://www.acctbief.org/publica/anuinfsc.htm

This directory, originally published in print form in 1996, has been converted into a searchable Web database by the publishers, Canadian-based BIEF (Banque internationale d'information sur les États francophones). The directory includes basic contact information for the national archives and libraries of forty-seven francophone countries. Further descriptive information about the listed institutions can often be found in a BIEF companion Web site, titled *Profis géo-documentaires des états et gouvernements membres des sommets francophones*. Together, these databases are an important source of scarce information about archives for many smaller, non-Western countries.

Archivische Angebote im Internet (Archival Links in the Internet)

http:// www.uni-marburg.de/archivschule/deuarch.html

This list of archival resources, maintained by Dr. Karsten Uhde of the Archivschule Marburg in Germany, brings together links of interest to both archivists and researchers. Historians and genealogists will find the following pages particularly useful: *Archives in Germany*, listing German archives by type (state, city, church, etc.), *Archives in Europe*, *non-European Archives*, and *Genealogy*.

Archives and Library Resources

http://www.dcn.davis.ca.us/~vctinney/archives.htm

Created and maintained by V. Chris and Thomas M. Tinney, Sr., retired genealogical specialists, this Web site includes links to resources of particular interest to genealogists, including a link to the *Genealogy on the Web* site and the Salt Lake City LDS Family History Center. The Tinney Family organizes their links to archives, libraries, and many other types of resources in a variety of categories, from Business and Community and Geography to Religion and Surnames.

Archives of American Art

http://www.si.edu/organiza/offices/archart/start.htm

The Smithsonian maintains the Archives of American Art (AAA) and its Web site to provide researchers with access to "the largest collection of documents on the history of the visual arts in the United States." With thirteen million items, including the papers of artists, dealers, critics, art historians, museums, and art-related organizations of all kinds, the Smithsonian's claim can easily be believed. Moreover, the letters, sketchbooks, diaries, and other paper archives are supplemented with a large oral history interview collection and a sizable photograph collection. General collection descriptions of AAA treasures can be found in the Smithsonian online catalog (SIRIS) as well as RLIN, and the Smithsonian is beginning to make more detailed finding aids available as well.

Archives of Traditional Music

http://www.indiana.edu/~libarchm/home2.html

A Web site that provides information about an important and unusual archive of ethnographic sound materials housed at Indiana University. The largest such university-based archive in the United States, the Archives of Traditional Music preserves commercial and field recordings of vocal and instrumental music, folktales, interviews, and oral history from the state of Indiana, the United States, and the diverse cultures of the world. Holdings can be searched using the IUCAT online catalog.

ArchivesUSA

http://archives.chadwyck.com/

Chadwyck-Healey Inc. has developed a product that is an important tool for researchers interested in locating archival material in the United States. Although ArchivesUSA is a subscription service, and therefore not available for free over the Web, it is an important resource that some libraries and archives make available to the public. ArchivesUSA integrates the entire print edition of the National Union Catalog of Manuscript Collections with other sources of information to create a more complete record for a greater number of repositories than is available through RLIN AMC.

The Avalon Project at the Yale Law School: Documents in Law, History, and Government

http://www.yale.edu/lawweb/avalon/avalon.htm

Directed by William C. Fray and Lisa A. Spar, the Avalon Project is a major source of digital primary source documents in the fields of law, history, economics, politics, diplomacy, and government. Access to the documents is by time period (mainly century), author/title, and subject. Major collections include the Nuremberg Trials Collection and the Native American Treaty Collection. A recent addition to the digital repository is the Cuban Missile Crisis and Aftermath section, with over 250 documents (including editorial notes), prefatory essay, and lists of persons and abbreviations—a good example of the project's aim to not simply mount static text, but to add value.

Black Film Center/Archives

http://www.indiana.edu/~bfca/index.html

By and about African Americans, the historic 700 films housed at the Black Film Center/Archives at Indiana University consist of both Hollywood and independent efforts. Supplementing the films and videotapes are interviews, photographs, and other archival material. The Web site gives access to descriptions of the repository's holdings, the Frame-by-Frame database, and related Internet sites.

Canadian Archival Resources on the Internet

http://www.usask.ca/archives/menu.html

A comprehensive list of links to Canadian archives and associated resources on the Internet, this guide is the work of two Canadian archivists: Cheryl Avery of the University of Saskatchewan Archives, and Steve Billinton of the Archives of Ontario. Researchers can locate archives by name, type (provincial, university, municipal, religious, and medical), and Canadian region, or find links to archival educational resources, associations, listservs, and multi-repository databases.

Directory of Archives in Australia

http://www.asap.unimelb.edu.au/asa/directory/asa_dir.htm

The updated Web version of a directory originally printed in 1992, this directory of Australian archives allows researchers to browse archives alphabetically and by Australian states, and to search them by keyword. There are also handy lists of links to Australian archives and finding aids on the Web.

Directory of Corporate Archives in the United States and Canada

http://www.hunterinformation.com/corporat.htm

The fifth edition of this important print directory, put out by the Society of American Archivists, Business Archives Section, has recently moved to the Web. From Amgen to Walt Disney Corporation, each corporate archive entry supplies contact information, type of business, hours of service, conditions of access, and holding information. "Corporate" is interpreted broadly and includes "professional associations" ranging from the American Psychiatric Association to the International Longshoreman's Union. The directory may be searched by name of corporation, name of archivist, or geographical location.

DPLS Online Data Archive

http://dpls.dacc.wisc.edu/archive.html

The Data and Program Library Service at the University of Wisconsin is creating access to a large selection of archival machine-readable datasets (raw data and documentation files) that can be downloaded for use by social science researchers. The datasets are listed in reverse chronological order, or alphabetical by title, and cover raw data from an extremely diverse range of historical and current topics, such as French Old Regime Bureaucrats (1661–1790), Vegetation Change in the Bahamas (1972), and the effects of the Learnfare Program (1993–96).

EuroDocs: Primary Historical Documents from Western Europe: Selected Transcriptions, Facsimiles, and Translations
http://library.byu.edu/~rdh/eurodocs/
Aiming to provide digitized documents that shed light on "key historical happenings" in political, economic, social, and cultural history, EuroDocs links to a wealth of digitized resources organized under twenty-three Western European countries from Andorra to the Vatican City. Documents are also accessible from pages devoted to Medieval and Renaissance Europe and to Europe as a Supranational Region. EuroDocs is a project of Richard Hacken, European Studies Bibliographer, Harold B. Lee Library, Brigham Young University in Provo, Utah.

Guía preliminar de fuentes documentales etnográficas para el estudio de los pueblos indígenas de Iberoamérica
http://www.lanic.utexas.edu/project/tavera/
An important guide in the Spanish language, made available on the Web, the *Guia* describes the holdings related to indigenous peoples at hundreds of libraries and archives throughout Latin America, the United States, and Europe. A project of La Fundación Histórica Tavera in Spain, the Guía is organized by country and type of archive (civil or ecclesiastical), and provides contact information and holdings descriptions for all of the institutions listed.

A Guide to Uncovering Women's History in Archival Collections
http://www.lib.utsa.edu/Archives/links.htm
This guide to the archives, libraries, and other repositories on the Web with archival materials by or about women is maintained by the Archives for Research on Women and Gender Project at the University of Texas–San Antonio. Arranged by states in the United States (plus a link devoted to institutions outside of the United States), each listing includes annotations indicating which materials in a given collection may be of interest to researchers in the field of Women's History.

Historical Maps: The Perry–Castañeda Library Map Collection

http://www.lib.utexas.edu/Libs/PCL/Map_collection/Map_collection.html

A wonderful collection of digitized historical maps from all regions of the world offered by the Libraries at the University of Texas–Austin. Maps are organized by continent (including the polar regions and oceans) and each map listing gives both publication information and file size. Although most maps are in JPEG format in the 200–300K range, some map files are much larger, so expect some slow load times. The site also includes *Historical Maps at Other Web Sites* with links to other historical map collections.

International Institute of Social History

http://www.iisg.nl

Founded in 1935 in the Netherlands, IISH is one of the world's largest archival and research institutions in the field of social history, particularly labor history. Its 2,000 archival collections cover a range of topics not always well-represented in traditional archives, like anarchism, revolutionary populism from nineteenth-century Eastern Europe, the French revolution and Utopian socialism, and WWII resistance movements. Collections may be identified using an online catalog, a list of archival collections, or other finding aids. Other IISH resources include the William Morris Archive on the Web, Occassio, a collection of digital social history documents, and numerous electronic publications. The Institute's image collections are highlighted by a number of virtual exhibitions with titles like "The Chairman Smiles" and "Art to the People."

National Archives and Records Administration

http://www.nara.gov

NARA's Web site is a rich source of information for historians, genealogists, teachers, and students. For historians, the *Research Room* organizes information about historical archival records by branch of government and type of material. For genealogists, the *Genealogy Page* publishes not only practical information about using NARA's facilities nationwide, but also a growing list of "quick guides" on census, military, immigration, and other types of records. Teachers and students will appreciate the *Digital Classroom: Primary Sources, Activities, and Training for Educators and Students*, with reproducible documents and teaching activities. The *Online Exhibit Hall* is a showcase for NARA treasures. Finally, NAIL (NARA's Archival Information Locator) is a searchable database that contains more than 386,500 descriptions of selected NARA holdings in Washington, D.C., the regional archives and presidential libraries, including 106,215 digital copies of selected textual documents, photographs, maps, and sound recordings.

New York Public Library for the Performing Arts

http://www.nypl.org/research/lpa/lpa.html

"The world's most extensive combination of circulating, reference, and rare archival collections" in the performing arts, this Web site describes the library's important collections of recordings, videotapes, autograph manuscripts, correspondence, sheet music, stage designs, press clippings, programs, posters, and photographs in the areas of dance, music, and theater.

Online Archive of California

http://sunsite2.Berkeley.EDU/oac

The Online Archive of California, still in the pilot project stage, is an umbrella site bringing together information on a steadily increasing number of archival institutions in California. Its most important resource is a centralized database of 120 searchable electronic finding aids, which allows a level of precision searching for archival materials not available in more traditional online library catalogs, like RLIN AMC.

Portuguese Libraries, Archives, and Documentation Services on the Internet

http://www.sdum.uminho.pt/bad/bibpte.htm

This simple but useful Web site provides links to the thirty-three libraries, archives, and documentation centers in Portugal that have an Internet presence. Maintained by the Working Group on Information Technologies of the Associação Portuguesa de Bibliotecários, Arquivistas, e Documentalistas.

Social Science Data Archives—Europe

http://www.nsd.uib.no/cessda/europe.html

A map of Europe organizes links to fourteen important European social science data archives, with separate links to similar non-European institutions. Maintained by the CESSDA (Council of European Social Science Data Archives), this Web site also allows researchers to search the holdings of eleven electronic data repositories through its Integrated Data Catalogue.

A map of Europe organizes links to fourteen important European social science data archives, with separate links to similar non-European institutions. Maintained by the CESSDA (Council of European Social Science Data Archives), this Web site also allows researchers to search the holdings of eleven electronic data repositories through its Integrated Data Catalogue.

Special Collections Web Resources

http://info.lib.uh.edu/speccoll/specres.htm

The University of Houston Libraries pulls together a wealth of links related to special collections, mostly of use to librarians and archivists. However, historians will appreciate the links to antiquarian and rare book dealers and related sites not found on other archival metasites.

Television News Archive

http://tvnews.vanderbilt.edu

Vanderbilt University holds "the world's most extensive and complete archive of television news," including 30,000 evening news broadcasts and 9,000 hours of special news-related programming. These news broadcasts have been consistently recorded and preserved by the archive since 1968. The Web site makes several searchable indexes available, including Network Television Evening News Abstracts, Special Reports and Periodic News Broadcasts, and Specialized News Collections (containing descriptive summaries of news material for major events like the Persian Gulf War of 1991). The Archive is willing to loan videotapes to researchers worldwide.

United States Holocaust Memorial Museum

http://www.ushmm.org/misc-bin/add_goback/learn.htm

The Archive of the Holocaust Memorial Museum in Washington, D.C. has gathered together 1.7 million pages of microfilmed documents, 50,000 photo images, 200 hours of historical motion picture footage, 250 documentary or feature films, and 2,900 oral interviews—all related to the Holocaust, its origins, and aftermath. The document and photographic archives may be searched individually or together using the USHMM Information Access query form available at the Web site.

USIA Declassified Historical Information

http://www.usia.gov/admin/004/dchp/homepage.htm

Pursuant to Executive Order 12958, the USIA Declassification Unit prepares a listing of declassified documents in order to alert the general public—especially academic researchers—to information no longer classified. Researchers may do keyword searching of this listing, or browse by broad topic, from Africa to Youth, to find the titles of more than 5,300 classified and unclassified one-cubic-foot boxes of records coming from the National Archives and many other document-holding federal agencies.

WWII Resources

http://metalab.unc.edu/pha/index.html

"Dedicated to combating 'history by sound bites'," this electronic archive of documents related to all aspects of World War II is a project of the Pearl Harbor Working Group. Transcribed documents include speeches, treaties, official declarations, timelines, and testimony, ranging from documents from the German Foreign Office pertaining to Nazi–Soviet relations to the Pearl Harbor Attack Hearings.

ELECTRONIC REFERENCE DESK
Anne Rothfeld

METASITES

Encyberpedia

http://www.encyberpedia.com/ency.htm

A metasite of other dictionaries, encyclopedias, glossaries, languages, and thesauri. Some links are annotated.

Historical Society Page

http://wings.buffalo.edu/sa/ughc/links.html

A metasite of over 800 links to useful historical Web sites, including historical societies, history museums, and other history-related sites. This is the starting point for state historical societies and museums.

History Internet Resources

http://blair.library.rhodes.edu.histhtmls/histnet.html

Covering a wide range of areas and regions: general compilations, general WWW servers, and electronic texts, documents, exhibits and collections, and maps. Some links are annotated. Sponsored by Rhodes University.

Internet Public Library (IPL) Reference Center

http://www.ipl.org/ref

Provides links to general ready reference information and to specific subject areas. Click on topic and IPL takes you to additional subject-related sites. Links are subdivided and annotated. IPL is also creating subject pathfinders.

Research-It! Your One-stop Reference Desk

http://www.iTools.com/research-it/research-it.html

A meta search site for information, including dictionaries, thesauri, translations, biographies, and geographic tools. Each area has its own search screen.

WWW Services for Historians

http://grid.let.rug.nl/ahc/

A metasite with numerous links in the areas of history. Includes general sites, computing in the humanities links, calls for papers and conference announcements, and other history-related sites.

ARCHIVES

ArchivesUSA

http://archives.chadwyck.com

Fee-based service providing information and access to primary source holdings of over 4,800 repositories, indexes to over 109,000 special collections, and links to over 975 online finding aids. ArchivesUSA includes three major references: Directory of Archives and Manuscript Repositories in the United States (DAMRUS); National Union Catalogue of Manuscript Collections (NUCMC); and National Inventory of Documentary Sources in the United States (NIDS). ArchivesUSA on the Web is updated quarterly.

Historical Document Archives

gopher://musicbox.mse.jhu.edu/11/others/archives

Access to documents held by many North American universities via gopher and notice sites. Many of the sites on the gopher list now have Web pages and the notices direct you to access the site. Maintained by the Johns Hopkins University.

Historical Text Archive

http://www.geocities.com/Athens/Forum/9061

Organized by geographical and topical subject headings, this site provides links to other sites. Sites focus on the studying and teaching of history. Maintained at the University of Kansas.

Repositories of Primary Sources

http://www.uidaho.edu/special-collections/Other.Repositories.html

Over 3,000 Web and Gopher sites describing special collections holdings in the United States, including manuscripts and photographs. Repositories are divided geographically and subdivided by states. Additional links include other history-related Web sites with an international scope and subject specialty. Comprehensive and updated monthly. Maintained at the University of Idaho Library Special Collections and Archives.

ACRONYMS

Acronym Finder

http://www.mtnds.com/af

Searches over 116,400 common acronyms. Acronym Finder "is only designed to search for and expand acronyms and abbreviations." Contains search hints and links to other acronym sites. Updated weekly. Sponsored by Mountain Data Systems.

ALMANACS

The Almanac of Politics and Government

http://www.polisci.com

Covering U.S. political information: U.S. government; state and local government; political science; economics; and political history. Sponsored by Keynote Publishing Company.

CIA World Factbook 1997

http://www.odci.gov/cia/publications/factbook

Complete resource of statistics, maps, and facts for over 250 countries and other entities. Other excellent resources are linked, including Chiefs of State and Cabinet Members of Foreign Governments and selected task force reports.

Information Please

http://www.infoplease.com

This site is from Information Please LLC, which has been publishing almanacs for over 50 years. Features a daily almanac, a dictionary, and an encyclopedia. Nine subject categories available, including one specifically for the United States and United States history.

BIOGRAPHIES

Biographical Dictionary

http://www.s9.com/biography

Includes over 27,000 notable men and women from ancient times to the present day. Search the database by name, birth year, death year, and other keywords. Links to biography-related sites, arranged by subject. Tips for students and teachers on how to use this resource in the classroom. Sponsored by s9.com.

Biographical Sources and Reference Desk

http://www.lib.utulsa.edu/guides/

Links to other useful biographical resources. Maintained by the University of Tulsa, McFarlin Library.

Biography.com

http://www.biography.com

Searchable database with over 20,000 entries. Site is produced by A&E.

Women in Biography

http://w3.uwyo.edu/~prospect/bio-women.html

Links to electronic resources, including international directories, National First Ladies Library, and women in science and technology.

COPYRIGHT

Intellectual Property Law Hotlinks

http://w3.gwis.com/~sarbar/index.html

Connects visitors to numerous topics, including patents, trademarks, and copyright. Additional links to intellectual property law are provided. This site is a personal home page.

U.S. Government Copyright Office

http://lcweb.loc.gov/copyright

Describes how to file for a copyright, what can be copyrighted, and the terms of a copyright. Includes copyright information regarding digitalization, legislation, and publications.

CORPORATIONS

Corporations

http://w3.uwyo.edu/~prospect/company.html

Annotated links to corporate giving, company information, corporate directories, stock quotes and securities. Includes links to Companies Online, CorpTech, and manufacturers' profiles.

Locating U.S. Corporation Records Online: a Directory of State Web Sites and Secretaries of State Contact Information

http://w3.uwyo.edu/~prospect/secstate.html

Links to state Web sites providing information on corporations within selected states. Nonprofit databases for some states are available. Locator provides a search engine to browse through over one million entries.

DICTIONARIES AND THESAURI

The Alternative Dictionaries

http://www.notam.uio.no/~hcholm/altlang

Contains words and sayings that would not be found in a standard dictionary. Over 3,000 words and expressions.

A Web of Online Dictionaries

http://www.facstaff.bucknell.edu/rbeard/diction.html

A metasite linking multilingual dictionaries, thesauri, and other sites relating to words and phrases. Grammar guides in selected languages are also available.

Merriam-Webster Dictionary

http://www.m-w.com/

Sponsored by Merriam-Webster, Inc. Full definitions, with an online thesaurus available. Features new words recently added, word game of the day, and language InfoZone, which is a portal to additional online resources.

Online Computer Science Reference Resources

http://www.sc.edu/library/science/elcsref.htm

Provides links to searchable Computer Dictionary and to Free Online Dictionary of Computing (FOLDOC). FOLDOC provides links to other terminology contained in the dictionary.

Oxford English Dictionary Online

http://www.oed.com/dicts.html

Fee-based service.

Roget's Thesaurus

http://www.thesaurus.com

From the print version. Now online with links to other words and phrases.

Wordsmyth English Dictionary-Thesaurus

http://www.wordsmyth.net

Can search words exactly or as a phrase. Search returns definition and pronunciation guides. Provides access to additional dictionaries and to words of the week. Produced by Robert Parks and the ARTFL Project at the University of Chicago.

DISSERTATIONS AND THESES

Electronic Theses and Dissertations in the Humanities

http://etext.lib.virginia.edu/ETD/ETD.html

A directory and listing of electronic theses and dissertations currently in progress. Contains initiatives and a bibliography documenting arguments of electronic theses and dissertations.

Networked Digital Library of Theses and Dissertations

http://www.ndltd.org

A portal for dissemination of theses and dissertations.

UMIs Online Dissertation Services

http://www.umi.com/hp/Support/DServices

Link to published and archived dissertations and theses, which are available for purchase. Maintains a comprehensive bibliography for over 1.4 million doctoral dissertations and master's theses. Listing of best-selling dissertations is available.

ELECTRONIC JOURNALS (E-JOURNALS)

The World Wide Web Virtual Library: Electronic Journals

http://www.edoc.com/ejournal

Search for a journal by specialty—peer-reviewed—and connect to the site. Some have free access; others may be restricted. A search engine is available.

ENCYCLOPEDIAS

Encyclopedia Britannica Online

http://www.eb.com

This is a fee-based resource. Content is taken from the print edition and also includes *Britannica Books of the Year, Nations of the World, Merriam-Webster's Collegiate Dictionary,* 13,000 graphics and illustrations, and links to related Web sites.

Encyclopedia.com

http://www.encyclopedia.com

Free encyclopedia featuring more than 14,000 articles from "The Concise Columbia Electronic Encyclopedia, Third edition."

Funk and Wagnalls Multimedia Encyclopedia

http://funkandwagnalls.com

Includes the encyclopedia, a dictionary, multimedia index, and Reuters World News Service. Power search searches your term in all available resources. Free, but registration is required.

Symbols.com—Encyclopedia of Western Signs and Ideograms

http://www.symbols.com

Site contains over 2,500 Western signs, with discussions of histories, uses, and meanings. Search using the graphic index or the word index.

FAQS (FREQUENTLY ASKED QUESTIONS)

Encyclopedia Smithsonian

http://www.si.edu/resource/faq

Features answers to Smithsonian's FAQs, with links to available Smithsonian resources. Topics are filed alphabetically, A–Z.

FAQ Search Engine

http://www.cs.ruu.nl/cgi-bin/faqwais

This search engine allows users to search FAQs and other informative articles from a large database of newsgroups. Alphabetically indexed.

FLAGS

Flags of the World (FOTW)

http://fotw.digibel.be/flags

View more than 8,300 flag images.

GENERAL

AKA The Librarians' Guide to Internet Information Sources

http://www.sau.edu/bestinfo/index.html

A portal to resources on the Internet. Links include hot paper topics, national and international newspapers, search engines, and job-hunting guide. Geared for librarians and useful for historians.

CNET Shareware

http://www.shareware.com

Search engine listing over 190,000 shareware computer programs and links to sites where they can be downloaded.

Find-A-Grave

http://www.findagrave.com/

Locate the graves of famous people. Database is organized by last name and geographic location, and some photos of graves are included.

The HistoryNet

http://www.historynet.com

Contains an archive of different topical areas, including eyewitness accounts, historic travel, and people profiles. Provides links to history magazines on the Web and sponsors daily quizzes and factoids. Sponsored by the Cowles History Group.

Horus' History Links

http://www.ucr.edu/h-gig/

This Web page is designed to experiment in Internet historical teaching and research. Contents include histories of specific countries, times, and places; areas of history; online services about history; Web tools; and searching hints.

HyperHistory Online

http://www.hyperhistory.com/online_n2/History_n2/a.html

A 3,000-year timeline is available to access relevant maps, biographies, and brief histories of people, places, and events.

The Scout Report

http://scout.cs.wisc.edu/index.html

Published every Friday on the Web and by e-mail, this report provides valuable information on new electronic and online resources. General interest areas include social sciences; science and engineering; and business and economics.

GEOGRAPHIC NAMES AND MAPS

Getty Thesaurus of Geographic Names

http://shiva.pub.getty.edu/tgn_browser

Sponsored by the Getty Information Institute. Currently has information for over 900,000 geographic names and places. Search displays by using geographic hierarchy displays, definition/description of term, other known names, and sources.

Historical Map Web Sites

http://www.lib.utexas.edu/Libs/PCL/Map_collection.html

Links to historical maps at other Web sites.

U.S. Geological Survey—Geographic Names Information System

http://mappings.usgs.gov/www/gnis

Contains over two million physical and cultural geographic features in the United States. Supplied by the Geographic Names Information System (GNIS) and the U.S. Board on Geographic Names (BGN). Includes a search engine and links to online geographic resources.

GOVERNMENT AND STATE RESOURCES

FedStats

http://www.fedstats.gov

Statistical information from government agencies and departments. Search FedStats by topic, such as demographic, education, and labor, and listing provides annotated links.

Social Statistics Briefing Room

http://www.whitehouse.gov/fsbr/ssbr.html

Access statistics on crime, demographics, education, and health. Links are provided to selected federal agencies. Graphics are available.

Thomas (Legislation Information)

http://thomas.loc.gov/

Search for congressional bills, the Congressional Record, committee bills, and historical documents. FAQs regarding Thomas are available. Links to other government agencies.

GRANTS

FinAid! The Smart Student Guide to Financial Aid

http://www.finaid.org/

Sponsored by the National Association of Student Financial Aid Administrators. Includes links to indexes of grant information, grant writing, and government grants.

Foundation Center

http://fdncenter.org

Foundation Center provides grant information, funding trends and analysis, libraries and locations, and Foundation Center publications. Searchable links to over 160 sources of private, commercial, and corporate funding. Ranks foundations by assets and total giving.

Foundation/Grants Reference Desk

http://w3.uwyo.edu/~prospect/found.html

Provides links to U.S. sources, including private funding, grants and sponsored research, nonprofit information, and fundraising news online. Includes international funding, both private and government.

Internet Prospector Reference Desk

http://w3.uwyo.edu/~prospect

Portals to information on nonprofit organizations and nonprofit research.

INDICES

Cool History Resources

http://www.teleport.com/~barell/history.phtml

Annotated links to American and world history, general history, and related sites. Each site is ranked, and information is available about the methodology of the ranking.

Indexes, Abstracts, Bibliographies, and Tables of Contents Service

http://info.lib.uh.edu/indexes/indexes.html

Includes links in the areas of North American history, European history, and multinational and other history.

Librarians' Index to the Internet

http://sunsite.berkeley.edu/InternetIndex.html

Arranged by subject. Click on History and the index is linked to over 300 history-related sites. Search can be focused by using the available search engine.

Multidisciplinary WWW Subject Directories for Scholars

http://info.lib.uh.edu/wsub.htm

Access selected subject guides and resources on the Internet. Some databases are free; others are restricted. Sites include many universities, and guides have been developed by libraries and history departments.

The WWW-VL History Index

http://history.cc.ukans.edu/history/WWW_history_main.html

A portal to over 3,500 electronic resources arranged by different areas of history.

INTERNET TUTORIALS

Evaluating Internet Resources

http://www.albany.edu/library/internet/evaluate.htm

Discusses what elements should be included in a reliable Web site and why. For example, the intended audience, the source of the content, the accuracy and comprehensiveness of the content, and the style and functionality of the page.

Searching the Internet: Recommended Sites and Search Techniques

http://www.albany.edu/library/internet/search.html

Discusses and describes searching hints and tips for successful usage of subject directories and search engines within Web pages.

LISTSERVS

Tile.Net: the Comprehensive Internet Reference

http://tile.net

Search for discussion lists, newsgroups (Usenet), and FTP sites by entering a subject search. All of the results are linked to a page describing the listing and how to subscribe.

QUOTATIONS

John Barlett's Familiar Quotations (1901)

http://www.bartleby.com.99/

The ninth edition is available online. It was published in 1901, whereas the print version is available in its 16th edition. Includes English and French writers and wisdom from the ancients. Browse by author or search by keyword. Indices are available to browse by author, both alphabetical and chronological.

Quotations Home Page

http://www.geocities.com/Athens/Acropolis/2012/quote.htm

Use this home page to find twentieth-century quotes arranged by topics from contemporary authors and orators. Provides specialized databases of quotations, including Alternative Definitions, Serious Sarcasm, Childsong, Film, and Good Starts. Site contains over 21,000 quotations.

The Quotations Page

http://www.starlingtech.com/quotes

Read quotes of the day and motivational quotes of the day. Site can also be searched, and there are links to other quotation sites.

STATISTICS

Statistical Abstracts of the United States

http://www.census.gov/statab/www

Excellent resource for statistical information: demographics, employment, industrial production statistics, and government financial information.

Statistical Resources on the Web

http://www.lib.umich.edu/libhome/Documents.center/stats.html

A metasite of statistical information. Search by categories, including business, demographics, labor, education, and sociology. Links to government resources on the Web. Links are annotated. Maintained by the University of Michigan Documents Center.

U.S. Census Bureau: U.S. Gazetteer

http://tiger.census.gov/cgi-bin/gazetteer

Census data on all incorporated municipalities in the United States. Maps provided.

U.S. Historical Census Data Browser

http://fisher.lib.Virginia.EDU/census

Descriptions of people and economy of the United States for each state and county from 1790 to 1970.

STUDENT AND SCHOOL INFORMATION

American Universities

http://clas.ufl.edu/CLAS/american-universities.html

A metasite listing universities and colleges in the United States.

CollegeNet

http://www.collegenet.com

A search engine allows you to find the ideal college by using such categories as region, sports, major, and tuition. Also find scholarships and financial aid; college Web applications; and college recruiting. Virtual tours allow you to see campuses from your desktop, with links to the schools' Web sites.

History Departments around the World

http://chnm.gmu.edu/history/depts

Alphabetical listing of links to history departments' home pages. Maintained by the Center for History and New Media at George Mason University.

Peterson's College Search (undergraduate)

http://www.petersons.com/ugrad/ugsector.html

Find your ideal college by major, region, and size of student population. Search results provide a link to an institution's profile, not Web site.

Peterson's Guide

http://www.petersons.com

Education resource with links to colleges and universities, graduate programs, and international programs. Search the database by keywords and subject specialty.

U.S. News and World Report Online: Undergraduate School Ranking

http://www.usnews.com/usnews/edu/college/corank.htm

Locate a school using categories provided from the most expensive school to the one with the best marching band! Includes methodology of rankings.

U.S. News and World Report Online: Graduate School Ranking

http://www.usnews.com/usnews/edu/beyond/bcrank.htm

Find graduate programs meeting your requirements. Includes methodology of rankings.

STYLE MANUALS AND USAGE

Citing Electronic and Print Resources

http://www.lib.ucdavis.edu/citing/Turabian.html

Citation information for Modern Languages Association (MLA), American Psychological Association (APA), Turabian Style, Chicago Style Manual, and government information. Includes thorough discussions and examples.

MLA Style

http://www.mla.org/main_stl.htm

Portions of the book are available online, especially citing electronic resources. Official site for Modern Languages Association (MLA).

Strunk's Elements of Style

http://www.bartleby.com/141/index.html

The print edition is now available online.

The Writer's Handbook

http://www.wisc.edu/writing/Handbook

Includes handouts on academic writing, documentation styles, grammar and style, and letters and application essays. Sponsored by the Writing Center at the University of Wisconsin–Madison.

VIRTUAL LIBRARIES

CARRIE: A Full-Text Electronic Library

http://www.ukans.edu/carrie/docs_main.html

Besides an electronic reference desk, this site contains selected full-text documents from the Catholic Church, the United Nations, U.S. Documents, World Constitutions, and documents of World War I. Sponsored by the University of Kansas.

Sites in the News

http://www.albany.edu/library/references/sites.html

Includes "sites in the news" that are hot topic sites; reference section is subdivided into subject areas; subject and library catalogs, which include Internet resources and research databases; electronic publications; and fee-based services. All sites are linked, some with descriptions.

Thor: The Virtual Reference Desk

http://thorplus.lib.purdue.edu/reference

Lists dictionaries, thesauri, zip code directories, and other useful reference sources.

Glossary

ActiveX: This is a Microsoft technology used on the Internet. ActiveX controls can be downloaded from the Internet. These controls are "activated" by the Web browser and perform a variety of different functions. There are ActiveX controls that allow you to view Microsoft Word documents via the Web browser, play animated graphical effects, and display interactive maps. As the name suggests, they make the Web page "active"; they provide the same functions as Java Applets.

Animated GIF File: A special type of GIF File. It gives the impression of a video. A collection of GIFS, presented one after the other, with each picture slightly different from the previous.

Alias: A name used in place of a Areal@ name. Aliases are often shorter or more clever than a person's real name.

Applet: An applet is a brief program written in the Java programming language that can only be used as part of a Web page.

ASCII: The American Standard Code for Information Interchange. This a way of formatting data (text only) so that it can be read by any program, whether DOS, Windows, or Mac.

Bit: A bit is the smallest unit of information understood by a computer. A bit can take a value of 0 or 1. A byte is made up of eight bits, which is large enough to contain a single character. A Kilobyte is equivalent to 1,024 bytes. A Megabyte is equivalent to 1,024 Kilobytes. A Gigabyte is equivalent to 1,024 Megabytes.

BBS: Bulletin Board System. This term usually refers to small, dial-up systems that local users can call directly.

Browser: A program used to access the World Wide Web. The most popular browsers—Netscape and Mosaic—allow users to interact audiovisually with the World Wide Web.

Client: A synonym for web browser or browser.

Domain Name System (DNS): DNS is the system that locates addresses on the World Wide Web. When a DNS error message is given by a browser, it means the address it is looking for cannot be found.

Document: On the World Wide Web, a document can be either a file or set of files that can be accessed with a Web browser.

Download: The process of getting a file or files from a remote computer— that is, a computer other than the one on your desk or local area network.

Electronic Mail (e-mail): Sending typed messages and attachments through an electronic mail network.

Encryption: A method of converting data into "unreadable code" so that prying eyes cannot understand the content.

FAQ: Frequently Asked Questions. A FAQ is a document that contains answers to the most frequently asked questions about a given topic.

Flame: This refers to the practice of sending negative or insulting e-mail.

File: A file is a collection of data stored on a disk or other storage device under a certain name.

File Transfer Protocol (FTP): FTP is a tool for moving files from another computer site to your local service provider's computer, from which it can be downloaded.

GIF: Graphic Interchange Format. A set of standards for compressing graphic files so that they occupy less space in a computer's memory or on a storage device. GIF was developed by CompuServe and Unisys.

Gopher: An older method of navigating the Internet developed at the University of Minnesota (where the mascot is the Golden Gopher). It displays information and links to documents, but is not graphics-based and is more difficult to use than the World Wide Web. Gopher is rapidly being replaced by the World Wide Web.

H-Net: The Humanities Network, or Humanities Online Initiative. H-Net is an organization dedicated to exploiting the potential of electronic media for history. It is supported by the National Endowment for the Humanities, the University of Illinois–Chicago, and Michigan State University. H-Net sponsors discussion lists, Web sites, book reviews, conferences, and other activities.

Hits: This is Internet slang for both the number of times a site is accessed by a user and for the number of sites found when using any Web search engine.

Home Page: A home page is the designated beginning point for accessing a World Wide Web Site.

Hypermedia: Computer-generated displays that combine text, images, and sound.

Hyptertext: Data that provides links to other data allowing a user to move from one resource to another.

HTML: Hyptertext Markup Language. This is the computer language used to construct documents on the World Wide Web. Most home pages are written in HTML.

HTTP: Hypertext Transfer Protocol. This is a method of coding information that enables different computers running different software to communicate information. It permits the transfer of text, sounds, images, and other data.

Icon: A graphic image that is used to represent (and usually activate) a file or program.

Internet: The Internet refers to the worldwide network of computers that is linked together using the Internet Protocol, TCP/IP.

Java: A new programming language developed by Sun Microsystems that allows programmers to create interactive applications that can be run within Web browsers on any type of computer. Java programs are referred to as applets.

JavaScript: A programming language for developing Internet applications. A Web browser interprets JavaScript statements embedded in an HTML page to create interactivity.

JPEG: Joint Photographic Experts Group. This is now the standard format for compressing graphic files so that they occupy less space in a computer's memory or on a storage device.

Kbps: Kilobits Per Second. The unit used to measure how fast data is transferred between devices on a network. One kilobit is 1,024 bits.

Link: A connection point, which might take you from one document to another or from one information provider to another.

Local Area Network (LAN): A group of computers connected together by cable or some other means so that they can share common resources.

Log in: The process of gaining access to a remote computer system or network by typing one's login name and password.

Listserv: A computer that serves a discussion group by processing, distributing, and storing messages and files for all members of the list.

Login name: This is the name you use for security purposes to gain access to a network or computer system.

MPEG: Moving Pictures Expert Group. This is the standard for compressing video images so that they occupy less space in a computer's memory or on a storage device.

Netiquette: Etiquette for the Internet.

Network: A group of interconnected computers.

Page: Page can refer to either a single screen of information on a Web site or it can refer to all of the information on a particular site.

PDF: Portable Document Format. A file type developed by Adobe Systems to allow the preservation of complex formatting and symbols.

POP: Post Office Protocol. A standard for exchanging e-mail between a user's PC and their Internet Access Provider.

RAM: Random Access Memory. RAM is the memory your computer uses to temporarily store and manipulate information. RAM does not hold information after your computer is turned off.

RealAudio: Software that allows sound files to be transmitted from the Internet back to the user's PC in streams, allowing the experience of immediate and simultaneous playing.

Service Provider: Any organization that provides connections to the Internet.

SLIP/PPP Serial Line Internet Protocol/Point to Point Protocol: This is a connection that enables a home computer to receive TCP/IP addresses. To work with the World Wide Web from home, via a modem, a SLIP or PPP connection is necessary.

SMTP: Simple Mail Transfer Protocol. An accepted standard used extensively on the Internet to allow the transfer of e-mail messages between computers.

Snail Mail: A term that e-mail users employ to describe the traditional mail or post office service.

Spam: To send e-mails to people who in no way asked you to send that information. Spamming is usually done as bulk e-mailing to promote a product.

TCP/IP Transfer Control Protocol/Internet Protocol: Essentially this is the most basic language on the Internet. The rules of TCP/IP govern the sending packets of data between computers on the Internet, and they allow for the transmission of other protocols on the Internet, such as http and FTP.

Telnet: This is an Internet protocol that enables you to log on to a remote computer.

T-1 Line: A leased Internet line connection. The speed at which data can be transmitted is 1.45 megabits per second on a T-1 line.

UNIX: Like DOS or Windows, UNIX is an operating system run by most of the computers that provide access to the Internet.

URL: Uniform Resource Locator. This is the address for an Internet site.

Web Bot: A search engine that obtains its information by starting at a specified Web page and visiting each Web page that has a link to it. Web bots are used by the large databases such as Yahoo! to create their database. Also called spiders, bots, and robots.

Web Browser: A program used to access the World Wide Web. The most popular browsers—Netscape and Mosaic—allow users to interact audiovisually with the World Wide Web.

Winsock: A program that runs in the background on a Windows-based personal computer, allowing one to make a SLIP/PPP connection to the Internet and to use the TCP/IP protocols.

World Wide Web (WWW): An Internet service that enables one to connect to all of the hypermedia documents on the Internet. The Web is like a network within the Internet.

Zip: Zip (or zipped) files are files that have been compressed by a software package to reduce the amount of space that the data take up. This file type is popular on the Internet because smaller files can be sent faster. To create or open a Zip file one needs a special software package such as WinZip or PKUNZIP. The .zip extension indicates a Zip file.

About the Contributors

Jeffrey Barlow is the Matsushita Chair of Asian Studies at Pacific University in Forest Grove, Oregon and editor of the *Journal of the Association for History and Computing* (http://mcel.pacificu.edu/JAHC/). He has written four books and a number of articles on Chinese and Chinese-American history. He is a frequent traveler to Asia, and has lived in China for more than six years, one year of which was spent working on a 64K Kaypro computer with a voltage regulator somewhat smaller than a Volkswagen. He is also the Webmaster for the Association of Asian Studies on the Pacific Coast (ASPAC), whose site can be found at: http://mcel.pacificu.edu/aspac/home/aspac.html.

Marilyn Dell Brady received her Ph.D. from the University of Kansas and was an Associate Professor of History at Virginia Wesleyan College. Her publications include articles dealing with African American women. She now resides in Alpine, Texas, where she teaches part time at Sul Ross State University. In addition, she is writing an overview of African Americans in the Trans–Pecos for the Center for Big Bend Studies.

Susanna Betzel is a bookseller and freelance writer, with a particular interest in revolutionary France. She is currently working on her second novel about the French Revolution and hopes soon to have *Keystone of the Terror*, her translation of the memoirs of the executioner of Paris, published by a university press.

Patrick Callan is a Deputy Principal and Lecturer at Maynooth–National University of Ireland. He received his B.A., M.A., and Ph.D. from University College, Dublin, and he is a frequent speaker, writer, and lecturer in Ireland on the future of education and technology.

Solomon Davidoff is an Instructor for the Department of Ethic Studies and a doctoral candidate in the American Culture Studies Program at Bowling Green State University.

Christine de Matos has taught history and computing for the past six years at the University of Sydney; the University of Technology, Sydney; and the University of Western Sydney, Macarthur. She is currently a doctoral candidate at the University of Sydney. Her dissertation explores Australians and the Left in Japan during the Allied Occupation of 1945–49.

Lloyd deMause is the Director of the Institute for Psychohistory and editor of the *Journal of Psychohistory*. He has written widely on psychology and psychohistory, including two books: *Foundations of Reagan's America*, *Psychohistory*, and *Childhood and History*.

Sam Dicks holds a doctorate from the University of Oklahoma and has been a member of the history faculty at Emporia State University since 1965. He is the publication director of *Teaching History: A Journal of Methods*, and edits its Internet Web site. In addition to courses in Ancient and Medieval History, he also teaches Historiography and an introductory class in Genealogy.

Bambi L. Dingman is a freelance writer from New Jersey. She has been the French and Indian War editor for *Smoke and Fire News*, an internationally recognized living history newspaper, and has also written for *Recreating History Magazine*. She currently serves as the Regimental Adjutant for the 7th Vermont Infantry Regiment as part of the Web-based project Vermont in the Civil War.

Kenneth R. Dvorak is the Secretary-Treasurer of the American Association for History and Computing and a doctoral candidate in American Culture Studies at Bowling Green State University. He is the co-director of two nationally honored Web sites—"America in the 1890s" and "1890s Bowling Green, Ohio," and he has written numerous articles that have appeared in the *Journal of Film and History*, the *Journal of Popular Culture*, and the *Journal of American Culture*.

Susan Ferentinos is the Assistant Editor of the *OAH Magazine of History*, published by the Organization of American Historians. She holds an M.A. in history and an M.L.S., with a concentration in special collections. She is currently a Ph.D. student at Indiana University and conducts occasional workshops on information resources at the IU Undergraduate Library.

Claire Gabriel is Librarian for United States and World History at New York University and has worked previously for the Humanities and Social Sciences Library of the New York Public Library. She holds an M.L.S. from Columbia University and an M.A. in History from New York University. Past projects

include a Web history tutorial designed for students at NYU and other historical researchers.

Kathryn L. Green is an Assistant Professor of History at California State
University, San Bernardino. She received her M.A. and Ph.D. from Indiana
University and has published numerous articles on African history. Her cur-
rent research involves a study of Islam and political ideology in precolonial
West African savanna states, and she is the co-director of the Africa Research
Central project (http://africaresearch.csusb.edu/).

Ernest Ialongo is a doctoral candidate at the Graduate Center of the City
University of New York. His research focuses on the poor and working class in
post-unification Naples.

Jone Johnson is a minister, ethical culture leader, teacher and Web site designer. She has taught at Meadville/Lombard Theological School and served
as a faculty member of the Humanist Institute. She has a special research
interest in the life of Anna Garlin Spencer (1851–1931) and in nineteenth-
century religious and social reform history and is currently the Miningco Guide
for Women's History, http://womenshistory.about.com/.

James E Jolly is a doctoral student and Adjunct Professor of American history at Middle Tennessee State University.

Ken Kempcke received his M.A. in American Studies from Purdue University and his M.L.S. from Indiana University. He is currently the Social Science Reference Librarian and Coordinator of Library Instruction at Montana
State University, Bozeman.

Andrew E. Kersten has taught at the University of WisconsinGreen Bay since
1997. He earned his B.A. at the University of Wisconsin, Madison, and he
received the M.A. and Ph.D in United States history from the University of
Cincinnati. He has published in the *Queen City Heritage*, *The Michigan Historical Review*, and *The Missouri Historical Review*, and has contributed to
several anthologies. He is currently working on a book-length study of President Franklin D. Roosevelt's Fair Employment Practice Committee.

Stephen Kneeshaw is Professor of History at College of the Ozarks in southwest
Missouri. He is also involved with the teacher education program, specifically
history and social studies education. He completed his B.A. in history and English at the University of Puget Sound and his M.A. and Ph.D. in American

history at the University of Colorado, Boulder. Since 1972 he has been on the history faculty at College of the Ozarks, where he was named the first recipient of the college's Distinguished Faculty Award for excellence in teaching, scholarship, and service. He has held fellowships for study and research at the Newberry Library, Harvard, MIT, and the U.S. Military Academy at West Point. Steve is the Founder and Editor of *Teaching History: A Journal of Methods* and for several years has presented workshops on "Active Teaching and Learning" at high schools and colleges. His publications cover a wide range of topics from diplomatic history to history education, active learning, and writing to learn.

David Koeller received his M.A. and Ph.D. from the University of California, Berkeley and is a specialist in the German Enlightenment. He is an Associate Professor of History at North Park University, and has taught world history for many years. He also serves as a member of the World History Association and recently won a grant from the Ameritech corporation to help develop the WebChron Web Chronology Project.

Leo E. Landis is Curator of Agriculture at Henry Ford Museum and Greenfield Village in Dearborn, Michigan. He launched the Web site for the editorial office of Agricultural History in October 1995. He often provides content for the museum's Web site (http://www.hfmgv.org) and is working towards a Ph.D. in Agricultural History from Iowa State University. His research interests are Midwestern agriculture and social and cultural history. He is author of *Building Better Roads: Iowa's Contribution to Highway Engineering*.

Julia Landweber is a doctoral candidate in early modern European history at Rutgers University. She is currently at work on her dissertation, "French Delight in Turkey and the Genesis of National Identity," a study of French national identity formation through an examination of France's cultural relations with Turkey in the late seventeenth- to mid-eighteenth centuries.

Todd E.A. Larson is a doctoral candidate in modern British history at the University of Illinois at Urbana–Champaign. He has been deeply involved in academic technologies and has held technology appointments at the National Center for Supercomputing Applications (NCSA), the Division of Guided Individual Study, and the University of Illinois Provosts' Office. Currently he is the first historian to be named an associate fellow of the Merriam Laboratory for Analytic Political Research. He was the co–author of *The History Highway* (M.E. Sharpe, 1997) and the editor of the forthcoming *Very Victorian: Essays in Honour of Walter L. Arnstein* (Ashgate Press, 2000).

Charles H. MacKay is an Assistant Professor of history at Morehead State University. He received his B.A. from the University of Arkansas and his doctorate from Florida State University. He has served as on the Executive Board of the American Association for History and Computing and spoken widely on teaching and technology.

Margaret M. Manchester is an Assistant Professor of History and Director of the American Studies Program at Providence College.

Mary K. Mannix is the Maryland Room Manager for the C. Burr Artz Library, Frederick, Maryland and the Co-Moderator for H–LOCAL and H–MARYLAND. She received her M.A. in American History and Museum Studies from the University of Delaware and her M.L.S. from the University of Maryland, College Park. She has spoken and published widely on issues relating to archive, library, museum, and local history activities in the electronic age.

Robert M. S. McDonald is Assistant Professor of History at the United States Military Academy, West Point. A specialist in the revolutionary and early national United States, he holds degrees from the University of Virginia, Oxford University, and the University of North Carolina at Chapel Hill, where he received his Ph.D. He is currently at work on a book about Thomas Jefferson's public image, 1776-1826.

Scott A. Merriman is a doctoral candidate in modern American history at the University of Kentucky. He has previously taught history at the University of Cincinnati, Northern Kentucky University, and Thomas More College. He is also the co–author of *The History Highway: A Guide to Internet Resources* and an associate editor for *History Reviews Online*. He has contributed to the *Historical Encyclopedia of World Slavery*, *American National Biography*, and *Buckeye Hill Country*.

Charlene Mires is an Assistant Professor of History at Villanova University. She received her M.A. from the University of Pennsylvania and her doctorate from Temple University. She has published widely on American Culture and Material Culture and serves as the project coordinator for The Centennial Exhibition of 1876 Project (http://www.villanova.edu/~his2998cm/).

Richard P. Mulcahy is currently an Associate Professor of History and Director of the Division of Social Sciences with the University of Pittsburgh, Titusville. The author of a number of refereed articles and book chapters, he currently has a book dealing with social policy in Appalachia.

Keith Nightenhelser studied at Wabash College and Princeton University, and now teaches Classics and Philosophy at DePauw University.

Bente Opheim teaches at the Department of History at the University of Bergen, Norway. She has a Master of Philosophy in medieval history, but has mainly been involved in developing pedagogical programs for using technology in teaching. She has previously worked as administrator for the thematic network Advanced Computing in the Humanities and is still involved in the work of the history sub-group of the network.

Edward Ragan is currently a Ph.D. candidate at Syracuse University, where he is studying early American and native American history. His dissertation explores Anglo-Indian relations in Virginia. Through his research, Edward has become involved with Virginia's Indians in their efforts to gain federal recognition.

deTraci Regula is the author of *The Mysteries of Isis*, which explores the religion of Isis in Greece, Ptolemaic Egypt, and in modern revivals. She has written dozens of articles on Greece, ancient and modern. She is presently the Greece for Visitors Guide at the Miningco, http://gogreece.miningco.com.

J. Kelly Robison is an American Studies Fellow and the Academic Computing Specialist at the Center for U.S. Studies, Martin-Luther-University Halle–Wittenberg, Wittenberg, Germany. He holds a Ph.D. in American History from Oklahoma State University and an M.A. in American History from the University of Montana. His research and teaching focus is the history of the American West and Native America, with a special emphasis on the Spanish Borderlands and cross-cultural acculturation. He is also interested in the use of computer technology in teaching and researching history. He is a consulting editor for the *Journal of the Association for History and Computing* and is member of the Executive Board of the American Association for History and Computing.

Anne Rothfeld is an Information Specialist at the University of Maryland, Baltimore. She earned her M.A. in library science from the Catholic University of America, concentrating in special collections and archives. Previously she was the Archivist Technician at the U.S. Holocaust Memorial Museum in Washington, D.C.

Kalpana Shankar is a doctoral candidate in library and information science at the University of California, Los Angeles. Her particular interest is in scientific recordkeeping, scientific archives, and their relationship to historiography of science.

Christopher A. Snyder is currently Acting Chair of the Department of History and Politics at Marymount University in Arlington, Virginia. He taught at Emory University and the College of William and Mary before coming to

Marymount, and he is a Fellow of the Society of Antiquaries of Scotland. His books include *Sub–Roman Britain (A.D. 400–800): A Gazetteer of Sites* (Oxford, 1996) and *An Age of Tyrants: Britain and the Britons, A.D. 400–800* (Penn State, 1998)

Eric G. Swedin holds a Ph.D. in history from Case Western Reserve University. He currently works as the Webmaster at the Thiokol Propulsion Division of Cordant Technologies and as Adjunct Professor of History at Weber State University in Ogden, Utah.

H. Micheal Tarver is currently Assistant Professor of World History at McNeese State University (Lake Charles, Louisiana) and Profesor Invitado at the Centro de Estudios Históricos "Carlos Emilio Muñoz Oráa" at the Universidad de Los Andes (Mérida, Venezuela). He received his M.A. from the University of Southwestern Louisiana and his Doctorate from Bowling Green State University.

Gunnar Thorvaldsen is the Manager of Research at the Norwegian Historical Data Center, The University of Tromsoe, with a speciality in migration studies and the computerization of historical microdata. He is currently a member of a research team in the Center for Advanced Study in the Norwegian Academy of Sciences and Letters, studying the mortality decline in Norway 1770–1920. He also has spent a sabbatical at the Census Projects, the University of Minnesota, and has been a guest researcher at the Demographic Database, The University of Umeå and at the Stockholm Historical Database.

Dennis A. Trinkle is an Assistant Professor of History and Associate Director of Faculty Development at DePauw University. He serves as the Executive Director of the American Association for History and Computing (http://www.theaahc.org), and he has published widely on technology, teaching, and history. His books include *The History Highway: A Guide to Internet Resources; Writing, Teaching, and Researching History in the Electronic Age*; and *History.Edu: Essays on Teaching with Technology.*

Keith C. Trinkle is the chief financial officer for ETC: The Educational Technology Consulting Group. He majored in history at Indiana University and is nationally-recognized pioneer in the development of interactive computing environments such as bulletin boards, newgroups, and chat sites. He is currently completing an M.B.A. at Indiana State University.

Susan Tschabrun is Reference and Electronic Resources Librarian at the California State University, San Bernardino. She holds a Ph.D. in History from University of Wisconsin, Madison and a M.L.S. from UCLA. She is currently the project director for a Getty-funded grant to catalogue and digitize the holdings of the Center for the Study of Political Graphics, an educational archive of domestic and international political and protest posters in Los Angeles. Other projects include work on a set of multimedia learning modules to teach History majors information competency skills and co-authorship of the Web site, Africa Research Central: A Clearinghouse of African Primary Sources.

Frode Ulvund is an Assistant Professor at the History Department, University of Bergen, Norway. His field of work is mainly developing and implementing information technology as a tool in teaching history, as well as teaching Computing and History.

Laura Winninghoff is the Evening Circulation Librarian at Indiana University–Bloomington's Law Library. She has also worked in the Curatorial and Collections Departments of the Houdini Historical Center and the Children's Museum of Indianapolis and has taught History and English at Notre Dame Girls Academy in Chicago. Her research interests include the interaction of museum visitors and Web–based exhibits. She earned her M.L.S. and M.A. in history at Indiana University–Bloomington.

Igor Yeykelis received his Ph.D. from the University of Melbourne. His dissertation examined Odessa, 1914–1922. The Reassertion of Traditional Social and Cultural Values at the Times Of Upheaval, and his published works include *The Odessa Maccabi 1917–20: The Development of Sport and Physical Culture in Odessa's Jewish Community* and *Artur Anatra, Odessan Entrepreneur, 1914–1919.*

Index

Entries in *italics* are internet sites.